U0509406

《瑷珲海关历史档案辑要》编委会

主　编：石巍巍
副主编：魏　巍
编　辑：杜　晔　张　念　张丽娜　陈　頔

瑷珲海关
历史档案辑要

海务港务（上）
（第五卷）

黑龙江省档案馆　编译

社会科学文献出版社
SOCIAL SCIENCES ACADEMIC PRESS (CHINA)

目 录

专题一

黑龙江航务

1. 为开设哈尔滨江关、拉哈苏苏分关和三姓分关事

Sungari and Amur: Status of River Trade on application of I. W. S. W. rule, to Sungari and of ordinary treaty Port treatment on Amur; suggesting various suggestions, in re duty treatment of goods, issue of various documents, Tariffs, Regulations, opening of Harbin River Customs, Sansing & Lahasusu offices, submitting.

Copy
No. 164.

I. G.

Harbin, 7th January, 1909.

Sir,

1. I have the honour to acknowledge the receipt of your despatch No. 223:

instructing me to take in hand the matter of establishing Customs on the Sungari and to report on the question in connection with the Russian Minister's enquiry addressed to the Board as to the future functions of the offices to be established:

and the preceding ones, Nos 110, 159 and 201, on the same subject.

2. In my despatch No. 60 I have already, in reply to your despatch No. 110, submitted an outline of Customs programme on the Sungari the main point of which was the recommendation to make a start at Harbin and supplement the Harbin establishment with branches at Sansing and Lahasusu. The proposal has already been considered by the Manchurian Authorities and the Boards at Peking and generally approved.

3. On his way to Aigun the conditions on the river have been studied by Mr. Schmidt, acting Deputy Commissioner; whose report forwarded in my despatch No. 132, tends to confirm the advisability of proceeding in the manner indicated above.

Sir Robert E. Bredon, K.C.M.G.,
Acting Inspector General of Customs,
Peking.

4.

4.

**Control and
Treatment of
Steamers.**

Native shipping on the river amounts to very little at present, and steamers and their tows do most of the carrying trade. These <u>steamers</u> can be divided into two categories, <u>viz</u>:

A) river steamers running chiefly between Harbin and Sansing and a few other places on the river; and

B) <u>foreign going steamers</u>, <u>i.e.</u> steamers which run between the Amur ports (Habarovsk, Blagovestchensk) and Sungari ports (Harbin, Sansing, etc.).

The Russo-Chinese Treaty stipulations, of dates anterior to the recent Komura Convention of Peking (1905) by which Harbin and Sansing were opened to trade, restrict the navigation to ships of the two countries but allow them to trade everywhere and not only at specially opened places — "<u>de faire le commerce avec les populations des localités riveraines</u>" (Art. 1 and 2 of the Aigun Treaty of 1858, Art. 4 of the Peking Treaty of 1860 and Art. XVIII of the St. Petersburg Treaty of 1881) — and not only on the Sungari but also on the Amur and the Oussuri; so that the ordinary regulations in force elsewhere in China do not seem to apply here in full measure. It would be too serious a task to elaborate special regulations based upon these treaties, and a simple adaptation of what is in force elsewhere might be preferable from all points

of

of view. I would therefore apply to the first category, i.e. steamers running on the Sungari between open and "nei ti" places, the ordinary Inland Waters Steam Navigation Regulations in a provisional and experimental way until the necessary changes and modifications have suggested themselves. The exhibition of an I. W. S. N. Certificate, when calling at inland places, would, or should, prevent any misunderstanding with the taxation offices at those places. As regards the second category of steamers, whether those regularly running to and from, the Russian Amur ports, or those of the first category occasionally engaging in that trade, Amur being as much Chinese as a Russian river, the same I. W. S. N. Regulations could, for the sake of uniformity, also be applied to them if it were not against the spirit of the I. W. S. N. Regulations to allow such vessels to touch at foreign ports. On the other hand, the rule forcing steamers to deposit their ship's papers at the port of registration when taking out an I. W. S. N. Certificate and the necessity of producing these papers when entering Russian ports make a distinction advisable and a change of status on each such occasion. For the second category the ordinary treaty port treatment of non- I. W. S. N. steamers must therefore be reserved

reserved.

5.

Tonnage Dues

In the matter of Tonnage Dues all steamers will have to be treated alike, i.e. Tonnage Dues to be paid every four months at the usual rates of one mace per ton if 150 tons, or under, and of four mace if over 150 tons. The ordinary Tonnage Dues Regulations in force elsewhere would most probably suffice for our guidance, and the question of the extension of Certificates for the time vessels are docked on the Sungari during the winter can be dealt with separately. The introduction of this new charge on shipping will be, I understand, protested against by the Russian Authorities on the ground that no such dues are leviable on Chinese or Russian steamers running on the Amur even between Habarovsk and Nicolayevsk, i.e. on the Russian Amur which corresponds to the Chinese Sungari. Such question, if it should be raised, will have to be settled of course at Peking, and meantime a local temporary arrangement should be possible to enable us to collect Tonnage Dues on deposit

6.

Duties on Cargoes

Another question to which the ordinary treaty port practice cannot be fully applied concerns the duties leviable on cargoes carried. Presumably no duties can be levied at Lahasusu as situated within the 50-versts free trade frontier zone, if the

the validity of Articles quoted in
§ 4 in this region be admitted. The
river taxation will have therefore to
be attended to by the Harbin and Sansing
offices and Lahasusu can only
undertake a certain control. The
following categories of duties should be
levied

A) Import duty on cargoes brought to
Harbin, or Sansing, from other river
places, or from Chinese and Russian
Amur ports.

B) Export duty on exports from Harbin, or
Sansing, to other river places, or to
Chinese and Russian Amur ports.
Inter-mart cargoes to be dealt with
similarly.

C) Coast Trade duty on native re-imports
which had paid Export duty at the
other mart. Coast Trade duty to be
refunded by drawback when goods are
re-exported abroad.

D) Transit dues on duty-paid foreign goods
sent to inland places or inland taxation
en route in lieu thereof.

E) Transit dues, etc. on native produce
brought from the interior under Transit
Certificates.

F) Tungshui tax on Native Opium.

Besides the collection of the above the
offices will have to issue

G) Special Manchurian Exemption Certificates
(Cir. Nos. 1472 & 1499) for Import duty-paid
foreign

foreign goods, and Export plus Coast
trade duty-paid native goods, as well
as for duty-free goods. (Cir. No. 1544).

H) Drawbacks for Import duty on foreign
goods, and for Coast Trade duty on
native goods re-exported abroad.

Tariffs and D.F. List.

7. The Tariffs to be followed by the Harbin
and Sansing offices would be

the Revised Import Tariff of 1902
for Imports & the General Tariff
of 1858 for Exports

and only such articles to be passed
duty-free as are exempted at other Chinese
ports, i.e. not all those that are
enumerated in the Duty Free List of the
1881 Land Trade Regulations, as not
applicable to water-borne trade.

Proposed Regulations

8. In order to acquaint steamer owners
and merchants with the character of the
taxation now described. I beg to solicit
your authority to issue a series of Customs
Notifications in Chinese, English and Russian
and to supplement them eventually with
Notifications regarding
1) Harbour Regulations for each place;
2) Sanitary Regulations;
3) Regulations governing the issue of, and
fees for, Special Permit Fees;
4) Regulations concerning issue of Arms
Certificates for Arms carried on board the
steamers;
5) Regulations concerning Inspection of Boilers
and the number of passengers that might
be

be carried;

6) Rules for <u>prevention of collisions</u> and right of way in which, for safety sake, we might follow to a reasonable extent the Russian Rules on the Amur until the Special Russo-Chinese Commission has met and agreed upon a special set of Rules for the Amur.

9.
Harbin River Customs.

As soon as the river opens an <u>active start</u> should be made by establishing an office on the river at Harbin which should be styled the <u>Harbin River Customs</u> (哈爾濱工關) The foreshore within the limits of the Railway territory is the centre of the Harbin river trade and our office should obviously be established there. In view, however, of the present attitude of the Railway Company in the question of the <u>Harbin Railway Custom House</u>, we must be prepared to face similar obstacles on the river, and I should therefore recommend mobile arrangements at the start. The best plan would be to hire a barge for the first summer's work, fit it up to suit our requirements and moor it in the most suitable locality. With such a floating office any errors of judgment, changes caused by unexpected alterations in the channel, etc. could be easily remedied by simply shifting berth.

10.
Lahasusu Office

The next step should be to <u>send Staff to Lahasusu.</u> The negotiations conducted here, and at Peking, have resulted in the closing of the Russian Customs office which hitherto functioned

functioned at Lahasusu. The buildings used
for offices and quarters were inspected by Mr.
Schmidt and found adequate for our needs.
As it is impossible to send Staff to Lahasusu
during the winter, I am requesting the
Superintendent to ask the Linchiang Chou
(臨江州) by telegraph to take charge of them
until the spring. After consulting with the
Superintendent I hope to be able to arrange
about the payment for the buildings
through the intermediary of the Russian
Consul General. The functions of the
Lahasusu establishment, to be styled a
fên ch'ia (分卡), would be of a preventive
and controlling nature. Incoming steamers
would be searched for contraband and be
required to produce their ship's papers
and manifests (in duplicate). After
checking the latter with the cargo, etc.,
the manifest would be sealed by the
Lahasusu office, supplied with any
remarks that may be called for and
placed in a sealed cover to be delivered
by the steamer at Harbin (or Sansing) while
the duplicate copy would remain in the
Lahasusu archives. Outgoing steamers
will present any documents issued by
the Harbin and/or Sansing offices and,
after cargo and documents have been
found in order, they will be allowed
to proceed outwards. Detailed regulations
for the guidance of masters of vessels
as well as for the Customs employés
will

will have to be drawn up, the practice and procedure to be as simple as possible. For these simple functions it is <u>not necessary</u> to place any <u>Assistants at Lahasusu</u>. Mr. Schmidt, having studied the conditions there, considers that <u>two foreign Tidewaiters</u> and <u>half a dozen Chinese boatmen or soldiers</u> would suffice. It will however be advisable to detail an Assistant, or even the Deputy Commissioner, to take over the property, establish relations with the local authorities and to start the work generally.

11.

Sansing Office.

After the Harbin River Customs and the Lahasusu Controlling Station have been started, arrangements can be made to <u>supply Sansing</u> with a sub-office (分關) <u>of Harbin</u>. A preliminary study of that Trade Mart will have to be made before submitting any definite proposals. <u>The functions of the Sansing sub-office</u> will be similar to those of Harbin i.e. levy of duties and Tonnage dues, checking and issue of documents for cargoes landed and shipped, as well as control of transit cargoes emanating from inland places below Harbin and above Lahasusu. An <u>Assistant will have to be stationed at Sansing</u> especially as questions will often arise in connection with our control of the navigation aids. <u>The strength of the Staff</u> cannot be determined at present, but

but the establishment will have probably to count 1-2 Chinese Clerks, 1-2 Shupan and 3-4 Tidewaiters and/or watchers, besides boatmen, etc.

12.

Aids to Navigation on Sungari

In addition to the revenue work dealt with above, the control of the Aids to Navigation will have to be organised and maintained. In my despatch No. 60 I have already mentioned that a River Committee was in charge of the Aids temporarily and its organisation is fully described in Mr. Schmidt's report (Harbin despatch No. 132). By an arrangement come to at an interview held on the 21st October between the Superintendent and myself, on one side, and General Horvat and the Chairman of the River Committee, on the other, the Committee has ceased its function on the 28th October from which date the Customs may be considered as having assumed them. A sum of Roubles 3,000-, representing part of the available balance of the Committee's last season's working account has since been handed over to me on the understanding that the money would exclusively be used for river expenditure. The plant consisting of shore beacons is also placed at our disposal by the Railway Company to whom it belongs, but the sum to be paid for it remains to be settled. At least two launches will be required for the river work and, on the authority

of

of your semi-official letter of 30th
October, 1908, I am already in
communication with the Coast Inspector
about the provision of one. One or more
motor launches (at Newchwang at present)
have since been offered by the Viceroy
and the Newchwang Harbour Master has
been asked to inspect them and report
on their suitability. As will be seen
from Mr. Schmidt's report, already
alluded to, this new duty presents
little difficulty once properly started.
The _work_ however _is of some magnitude_
considering its novelty, length of the
river and the desert character of its
banks. During the last few years
the river aids were satisfactorily
maintained by the Russians, and the
Customs to whom the duty has now been
entrusted by the Government, must be
prepared to be, from the very beginning,
severely criticised for any faults or
mismanagement and any accidents to
shipping arising therefrom. Under the
circumstances, I consider it my duty
to request you to _detail either Captain_
Tyler or Captain Eldridge for a couple
of weeks in April to initiate the control
and thus give to all concerned the
immediate impression of the work being
in competent hands and not likely to
suffer through the change of Administration.
Good many things will have to be settled
on the spot and I cannot think of
anyone

anyone else who has the requisite authority, training and qualifications. Mr. Jacobson, 2nd Class Tidewaiter, will probably be able to carry on the work afterwards. Just before the closing of the river he has made a trip by steamer down the Sungari and Amur and acquired a slight knowledge of the river and the old system of marking the channel.

13.
Sansing Channel.

I have to mention in this connection that it was the intention of the former Committee to utilize the surplus funds in _deepening and cleaning_ a part of the channel near Sansing by blasting during the winter when the water is low, and it is quite possible suggestions will be made to us to do something with the amount paid over to us.

14.
Carriage of
I-P-O. Mails
by Steamers.

The _I.P.O._ has extended its operations as far as Sansing and it would be advisable to endeavour to make the _Sungari steamers carry the Imperial Mail_. The two-three Chinese running as far as Hulanfu will undoubtedly undertake this duty on their route (Cir. No. 1167), and by refunding one half of the Special Permit Fees we should be able to secure the cooperation of Russian vessels as well.

15.
Accounts.

The extra _expenditure involved_ by this extension of work will have to appear, I suppose, in the Harbin General Account (A/c _D_) but a

sub-schedule

sub-schedule would be necessary in connection with future appropriations from the river collection for initial and current expenses. The <u>outlay on river aids</u>, etc., and the <u>Tonnage Dues</u> collected would constitute A/c <u>C</u> payments and receipts.

        I have the honour to be,
        Sir,
        Your obedient Servant,
        (signed) N. A. Konovaloff
        Commissioner.

True Copy:

C.B.Jo
2nd Assistant, <u>A</u>

呈海关署总税务司公署 <u>164</u> 号文　　　　　　哈尔滨关 1909 年 1 月 7 日

尊敬的海关署总税务司（北京）：

1. 根据海关总税务司署第 223 号令：

"请着手办理于松花江沿岸设立分关事；另请针对俄使向税务处致函询问拟建海关分关之职能事呈交报告；"

及与此相关之海关总税务司署第 110 号、159 号及 201 号令，特作如下汇报。

2. 本署已于哈尔滨关第 60 号呈（回复海关总税务司署第 110 号令）中汇报了于松花江沿岸设立分关的计划，建议首先在哈尔滨关设立江关，以此作为松花江上的其他两处分关（即三姓分关和拉哈苏苏分关）之补充。该提议已汇报至满洲当局和北京税务处，并已批准通过。

3. 哈尔滨关署副税务司式美第（A. Schmidt）先生前往瑷珲视察途中已考察过松花江沿岸情况，并已于哈尔滨关致海关总税务司署第 132 号呈中呈交考察报告，报告内容与上述设立哈尔滨江关之建议一致。

4. 现今在松花江上航行船只极少，往来船只大多为运输货物之轮船，可分为两类：

（1）华籍轮船，即主要往来于哈尔滨关和三姓分关之间的轮船（有时也前往松花江沿岸的其他地方）；

（2）外籍轮船，如往来于黑龙江各口岸哈巴罗夫斯克（Habarovsk）①和布拉戈维申斯克（Blagovestchensk））和松花江沿岸海关（哈尔滨关、三姓分关等）的轮船。

依据 1905 年《中日会议东三省事宜正约》规定，哈尔滨和三姓两地需开埠通商。此外中俄条约规定，华方则应允许两国货船与界河沿岸所有地区（不仅限于已开放地区）进行贸易。"与界河沿岸居民开始通商"（参见 1858 年《瑷珲条约》第一款和第二款，1860 年《北京条约》第四款，1881 年《圣彼得堡条约》第十八款）- 即除松花江沿岸开放通商外，黑龙江和乌苏里江沿岸也需照办。有鉴于此，中国其他海关实施的贸易章程并不适用本关区，但本署亦认为不必大费周章地制定特别章程以符合上述条约规定，只需将其他口岸章程作适当改动即可。以上述甲类往来于松花江上贸易开放地区和"内地"的轮船为例：原《内港行船章程》为临时试用章程，在做必要的修订后便可于本关区正式颁布生效。凡轮船在本关区内陆地区停靠者需出示"内港行船执照"（I.W.S.N.Certificate），以防止当地

---

① Habarovsk 现在一般翻译为哈巴罗夫斯克，还有另外一个非常有名的中文名"伯力"。

税捐局误征税款。此外，因黑龙江为中俄两国界河，根据《内港行船章程》规定，华方也可对频繁往来于黑龙江俄岸港口且未违反该章程的华籍轮船签发"内港行船执照"，并准许该轮船停靠俄国港口。另外，船只领取"内港行船执照"时须在注册港口上交船舶证件登记，驶入俄国港口时还须出示船舶证件。此举便于海关区别中俄两国船只，并保证船只在任何情形下均无法改变国籍。对于乙类轮船而言，凡未持有"内港行船执照"者，须得到通商口岸批准后方可进出港口。

5. 至于缴纳船钞一事，兹认为对所有轮船应一视同仁。如船只每四个月支付一次船钞，凡船只载重超过 150 吨以上者，其税率为每吨 4 钱；凡船只载重低于或等于 150 吨者，其税率为每吨 1 钱。其他地区所施行的《船钞章程》可为本关区提供参考。至于为冬季停靠在松花江上的船只延长签发内港行船执照（Certificate）的期限一事可不与船钞问题一同处理。本署认为，俄国当局必然会反对海关对货运船只征收船钞，原因是此前并无对黑龙江上往来的中俄船只征收税捐之先例，即使是对往来于哈巴罗夫斯克和尼古拉耶夫斯克（Nickolaevsk）[①]的船只（需取道中国境内的松花江），华方也未征收过税捐。若俄方当局对征收船钞一事提出质疑，则需中俄双方于北京协商解决；同时地方海关可做临时安排，仅对长期停靠在口岸的船只征收船钞。

6. 此外，通商口岸之征税方法并不完全适用于对本关区船只运送之货物征税。鉴于拉哈苏苏分关位于 50 俄里边境免税贸易区内，因此如若施行通商口岸章程之第四款，则该分关必然无税可征。因此在哈尔滨关江关、三姓分关和拉哈苏苏分关实施之江捐规定须作适当修改，此三关仅对往来船只进行适当管控。海关应对符合下列规定之货物征收税款：

（1）对凡货物自松花江沿岸或中俄港口运至哈尔滨关或三姓分关者征收进口税。

（2）对凡出口货物自哈尔滨关或三姓分关运往松花江沿岸或中俄港口者征收出口税。凡货物运往国内市场者，其征税办法须照此办理。

（3）对反复进口土货在其他海关缴纳过出口税者征收土货复出口半税。货物复出口至国外后可退还土货复出口半税。

（4）对凡洋货运往内陆地区，且已缴纳过税款者征收子口半税，以此替代运输沿途税捐局征收之税捐。

（5）对凡土货来自于内陆地区，且持有运照者征收子口半税等税。

---

① Nickolaevsk 现在一般翻译为尼古拉耶夫斯克，还有另一个非常有名的中文名"庙街"。

（6）对凡鸦片自中国出产者征收统税（T'ungshui）。

海关除征收上述税款外，还具有下列职能：

（7）凡洋货已缴纳进口税者、土货已缴纳出口税和土货复出口半税者（参阅海关总税务司署第1544号通令）签发满洲特别免重征执照（参阅海关总税务司署第1472和第1499号通令）。

（8）为已缴纳进口税之洋货退税；为已缴纳子口半税并已复出口至国外之土货退税。

7.哈尔滨关和三姓分关征收税款需遵循以下税则：

对进口货物征收税款需遵循1902年《进口税则修订》（Revised Import Tariff of 1902）；对出口货物征收税款需遵循1858年《通用税则》（General Tariff of 1858）。

凡货物在其他中国口岸可免税过关者，方可免税通过哈尔滨江关和三姓分关，但因1881年《通商章程》中免税清单上并非全部适用于水上贸易，故而并非所有列于该清单之货物均可免税过关。

8.为使轮船主和商人了解海关现行条例及征税办法，兹请贵署批准以汉文、英文和俄文三种文字发布下列海关公告：

（1）《理船章程》；

（2）《防护染疫章程》；

（3）《管理和收取特别准单费章程》；

（4）轮船携带的武器需有军火准照之章程；

（5）巡查边境章程以及轮船搭乘乘客数量章程；

（6）避碰规则：为保证航行安全，在中俄委员会就《黑龙江航行规则》达成一致前，凡华籍船只于黑龙江上航行者应遵循俄国制定的航行规定。

9.兹建议，待今年松花江开江后，海关便应积极筹备在哈尔滨设立江关之事，并将其命名为哈尔滨江关。铁路沿线的堤岸为哈尔滨江上贸易之中心，因此哈尔滨江关办公楼也应在此修建。但是鉴于中东铁路公司对于修建哈尔滨铁路海关办公楼的态度，本署认为海关应做好面对困难之准备（与在松花江堤岸修建哈尔滨江关办公楼之困难相似）。有鉴于此，兹建议海关可暂设流动分关，即最好于今年夏季在松花江上租用一艘驳船，修整后停泊于最适宜海关工作之位置，以此充当哈尔滨江关办公室。如此一来，如遇因河道变化而出现的停靠位置错误、航道改变等问题，海关也可通过转改变驳船停泊位置来解决。

10.哈尔滨江关设立后，海关需派遣关员前往拉哈苏苏分关任职。中俄代表已在北京和哈尔滨进行协商，双方同意关闭位于拉哈苏苏的俄国海关，并由华方在此地设立分关。

因冬季无法派遣关员前往拉哈苏苏分关任职，因此本署请求海关监督向临江州（Linchiang Chou）当局发送电报，请其在今年春季前代管拉哈苏苏分关。式美第（A. Schmidt）先生在拉哈苏苏视察后，认为俄国海关在此修建的办公楼和宿舍足以为中国海关所用。在与海关监督沟通后，本署希望以俄国总领事为中间人，将俄国海关在拉哈苏苏修建之房屋买入。中国设立的拉哈苏苏分关为海关分卡，其主要工作为预防走私和管控往来货物。凡轮船驶入上游地区者，均须接受关员查验，即检查船上是否存有走私货物，并须出示船舶证件和载货清单（一式两份）。待货物查验完毕后，关员将可能需要的货物信息详细记录在载货清单上，并铅封盖章，随船送至哈尔滨关（或三姓分关）以便核查，载货清单之抄件则保存于拉哈苏苏分关档案室中。凡轮船驶往下游者，均须出示哈尔滨关或三姓分关签发的所有海关凭证，待关员核查过货物和凭证后方可离港。详细的《拉哈苏苏分关章程》不日将起草完毕，其中轮船过关和关员查验之手续应尽量简化，以便拉哈苏苏分关据此指导船主有序过关，规范关员查验货物。鉴于拉哈苏苏分关之工作并不复杂，故不必派遣帮办前往此地任职。在研究过当地之情形后，式美第（A. Schmidt）先生认为派遣两名洋籍铃子手和六名华籍水手或士兵即可。但本署认为，需由一名帮办甚至是副税务司负责接管拉哈苏苏分关关产、与当地政府沟通以及逐步开展工作等事。

11. 待哈尔滨江关和拉哈苏苏分关开展工作后，便可筹备设立三姓分关。在筹建三姓分关之前，本署将就三姓贸易市场一事呈交初步研究报告，供贵署参考。三姓分关之工作与哈尔滨关其他分关类似，如征收税款和江捐，查验装卸货物并为货物签发海关凭证以及管控来自上游哈尔滨和下游拉哈苏苏内陆地区的货物。三姓当地时常出现航运管控问题，因此需一名帮办在此任职。现今还不能确定此地所需关员几何，但预计设立海关需有一到两名华籍供事、一到两名书办、三到四名铃子手或巡役及若干水手等在此任职。

12. 除上述工作外，新设立的分关还负责组织修建和维护航路标志。本署已在哈尔滨关致海关总税务司署第 60 号呈汇报过，此前航路标志相关事务由"河道委员会（River Committee）"暂管（该委员会的详细介绍可参阅哈尔滨关致海关总税务司署第 132 号呈中式美第（A. Schmidt）先生之报告）。10 月 21 日，海关监督和本署与郝沃斯（Howarth）将军和"河道委员会"主席商讨松花江上的航路标志问题，最终商定"河道委员会"于 10 月 28 日停止对航路标志之管理，并自当日起将管理权移交海关。"河道委员会"已在移交管理权的当日将上一季度工作账户余额 3000 卢布转交至本署，并称此笔款项为河道专用开支。河道沿岸的灯塔等航务设备本属中东铁路公司，现已移交海关，但尚未支付购置费用。本关区至少需要两艘摩托艇用以处理河道工作，依据贵署在 1908 年 10 月 30 日的半官函中的批复，本署已与巡工司联系借用一艘摩托艇。此外，东三省总督另为哈尔滨关提供一艘（或多艘）摩托艇（现停靠于山海关），现已命令山海关理船厅仔细检视，并汇报是否可用。式美第先生认为，待征税开始后便可减轻海关现今面临的财务困难（参阅式美第先生报告）。然而于海关而言，航务工作较为陌生，海关不了解河流长度以及江岸沙化特质等问题，因此修建航路标志工程难度较大。过去几年来，航路标志由俄国方面负责维护且保存完好，现中国政府将维护航路标志一事委托给海关，海关需早作准备，以免因工作失误或管理不周引来外界严厉批评。因此请贵署批准，派遣泰勒（Tyler）船长或额得志（Eldridge）船长于4月前往哈尔滨关任职数周，以便指导航务关员了解航务工作，同时防止因管理部门变化而影响航务工作进度。此时虽有较多航务工作急需处理，但本署不知何人接受过专门培训或是有此能力和资格可代为处理。在航运季结束前二等钤子手雅克森（Jacobson）先生曾乘坐轮船巡视了松花江和黑龙江，初步了解了河道情况和河道上的原有标记。因此本署认为雅克森先生或可负责航务工作。

13. 前"河道委员会"（River Committee）原计划于冬季水位较低时拓深和疏浚三姓分关附近一条航道（具体计划为使用工作账户余额购置炸药，利用炸药爆破），但并未实施。兹建议待哈尔滨关接管工作账户余额后不必按照原计划继续执行。

14. 邮政局早已在三姓开展业务，兹建议松花江轮船可为邮局运送信件。由两至三名往来于呼兰府和三姓的华籍信差可负责于沿途送信之事（参阅海关总税务司署第1167号通令），海关也可通过为俄籍船只退还一半特别准单费的做法确保其帮助邮政局运送信件。

15. 本署认为，凡因哈尔滨关管理航务而产生的额外费用均以哈尔滨关总账户支付；另将管理未来从江捐收入中的拨款和当前开支计入子目录项下；至于修建和维护航路标志的支出以及船钞之收入，可由C账户人账。

您忠诚的仆人

（签名）葛诺发（N.A.Konovaloff）

哈尔滨关税务司

该抄件内容真实有效，特此证明：
录事：周骊（C.H.B.Joly）二等帮办前班

2. 为瑷珲设立港务课及维护黑龙江航路标志事

Amur River Navigation.
Establishment of harbour office at Aigun and
repairs to aids to navigation: report on, requested

No. 2339   Commrs.

Harbin.   No. 79,904

INSPECTORATE GENERAL OF CUSTOMS.

PEKING, 30th August, 1920.

Sir,

       With reference to previous correspondence on the subject of :

       Amur River Navigation:

I append for your perusal copy of Shui-wu Ch'u despatches Nos.1192 and 1254 from which you will see that the question of establishment of a Harbour office at Aigun and of repairing the aids to navigation on the Amur by the Chinese Government are again raised.

       You are accordingly requested to express your views on both these questions and to report in particular if in your opinion the conditions prevailing along the Amur justify the enormous expenditure which will be involved in case China undertakes to restore and maintain the aids to navigation on that River. I have to remark that a Harbour Office at Aigun would appear to be of little value to shipping unless the question of the aids was first settled.

       Your despatch in reply should be accompanied by a Chinese version in duplicate.

               I am,

                  Sir,

           Your obedient Servant,

         (Signed) Cecil A. V. Bowra,

           Officiating Inspector General,
              ad interim.

True Copy:
3rd Clerk, B.

The Commissioner of Customs,

    H A R B I N.   APPENDIX.

<u>Translations of Shui-wu Ch'u Despatches Nos. 1192 and 1254. to the</u>

<u>Inspector General of Customs.</u>

No. 1192.   3rd   August, 1920.

The Wutung Steam Navigation Co. in their despatch report

"a confidential telegram has been received from the
Manager of our Branch Office at Habarovsk stating
that Jaopan is endeavouring to exclude Chinese
vessels from navigating the Amur between Habarovsk
and Nikolaivsk and that negotiations between Japan
and Russia are at present in progress by which the
Amur between Habarovsk and Nikolaivsk is only to
be open to Russian and Japanese vessels, and that
if an agreement be once made by these parties there
would be no hope of restoring our rights; requesting
that the Government be asked to inform the Diplomatic
representatives of both the parties concerned that
in accordance with the treaty provisions only
Chinese and Russian vessels are permitted to
navigate the Amur down to its mouth and that any
agreement between Japan and Russia cannot in any
way affect China's original rights etc. According
to Article I of the Aigun Treaty of 1858 the navigation of the Amur, Sungari and Ussuri Rivers is
only permitted to Russian and Chinese shipping,
vessels of other nationality not being permitted.
Amur River indicates the section from the Upper
Argun River ^(?) down to Nikolaivsk. As the Treaty
is in existence Russia could not in any way alienate
arbitrarily the right to Japan. Again, Russia's
former refusal to allow Chinese vessels to navigate

                                                        the

~~the navigate~~ the Amur was made under pretext of our
having spent nothing in the establishment of lights
etc. ~~How~~ Most of the aids to navigation have now
become dilapidated owing to the disturbed condition
of Russia during these last years. Russia would
evidently agree that we should do the necessary
repairs to them and by this means not only the share
which we should have paid in the establishment of the
aids would be offset but also the navigation rights
on the several thousand li of the Amur River would
be secured. Taking advantage of the Customs station
at Aigun, we should have to establish a Harbour Office
there to which the business of repairing the Aids to
navigation might be entrusted. The expenditure might
be defrayed by a contribution to be imposed upon
vessels. The shipping firms on the other hand must
show their patriotism and pay the contribution
obediently. The above being a scheme concerning the
defence of the nation and the rights of navigation,
merchants do not seem to be in a position to make any
proposition, but in view of the above mentioned
conditions we could hardly remain silent. Although
our vessels navigating the Amur, Argun (?) and Ussuri
Rivers have lately suffered dangers and losses very
frequently, yet we have never been discouraged from
the purpose of preserving our rights. We therefore
beg that the provisions of the Aigun treaty be re-
announced to Japan and Russia lest they come to an
agreement permitting no Chinese vessels on the Amur
below Habarovsk in which case it would be difficult
to restore our rights. With regard to the establishment of a Harbour Office we also hope that it will
meet with your kind consideration."
According to the Inspector General's previous despatch No.

No. Ying 82, it would seem unnecessary to establish a
Harbour Office at Aigun, but in view of ~~thexfxmts~~ having
the advantage of a Customs station there etc. as stated
above by the Wutung Co. this question seems worthy of
consideration. The Ch'u is writing to Wai-chiao Pu and also
requests you to submit your views on this question.

No. 1254.   21st August, 1920.

With reference to the Chiao-tung Pu Despatch:
     "regarding the establishment of a Harbour Office
     at Aigun the Ministry communicated to you the
     repeated request of the Heilungchiang Tuchun and
     you subsequently appointed the River Inspector,
     Mr. Garden, to make an inspection, and the
     Inspector General was also instructed by you to
     instruct Mr. Garden to discuss the matter with
     the Heiho Taoyin and the Senior Assistant of the
     Aigun Customs, Mr. Mansfield. In the opinion of
     the Inspector General and Mr. Garden the joint
     administration of the aids to navigation is not
     advisable, but in view of the proposed Harbour
     regulation for Taheiho drawn up by Mr. Garden and
     submitted to the Ministry through the Taoyin at
     the time when the negotiations for an arrangement
     for the nivigation of the Amur, Sungari and Ussuri
     Rivers by Chinese vessels was in progress, the
     establishment of a ~~Six~~ Harbour Office had been laid
     down so to speak. The reason of Mr. Garden's
     strong objection to the joint administration was
     that the lights had all been established by Russia
     and that if the joint administration of aids to

to navigation should be suddenly effected there
would be difficulty in taking over. Most of the
lights have now been dilapidated and if China
on one hand raises funds to repair them and on
the other to establish a Harbour Office to control
them there would evidently be no objection on
the part of Russia. You are therefore requested
to ask the I.G. to instruct the Aigun Assistant to
discuss the matter with the Harbin Commissioner
and make careful arrangements in order to preserve the national rights."

In view of the Wutung Co's despatch regarding the repairs
to the aids to navigation and the establishment of a
Harbour Office at Aigun, which has been brought to your
notice by despatch No.1192,and the above despatch to the
same effect you are to instruct the xhx Customs stations
concerned to take the necessary steps in this matter and
report to the Shui-wu Ch'u for approval.

True Translations:

3rd Clerk, <u>B</u>.

致哈尔滨关第 <u>2339/79904</u> 号令　　　海关总税务司署（北京）1920 年 8 月 30 日

尊敬的哈尔滨关税务司：

　　根据此前与黑龙江航务有关的往来函文，兹附上税务处第 1192 号及 1254 号令抄件，以供详阅。从中可知，中国政府已再次提及于瑷珲设立港务课及维护黑龙江上的航路标志事。

　　请对该两项事宜给出意见，尤需说明以黑龙江上当前的贸易情况来看，是否值得中国政府投入大量经费开展相应的航路标志重建及维护工作。如果航路标志问题不能得以解决，于瑷珲设立港务课，于船运而言，亦是毫无意义。

　　呈交报告时，请随附中文译本，一式两份。

您忠诚的仆人

（签字）包罗（C. A. V. Bowra）

暂行代理总税务司

该抄件内容真实有效，特此证明：

录事：三等同文供事副前班

附录

税务处致海关总税务司第 1192 号及 1254 号令译本

税务处令第 1192 号

前据戊通航业公司呈报：

"据本公司［哈巴罗夫斯克（Habarovsk）］分部经理密电称，日本试图剥夺中国船只于黑龙江自哈巴罗夫斯克至尼古拉耶夫斯克（Nickolaevsk）河段航行的权利，现正与俄国商议将此河段仅对俄日两国船只开放。双方一旦达成协议，中国将再无希望夺回于此河段航行之权利。恳请政府警告日俄两国外交代表，依照条约规定，仅中俄两国船只有权于黑龙江上航行至入海口，无论日俄两国达成何种协议，均不得侵害中国原有之权利。1858 年《瑷珲条约》第一条规定："黑龙江、松花江、乌苏里江，此后只准中国、俄国行船，个别外国船只不准由此江河行走。"黑龙江即指自上游额尔古纳河至下游尼古拉耶夫斯克（Nickolaevsk）河段。鉴于此条约仍有效力，因此俄国无论如何都不得擅自将此权利转让给日本。另外，俄国此前拒不允许中国船只于黑龙江上航行，是以中国从未参与于江上修建灯照标杆等事为由，而近年来，俄国政局动荡，此前所建航路标志如今已是破旧不堪。相信俄国定会同意由中国出资修缮航路标志，而中国亦可借此机会弥补初建航路标志时未能摊付费用之缺憾，还可获得于黑龙江数千里航道上航行的权利。而且瑷珲已设有海关，借此设立港务部门负责航路标志的维修工作，应非难事。经费方面或许可由船只摊付一部分，船运公司也应发扬爱国主义精神，积极承担相应的费用支出。以上所涉关乎对国家利益及航行权利的维护，商人似乎无权提出意见，然基于上述种种，吾等亦无法保持沉默。近日来，公司船只在黑龙江、额尔古纳河及乌苏里江上航行时，屡屡遇险，损失惨重，但即便如此，吾等也从未有过放弃航行权利的念头，遂恳请向日俄两国重申《瑷珲条约》之规定，以防该两国达成协定，不再允准中国船只于黑龙江哈巴罗夫斯克下游河段航行。若如此，中国再想重获于此河段航行的权利，只怕会更加困难。另望酌情考虑设立港务部门一事。"

据总税务司盈字第 82 号来呈所述，于瑷珲设立港务课似乎无甚必要，然如戊通航业公司所言，当地已设有海关，此事似乎值得商榷。已致函外交部，相应令行总税务司酌核呈复可也。此令

1920 年 8 月 3 日

税务处令第 1254 号

前据交通部咨称：

"此前黑龙江督军再三提及于瑷珲设立港务部门一事，本部已据实传达，而税务处业已相应任命巡江工司贾登（H.G.Garden）先生前去调查，同时令总税务司指示贾登先生与黑河道尹及瑷珲海关超等帮办满士斐（R. D. Mansfield）先生商议此事。虽然总税务司与贾登先生皆认为由中俄两国联合管理航路标志事宜并不可行，但当时中国船只于黑龙江、松花江及乌苏里江上的航行事宜已在协商当中，而且由贾登先生为大黑河海关草拟的《理船章程》已由道尹呈交至本部，可以说设立港务课之事已基本落实。贾登先生强烈反对由中俄两国联合管理航路标志事宜，无非是考虑到黑龙江上的航路标志皆是由俄国修建，如果突然由两国联合管理，工作交接方面将会面临诸多麻烦。但如今这些灯罩标杆大多已是破旧不堪，倘若中国能够筹集资金予以修理，同时设立港务部门负责监管，相信俄方应不会有何异议。故请令总税务司指示瑷珲海关帮办与哈尔滨关税务司商议此事，做出妥善安排，以维护国家之利益。"

如第 1192 号令中所述，戊通航业公司已呈请对修理航路标志及于瑷珲设立港务课等事酌情考虑，今交通部又有此意，故请指示该处海关采取必要措施妥善安排并呈报税务处批准。此令

1920 年 8 月 21 日

该抄件内容真实有效，特此证明：

录事：三等同文供事副前班

3. 为《临时理船章程》之修改事

PROVISIONAL HARBOUR REGULATIONS FOR AIGUN(TAHEIHO):
replies to I.G.'s queries in re and Commissioner's
recommendation to postpone promulgation of, until
appointment of River Inspector: Aigun Despatch No. 306
and Notification No.261, submitting.

No. 2343.

I. G.   Harbin, 21st March, 1921.

        Sir,

                I have the honour to acknowledge receipt

        of your Despatch No. 2482/82,695 (in reply to

        Harbin Despatch No. 1970 of the 15th August,

        1919),

                        informing me that the draft of
                        proposed Provisional Harbour Regulations
                        for Aigun (Taheiho) will be recommended
                        to the Chinese Government with some
                        alterations, asking for explanation
                        concerning the terms "River Authorities"
                        and "Special Navigation Regulations"
                        and their equivalent in Chinese which
                        appear in the draft of the proposed
                        regulations and asking to be supplied
                        with copies of the "Special Navigation
                        Regulations" if any have been pro-
                        mulgated,

        In reply I beg to report that these matters

        have been referred in turn to the Aigun

                                                Assistant

The Inspector General of Customs,

                PEKING.

Assistant whose reply (Aigun Despatch No. 306) will be found appended to this Despatch, together with one copy in English and two in Chinese of Customs Notification No. 261 - Taheiho Harbour Anchorages - the only notice that might come under the heading " Special Navigation Regulations ".

The terms 航路廳 and 行駛章程 employed in the draft may be recognized as the Chinese equivalents of the "River Authorities" and "Special Navigation Regulations". I would like to say however that article 22 of the proposed draft appears to me superfluous and might be expunged.

Mr. Talbot in his despatch No. 306, folio 2, under "Anchorages" points out that if a winter harbour is established at the lower end of the island the lower limits could be extended to Chia Hsin-tze (夾信子) with the understanding that vessels still anchor in the summer within the limits established at present.

Mr.

Mr. Talbot also points out that it would be well to define the limits of Chinese jurisdiction within the waters of the Harbour. My ideas on these points are that in the absence of a Harbour Master $^{and}_{or}$ River Inspector for the port of Aigun (Taheiho) or of someone competent in Harbour matters and until the appointment of such a competent person no Harbour Regulations should be promulgated. I would also like to remark that the contemplated survey of the Harbour has not been taken in hand and that this matter might bear on the question of anchorage and harbour limits. Another question which will need consideration when the proposed Harbour Regulations come into force is the provision of boarding facilities for which either a gig or preferably a steam-launch on account of swift current will have to be purchased. This difficulty may perhaps be met when selling the Heilung by purchasing locally a steam

launch

launch with part of the proceeds of the sale.

In conclusion and unless the Inspectorate has special reason to enforce Harbour Regulations at Taheiho without delay, I would recommend that this matter be postponed until after the appointment of the River Inspector (Harbour Master) in place of the late Mr. Garden and after the completion of the survey of the Harbour.

A copy of this Despatch is being forwarded to the Coast Inspector.

I have the honour to be,

Sir,

Your obedient Servant,

(Signed)   R. C. L. d'Anjou,

Commissioner.

APPENDIX.

APPENDIX. No. I.

Aigun Despatch No. 306 to Harbin Commissioner.

Aigun/Taheiho, 7th March, 1921.

Sir,

  With reference to Harbin Despatch No. 189 to Aigun:

    Provisional Harbour Regulations for Aigun (Taheiho): information concerning required by I.G., requesting:

and enclosing copy of I. G. Despatch No. 2482 to Harbin in this connection, I have the honour to reply as follows.

  The term "Special Navigation Regulations" is understood by this Office to mean "Harbour Notifications" when applied to the Harbour or "Notice to Mariners" when applied to the Amur River in general. By "River Authorities" is meant local Customs authorities in charge of the River affairs (including Harbour Master) and would appear to mean that the appointment of a River Inspector, Harbour Master, etc., was contemplated at the time the Regulations were drafted.

  The only notice that has been posted in this sub-district that might come under the heading "Special Navigation Regulations" is Customs Notification No. 261 - TAHEIHO HARBOUR ANCHORAGES - issued by Harbin on the 5th September, 1919.

I

I have carefully gone over the Regulations forwarded in Aigun Despatch No. 250 with Messrs. Wahlgren and Grundt and find that there is nothing radical to suggest in the way of alterations but there are certain minor points that might be made more clear.

ANCHORAGES.

2. In fixing Harbour Limits would it be well to say anything about the limit of Chinese jurisdiction with respect to the middle of the River? If a winter harbour is established at the lower end of the island and it is necessary to establish control over it, the lower limits could be extended to Chia Hsin-tze（夹信子）with the understanding that vessels still anchor in the summer within the limits as established at present.

CONSERVANCY.

17. The phrase "without permission of the Harbour Master" might be extended to include the words "and continued to his satisfaction".

19. (Second Paragraph). The last sentence might better read "Neither is cargo to be stored on the foreshore or bund or buildings of a permanent or temporary nature erected without

special

special permission of Customs
authorities". This would do away wit
the practice of erecting sheds promis
cously along the foreshore.

MISCELLANEOUS.

32. The term "prosecuted before his
national authority" would have to
be defined as applying to Taheiho.

It is noted that these Regulations apply
only to Taheiho but provision should be made
to include Aigun and it might be said that
the same regulations shall apply there with
the exception of the Harbour Limits "which
will be duly notified to the public by special
notification". (This might appear, however, as
putting the cart before the horse as, strictly
speaking, Aigun is the open port and Taheiho
but a barrier - moreover the fact that Taheiho
has never been "opened" would have to be
thought of in connection with MISCELLANEOUS 32).

I have considered the question of the
new taxation of Amur traffic as effecting the
proposed Regulations and cannot see that it
need be taken specially into consideration.
Rafts will be regulated under Rule 1, as will
other native craft, and Foreign steamers on the
Amur will come under the same category as any
others.

I have, etc.,

(Signed)   R. M. Talbot,

2nd Assistant, A.

APPENDIX.

APPENDIX NO. II.

Copy of Harbin Customs Notification No. 261.

TAHEIHO HARBOUR ANCHORAGES.

The Upper and Lower limits of the Harbour are respectively from Shih Shan T'ou Hill to below the Public Park.

The anchorages for foreign-type vessels are:-

(a) For vessels other than those provided for in (b), for which special anchorages have been assigned, between the Upper and Lower limits of the Harbour as defined above.

(b) For vessels carrying mineral oil and explosives, and those subject to quarantine regulations, outside the Upper limits of the Harbour.

Vessels shall moor in accordance with instructions from the Harbour Master, and shall not shift their berths without a special permit, except when outward bound after having obtained their clearance papers.

Vessels may not lie in the stream at single anchor.

(Signed) P. Grevedon,
Commissioner of Customs.

Office of the Commissioner of Customs,   True Copy:

Harbin, 5th September, 1919.

3rd Clerk, B

哈爾濱關稅務司柯佈告 第二百六十一號

為佈告事案據大黑河分關規定船隻拋錨界限呈請公佈等情前來合亟佈

告各船戶人等一體遵照毋違此佈

計開

大黑
河關 停泊界限

界限 圍後身
拋錨 頭下至公
河關 上至兩山

甲凡船為洋式
而非屬於乙
乙凡裝煤油爆
裂物料及應
候查驗有無
疫症應行隔
離之船隻應
均應於前條
所規定之界
限內下椗
在上界之外
泊時不准只下一錨

凡船隻停泊事宜均須聽由理船
廳指示所有停泊之船隻除已
領有海關准放行之紅單者可以任
便開行外其餘並未領有特發准單
各船隻均不得擅自移泊凡船隻停

中華民國八年九月五日

呈海关总税务司署 <u>2343</u> 号文　　　　　　　哈尔滨关 1921 年 3 月 21 日

尊敬的海关总税务司（北京）：

　　海关总税务司署第 2482/82695 号令（为回复 1919 年 8 月 15 日哈尔滨关第 1970 号呈）收悉：

　　　　"瑷珲分关（大黑河）《临时理船章程》草案稍作修订后可呈交至中国政府；要求说明草案所载'River Authorities'和'Special Navigation Regulation'对应之汉文，如果此章程已经颁布，需呈交抄件。"

　　兹汇报，上述问题已请瑷珲分关帮办协助解答。据其所述，于瑷珲关区而言，唯一可划归为"Special Navigation Regulations"的便是哈尔滨关税务司布告第 261 号，兹附上此布告英文版抄件一份，中文版抄件两份，及瑷珲分关致哈尔滨关第 306 号呈抄件一份。

　　临时章程草案所载"River Authorities"和"Special Navigation Regulations"对应之汉文可为"航路厅"和"行驶章程"，但依吾之见，章程草案第二十二条略显赘余，或应删去。

　　铎博赉（R. M. Talbot）先生于瑷珲分关第 306 号呈第 2 页"锚地"项下指出，如于下流小岛低洼处设置冬季停泊处，为便于管理，港口下限或许可延伸至夹信子，惟须提前声明夏季船只仍于当前所定停泊界限以内下碇，还提出最好增加限制地方政府于港口水域内之管辖权的相关内容。对此，兹认为，在没有为瑷珲分关（大黑河）任命理船厅及/或巡江工司，或者任何有能力处理港口事务的人员之前，《理船章程》暂无颁布之必要。此外，原定的港口测量工事还未着手处理，此事或许会影响锚地及港口界限的划定。如果拟议之《临时理船章程》付诸实行，为便于关员登船检查，还需考虑购置一艘小艇，当然最好是汽艇，以适应港口内湍急之水流。届时或许可将"黑龙"（Heilung）号卖掉，再使用所得收益于当地购入一艘汽艇。

　　总之，如果海关总税务司署无特殊原因要求大黑河口岸立即施行《理船章程》，则建议暂缓此事。待任命巡江工司（或理船厅）接替已故贾登（H. G. Garden）先生之职务，完成港口测量后，再行斟酌决定。

　　此抄件发送至巡工司。

您忠诚的仆人

（签字）覃书（R. C. L. d'Anjou）

哈尔滨关税务司

附录 1

瑷珲分关致哈尔滨关税务司

呈哈尔滨关 306 号文   瑷珲分关 / 大黑河 1921 年 3 月 7 日

尊敬的哈尔滨关税务司：

根据哈尔滨关致瑷珲分关第 189 号令：

"为瑷珲分关（大黑河）《临时理船章程》事：要求呈交总税务司所需信息；"
及随附之海关总税务司署致哈尔滨关第 2482 号令抄件，特作如下回复：

本分关对 "Special Navigation Regulations" 的理解为，如涉及港口，则为《港务通告》，如涉及黑龙江航道，则为《航船布告》。至于 "River Authorities"，则为负责江上事务的地方海关关员（包括理船厅），即在起草《理船章程》时考虑任命之巡江工司、理船厅等。

本分关所颁布的章程中，唯一可划归为 "Special Navigation Regulations" 的便是哈尔滨关 1919 年 9 月 5 日颁布之海关布告第 261 号——大黑河港口抛锚界限。

兹已与华格伦（O. W. Wahlgren）先生和谷兰体（H. Grundt）先生详阅瑷珲分关致哈尔滨关第 250 号呈随附之《临时理船章程》草案，认为并无需要大改之处，惟有一些细节表述或需调整，以使表意更加明确。

具体列下：

锚地

第二条：如于此增加限制地方政府在港口水域内之管辖权的相关内容，是否于停泊界限之划定更为有益？如于下流小岛低洼处设置冬季停泊处，为便于管理，港口下限或许可延伸至夹信子，惟须提前声明夏季船只仍于当前所定停泊界限以内下碇。

河港管理

第十七条："未经理船厅批准" 之后或应补充 "如有以上各事，必须具呈理船厅批准"。

第十九条：第二段最后一句应改为 "未经海关特许，商人之货物不准堆积江岸，亦不准于该处建筑永久或暂时之房屋"。如此便可杜绝商人沿江岸乱建棚屋之行为。

杂项规定

第三十二条："可向其本国官吏控告" 应定义为适用于大黑河。

值得注意的是，此临时章程虽是为大黑河口岸所拟，但其实瑷珲口岸亦应包含在内，甚至除港口界限"将另由专项公告公布"外，余下条款皆应适用。当然，如此一来似有本末倒置之嫌，毕竟严格来说，瑷珲才是通商口岸，而大黑河不过是一处分卡而已。更何况大黑河口岸实际尚未确立"通商"之地位，上述第三十二条所定不免要将此情况考虑在内。

另外，对于临时章程施行后开始对黑龙江往来运输征税一事，兹认为暂无需特别考虑。木筏及其他华式船只将遵循同一规章办理，黑龙江上往来之外国轮船将与其他轮船划归为一类。

您忠诚的仆人

（签字）铎博赉（R.M.Talbot）

二等帮办前班

附录 2

哈尔滨关税务司布告第 261 号抄件

大黑河港口抛锚界限

停泊界限上至西山头，下至公园后身。

洋式船只抛锚界限：

（1）凡船为洋式而非属于乙款内所指者，均应于前条所规定之界限内下碇。

（2）凡装煤油爆裂物料及听候查验有无疫症应行隔离之船只，应在上界之外。

凡船只停泊事宜，均须听由理船厅指示。所有停泊之船只，除已另有海关准放行之红单者可以任便开行外，其余并未领有特发准单各船只均不得擅自移泊。凡船只停泊时，不准只下一锚。

（签名）柯必达（P. Grevedon）

哈尔滨关税务司

1919 年 9 月 5 日

该抄件内容真实有效，特此证明。

录事：三等同文供事副前班

4. 为俄方提议管理黑龙江航路标志工作并征收江捐以支付航路标志维护费用事

834.

4.C.

Harbin   5th May, 1922.

SIR,

    With reference to Aigun Despatch No. 44 to
the address of the Inspector General :

            concerning the Russian proposal to
            operate the Aids to Navigation on
            the River Amur, collecting river
            dues for the upkeep of same, and
            the Aigun Commissioner's remarks and
            recommendations in re :

I beg to offer the following remarks based on my
experience in this district and the study of this
question in 1919 when appointed on the Sino-Russian
Commission.

    The most satisfactory solution of this
problem of upkeep of Aids to Navigation on the
Sino-Russian river frontiers consists in the division
of the jointly - owned rivers into two portions to
be determined by a Sino-Russian commission, one

                                    portion

The Inspector General of Customs,

    PEKING.

portion of which would be administered by China and the other by Russia, each country defraying the cost of the upkeep of its own section, while the cost of important engineering works, etc., mutually agreed upon would be shared by both. It would also be fair if China were to reimburse Russia for a share of the Aids to Navigation, such as buoys and beacons, put up by Russia on the basis of their present value.

In the present financial stress of the Chinese Government this proposal cannot probably be immediately realised. Owing to the immediate necessity of re-establishing Aids to Navigation on the Amur the most practical solution for the present would be to accept temporarily, and for the year 1922, the Russian proposal to undertake this work, China defraying a certain sum towards expenses, a sum which it would be well to determine beforehand in consultation with the Russians and not to exceed $50,000.00. The idea of the Russians collecting taxes on the Chinese side

side cannot be possibly entertained. They should collect whatever taxes they like on their own vessels and their cargoes, and China would devise means, in consultation with the Aigun Authorities, Chambers of Commerce, Shipping Companies and the Aigun Commissioner, to raise the sum necessary to pay for her share of expenses (a maximum of $50,000.00). To obtain this sum some charges as in force on the Sungari, for the sake of uniformity, should be collected on steamers according to horse - power, on junks and barges according to tonnage, and on Amur river-borne cargoes per pood and per distance. The collection of these taxes and the payment of China's contribution towards the upkeep of the Aids should be in the hands of the Aigun Customs, the latter on receipt of detailed accounts and inspection of Aids to Navigation on the jointly-owned section.

The question of Aids to Navigation on the River Ussuri, which more directly concerns this office, should be left in abeyance until conditions

in

in that district are more settled. Our Harbour
Master could collect during the next winter some
information concerning that river and an inspection
might be prepared the following season under the
guidance of the Coast Inspector.

A copy of this despatch is being sent to
the Aigun Commissioner.

I have the honour to be,

Sir,

Your obedient Servant,

(Signed) R.C.L.d'Anjou.

Commissioner.

True Copy:-

2nd Assistant A:

呈海关总税务司署 <u>2634</u> 号文　　　　　　　哈尔滨关 1922 年 5 月 5 日

尊敬的海关总税务司（北京）：

　　根据瑷珲关至海关总税务司署第 44 号呈：

　　　"关于俄方提议管理黑龙江航路标志工作，并于黑龙江航道征收江捐以支付航路标志维护费用事宜，以及瑷珲关税务司之回应意见及提议。"

　　根据本署在大黑河地区之经验以及于 1919 年参加中俄委员会之时对此问题之研究，兹提出以下意见。

　　中俄边界河道航路标志维护问题最适宜之解决办法应为，由中俄委员会决定将共同拥有之河流分为两部分，一部分由中国管理，另一部分由俄国管理，双方承担各自管理部分的维护费用，而经双方同意的重要工程及工作等之费用由双方共同承担。若中国欲按当前价值偿还俄国所立浮标及标桩等航路标志费用，亦为公平之举。

　　中国政府目前面临财政压力，恐难以立即实现此提议。然而，鉴于需立即于黑龙江航道重建航路标志，因此目前最切实有效之解决办法应为，接受暂时及 1922 年由俄方承担此工作之提议，而中国则摊付一定数额的费用，但应提前与俄方议定金额，不可超过 50000.00 银圆。至于俄方欲于航道华岸征税之想法，则不予考虑。俄方可随意向其本国船只及货物征税，而中国政府将与瑷珲县政府、黑河商会、船运公司以及瑷珲关税务司商定如何筹集需要支付的费用（最多 50000.00 银圆）。为筹得此款，可遵循统一原则，按照松花江现行征税标准，按马力向轮船征税，按吨位向民船及驳船征税，按普特及距离向黑龙江沿岸货物征税。此外，所征税额及中国应付之航路标志维护费用（待收到俄方账款明细并检查联合维护河段的航路标志后再行支付）皆应由瑷珲关管理。

　　乌苏里江航路标志问题与哈尔滨关有更直接之关系，但待其状况更为稳定之时，再行处理。哈尔滨关理船厅可于明年冬季收集一些乌苏里江航道的信息，或可在巡工司指导之下，准备明年航运季的巡查工作。

　　此抄件发送至瑷珲关税务司。

　　　　　　　　　　　　　　　　　您忠诚的仆人

　　　　　　　　　　　　　　　（签字）覃书（R. C. L. d' Anjou）

　　　　　　　　　　　　　　　哈尔滨关税务司

5. 为黑河道尹与俄阿穆尔政府之间讨论关于界河航行的协议事

47.

I. G.   Aigun / Taheiho 5th May, 1922.

Sir,

1.   In continuation of my despatch No. 44, and
in amplification of my telegram of this day :

            concerning   the Aids-to-Navigation on
            the Amur,

I have the honur to report that a meeting to
discuss this question was held in Blagovestchensk
on 2nd May, at the premises of the Russian Navigation
Office. - The representatives on the Russian side
were chiefly the Directors of the Nagivation Office,
the Emissar, the Shipowners' Association, the Chamber
of Commerce and the Customs; on the Chinese side,
the Garrison Commissioner (鎮 守 使), the Taoyin,
the Consul General in Blagovestchensk, the President
of the Chamber of Commerce, the Wutung Co. and myself.

            The discussion lasted over three hours; the

                                        Taoyin

The Inspector General of Customs,

            PEKING.

Taoyin, recognising the urgency of the upkeep of the "Aids", agreed in principle to a Convention of a purely local and temporary nature, which mainly consists of the following points :

Validity for 1922

The work to be undertaken by the Russian Navigation Office

A Commission composed of an equal number of Chinese and Russians to authorize all the work and expenditure

Uniform levy of duties on both sides, the proceeds going in toto towards the upkeep of the "Aids".

2. The Russians proposed a Tariff which shows certain modification of the terms reported in my despatch No. 44 ; it would be now as follows :

Building Materials, Iron, Cast Iron and Steel, lead, cereals, vegetables, salt, coal, agricultural implements and machinery other than wooden, to pay 1 cent per pood

Firewood, Timber, Cattle and Horses, Sheep and Pigs, to pay as already reported

Fowls of all description, 1 cent a piece

All other goods (including therefore Piece-Goods) to pay 2 cents per pood

Besides, they now intend to levy on cargo carried by Ferries and on re-exports. The collection

in

in this case may amou t to 50,000 or 60,000 dollars.

But at the meeting nothing was definitely settled about the Tariff, and it was only agreed that representatives of both parties would meet at an early date, and work out the details of the Tariff and of the working of the Commission. The Russians wanted to fix the 5th of May as the date for signing the Agreement, but the Taoyin wisely objected, and proposed that it be signed "as soon as possible".

5. It was also proposed that the Agreement be signed for China by the Taoyin and the Commissioner of Customs; but, in the absence of instructions, and thinking that this may mix me up with political issues which are beyond the scope of the Customs, I called the following day on the Taoyin and persuaded him that my signature would add nothing to his, while requiring your authority and perhaps a long time to get it. At the same interview the Taoyin asked who would be the fittest representative of China in the future Commission, and

and I suggested a River Inspector, as possessing adequate technical skill, and as benefiting by the work previously done by the late Mr. Garden.

4.   This morning, at the Taoyin's Office, took place a meeting of Chinese commercial and shipping interests; the usual conflict between shipowners and merchants was evident, the former opposing Tonnage Dues because they do not want to take the risk of a lean year; the latter saying that the chief burden should fall on the vessels, which derive more direct benefit from the "Aids". Finally, considering that the work is urgent for the common welfare, and cannot be undertaken except with the assistance of the Russians who have an organisation ready, it was concluded that, provisionally, it would be better to give way to the russian point of view, and agree to the collection of River Dues. But, instead of a single rate for the whole River, it should be proposed to divide its length into four sections, with different rates according to the number of sections travelled. Another meeting will be held on the 8th instant.

5.   I have sent you to-day a telegram asking

a) whether

a) whether the Customs may collect dues under this local Agreement ; it is my opinion that our abstention would constitute a diminutio capitis and a bad precedent

b) whether Lahasusu could collect on cargo and passengers from or for points below Aigun; collection at Lahasusu is essential to any scheme. I have also wired to the Harbin Commissioner, asking whether he would consent, with your approval

c) whether collection of duty on passengers' tickets may be made through the Shipping Cos., on inspection of their Books, which the Taoyin guarantees; it is entirely a departure from our practice, but is the only way, especially for passages between points where there is no Custom House. This duty on tickets is objectionable, and should be done away as soon as possible

d) whether the Tariff can be fixed in Dollars; this for uniformity's sake, and for simplicity of calculation. In my opinion, these moneys may be considered not as collection, but as Local Moneys, until an Agreement is concluded between the two Governments, and collection is started by direct order from Peking

e) whether the total collection may be surrendered without deduction;this in view of the meagre resources and the magnitude of the task, especially the first year, when the "Aids", neglected for several years, will require very important repairs and modifications.

As

As to the way of ascertaining the weight in poods, I propose to accept the figures of the Shipping Orders; in this case, not very much extra work will be involved on the part of this Office; the Bank of China agrees to collect without fee or commission.

6.   It would have been certainly preferable for the Customs, had Tonnage Dues been adopted; but certain considerations make it imperative to accept for the present an imperfect agreement, rather than none at all. In fact, neither the Russian, nor the Chinese Government, are in a position to guarantee a certain sum for the upkeep of the "Aids"; the Chinese Government even does not want to have an Official Agreement for the present. Under these conditions local resources are only to be counted upon, and it is natural that the same kind of duty, at the same rate, be levied on both sides. The Russians do not agree to Tonnage Dues, partly through habit, partly by interest; as they have the materials and organisation, which China could not improvise, even if the money were at hand, it is hard to oppose them.

But

But my ideas as to a future and permanent Arrangement are these :

a) an estimate should be made, beforehand, of the expenditure necessary for one season

b) this amount should be apportioned between China and Russia - with perhaps a larger share to China, in consideration of the Russians supplying the materials

c) each contry should be free to levy the necessary amount with whatever kind of taxation is deemed most suited. If the collection falls short of the required amout, - due to heavy slump in trade - the Government is to make good; if there is an excess, it is laid aside for the following year.

On the Chinese side

1) the Tax should be calculated so as to cover the amount allotted to China

2) it should preferably take the shape of an ad valorem duty on cargo - plus Tonnage Dues on a normal basis, in order to have the vessels share the burden. Tonnage Dues should possibly be collected also on the Russian side, at the same rate.

As to the ad valorem Tax, I have calculated that, for 1921, goods for a value of Hk. Tls. 4,500,000 were carried by water from or to Aigun/Taheihe; Dues at the rate of 1 % would yield

about

about $ 70,000. - Tonnage Dues should be preferably
collected every month, or every two months, owing
to the facility of a steamer being laid up; and
extension should be granted, not only for the time
of undergoing repairs, but also for the time spent
on the Sungari (or other rivers not included in
the Arrangement, such as the Zeia, Ussuri, the Amur
below Habarovsk (Kasakevitch) to be recorded on the
Certificates by the Lahasusu or other Office. Probably $ 10,000 could be easily collected on this
side. The amount necessary to the upkeep of the
"Aids" on very economical lines can best be ascertained after one year's working.

7.   I am practically sure that my view would
meet with the approval of the local Officials and
Merchants; kindly let me know whether you agree with
them, or else on what principles you would like me
to work for a possible definite Agreement in the
years to come.

8.   The text of the Agreement not being definitely decided upon, I am not sending copy of it.

                    I have the honour to be, Sir,

                         Your obedient Servant,

                              Acting Commissioner.

呈海关总税务司署 <u>47</u> 号文 　　　　　　瑷珲关 / 大黑河 1922 年 5 月 5 日

尊敬的海关总税务司（北京）：

1. 根据瑷珲关第 44 号呈 1922 年 5 月 5 日电报：

"关于黑龙江航务。"

兹汇报，布拉戈维申斯克（Blagovestchensk）俄阿穆尔水道局已于 5 月 2 日召开会议讨论黑龙江航务相关问题。俄方代表主要有俄阿穆尔水道局各督办、密使、船主协会、商会及俄国海关；华方代表有镇守使、道尹、驻布拉戈维申斯克总领事、商会主席、戊通公司及瑷珲关署理税务司。

此次会议讨论持续三个多小时；道尹承认"航路标志"维护工作十分迫切，原则上同意签订一份仅限于地方的临时性协议，主要包括以下几点：

协议仅于 1922 年有效；

航路标志维护工作由俄阿穆尔水道局执行；

中俄双方以等量人员成立委员会，由该委员会对所有工作及支出予以批准。

双方统一征税，税款完全用于"航路标志"维护工作。

2. 俄方所提议之关税对瑷珲关第 44 号呈中所报告各项有所修改；现关税标准如下：

建筑材料、铁、生铁、钢、铅制品、谷物、蔬菜、盐、煤炭、非木质农业用具，税率为每普特 1 分；

木桩、木料、牛和马匹、羊和猪，税率与之前报告相同；

各种家禽，税率为每只 1 分；

其他所有货物（包括按件货物），税率均为每普特 2 分。

此外，双方现欲向渡船所运货物及复出口货物征税。于此征税总额可达 50000 至 60000 银圆。

但会议并未对关税事宜做出任何明确决定，仅协定双方代表尽快会面制定详细关税标准，研究中俄黑龙江水道委员会之具体工作内容。俄方希望定于 5 月 5 日签署协议，但道尹明智地提出反对，提议"尽快"签署协议。

3. 双方于会上提议，华方由道尹及海关（瑷珲关）税务司签署协议；但因本署尚未获得贵署指示，同时考虑到会因此卷入政治问题，超出了海关的职责范围，故于次日拜访道尹，劝说道尹本署之签字并无任何意义，且需向海关总税务司署请求批准，可能尚需一段时日。道尹同时问及将来若成立委员会，华方代表最适合之人选应为何人，本署建议巡江工司，因其不仅技术能力相当，还可得益于已故贾登（H. G. Garden）先生前期之功。

4. 今晨,道尹召集商会及船运公司于道尹公署举行会议;会上,船主及商人之间的冲突显而易见,船主因不愿冒一年欠收之风险,而反对船钞;商人则认为船只更直接受益于"航路标志",应承担主要责任。最后,鉴于此项工作宜于共同福利,实为迫切,但若无俄方(已有组织机构)协助,将无法进行,遂决定,暂时听凭俄方之意见,同意征收江捐。但税率方面,会上提出不应于整条航道使用单一税率,而是将航道分为四段,按照航行距离,制定不同税率。本月 8 日将再次召开会议。

5. 瑷珲关 5 月 5 日电报内容如下:

（1）海关是否可以按此地方协议征收江捐;兹认为,若弃权可能会削减海关权利,若开此先例亦为不妥。

（2）拉哈苏苏分关是否可以向瑷珲关下游往来货物及乘客征税;拉哈苏苏征税于任何方案而言均至关重要。本署亦向哈尔滨关税务司发送电报,询问若有海关总税务司批准,其是否会予以同意。

（3）可否由船运公司代行向乘客征税,道尹保证会检查其账簿;虽与海关惯例相悖,但此为唯一之法,尤其当乘客往返之地未设海关之时,海关便无法向其征税。按照票面征税可能会引起反对,应尽快取消。

（4）可否使用银圆制定关税;既为统一,亦为计算简便。兹认为在双方政府签订协议,乃至北京直接下令开始征税之前,所征税款皆可不计入税收一项,而计入地方公款。

（5）可否不扣除海关征税佣金而直接上交全部税收;鉴于目前资源紧、任务重,且此为签订协议之第一年,"航路标志"因已搁置数年,定需重大维修或改动。

关于以普特确定重量之方法,兹提议以装货单上的数据为准;于此海关不会涉及太多额外工作;中国银行同意不收取佣金。

6. 于海关而言,征收船钞本应为最佳选择;但全面考虑过后,发现此项临时协议虽不完善,但亦强于不签订协议,故应暂予接受。实际上,中俄双方政府均无法保证"航路标志"维护费用所需之金额;中国政府甚至不希望当下签订正式协议。鉴于此,地方经费成为唯一经济来源,且中俄双方必然要以相同税率向两岸征收同种关税。俄方不同意征收船钞,一部分源于习惯,一部分源于利益;俄方有物料、有组织,皆非中国可临时拼凑而成,即使收到税款,亦难以处置。

但本署认为可为将来做如下长久安排:

（1）应提前制定航运季所需的支出预算。

（2）由中俄双方分摊预算金额——鉴于俄方会提供物料等,中国或可摊付较大份额。

（3）中俄双方均有可采用最适合的税收方式来征收所需经费。若因贸易严重衰退等事，以致所征税款未能达到要求之金额，政府应予以补偿；若所征税款超过要求金额，留用于下一年。

华岸征税事项：

（1）税收预算应足以支付华方所摊金额。

（2）更宜向货物采取按价征税之方式——在常规基础上加征船钞，以使船只分担税负；俄岸或可以相同税率征收船钞。

关于按价征税，本署已计算出 1921 年经水运运自或运至瑷珲关 / 大黑河的货物价值约为 4500 海关两；按照 1% 的税率，税收约为 70000 银圆。鉴于轮船可能闲置，船钞更适宜于每月或每两月征收一次；除应于维修时准予延期征收外，船只于松花江（或此项安排以外的其他河流，如结雅河、乌苏里江、哈巴罗夫斯克（嘎杂克维池]）下游的黑龙江）上航行之时间，若由拉哈苏苏或其他分关记录在检查凭证之上，亦应准予延期征收。如此或可征税约 10000 银圆。一年之后，便可筹得"航路标志"维护工作所需之金额。

7. 兹确定，上述观点可获地方官员及商人的认可；望贵署告知是否同意如此安排，若希望海关将来可促成中俄双方签订确切之协议，兹请告知谈判之准则。

8. 因未确定协议文本，故未发送其抄件。

您忠诚的仆人

包安济（G. Boezi）

瑷珲关署理税务司

6. 为委任易保罗先生为黑龙江航务专门顾问事

COMMRS.   INSPECTORATE GENERAL OF CUSTOMS,

No. 90,949   PEKING, 2nd September 1922.

Sir,

    I am directed by the Inspector General
to append copy of his despatch No. 2928/90,948 to
the Harbin Commissioner from which you will see
that Mr. Ignatieff has been appointed to the
Aigun Customs as Technical Adviser on Amur Aids
to Navigation on a 3 years' Agreement, to date
from 16th September, with pay at the rate of
Hk.Tls.350 during the first year and Hk.Tls. 375
and 400 during the second and third years
respectively to be issued by your office.

    Mr. Ignatieff is to be provided with
unfurnished quarters, in accordance with the
information supplied in your telegram of 31st
August.

      I am,
        Sir,
    Your obedient Servant,

              Chief Secretary.
The Commissioner of Customs,

   AIGUN.   Appendix.

2928

Appendix.

I. G. despatch No.75/90,949 to Aigun.

from   90,948   2nd September 1922.

Sir,

       With reference to I. G. telegram of 26th

August :

           you are authorised offer to Ignatieff

           appointment under three years agreement

           as Technical Adviser on Amur Aids to

           Navigation to Aigun Customs on following

           terms: Hk.Tls.350 first year 375 second

           year and 400 third year with quarters

           or Rent Allowance in lieu thereof.

           Wire if willing accept and when available;

and to your telegram, in reply, of 28th August:

           Ignatieff accepts and will be available

           two weeks after receipt of definite

           appointment;

I am now directed by the Inspector General to

request you to notify Mr. Ignatieff of his

appointment, on a three years' agreement, as

Technical Adviser on Amur Aids to Navigation to the

                                  Aigun

The Commissioner of Customs,

    HARBIN.

Aigun Customs, from the 16th September 1922, with pay at the rate of Hk.Tls.350 during the first year and Hk.Tls.375 and 400 during the second and third years respectively.

Mr. Ignatieff will be further entitled to unfurnished quarters or to a rent allowance <u>in lieu</u> thereof.

A draft agreement is appended to be drawn up in duplicate, one copy being retained by Mr. Ignatieff and one copy being sent to the Inspectorate, which is to be signed by yourself, as Agent for the Inspector General, and by Mr. Ignatieff.

You are further authorised to issue to Mr. Ignatieff a passage and travelling expenses to Aigun according to standing instructions, no transfer allowance being however issuable in this case.

A copy of this despatch is being sent

to

to the Aigun Commissioner.

I am,

Sir,

Your obedient Servant,

(Signed) C. A. V. Bowra.

Chief Secretary.

Appendix.

Appendix.

I. G. despatch No. 2928/90,948 to Harbin.

————

A G R E E M E N T.

Harbin,　　　September 1922.

Sir,

1.　　　Acting under instructions from Sir Francis
Aglen, K. B. E., Inspector General of Chinese
Customs, I hereby offer you an appointment to the
Chinese Customs Service as "Technical Adviser on
Amur Aids to Navigation" in the Aigun Customs on
the following terms:-

　　The appointment to be for three years on a
　　salary at the rate of Haikwan Taels 350 a
　　month for the first year and Haikwan Taels
　　375 a month for the second year and Haikwan
　　Taels 400 a month for third year.
　　Unfurnished quarters will be provided or a
　　rent allowance of Hk.Tls.50 a month will be
　　issued in lieu thereof, should quarters be
　　unavailable.

2.　　　The appointment may be determined without
notice by the Inspector General at any time owing
to misconduct on your part or conduct in
contravention of Service rules and regulations; or
for any other reason on giving three months'
Notice in writing or an allowance of three months'
salary in lieu of notice.

3.

Ignatieff,

H A R B I N.

3.   In making this offer, I am acting on behalf of the Inspector General as Agent for the Chinese Government. But neither the Inspector General nor myself come under any personal liability whatever.

4.   If you accept the appointment, you will be required to proceed to Aigun by the first opportunity after the 16th September, and upon arrival there to report yourself for duty to the Commissioner of Customs. Pay will be issued from the 16th September 1922. from which date will be calculated the annual increases in pay and the termination of this agreement.

I am,

Sir,

Your obedient Servant,

Commissioner of Customs.

I accept the appointment offered in the foregoing letter on the terms and conditions set forth therein.

True Copy:

A.A. Forbes.

Acting Assistant Secretary.

致瑷珲关第 <u>75/90949</u> 号令　　　　　海关总税务司署（北京）1922 年 9 月 2 日

尊敬的瑷珲关税务司：

　　奉总税务司命令，兹附第 2928/90948 号令副本。据该令所示，委任易保罗先生（Ignatieff）担任瑷珲关黑龙江航务专门顾问，任期三年，自 9 月 16 日起生效。由贵署发放薪俸：第一年月薪为 350 海关两，第二年月薪为 375 海关两，第三年月薪为 400 海关两。

　　根据贵署 8 月 31 日电呈信息，同意给易保罗先生分一间不带家具的宿舍。

您忠诚的仆人

包罗（C. A. Bowra）

总务科税务司

海关总税务司署致瑷珲关第 75/90949 号令附件

尊敬的哈尔滨关税务司：

根据海关总税务司署 8 月 26 日电令：

"授权贵署委任易保罗先生（Ignatieff）担任瑷珲关黑龙江航务专门顾问，任期三年，合同附带以下条件：第一年月薪为 350 海关两，第二年月薪为 375 海关两，第三年月薪为 400 海关两，并为其提供宿舍或者发放租房津贴。如易保罗无异议，请电报通知本署。"

贵署 8 月 28 日回电：

"易保罗先生（Ignatieff）同意任职，将于收到正式委任书两周之后上任。"

奉总税务司命令，请贵署通知易保罗先生（Ignatieff）担任黑龙江航务专门顾问，任期三年，合同自 1922 年 9 月 16 日起生效。第一年月薪为 350 海关两，第二年月薪为 375 海关两，第三年月薪为 400 海关两。

易保罗可以选择一间不带家具的宿舍，也可选择领取租房津贴。

随函附上合同草稿，一式两份，其中一份由易保罗（Ignatieff）保留，另外一份将寄至海关总税务司署，您需代表总税务司，与易保罗一起在合同上签字确认。

此外，授权贵署根据现行规定，为易保罗发放前往瑷珲关的差旅费，无需给予调口津贴。

同时，此令副本已抄送至瑷珲关税务司。

您忠诚的仆人

包罗（C. A. V. Bowra）

总务科税务司

海关总税务司署致哈尔滨关第 2928/90948 号令附件

合同

1922 年 9 月, 哈尔滨关

尊敬的哈尔滨关易保罗（Ignatieff）先生：

1. 奉中国海关总税务司安格联爵士（Francis Arthur, K.B.E.）的指示, 兹传达一份中国海关委任书, 现委任您为瑷珲关黑龙江航务专门顾问, 并附以下条件：

> 任期三年, 第一年月薪为 350 海关两, 第二年月薪为 375 海关两, 第三年月薪为 400 海关两。

> 提供一间无家具的宿舍, 如无空余宿舍, 可每月发放租房津贴 50 海关两。

2. 若您有任何不当或者违反海关法规章则的行为, 总税务司即可终止任命, 且不发出通知; 若海关出于其他原因终止协议, 会提前三个月给出书面通知, 或补偿三个月津贴。

3. 谨代表海关总税务司, 向您传达此份录用通知。但是, 无论总税务司还是我本人, 均对此不承担任何个人责任。

4. 如果接受此项任命, 请于 9 月 16 日前往瑷珲关税务司处报到。薪俸将于 1922 年 9 月 16 日起开始发放, 隔年涨薪日期以及合同终止日期都将按 9 月 16 日计算。

您忠诚的仆人
哈尔滨关税务司

本人同意并接受上述信函中的委任及所列各项条件。

此副本内容真实有效, 特此证明。

确认人签字：福贝士（A. H. Forbes）

代理总务科副税务司

7. 为与道尹商议 1923 年中俄临时航务协议及航运开通时征收江捐事

```
                97

I. G.
                            Aigun / Taheiho 24th February, 1923.


        Sir,

                In continuation of my despatch No. 91:

                        concerning Amur Aids to Navigation,

        I have the honour to inform you that the Taoyin-

        Superintendent has asked me to investigate into the

        possibility of concluding an agreement, permanent or

        temporary, on Aids to Navigation, and to make my

        suggestions for the future.

                I have complied with his request in a

        despatch which is herewith appended for your

        information and which may be summed up as follows:

                a) The Commissioner has ascertained that the

        Russians are not willing, for the time being,

        to come to a local Agreement, preferring to

        leave the matter of navigation and Aids on

        the Amur to be discussed with the Peking

        Authorities in connection with the conclusion

        of a General Treaty between the two Nations;
                                                    b)
The Inspector General of Customs,

        P E K I N G.
```

道字第五十五號

b) if no agreement is reached in Peking
before the Navigation opens, it is possible
that the Russians will at the eleventh hour
propose a temporary arrangement similar to the
one in force for the year 1922; in which
case it would be advisable to ascertain in
advance the views of the competent Boards, so
that an Agreement may be concluded here, if
necessary, with the least delay. The Commissioner has on his side applied for instructions
from the I. G., and cannot suggest anything
definite before receipt of a reply;

c) the principal modifications to be suggested to an Agreement on the lines of the one
for 1922 are (as reported in Aigun despatch
No. 91):

1) China to contribute a fixed percentage
of the expenses, in accordance with estimate
to be fixed beforehand, not in proportion of
Dues collected, which implies an impossible
check on collection of Dues on the Russian
side.

2) Estimates should not exceed Gold Roubles
50,000, plus $ 8,000 for the Office of
the

the Technical Adviser to the Chinese
Commission in Taheiho.

3) China should pay more than 50%, say
60% in return for the Russians supplying
the organisation, materials, boats, etc.,

4) precautions should be taken to see
that goods, once having paid River Dues on
one shore, be entirely exempt from further
levy on arrival, within the limits of the
Frontier Waters,

5) the tax on passengers tickets should
be replaced by a Clearance fee,

6) Russian accounts should be checked more
rigourously: it should be agreed that only
half the Chinese share of estimated expenses
can be advanced each month, the other half
to be paid after accounts have been audited
and found correct.

d) in the event of China taking up the
works on one division of the River, rough
estimates of the cost of operation by the
Customs are submitted 1) supposing operation
by means of local repair parties, 2) in the
case of operation by parties working in two
steam launches;

e) the estimated River Dues Collection by
the C. M. Customs could cover the ordinary

cost

cost of maintenance; but to meet initial
expenses, especially heavy in the case of
purchase of steam launches, there is only the
surplus of 1922, which can be estimated at
7,000 to 8,000 dollars.

In this connection I would like to suggest
that collection be started anyhow at the beginning
of the navigation season and that possibly an
understanding be arrived at with the Amur Navigation
Office in order to avoid double collection of
Dues: if an Agreement is concluded later on in
the summer, it is necessary that River Dues be
collected for the whole season in order to fully
meet expenses. If an Agreement is not arrived
at in 1923, and there is no contribution towards
the Aids on the part of China, the funds collected may be set aside and used, either for purchasing the steam launches (in the following year, or
whenever the Customs may take over the working
of part of the River), or be devoted in promoting
studies and doing preliminary work for the improvement of the Saheiho Harbour which is slowly

silting

silting up and becomes every year more difficult to navigation.

If you agree to my suggestion, I will put it before the Taoyin and, if necessary, the Chamber of Commerce.

I have the honour to be,

Sir,

Your obedient Servant,

Acting Commissioner.

呈海关总税务司署 <u>97</u> 号文　　　　　瑷珲关／大黑河 1923 年 2 月 24 日

尊敬的海关总税务司（北京）：

　　根据瑷珲关第 91 号呈：

　　　　"关于黑龙江航务；"

　　兹汇报，应道尹兼海关监督之要求，本署已调查是否有签署长期或临时航务相关协议之可能，并附相关建议。兹附本署致道尹之函文（道去字第五十五号），以供参考，大致内容如下：

　　1. 税务司已确认俄方目前不愿签订地方协议，更倾向于与北京政府讨论黑龙江航运及航路标志问题，意欲由两国政府缔结总协约。

　　2. 若航运季开始之前，北京方面未能达成协议，俄方最后可能会提出按照 1922 年之安排签订临时协议；若如此，可提前向税务处征询意见，以便必要时，可立即于本地签订协议。税务司方面已向海关总税务司署申请指示，然未收到回复之前，无法给出确切建议。

　　3. 关于 1922 年协议，兹提出如下改动建议（参阅瑷珲关第 91 号呈）：

　　（1）华方应按照前期议定之预算，以固定比例摊付支出，因无法核查俄方江捐征收情况，故不以江捐征收比例支付。

　　（2）预算不应超出 50000 金卢布，外加大黑河中国委员会航务专门顾问办事处经费 8000 银圆。

　　（3）华方摊付之比例应超过 50%，比如 60%，而俄方则相应提供管理机构、物料、船只等。

　　（4）应做好预防措施，确保边界河道范围内之货物于一岸完纳江捐后到达另一岸时免于再次征税。

　　（5）乘客票税应由出港费取而代之。

　　（6）对于核查俄方账户一事，应更加严格；中俄双方应协定俄方每月只可从华方摊款半数中预支费用，待账户审计结束，确认无误后，方可支付另外半数金额。

　　4. 若中国接管黑龙江某一段边界河道的航路标志工作，海关应根据以下两种情况制定初步预算，①由驻守职员组成施工队进行航路标志维修事宜，②由施工队乘坐两艘汽艇进行航路标志维修事宜；

　　5. 中国海关江捐税收预算仅够支付常规维修费用，因此初期经费只能使用 1922 年税收之结余支付，然若有购置汽艇之需，此项费用将极高，而 1922 年税收之结余预计仅有约

7000 至 8000 银圆。

鉴于此，兹建议，于 1923 年航运开通之时开始征收江捐，相信为避免重复征税，阿穆尔水道局亦会表示赞同；但若至今夏方能签订协议，则只有于整个航运季均征收江捐，方足以支付全部费用。然而，若 1923 年中俄双方未能达成协议，中国则无需承担航路标志相关费用，所征金额便可留用，或购置汽艇（明年或待海关接管一段航道之时），或用于大黑河港口改建所需的研究及初步工作，目前大黑河港口堵塞日益严重，航运工作日益困难。

若贵署同意此建议，本署将提交至道尹，如有必要，亦会提交至商会。

您忠诚的仆人

包安济（G. Boezi）

瑷珲关署理税务司

8. 为黑龙江航务 1922 年及 1923 年的工作及规划事

101

I. G.

Aigun / Taheiho 20th March, 1923.

保存

爱珲阅
文 第102-64 号

Sir,

I have received copy of the Harbin Commissioner's comments on my despatch No. 91:

concerning Aids to Navigation on the Amur.

Chief Tidesurveyor Abrahamsen's Memorandum contains many useful suggestions, especially as to contributions towards expenses for the upkeep of the Aids by the Russian Navigation Office, Hospital attendance, exclusion of conservancy work, unification of navigation rules and control of Masters, Officers and Pilots on the Amur and Sungari; but certain assertions call for replies and explanations, which I have the honour to submit herewith.

1.   It has never been suggested that China take up the upkeep of the Aids on one division of the Amur by force of a local Agreement; but only, eventually, by virtue of an Agreement or Treaty

concluded

The Inspector General of Customs,

PEKING.

concluded between the two central Governments. In this case, it is difficult to understand why there should be any danger of a "retraction", or a loss of face caused by the Russians taking back what they may have granted, any more than for the eventual settlement by Treaty of all questions outstanding between China and Russia (status of Mongolia, Chinese Eastern Railway, etc.).

2.   It would be preferable, as already stated in the despatch, to receive the Division from Tahaiho to Kasakevich (not to Iahasusu only). But the linking of the Sungari system to the Amur is not essential, in the opinion of this Office, especially if the proposed unification of Regulations and methods on all the waterways of the Amur Basin, whether controlled by Russia or by China, could be obtained. - It is further to be remarked that the nature of the two Rivers differs considerably, and that absolute uniformity is impossible. - The reason for fixing the limits of the Lower Division to Kasakevich, not to

Iahasusu,

Lahasusu, is that China should operate the Aids on half the length of the frontier Rivers, when she should contribute nothing towards the operation of the other half by Russia; while if less than half the stretch is controlled by China, she will have to compensate Russia for part of her expenses in operating more than half of the River, thus defeating one of the main advantages of taking over the works on one Division. -

3.   The greatest economy on the part of the Amur (Russian) Navigation Office, has already been enforced in 1922; water gauges, signal stations, traffic stations, lighted shallows, have already been reduced to a minimum, and the strictly necessary expenditure has been entered in the estimates for the future, presented in Aigun despatch No. 91. - As to the Amur Navigation Office, it must be remarked that where they had about 200 employees, they have now little over 50; again, that out of these, only 23 have been taken in 1922 as working for the Aids to Navigation, as will appear in Enclosure No. 4 of

my

there

my despatch. All those who draw maps, who attend to archives, in a word those who do not directly contribute to the working of the Aids, have been excluded from the estimates for 1922, and, of course, for 1923. That is why those estimates have been headed "Blagovestchensk Technical Section", not "Central Office of the Amur Navigation Office".

4.   My despatch has been misread on one point: the salary of Rbls. 75 a month paid to the Director General of Navigation, appears in the estimates prepared (for 1922 and also for 1923) for the upkeep of the Aids entirely by the Russians (Enclosures Nos. 4d and 8 of Aigun despatch No. 91): our own estimates for the event of the Customs taking over the exploitation of one Division (Enclosure No. 9 of the above despatch) are established on the basis of salaries paid before the Revolution, with the exception of the District Surveyors whose proposed salary is $150 a month (equal to the maximum salary paid to a Captain by the Wut'ung S. N. Company) while their former pay ranged from Rbls. 200 to 350 (in very exceptional cases). In the estimates for the Customs there

there is no Director General, but an Inspector, at a salary of Hk. Tls. 350 - 400 per month. - Thus it will be seen that the cost of the upkeep by the Customs will probably remain the same for several years, while on the Russian side increases of salaries are to be expected.

5.　　　As to the share of expenses of the Russian Central Navigation Office debited to the account of the Joint Commission (which has been reduced to a "Blagoveschensk Technical Section", as reported above), it is to be noted that in 1922 the Amur Navigation Office undertook the upkeep of the Aids on the following Rivers:-

Amur, from Pokrovka to Harbarovsk 1768 verst

　　　　Total frontier rivers 　1768 　"

Shilka 　　　　　　　　　　　 373 　"
Lower Zeya 　　　　　　　　　 604 　"

　　　　Total inland waters 　977 　"

This means that over 2 3rds of the work was done on frontier waters, and therefore the debiting in 1922 to the account of the Sino-Russian Commission for the frontier Waters of 2/3rds of the expenses

of

of the Technical Section is not unfair; but in future the Russian Navigation Office should work also on other inland rivers, and the proportion for 1926 may be established at 50% Frontier Waters, and 50% Inland Waters, by the addition to the latter of the Amur from Harbarovsk to Nikolaievsk (876 verst). -

6.　　It is probably true that a non-Russian (preferably British) Inspector, would have a more independent position vis-à-vis the Russians; but on one hand, the Russian Inspector is backed by the Customs and the Non-Russian Commissioner; and on the other it would be most difficult to find a non-Russian with sufficient knowledge of the language, the Russian methods and Russian accounting, to enable him to either control the works and expenses, if entirely undertaken by the Russians, or to start an organisation for China, with the same efficiency as a Russian of undoubted honesty, totally extraneous to politics, with an experience of over 15 years on the Amur. -

　　　　　　　　　　　　　　7.

7.   I have no objection, in itself, to the
upkeep of the Aids on the whole Amur by the
Russians; but I must express my disbelief of
such theoretical abstractions as "a committee
appointed by the two Governments, purely technical
and void of political character", and "undertakings
.... strictly neutral in political matters";
I believe that joint Commissions are in practice
always a nest of intrigues and difficulties, more
or less under the influence of politics, which
are those of the Governments to which the
members of the Commission belong; also that, by
their discussions, difficult to conclude in the
absence of a neutral arbitrator, they are the
source of delays and great loss of time.

          This Office has had experience in 1922,
such as to justify a distinct preference, all
other conditions being the same, for a solution
which would leave both parties as independent as
possible of the other in their respective fields
of action.

                                        Copies

Copies of this despatch are forwarded to the Coast Inspector and to the Harbin Commissioner.

I have the honour to be,

Sir,

Your obedient Servant,

[signature]

Acting Commissioner.

呈海关总税务司署 <u>101</u> 号文　　　　　　瑷珲关 / 大黑河 1923 年 3 月 20 日

尊敬的海关总税务司（北京）：

哈尔滨关税务司关于瑷珲关致海关总税务司署第 91 号呈的意见收悉：

"关于黑龙江航务；"

超等总巡阿布兰森（H.Abrahamsen）先生在其报告中所提之建议的确非常有益，尤其是关于如何向俄阿穆尔水道局支付航路标志维护费用摊款，是否应为职员提供医疗护理、是否应接管部分黑龙江航路标志维护工作，以及是否应统一黑龙江和松花江两条航道上的航务条例以便于管理等方面的意见，均颇有价值；但对于其中某些观点，本署仍需做出补充说明，具体列下。

1. 关于中国接管部分黑龙江航路标志维护工作一事，须说明，本署从未提出要通过签订地方协议来实现此事，只是希望中俄两国政府最终可签署相关协议或条约。地方协议亦不过是协定等待中俄两国政府通过签署条约来解决两国之间的各项重要问题（如外蒙地位问题、中东铁路问题等），既如此，又何须担忧俄方会"食言"，中国又何以会颜面受损。

2. 兹认为，中国若要接管黑龙江某一段边界河道，最佳选择依然是大黑河至嘎杂克维池（Kasakevich）河段（参阅瑷珲关第 91 号呈），而非仅到拉哈苏苏，如此方可确保中国所负责的航道长度不低于整条边界河道的半数，亦只有如此，中方无需向俄方支付额外摊款，否则俄方所负责的航道长度将超出整条边界河道之半数，中国亦需支付多出之款，如此一来，中国独自管理一段航道的益处便会大打折扣。此外，于瑷珲关而言，松花江与黑龙江两条航道的管理制度并无统一之必要，尤其待将来可在黑龙江流域内中俄两国所管辖之水道上施行统一的航行章程和管理办法时，更无此必要。另外，黑龙江与松花江两条航道的性质完全不同，无法实现绝对统一。

3. 1922 年，俄阿穆尔水道局已在最大程度上削减了开支，水位观测站、水深信号站、通行信号站以及设立灯塔之浅滩的数量均已降至最低，所编制的预算亦仅为必要支出（预算明细已随附于瑷珲关第 91 号呈）。值得注意的是，俄阿穆尔水道局曾拥有雇员 200 余名，但现在却仅余 50 人左右，其中亦只有 23 人被列入 1922 年航路标志维护工作预算之中（详见瑷珲关第 91 号呈附件 4）。总而言之，诸如绘图工程师、档案管理员等与航路标志维护工作无直接关联的职员，均未列入 1922 年预算之中，1923 年亦是如此。此亦为俄方未将该两年的预算列入俄阿穆尔水道局名下，而是列入布拉戈维申斯克（Blagovestchensk）技术部名下之原因。

4. 本署于 1922 年及 1923 年航路标志维护工作支出预算中所列之"督办薪俸每月 75 金卢布"（参阅瑷珲关第 91 号呈附件 4 和附件 8）一项，乃指黑龙江航路标志维护工作由俄方全权负责之情况；至于中国海关独立维护黑龙江一段边界河道航路标志所需之支出预算（参阅瑷珲关第 91 号呈附件 9），则主要基于大革命爆发之前的薪资水平计算得出，唯有测量师之薪俸（每月 150 银圆）是依照戊通航业公司船长的最高月薪标准而定，测量师此前之薪俸水平曾在 200 金卢布至 350 金卢布（极少数情况下）之间。海关预算中无"督办"一职，只有"巡江工司"一名，其月薪为 350 海关两到 400 海关两之间。由此可以推断，海关维护航路标志所需之费用或可于数年内保持不变，但俄方所需费用中职员薪俸一项却极有增加之可能。

5. 关于俄阿穆尔中央水道局（目前已被降为"布拉戈维申斯克 Blagovestchensk"技术部）计入中俄水道委员会账户的支出，特此列出 1922 年俄阿穆尔水道局航路标志维护工作所涉之河流。

河流	长度（俄里）
黑龙江：自波克罗夫卡（Pokrovka）起 至哈巴罗夫斯克（Habarovsk）止	1768
黑龙江边界河道总长：	1768
石勒喀河	373
结雅河下游	604
俄国内陆河道总长	977

由上表可知，俄阿穆尔水道局 1922 年航路标志维护工作中有三分之二与边界河道相关，因此将 1922 年布拉戈维申斯克技术部的三分之二支出计入中俄水道委员会账户，实属公平合理之举。不过，俄阿穆尔水道局今后负责的内陆河道数量必会有所增加，1923 年，黑龙江自哈巴罗夫斯克至尼古拉耶夫斯克（Nickolaevsk）河段（876 俄里）便划入其须负责的内陆河道之列，因此其 1923 年的航路标志维护工作分配比例应为边界河道和内陆河道各占百分之五十。

6. 至于巡江工司的人选，非俄籍（最好是英籍）人员或许可以在处理有关俄国事务方面保持更加客观公正的立场，但若要其既精通俄语又熟悉俄国办事方法和会计制度，未免难以实现；然若无此等能力，其如何能在由俄方全权负责航路标志维护工作的情况之下，有效地管理工作，控制支出，又如何能在由中国独立维护黑龙江一段边界河道的情况之下，为中国建立一个航路标志管理机构。相对而言，一名对中国海关绝对忠诚，与政治毫无干系，在黑龙江上又有 13 余年工作经验的俄籍人员，应该更能胜任巡江工司一职，且海关和非俄籍税务司还可襄助。

7. 对于由俄方全权负责黑龙江航路标志维护工作一事，本署并无异议，但是对于"由双方政府委派并组建纯粹技术性质的、不带有任何政治色彩的水道委员会"以及"在管理……时，于政治立场上保持绝对的中立"这两种近乎空谈的主张，本署则实在难以采信。

兹认为，中俄水道委员会实际上就是一个酝酿阴谋和妨碍工作进程的组织，双方委员既由两国政府任命，那么，该委员会或多或少都会受到政治因素的影响；而且中俄双方之间的协商，若无一个客观中立的仲裁者来裁决，实难达成共识，如此，中俄水道委员会便成了贻误时机和浪费时间的根源。

瑷珲关 1922 年的经历已然证明，其他条件均可保持不变，但中俄双方最好在各自管理领域内独立行动。

此抄件发送至哈尔滨关税务司及巡工司。

您忠诚的仆人

包安济（G. Boezi）

瑷珲关署理税务司

9. 为汇报中俄地方政府就签订新协议进行协商事

NO. 110

I. G.

CUSTOM HOUSE,

Aigun, Taheiho, 5th May, 1923.

Sir,

1.   With reference to previous correspondence concerning Aids to Navigation on the Amur,

I have the honour to report that, since early in the year, after consultation with the Taoyin-Superin-tendent, I tried to ascertain the views of the Russian Amur Navigation Office and Amur Water Transports concerning the renewal of the 1922 Agreement for the upkeep of the Aids. - I also raised the question with the members of an Inspecting Commission despatched by the Moscow Ministry of Communications to deal with all traffic problems in Eastern Siberia, which visited Taheiho between the 16th and 22nd January; but both the Local Russian Authorities and the Moscow Commission said they had orders not to conclude any agreement locally, since all the questions should be reserved for a Conference between the Central Governments of China and Russia.

I reported

The Inspector General of Customs,
    P E K I N G.

I reported to the Taoyin the negative results of my steps, and I suggested to him to apply for instructions from the competent Boards in Peking.

2.   Later, however, probably coincident with Mr. Joffe's departure from Peking and the prospects of a Sino-Russian conference indefinitely postponed, I got information that the Russian point of view had undergone a change. But the Acting Director of the Amur Navigation Office and Water Transports, was away from Blagovestchensk, and no discussion could be started. - On 23rd March the Acting Director returned, in a new capacity as Technical Adviser, with the Head of the Inspecting Commission, (Mr. N. K. Marshan), newly-appointed Director General, On the 26th I went to see them, and they expressed willingness to discuss an Agreement similar to the one for 1922. At the same time they tackled the problem of Navigation of the Sungari by steamers of the Water Transports (flying the Red Flag); but I replied that this matter was entirely out of my province, and that they may take it up with the Taoyin as Commissioner for Foreign Affairs, which they said they would
do.

do.

I informed the Taoyin of the conversation held, and **again** showed him the Draft of Navigation Regulations which you sent in your S/O letter of 24th May, 1922, prepared by the various Boards concerned, and advised him to follow the draft if the Russians were to take up with him the question which they had raised with me.

3. In the meantime, a brisk exchange of views was taking place between the Customs (Mr. Ignatieff and myself) and a representative of the Amur Navigation Office, so that a general understanding was reached on the clauses of the proposed agreement. I also prepared a draft, embodying all the changes suggested in Aigun despatch No. 91. I had however to give way in the matter of the levy of Clearance Fees instead of Dues on Passengers' tickets: the Russians said that they could not change the Tariff on their side, which is fixed by Regulations of the (ex) Chita Government: the Taoyin thought the Clearance Fees harmful to Chinese steamers, which are this year in such distressing financial conditions. In vain I argued that the

S.S.

S.S. Companies would recover the fee somehow on the
passengers or cargo, and that the burden would fall
on Russian and Chinese steamers alike; that the fee
was already in force on the Sungari; that collection
of dues on passengers' tickets is impossible, and
constitutes a loss of face to the Customs: - not
being arbiter in the matter, I had to give way.

4.   March 30th was the day fixed for discussing
the Chinese draft. My draft had to be completely
remade, because the Taoyin wanted to preserve as
much as possible the <u>form</u> of the 1922 Agreement,
saying that it would be more easily approved,
notwithstanding all the changes, especially by the
Provincial Authorities, whose opinion and decision
he had to take seriously into consideration. At
the same time, he decided to add to the Technical
Agreement the whole draft of Navigation Rules as
shown to him by myself, thus taking the initiative
of negotiations himself. The Russians, probably
instructed from Moscow, had mentioned nothing to the
Taoyin of navigation on the Sungari. - I insisted
that it would be preferable to have the Navigation
Rules discussed separately, to form matter for

                                              another

another Agreement if possible. But the Taoyin insisted that the Navigation Rules should form part of a general Agreement, and I could not oppose his wishes. - I confined my attention, however, to the Technical side only, and left the Taoyin to prepare copy of the Russian translation with regard to the Agreement itself, while I had the translations prepared for the Annexes, which deal exclusively with Technical matters. The draft, as finally agreed between the Taoyin and the Customs, is herewith appended. I succeeded however in suppressing in the Russian text Article No. 22 which stipulates that Steamers can <u>in no case</u> be detained or confiscated for any liability of the Owner or Agent. The article was introduced as a protection to the Wut'ung S.S. Company, which had one of their vessels locally detained by a Russian Court as security for the payment of wages due to the Officers and Crew. I remonstrated that no such privileges could be accorded a steamer, and that Laws in every country (including Russia) make the salaries of Officers and Crews a first lien on steamer; that Russian Laws, and especially a very

good

good one like this, could not possibly be altered.

5.   The broad outlines of the Agreement (Technical Part) as proposed by us, are :

    1) Levy of Dues and work to be on the same standard as last year and to include the Amur from Pokrovka to Habarovsk.

    2) Rough estimates and plans of work to be fixed beforehand, on most economical basis, and only $\frac{1}{2}$ expenses of Technical Section to be included in Russian estimates.

    3) China to contribute a fixed percentage (50 %) but not to be responsible for any amount over the River Dues collection for the season, less 10 %.

    4) The Chinese Technical Adviser's Office and President of the Commission's Office to be paid first (monthly) out of Chinese collection, the balance only being available for paying the share of Russian estimates.

    5) Part (50 %) of China's share towards Russian estimates to be paid in advance at beginning of each month, the balance on production of proper accounts.

    6) Mutual right of supervision of collection and expense.

6.   The draft, in Russian, was sent by me to

the

the Water Transports and the Amur Navigation Office
on the 12th April through Mr. Ignatieff, who gave
also explanations on the Technical part.

On the 14th April, Representatives of the
Water Transports, Amur Navigation Office, and Taoyin
met in the Custom House, and discussed thoroughly
the technical part of the draft Agreement. The
principal modifications proposed, and, in principle,
accepted, were the following :

Works and levy of duty within the scope
of the Agreement to be limited to strictly frontier
waters, i.e. Amur from Pokrovka to Kasakevich.

The surplus of Chinese collection on Chinese
side for 1922 (about $ 10,000) to be used as a
"reserve fund", in case 1923 collection should not
be sufficient to pay the whole Chinese share of
Russian expenses, according to estimates submitted
and approved as per Agreement.

In view of the purchase of materials to be
effected in advance by the Navigation Office, 75
per cent. of the Chinese share towards Russian
estimates to be advanced at the beginning of each
month, the balance of actual expenditure to be

paid

paid when proper accounts have been presented, or when the Chinese Commission is otherwise satisfied of the correctness of the amount reported as spent.

The division of the River into sections for each of which only half the Tariff duty is collectable, to apply only to the Chinese side. (so was done in fact in 1922.)

7. Concerning the Navigation Rules, the Russian representatives declared themselves incompetent. They even asked whether the Taoyin had power to discuss navigation on the Sungari, whereupon the Taoyin's representative replied that the Taoyin's jurisdiction extended only as far as the mouth of the Sungari.. ....

With the consent of the Taoyin, shortly afterwards I informed the Russian Authorities concerned that the Taoyin as representative - and with the consent - of the Ministry of Foreign Affairs, could come to Agreements covering a larger field than his province as Taoyin, and asked if the Russian Navigation Office could, likewise, obtain authority from Moscow for discussing the Navigation Rules as well. This they did, but the results were

unfavourable:

unfavourable: instructions were to the effect that, preparations having been resumed for an early Conference in Peking, these questions should be left to the Conference to discuss. - The Taoyin approached the Head of the Revolutionary Committee (Highest political authorities in Blagovestchensk), but he had the same answer; however Mr. Marshan left recently for Chita, and there is a chance - but very slim, - of his getting fresh instructions.

8.   The Taoyin was at first of opinion that the Agreement should be signed in its entireness, or not at all. But he was soon persuaded that there are too many reasons, technical and political, which make the conclusion of an Agreement, even exclusively technical, highly advisable, so that he has reported the whole question to the Various Boards in Peking and to the Heilungchiang Authorities. I must add that he has sent copy of the Draft as prepared (and as appended to this despatch) without mentioning the modifications accepted in principle.

If the Taoyin receives, as probable, a reply favourable to the conclusion of an exclusively Technical Agreement confined to the upkeep of the

Aids,

Aids, I think discussion will last very little, and the Agreement will be signed shortly.

Under the circumstances and seeing that the Navigation season is about to open at Lahasusu, and that any delay means a big loss in River Dues Collection, I have the honour to solicit your telegraphic authority to start collection of River Dues on last year's Tariff, possibly slightly modified, as soon as an eventual Agreement is signed, based on the one for last year, with the reported modifications, - I would also be much obliged if the Harbin Commissioner could receive similar telegraphic instructions as regards collection of Amur River Dues at Lahasusu. Last year, through collection at Lahasusu starting only on 17th June, the Revenue suffered a loss of a few thousand dollars.

I must add that the proposal to start collection at the beginning of the Navigation Season irrespective of the conclusion of an Agreement (Aigun Despatch No. 97) has not been accepted by the Taoyin, who says he has no power to enforce it.

Copies

Copies of this despatch are sent to the

Coast Inspector and the Harbin Commissioner.

I have the honour to be,

Sir,

Your obedient Servant,

(Signed) G. Boezi,

Acting Commissioner.

True copy

Wong yue sih

3rd Clerk, C.

Append

呈海关总税务司署 110 号文　　　　　瑷珲关/大黑河 1923 年 5 月 5 日

1. 根据此前函件：

　　"关于黑龙江航务；"

　　兹汇报，今年年初，在与道尹兼海关监督商议后，本署试图确定俄阿穆尔国家水道局和水运局对于续签 1922 年《联合维护航路标志协议》一事的态度，为此还询问了莫斯科交通部派遣来解决东西伯利亚交通问题的监察委员会成员（于 1 月 18 日至 22 日期间来访大黑河）；当地俄国政府和莫斯科监察委员会均表示已接到不得在当地签订任何协议之命令，一切问题均须由中俄双方的中央政府会议裁决。

　　本署已将此次试探结果告知道尹，并建议其向拥有决定权的北京税务处请求指示。

2. 但之后，或因越飞（即阿道夫·阿布拉莫维奇·越飞，Adolf AbramovichJoffe）先生已离开北京，中俄会议可能会无限期推迟。据悉，俄方对续签 1922 年协议一事的态度已有所转变，但因俄阿穆尔国家水道局和水运局署理督办目前未在布拉戈维申斯克（Blagovestchensk），故无法与之进行协商。3 月 23 日，署理督办以专门顾问的身份，随监察委员会主席马山（N.K.Marshan）先生（新任俄阿穆尔国家水道局和水运局督办）一同返回。3 月 26 日，本署前去拜访，二人表示愿意协订一份与 1922 年协议相类似的新协议，同时还欲解决俄阿穆尔水运局的轮船（悬挂红旗）在松花江上的航行问题；但本署表示此事已完全超出本署的职权范围，建议与道尹兼交涉司商议此事，二人皆表示同意。

　　本署已将此次会谈内容告知道尹，并再次向其出示海关总税务司署 1922 年 5 月 24 日机要信函随附之《航行章程》草案，建议其根据草案回复俄方关于轮船在松花江上航行之问题。

3. 与此同时，易保罗（P.I.Ignatieff）先生和本署代表海关与俄阿穆尔水道局代表交换了意见，以确保双方对拟订协议条款达成基本共识。本署亦就瑷珲关第 91 号呈中所建议之改动草拟了一份文件。然在以结关费代替乘客船票税的问题上，本署最终做出了让步。俄方坚称，该乘客船票税乃由（前）赤塔政府所定，其无法更改；道尹亦认为结关费有损中国轮船的利益，况且今年的经济状况已然十分惨淡；本署提出，轮船公司在支付结关费后，可从客运及货运方面将这些费用赚取回来，俄国轮船和中国轮船皆可如此；而且松花江上已开始征收结关费；征收乘客船票税实不可行，亦有损海关形象；然而，本署对此事并无决定之权，此番争辩亦属徒劳，唯有让步。

4. 商议华方协议草案的日期定在 3 月 30 日。道尹认为，应尽可能保留 1922 年协议的模式，虽然可能需要进行诸多修改，但却更容易获得省政府的批准，毕竟于其而言，省政府的意见及决定十分重要；如此一来，本署所拟之草案则须全部重改。与此同时，道尹决定将《航务条例》草案的全部内容加入《工程协议》中，以获取谈判中的主动权。俄方或已收到莫斯科方面的指示，并未向道尹提及俄国轮船在松花江上的航行事宜。本署提出，最好可以将《航务条例》与《工程协议》分开讨论，若情况允许，不妨就《航务条例》再另行签署一份协议。但道尹坚持将《航务条例》纳入整个协议之中，本署无力反对，只得专注于工程方面的问题，负责工程部分的翻译工作，而协议俄文译本的翻译工作则由道尹负责。随呈附上道尹与海关最终协订的协议草案。

道尹俄文译本的第 22 条条款规定，"不得因船主或代理船主有负债行为而扣押或没收其轮船"，本署已将此条成功驳回。道尹列出该项条款，意在保护戊通航业公司，因俄国法庭曾扣押过该公司的一艘轮船，以确保该船驾驶员和船员的薪俸能够得到支付。本署提出，协议不应赋予轮船此等特权，因为任何国家的法律（包括俄国）在处理轮船的留置问题上均以船员的薪俸为优先考虑，素以完善见称的俄国法律更是如此。

5. 对于协议的工程部分，提议如下：

（1）征税标准及航路标志工作标准均与去年相一致，包括黑龙江自波克罗夫卡（Pokrovka）至哈巴罗夫斯克（Habarovsk）河段；

（2）做好最符合经济原则的初步预算和工作计划，俄方预算中只包含工程部分的一半经费；

（3）华方按照固定比例（50%）支付摊款，但总金额不得超出航运季江捐税收扣除 10% 海关征税佣金后之数额；

（4）华方税收首先用于按月向中国航务专门顾问办事处与中国水道委员会委员长办事处提供经费，余下之款仅可用于支付华方摊款；

（5）华方应向俄方支付的（50%）摊款于每月月初提前支付，待俄方出示完整账簿后，再行支付尾款；

（6）双方对税收与支出情况共同享有监管权。

6. 本署已于 4 月 12 日通过易保罗（P.I.Ignatieff）先生将协议草案的俄文译本送交至俄阿穆尔国家水道局和水运局，易保罗先生已对工程部分予以解释。

4 月 14 日，俄罗斯阿穆尔国家水运局、阿穆尔水道局以及道尹代表在海关办公楼会面，对协议草案的工程部分进行了全面讨论，所提出的主要修改意见已基本通过，具体列下：

协议中的航路标志工作与征税范围应严格限制在界河上，即黑龙江自波克罗夫卡至嘎杂克维池河段；

　　华方应将于 1922 年在黑龙江华岸所征税款之盈余（约 10000 银圆）留作"储备金"之用，以防 1923 年所征之税款不足，无法按照协议规定之数支付摊款；

　　鉴于所需材料均须由俄阿穆尔水道局提前购置，因此华方应于每月月初预先分期支付应摊款项的 75%，实际支出的尾款，则应待俄方提交账簿，或中国水道委员会鉴定支出报表正确无误后，再行支付；

　　关于对黑龙江航道进行分段征税（每段航道仅征收半税）这一规定，将仅适用于黑龙江华岸（1922 年即是如此）。

　　7. 至于《航务条例》，俄方代表表示其无权过问，并询问道尹有无过问松花江航务的权力，道尹代表表示道尹的管辖范围仅至松花江口。

　　之后不久，本署经道尹许可向俄方说明，道尹亦为外交部代表，比起道尹之身份，可达成之协议范围更广，并询问俄阿穆尔水道局是否亦可从莫斯科政府得到类似的特许，从而与华方进行有关《航务条例》的协商。俄阿穆尔水道局确已照办，但结果却不尽如人意：莫斯科方面指示，已开始筹备将于北京召开的中俄会议，上述问题应留待会议上裁决。道尹又与革命委员会（布拉戈维申斯克最高政治权力机关）主席进行联系，得到的结果并无二致。尽管马山先生已于近日前往赤塔，但获得新指示的概率十分渺茫。

　　8. 起初，道尹认为必须签署完整协议，但转念又考虑工程和政治方面的影响因素过多，即使仅能敲定工程部分，亦大有裨益，故将此事据实呈报北京相关部门以及黑龙江省政府，并将协议草案（此呈附件）一并呈送，但却未提已通过之修改意见。

　　若道尹得到之回复为同意仅签署维护航路标志的工程协议，中俄双方所需讨论的时间将会很短，协议不日即可签署。

　　鉴于拉哈苏苏航运季即将开始，任何拖延都会令江捐税收蒙受损失，故特此申请贵署电令批准，待最终协议（基于 1922 年协议及上文汇报之修改内容）签订后，立即开始以去年之税率（可稍作调整）征收江捐。与此同时，还望贵署就于拉哈苏苏分关征收黑龙江江捐一事向哈尔滨关税务司发送电令指示。去年拉哈苏苏分关直到 6 月 17 日才开始征收江捐，因而导致了数千银圆的税收损失。

　　此外，关于瑷珲关第 97 号呈所提之无论缔结协议与否，均于航运季开始时征税之提议，道尹以无权执行为由未予同意。

此抄件发送至巡工司及哈尔滨关税务司。

您忠诚的仆人

包安济（G. Boezi）

瑷珲关署理税务司

该抄件内容真实有效,特此证明:

确认人签字: 王友燮三等同文供事后班

10. 为戊通航业公司轮船于叶卡捷琳尼斯基浅滩触礁沉船事

Chart(Separate)/6 Appendices.

AIDS TO NAVIGATION ON THE AMUR: Wu T'ung CO.'s S.S."Chi Yang" wrecked in the Ekaterininsky Shallows;Chamber of Commerce claim damages from Russian Amur Navigation Office;Commissioner support view of Technical Adviser & Harbour Master that accident due to negligence on part of Captain and Assistant Pilot; copy of reports & correspondence, enclosing.

180.

I.G.

Aigun 7th. August, 1924.

Entered in Card-Index.

Sir,   Replied to in No._____

1.   I have the honour to report the wreck

on the 3rd. of July, 1924, in the Ekaterininsky

Chart.
(Separate Cover)

Shallows, 50 versts above Taheiho, of the Wu T'ung

Company's S. S. " Chi Yang " which cleared at

this office for Moho on the 2nd. of July, 1924,

with 7,552 poods of general cargo. The cargo was

not insured and the Wu T'ung Company, through their

local manager, at once informed shippers that as

the vessel had struck a rock in the channel pre-

pared by the Russian Amur Navigation Office they

would be unable to accept any responsibility for

losses incurred.   The interested parties have now

placed the matter in the hands of the Chinese

Chamber of Commerce who have come to the conclusion

that the proper course to take is to attempt the

process

The Inspector General of Customs,

Peking.

process of forcing the Russians to pay.

2.   In their letter to the Chiao Shê Yüan
adix 1.   (Taoyin and Superintendent of Customs) the
Chamber of Commerce reason that the obligation
of merchants to pay River Dues is based on
the definite assumption that those who handle
the money and are entrusted with the responsibility
of maintaining the various channels in order will
carry out the obligations undertaken by them.
They contend that the Agreement entered into
with the Russians is essentially a conditional
Agreement and that the Russian Amur Navigation
Office, as the wreck of the " Chi Yang " in
the Ekaterininsky channel clearly demonstrates,
has violated the conditions which are its
foundation.   They criticise the faulty work
which has made possible so dangerous a situation,
and complain that the Agreement is now shown to
be one which confers upon Chinese merchants no
commercial advantages, and insist that it must be
held to be vitiated by being based on principles

                                        which

which the Russians have no intention of applying.
The Chamber of Commerce seize upon the occurrence
as a suitable text for a sermon on the wholly
inadequate acquittance by the Russian Amur Navigation
Office of its liabilities, and not only maintain
that the Russians are indifferent to the ruin of
Chinese merchants, but even go so far as to say
that they have shown by leaving stones in the
Ekaterininsky Shallows that they are taking steps
which clearly tend to bring about that result.
An attempt is also made to convey the impression
that both the Customs authorities and the Russian
Amur Navigation Office are agreed that the " Chi
Yang " was not out of her course when she struck
the rock and at the end of the letter emphasis is
thrown on the claim of the Chinese merchants to
compensation from the Russian authorities for the
loss of their cargo.

3.　　　　　　　　Both the Technical Adviser and the

Mix 2.
Mix 3.　Harbour Master hold that the Chamber of Commerce

are entirely wrong, not only in their conclusions,

　　　　　　　　　　　　　　　　　　　but

but in the evidence with which they seek to
buttress them. They are of the opinion that it
is not possible to blame the Russian Amur Navigation Office and that the accident was due to
culpable negligence on the part of the captain and
the assistant pilot and that against negligence
of such a kind there can be no protection.
The Chamber of Commerce, however, have committed
themselves to a certain line of conduct, and if
they are really determined to carry it out they
will presumably refuse to accept the decision of
this office as a final statement of the case.
This would be likely to render the relations
between the local Chinese and Russian authorities
not only a good deal worse than before, but
also a good deal more difficult to set right
because there is not the slightest prospect that
the Russian Amur Navigation Office will agree to
bear any portion of the burden caused by the
loss of the cargo and damage to the vessel.
The Russians insist that on all the points at

issue

issue they have the text of the Agreement at

their back and since the Technical Adviser, whose

ability and special experience on matters concerning

the navigation of the Amur are in combination

not to be found every day, states in his report

that the proper channels are well marked and that

the captain and assistant pilot of the " Chi Yang "

must be held to have acted wilfully and without

excuse, it would not be possible for this office

to accept the view that there has been any in-

fraction of the Agreement on the part of the

Russians.

4.   Our difference of opinion with the

Chamber of Commerce centres on the question whether

the " Chi Yang " was in the channel or not when

she ran on to a rock.   The Wu T'ung Company

say they can accept no responsibility for the

disaster because their vessel at the time of the

accident was in the channel and in nine feet of

water, but responsibility is not removed by merely

denying it and in view of the captain's two

statements and the pilot's report, it is difficult

to

to follow their line of thought in this matter.

Appendix 4. In his first statement the captain says that the " Chi Yang " was being steered from the front

Chart. white bearing line (_i.e._ White Beacon 75) to the white and red bearing lines (_i.e._ White Beacon 74

Appendix 5. and Red Beacon 74) whereas in his second statement he says that he did not himself verify the position of his vessel but left it to the assistant pilot to do this and concerned himself with taking note of the soundings only. The captain admits that he was on duty at the time of the accident and his responsibility would thus seem to be increased because his presence on the bridge gave him the opportunity to see with his own eyes that his vessel was not in position with the bearing lines. The pilot was not on duty when the accident occurred, but I submit

Appendix 5. that it is perfectly clear from his statement that the 9 feet of water found outside the proper channel unconsciously encouraged on the part of both the captain and the assistant pilot an unusually lax standard of navigation.

5.

5.   I venture the opinion that when the Chamber of Commerce proceed to object that the present Agreement serves no useful purpose they challenge criticism and proclaim only the narrowness of their own sympathies and understanding. Their argument, so it seems to me, should go on in exactly the opposite direction. If the *standard* of security is low, a way must be sought by which it can be raised and no one, of course, can be in any doubt of the ultimate effect of a demand for greater security. It means that we must increase the River Dues and make merchants pay more. The Technical Adviser, the calibre and honesty of whose mind may be judged to a great extent by the resentment which his careful and detailed investigation of accounts submitted by the Russian Amur Navigation Office has caused at Blagovestchensk, tells me that the expenses of management and maintenance under the present Agreement are so moderate that only work of the most urgent necessity can be carried out, and that if channels already sufficiently wide are to be

made

made still wider the Russians would not un-
reasonably ask where the money is to come from.
An important thing to remember is that the
precise definition of the duties of the Russian
Amur Navigation Office is a matter which was
determined by the representatives of the two
parties to the Agreement signed on the 28th.
of October, 1923, and that the balance of the
whole Agreement will be seriously upset unless
a distinction is made between the duties that
are the proper function of the Russian Amur
Navigation Office - the maintenance of Beacons
and Pyramids in a proper state of repair and
the maintenance of the channels between Head
and Stern Pyramids and Beacons in such a condition as to ensure the safe passage of vessels
proceeding through them - and other work such as
the removal of obstacles outside the channels.
The removal of stones which lie outside the
channels, no matter how great the additional
security that would be afforded by their removal,
is not, so I am advised, an actual necessity

and

un No.144.

and if this is the case I submit that their

removal remains a matter for proposal rather than

for demand. The Technical Adviser informs me

that the removal of stones may cost anything from

$200 to $1,000 per cubic sajen (7 English feet

and that under the Czar's régime, when a grant

ranging from 2,000,000 to 3,000,000 Gold Roubles

was allowed annually for the upkeep of the rivers

in the Amur basin, it was by no means unusual

for him to spend a sum varying from 50,000 to

100,000 Gold Roubles during any one year on

removing stones from the Zeya, the Selemdja, and

the Bureya, the three rivers in the Amur district

under his control. It was in 1922 that China

first began to pay her share towards the upkeep

of the Amur and her contribution for the 3 years

1922, 1923, and 1924 amounts to Gold Roubles 41,477.

A sum of $200 was spent during the winter of

1923/1924 on removing stones found actually in

the Soyous channel, but stones which lie outside

the channels have not been removed. There is

obviously

obviously something to be said for the contention that the wider the channel the greater the safety to shipping, but the Russians are forced to bring expenditure within the limits of greatly reduced resources and it is not reasonable to expect the whole of the Amur to be transformed into a perfect highway when those who do the work are paid only to keep a portion of it in a navigable condition.

6.   The Chamber of Commerce lay stress on the fact that the Russians have admitted that accidents have occurred in the Ekaterininsky Shallows, but I submit that there are three important considerations which should be borne in mind by those who seek to make a point of this circumstance - (1) that the stone which the "Chi Yang" struck lies from 30 to 40 sajens (from 210 to 280 English feet) outside the channel; (2) that in pre-war days this channel was considerably improved both by means of dredging operations and by the removal of stones in the channel, and that to guide vessels as they leave the

line

line of White Beacon 75 and turn in the direction of White Beacon 74, a Red Beacon 74, fronting White Beacon 74 on the opposite bank,

Chart.

has been specially erected by the Russian Amur Navigation Office so that the slightest deviation of a vessel from her proper course should be noticeable at once; and (3) that no complaint has ever been received at this office that the existence of stones near the Ekaterininsky channel makes navigation of the river at this point a dangerous matter.   It is the invariable practice of the Harbour Master to send on board every vessel which enters the Taheiho harbour a Complaint Book in which steamer captains are invited to enter suggestions and criticisms. Each entry is made in duplicate and one copy is passed on by the Harbour Master to the Technical Adviser who takes due note of the complaint in order that adjustments which may be found desirable and necessary may be brought about.   Now the captain of the " Chi Yang," who has been on the up river run for nearly 15

years

years, has never once lodged any complaint at the Harbour Office concerning the state of the Ekaterininsky channel and a fair inference is that he considered the Aids to Navigation in this section of the river adequate and that he was unable to suggest anything better. If this is the case, and that it is so would seem to follow logically, we have surely the right to argue that the captain of the " Chi Yang " could have insured his vessel against disaster if he had kept to the proper channel - as he must have been in the habit of doing on the numerous occasions when his ship negotiated these shallows without coming to grief.

7.   Towards the end of their letter the Chamber of Commerce hint that the Russians are doing their best to ruin Chinese shipping and that to accomplish this end they purposely leave the channels in a dangerous state. But this would not be a very clever move because Russian vessels also navigate the Amur and the notion that the Russian Amur Navigation Office is anxious

                                                        to

to sink its own ships is pure folly.

8.   I submit that the whole of this case as argued and examined by the Technical Adviser and by the Harbour Master shows that the essential facts have been subjected to impartial criticism and that this office is justified in coming to the conclusion that the captain and the assistant pilot of the " Chi Yang " have been guilty of an act of incompetence or negligence and that they cannot shield themselves from the proper consequences of their lapse.

9.   I append copy of my letter to the Taoyin.

Appendix 6.   In my reply I have supplied the Taoyin with -

Appendix 2(a).   1/ A translation of the Technical Adviser's report of the 9th. of July, 1924;

Appendix 2(b).   2/ A translation of §1 and of §7 of the Technical Adviser's report of the 1st. of August, 1924;

Appendix 3(a).   3/ A translation of the Harbour Master's report of the 9th. of July, 1924;

Appendix 3(b).   4/ A translation of an extract from the Harbour Master's report of the 17th. of of July, 1924 -¼4 And it must be noted......... a rise of 4 tenths only;

Appendix 4.

5/ A translation of an extract from the captain's first statement - On the 3rd. instant ......struck on a stone;

Appendix 5.
(First Sheet)

6/ A translation of an extract from the captain's second statement - All this time I stayed on the bridge .... but in my excited mood I did not give attention to the bearing lines;

Appendix 5.

7/ A translation of an extract from the assistant pilot's statement - On the 3rd. of July .... and took the helm; and

Appendix 5.
(Last Sheet)

8/ A translation of an extract from the Pilot's statement - About 8 a.m. I felt .... to direct the vessel to the right.

I have the honour to be,

Sir,

Your obedient Servant,

R. F. Chengelme

Commissioner.

APPENDIX 1.

AIGUN NO. 180 OF 1924.

APPENDIX 1.
(Translation)

Translation of letter from Taoyin (Commissioner for Foreign
Affairs and Superintendent of Customs) giving cover to a
communication received by him from the Chamber of Commerce
in re the sinking of the Wu T'ung CO.'s S.S. " Chi Yang."

The Taoyin (Commissioner for Foreign Affairs)
communicates to the Commissioner contents of a letter
which he has received from the Chinese Chamber of
Commerce in re the wreck of the S.S. "Chi-yang". The
Chamber of Commerce write thus-

It was decided at the Sino-Russian conference held
in the 11th. year of the Republic (1922) that
the money required for the upkeep of Aids to
Navigation on the Sungari and Amur Rivers should
be got from dues collected on cargo, and since
the object in view was the improvement of
navigation it was decided that the necessary money
should be found by the merchants. Notwithstanding
steps taken to give effect to the decision to
improve the condition of the waterway it remains
a fact that ever since the scheme started vessels
have constantly grounded in the lower section of
the Sungari, and this state of affairs has caused
rise in freight, delay, and general loss to
merchants. When the shallowness of the River is
due to lack of rain we recognise that we have
no cause for complaint. But this is not always
the case and on the 5th. July we received a
letter from the Wu-tung Company which reads as
follows -

The Company's S.S. "Chi-yang" left Taheiho on

the

the 2nd. of July for Moho. At 8 o'clock
in the morning of the 3rd. July, when
approaching Tayinshan, the "Chi-yang" suddenly
struck a rock when in 9 feet of water and
her hull was badly damaged. It was at once
apparent that a serious accident had occurred
and although every effort was made to save
the vessel by heading her for the ~~shallows~~ bank
in order to prevent her sinking, the water
poured in through the hole in her bottom and
when she was beached her hold was full of
water. Some of the cargo has been salved
but most of it is irretrievably damaged and
some totally destroyed. The vessel is still
submerged and the actual loss cannot as yet
be ascertained. We wish, however, to point
out that the wreck of the "Chi-yang" in 9
feet of water is an extraordinary occurrence
for which this company should not be expected
to accept any responsibility. We write this
letter so that there may be no misunderstanding
on the part of merchants as to the Company's
position in this case.

The local manager of the Wu-tung Company, Mr. Chên,
has also discussed this matter verbally with us
and he has told us that the Customs has been
asked to investigate the cause of the disaster.
He says that if it could be proved that the
accident was due to faulty navigation, and
consequently attributable to an error on the part
of the pilot, responsibility for damages would be
established, and in addition the pilot would be
liable to punishment. But Mr. Chên tells us that

on

on arrival with the Customs representatives at
the scene of the accident they were joined by
the Water Transport people and that as a result
of investigation both the Customs and Russian
representatives agreed that the "Chi-yang" was
not out of her course when she struck, and
that the accident was caused by a stone (in
the channel). The Russian Water Transport people
even went out of their way to volunteer the
information that there had been several accidents
at this place, and that the pilot was not to
blame. Now it is the duty of the Russian Amur
Navigation Office to provide shipping with the
facilities necessary to enable it to negotiate
those sections of the river where danger is
to be met with either by reason of lack of
water or presence of stones, and it follows
that lights and beacons should be established at
dangerous places. If it is held that there is
no danger to shipping at Tayinshan where the
"Chi-yang" was wrecked, how then is it that
there is a large stone in the channel at that
spot? Perhaps the Russian Navigation Office
who are responsible for the upkeep of Aids may
seek to avoid responsibility in this matter by
expressing ignorance as to whether this place
is dangerous or not, but we think they can
hardly do this because they have already
admitted that several vessels have come to grief
there. It thus follows that the stone should
have been removed, or the dangerous spot marked,
and that it is because neither of these
precautions have been taken that accidents have
occurred to so many of our Chinese vessels.
                                        Thus

Thus (the payment of river dues) is not only
a waste of money but also a source of danger
to life and property. During the 11th. and 12th.
years of the Republic (1922 and 1923) 71,000
gold roubles have been spent on the upkeep of
aids to Navigation but in spite of this large
expenditure there still remain places which are
a danger to shipping owing to the shallowness
of the water and the presence of stones.
Moreover, the Water Transport men have stated that
the pilot of the "Chi-yang" can not be blamed
and we therefore conclude that it is the intention
of the Russians to expose the lives and property
of Chinese to risk. If such is not their
intention, why did they not provide a proper
channel (at Tayinshan) where they knew a number
of accidents had occurred? They are pleased to
say that the pilot should not be blamed, but
it does not occur to them to say anything about
the heavy losses which Chinese merchants are
called upon to suffer. Now the merchants who
suffer all this loss are the very people who
put up the money which is intended to make the
river safe for navigation and it thus follows
that the more money they find for such a purpose
the more they must lose. Why should they submit
to such tyranny? Evil indeed is the intention of
the Amur Navigation Office! If we do not claim
damages for the loss of the cargo shipped by
the "Chi-yang" there will be no end to the
number of accidents which would never occur if
the Russians did their work properly. We write
                                              to

to ask you to assist us in this matter.
The Chiao-shê Yüan (Taoyin) will be obliged if
the Commissioner will let him know how this matter
really stands and what his views are.

APPENDIX 2.

AIGUN NO. 180 OF 1924.

APPENDIX 2.

(a) Technical Adviser's Report of the 9th. July,1924,
on the sinking of the Wu T'ung Company's S. S.
" Chi Yang " in the Ekaterininsky Channel.

Sir,

1/   I beg to submit my report concerning the
sinking on the 3rd of July 1924 in Ekaterininsky
Shallows on the Amur (50 versts above Taheiho) of
the S/S Chi-yang, belonging to the Wu-tung Steamship
Company.

2/   The investigation showed that on the 2nd of
July at 8.45 p.m. the S/S Chi-yang started from
Taheiho up the Amur to Moho (800 versts), loaded with
7,400 poods of cargo and 360 passengers, the draught
being 4½ feet. Most of cargo had destination only
to Humaho (265 versts). The shallowest water between
Taheiho and Humaho is to be found in the Karkovsky
Shallows (6 feet of water). On the upper Amur to
Chernayeva (425 versts) the level was lower and the
water continued to fall. From Chernayeva up river
commenced shoal water. The Beitonovsky Shallows showed
2½ feet of water, and the newly washed water-course
"Panga", 4½ feet; the other upper shallows, 5 feet
and over. At 11 p.m. owing to darkness and rain
the Captain stopped to await the day light, not
wishing to run the risk of negotiating the Belayevsky
Shallows (18 versts from Taheiho) in the dark.

3/   On the 3rd July at 3.30 a.m. the steamer
proceeded up river. At 4 a.m. the Assistant Pilot

Wang Tê-shêng

Wang Tê-shêng came on his watch, but owing to the dangerous sandy Markovsky Shallow(35 versts) from Taheiho), where the channel is narrow and there is less than 6 feet of water, the First Pilot Semeroff remained on the bridge, until the dangerous places were passed; then feeling unwell he went to his cabin, knowing that there were no more dangerous shallows. On the bridge remained the Captain and the Assistant Pilot Wang Tê-shêng, whose watch was from 4 a.m. to 12. About 8 a.m. the vessel began to enter the Ekaterininsky Shallows and according to his statement the Assistant Pilot Wang Tê-shêng, navigated according to the bearing line No. 75, when the sounding-rod showed over 10 feet of water. While passing in the line No.74 the leadsman began to cry: 9 feet, and the vessel struck. After that moment the soundings showed 7½ feet of water. Assistant Pilot Wang Tê-shêng immediately put the helm on the right. The Captain, at slow speed, ordered to investigate the holds and to start the pumps working. The First Pilot Semeroff, who came running, observed at once, that the vessel was to the left of the channel. He took the helm and kept on the right into the channel. Soon the leak was seen in the fireroom, where the water rose rapidly and came over the floor. The pumps could not help and the hole was difficult to find, as the fireroom was loaded with fire-wood. Then the Captain altered the course of vessel, and proceeded 200-250 sajens farther to the shore to beach his vessel. The water began to come through the partition between the fireroom and the hold and rose everywhere, putting out the fire in the boilers. The sailors cleared the fireroom and the Captain together with the Assistant Pilot found the hole under the boiler

boiler on the right, but in spite of all measures
taken, they could not close the hole, owing to 4½
feet of water in the fireroom and the vessel began to
sink. Most of the cargo in the hold got wet. At
this time the river began to fall. Not able to
rescue the vessel by his own means, the Captain sent
the First Pilot in a boat to inform the agent at
Taheiho of the accident and to request a steamer for
the wrecked passengers and for pumping the water from
the S/S Chi-yang.

4/   On the 3rd of July the S/S Aigun belonging
to the Wu-tung Steamship Company that had already
cleared for Harbin, was kept back and sent to take
the wrecked passengers and to proceed to Moho. The
pumps and salvage gear brought by the S/S Aigun,
proved useless, and the S/S Aigun herself had no
pumps. The S/S Shên-yang (also belonging to the
Wu-tung Company) which carries mails and passengers
down the Amur to Chi-ko-te (147 versts) was sent on
the 5th July to the S/S Chi-yang to load the
discharged cargo. I proceeded up-river on board this
vessel together with the Harbour Master, Mr. Baukham,
the Agent of the Wu-tung Company Mr. Chên, and his
Assistant, Mr. Tusoff. In due course we met the
surveying launch of the Amur Navigation Office,"Pioneer"
which attends to Aids to Navigation on both sides
of the Amur. We boarded this steamer and proceeded
up river to the Ekaterininsky Shallows. On arrival
there we kept   strictly in the bearing lines
No. 75 and No. 74, sounding along the channel and
getting over 10 feet of water. Then we altered
the course of vessel, dropping anchor in the line
No. 74 above the crossing of the line No. 75, and,
                                        turning

turning on the cable in all directions, sounded the
channel. In turning to the left we found the rock
bank where there was 7 to 9 feet of water. This
rocky shoal lies to the side of channel, marked by
bearing lines. In the channel we sounded, but could
not find bottom. The Surveyor of the Amur Navigation
Office who was sent on the "Pioneer" to sound the
channel of the Ekaterininsky Shallows reports that
the channel was clear of rocks and not less than
10 feet of water in any place. The steamer was
carried to the left by the current toward the rocky
bank (where she struck) which was not far from channel.
Arriving we immediately went aboard the wrecked steamer
to see the state she was in, and decided that in
order to raise her it would be necessary to send a
large steamer with powerful pumps, as soon as possible,
as the water from the 5th instant was rising and
if the decks became covered, it would be impossible
to pump her out and would then be necessary to send
barges to raise her.

5/ The Amur Navigation Office has erected Aids
to Navigation from 1896 to 1917, removing stones and
dredging channels on the rivers of Amur Basin, and
has expended over 38,000,000 Gold Roubles. The rocky
Ekaterininsky Shallows have been improved by dredging
and by the removal of stones. The cuts made by
dredges are still in a good state, and this channel
is considerably deeper than many others. The rocky
bank lying along the river is near the channel,
and the Amur Navigation Office has in the past removed
stones, with a view to clearing a part of the bank.
The large stone, on which the S/S Chi-yang struck

                is

is lying 30 - 40 sajens aside from the channel and
before the outbreak of the Great War it was not
found possible to remove it. However, the Amur Navigation
Office, after improving the channel in Ekaterininsky
Shallows, recognised the danger to navigation, owing to
the possibility of the broadside current carrying
vessels on the rocky bank while passing from the
line No. 75 to the line No. 74, and to guard vessels
against accidents the Amur Navigation Office purposely
erected red bearing line No. 74 corresponding to the
white ones No. 74, and left such a distance between
them, that the least deviation of a vessel from the
proper lines should at once be observed by the pilot.

The facts elicited force me to the conclusion
that the stone struck by the "Chi-yang" was <u>not in
the channel</u>, but that the vessel was out of her course
and too much to the left. The present accident to
the S/S "Chi-yang" is to be ascribed to <u>a possible
though entirely preventable error in river navigation</u>,
which must be held to be due both to insufficient
acquaintanceship with the navigation of the Amur on
the part of the Assistant Pilot Wang Tê-shêng, and
to lack of attention on the part of the Captain
Mr. Cherepanoff who should have taken into consideration
1/ the falling water; 2/ heavy (though allowed)
draught of his vessel; and 3/ the swift broadside
current in the vicinity.

(Signed) P. Ignatieff,

The Commissioner of Customs,
Aigun.

Technical Adviser on Amur
Aids to Navigation.

True Copy:- _Wangyuesik_ ,3rd. Clerk C.

(b)<u>Technical Adviser's Report of the 1st.August,1924.</u>

AIGUN NO. 180 OF 1924.

APPENDIX 2.

(b) <u>Technical Adviser's Report of the 1st. August,1924,</u>
<u>on the sinking of the Wu T'ung Company's S.S.</u>
<u>" Chi Yang " in the Ekaterininsky Channel.</u>

Sir,

1/   Cases of accidents to vessels on the Sungari,
before the erection and upkeep of Aids to Navigation
by the C. M. Customs, were much more frequent than
now-a-days. In the opinion of all specialists, Captains
and Pilots, the stony San-sing Shallows, as a result of
the work undertaken by the Customs, are far less
difficult than was the case previously, and the bearing
lines and lighting are excellent. Accidents on the Sungari
and especially on the San-sing Shallows are chiefly caused
by the owners of vessels or their agents, who
ignore the state of the river and in spite of
Customs regulations, compel the Captains to load
vessels to an excess, and do not comply with the
water level reports. The presence of **bandits**
(Hunghutze) in that district makes difficult both
navigation and the upkeep of Aids to Navigation, but
for this the Customs cannot be blamed. The main
features of the Sungari are a very low water level
and a changing channel. The vessels bought by the
Chinese from Russians were built for navigation on
Amur, where the depth of water is much greater.
Many steamers by their size, draught, and by the
great consumption of fire-wood, are quite unfit for
navigating the Sungari, e.g. S.S. "Fêng-tien" drawing
more than 3 feet, "Chên-chiang" which consumes some
36 sajens of fire-wood daily, and others. The Chinese
now propose to put into commission S.S. "Harbin"

(formerly

(formerly S.S. "Vasily Alexeeff") which measures 267 feet long. This was the largest steamer on the whole Amur Basin, and navigated only the lower Amur from Blagovestchensk to Nikolaevsk. I should not be surprised, if there were to be accidents caused by her running aground in shoal water, as it will be difficult for her to turn in the shoal and sandy banks of the Sungari.

2/ The collection of River Dues on the Amur was introduced on the 17th June 1922, the whole frontier section on the Amur being divided into 2 Districts: 1/ from Kasakevich to Taheiho and 2/ from Taheiho to Pokrovka. River Dues collected on a normal turnover of cargo - i.e. 3,000,000-5,000,000 poods of various cargo; 10,000-15,000 cubic sajens of fire-wood; and a great number of rafts - would be sufficient for the upkeep of and repairs to Aids to Navigation on the frontier section. The extraordinary circumstances which brought about the closing of the frontier and boycott decreased the turnover of cargo by more than 50%, and the collection of River Dues fell likewise. The Estimates prepared by the Amur Navigation Office were reduced to 60-75%, in view of the small amount of Dues collected. The amended estimates allowed only the most urgent work to be undertaken i.e., the verifying and sounding of channels and the maintenance of Aids to Navigation. In the winter season 1923-24, a sum of $ 200.00 was expended in removing stones in the Soyus Shallows which had been carried by the ice-floe too near to the channel. In 1922 estimates for Gold Roubles 32,000.00 were approved by the Sino-Russian Commission, the sum of Gold Roubles 13,978.20 being paid to the Amur

Navigation

Navigation Office according to Agreement. In 1923 estimates for Gold Roubles 19,250.00 were passed, the sum of Gold Roubles 9,623.97 being paid to the Amur Navigation Office. In 1924 estimates were approved for Gold Roubles 35,750.00, the sum of Gold Roubles 17,775.00 being paid to the Amur Navigation Office. During the three years the Agreement has been in force the total sum paid to the Amur Navigation Office from River Dues collected amounts to Gold Roubles 41,000.00.

3/ It was in 1896 that the Amur Navigation Office began work on the upkeep of Aids to Navigation, removing stones and dredging channels on the rivers of the Amur Basin, and from that year to 1917 they had expended for this purpose a sum over 38,000,000 Gold Roubles. The Amur River is known to have a rocky bed, and it is impossible to remove all stones from a river. And it is not necessary to do so in order to make navigation safe. The erection of Aids to Navigation, the dredging of the shallows, and the removal by the Amur Navigation Office of certain dangerous stones, are quite sufficient to make navigation along these rivers safe. Any one who understands the conditions prevailing on the river, should have no difficulty in navigating safely in high water if he keeps in the bearing lines. In the shoal water the navigation is much more difficult and it thus follows that Captains, Pilots, and Engineers should be people of knowledge and experience. Unfortunately the Chinese owners of steamers often appoint as employees persons who are not really competent.

4/

4/   As a result of accidents, which had taken place in the Ekaterininsky Shallows, the Amur Navigation Office undertook dredging operations there; and removed many stones thus improving and making the shallows navigable. The cuts **formed by** dredging in the channel are still in a good state, and the channel is much deeper than many others. The rocky bank lying along the river is near the channel. The Amur Navigation Office had undertaken the removal of stones with a view to clearing a part of the bank, near the channel, but the large stone on which the S.S. "Chi-yang" struck, could not be removed during the winter season. This stone lies 30-40 sajens away from the channel. Notwithstanding the improvement of the channel in the Ekaterininsky Shallows, the Amur Navigation Office recognised that navigation in the vicinity of the channel was risky owing to the broadside current, which tended to carry vessels on to the rocky bank, while passing from the line No. 75 to the line No. 74, and to obviate the likelihood of accidents, the Amur Navigation Office specially placed red bearing line No. 74, corresponding to the white one No. 74, and left such a distance between them, that the least deviation of a vessel from the bearing line, should at once be observed by the Pilot.

5/   After investigating this case and questioning all parties who were present at the time of the accident, I came to the conclusion that the Assistant Pilot Wang Tê-shêng, who was on watch when the "Chi-yang" entered the Ekaterininsky

Shallows,

Shallows, failed to appreciate the possible danger to navigation caused by a swift broadside current, and omitted to take into consideration the low level of the water and the heavy draught of the vessel. Being a young pilot, he probably did not know that there were stones in the bank near the channel, and thus failed to keep strictly in the bearing lines, and hearing the soundings and thinking that in 9 feet of water the way was clear, he proceeded in the direction of the rocky bank. Carried by the broadside current, the vessel struck her right side on a stone which was lying away from the channel. The damage was done forward of the boiler.

6/ The present accident to the S. S. "Chi-yang" must be attributed to an **explainable but entirely preventable error in river navigation**. I wish to remain quite impartial, and I cannot attribute blame to the Amur Navigation Office, which cannot be held responsible for the damage done. There are insurance companies established to cover risks of this kind.

7/ From 19th June to the 17th of July, I with the Russian River Inspector travelled in a launch on the whole frontier section for the purpose of investigating the nature of repairs being done by the Russians. Thanks to low water we verified bearing lines and sounded all shallows. Whatever changes were found to be necessary to the Aids to Navigation were at once carried out, and the channel is now in a good state.

The Commissioner of Customs,   Your obedient servant,
       Aigun.   (Signed) P. Ignatieff,

True Copy:-   Technical Adviser

    Wong Yusik ,3rd.Clerk C.   to Aigun Customs.

APPENDIX 3.

AIGUN NO. 180 OF 1924.

APPENDIX 3.

(a) Harbour Master's Report of the 9th. July,1924,
on the sinking of the Wu T'ung Company's S.S.
" Chi Yang " in the Ekaterininsky Channel.

Sir,

On the 5th instant, in accordance with your
instructions to investigate into the case of the
sinking of the S.S. Chi-Yang on the Ekerterininsky
Shallows on the 3rd instant, I beg to submit the
following report.

At 12.40 p. m., in company with the Technical
Adviser, Mr. Ignatieff, and the Manager of the Wutung
Company, Mr. Ch'ên, I boarded the S.S. Shên-Yang and
proceeded up river, On arriving at the Upper Markovsky
Shallows we met and hailed the Russian surveying
Launch S.S. Pioneer which came alongside of our vessel.
The Captain of the S.S. Pioneer informed us that he
had been sent up river by the Russian Authorities
to sound the Channels on the Shallows where the
S.S. Chi-Yang had sunk, and Mr. Ignatieff suggested
that we should board the S.S. Pioneer as she was
the faster of the two vessels and much more convenient
for sounding the Channels. As it was getting late,
already 6 p. m. , and we wanted to sound the Channels
before it got dark, the Captain having no objections
and quite willing to comply with our request, we
boarded the S.S. Pioneer and proceeded up river leaving
the S.S. Shên-Yang miles behind. Arriving at the
Ekerterininsky Shallows at 7.30 p. m. we sounded the
Channels in B/L 75 and B/L 74 and got a depth of

11'

11' of water and over everywhere along the Channels;
we then altered the course of the vessel back into
the Channel in B/L 75 and, instead of keeping
strictly in the Channel and bringing our vessel
in line with B/L 74, we turned to the left about
60 feet below B/L 74, bringing the vessel closer
into the bank on the Chinese side of the river,
and in doing so the strong current at this point
of the river drove our vessel closer into the bank
(which we assumed is what happened to the S.S.
Chi-Yang). Taking soundings in the vicinity of
this part of the river we got 9', 7'½ and then
6' of water with very large stones on the bottom
and laying everywhere on the bed of the river in
this particular point. Of course it is not disputed
that the vessel might have been in 9' of water
when she struck the stone and the stone turned
over on its side after the vessel had struck it,
and this particular stone may have been carried to
this point closer to the Channel by the heavy
Ice-floe in the spring, but it does not get away
from the fact that the Vessel was not in the
Channel. The Captain wrote in his statement, filed
in this office, that at the time of striking the
stone the soundings registered 9 feet, whereas if
he had been in the Channel he would have got 11
feet of water and more. This tends to show quite
plainly as I have already stated that the Pilot
instead of keeping strictly to the Channel in
B/L 75 until his vessel came in line with B/L 74
he altered the course of the Vessel too soon to
the left, as shown with a Red Dotted Line on the

attached

attached plan. And by doing so, I suppose to save
time, and not taking into consideration the low
level of the water, the heavy draft of the vessel
and the heavy current which caught the vessel
broadside on, when he turned drove the vessel still further
away from the Channel than he expected. It is
my firm opinion that when the Assistant Pilot who
was on watch at the time altered course of the
vessel leaving the channel too soon, sounded the
river, and getting 9 feet of water, thought the
road was clear and by using his own discretion and
ignoring the Bearing Lines led the vessel to
destruction.

Although the Assistant Pilot is solely to
blame for this disaster I do not wish to exonerate
the Captain from all blame. He was on watch at
the time and should have seen that the Pilot kept
his vessel in the Channel.

Summary of the Investigation.

Both myself and the Technical Adviser Mr.
Ignatieff have summed up the whole case very
carefully and come to the conclusion that the
sinking of the S.S. Chi-Yang on the Ekerterininsky
Shallows on the 3rd July 1924, was due to the
wilful negligence and carelessness of the Assistant
Pilot in not keeping strictly to Bearing Lines of
the Channels, and altering the course of the vessel
from B/L 75 to get into the Channel of B/L No. 74
too soon, and not taking into consideration firstly
the low water level, and secondly the heavy draft
of the vessel, $4\frac{1}{2}$ feet. In turning too soon in
B/L No. 75 and leaving the channel the strong current
carried the vessel farther into the Chinese side of

the

the bank than he had estimated and finally struck a stone, or some stones, which led to the destruction of the vessel.

The Captain cannot be exonerated from blame as he was on watch at the time the vessel struck, and being the Administrative Head of the vessel, he should have seen that the vessel was being navigated correctly and that the Pilot was keeping strictly to the Bearing Lines in the channels. He knew quite well that his vessel was fully loaded with a 4½ feet draft and that there were 350 Passengers on board, and especially with such a low water level he should not have allowed the Pilot to alter the course of the vessel too soon from bearing line No. 75, thus leaving the channel. On the other hand if he had been in doubt, and did not know this particular channel very well, he should have demanded a full explanation from the Pilot before leaving the channel.

I have the honour to be,
Sir,
Your obedient servant,
(Signed) G. E. Baukham,
Acting Harbour Master.

True Copy:-

_____,
3rd. Clerk C.

(b)Harbour Master's Report of the 17th. July, 1924.

呈海关总税务司署 <u>180</u> 号文　　　　　　　　　　瑷珲关 1924 年 8 月 7 日

尊敬的海关总税务司（北京）：

　　1. 兹报告，1924 年 7 月 3 日，戊通航业公司的"吉阳（Chi Yang）"号轮船在行至大黑河上游 50 俄里处的叶卡捷琳尼斯基（Ekaterininsky）浅滩时，触礁沉船。该轮船于 1924 年 7 月 2 日自瑷珲关结关驶往漠河，载有总计 7552 普特的普通货物，货物未投保。戊通航业公司随即通过其当地经理向发货人告知，由于轮船触礁地点乃是位于俄阿穆尔水道局所负责的航段之内，因此戊通航业公司对轮船在事故中所蒙受的损失并无责任。此事随后交由中国商会处理。商会经讨论后一致认为，可尝试通过法律程序强制俄方予以赔偿。

　　2. 中国商会在致瑷珲关交涉员（兼道尹及海关监督）的信函中说道，商人们之所以愿意缴纳江捐，是希望负责管理河道的有关部门能够尽心尽力地维护各条河道上的航运安全；事实上，这也正应该是中俄双方所签署的一系列有关边界河道之协议的一个理所应当的立足点。既然"吉阳"号轮船是在俄方所管理的河道上发生事故的，那么俄阿穆尔水道局就理应为这件事负责。而且中国商会认为，此次事故就是由俄阿穆尔水道局在工作上的失误所导致的，亦反映出俄阿穆尔水道局对中国商人合法权益的忽视，并坚称如果俄方无意为此次事故负上不可推脱之责任，那么中俄之间所签订的任何一份有关边界河道的协议，都将失去继续实施下去的意义。针对此次事故，中国商会除了斥责俄阿穆尔水道局对自身责任的认识甚不到位，对中国商人的损失无动于衷外，甚至怀疑俄阿穆尔水道局故意将石块留在"叶卡捷琳尼斯基"浅滩，意图使中国轮船发生意外。商会于信中认定，海关与俄阿穆尔水道局均已认同"吉阳"号轮船在触礁时并未偏离航路，并据此于信末强调，俄国政府应向中国商人赔付货物损失。

　　3. 航务专门顾问与理船厅皆认为商会的想法大谬不然，不仅得出的结论有误，甚至就连借以推导出该结论的依据都是不正确的。航务专门顾问与理船厅认为俄阿穆尔水道局无需对此次事故负责，因为此次事故乃是由船长及副引水员的疏忽所导致的，与航路标志无关。但商会向来有自己的一套行为准则，恐怕未必会完全听从本署之决定。然而，如果任由事态继续发展下去，势必会影响中俄两国政府之间的关系，甚至令二者间的关系恶化至再难恢复的境地，毕竟俄阿穆尔水道局绝不会同意为此次事故做出任何赔偿。俄方已明确表态，一切问题都早已在相关协议中列明。而且本署认为，航务专门顾问在黑龙江航务方面经验丰富，能力非凡，既然其报告中已很肯定地指出事故发生地点周围的航路标志并无不妥，"吉阳"号轮船触礁沉船一事便与航路标志无关，那么对于商会所述之俄方违反协议之观点，本署实难接受。

4. 本署与商会的意见分歧，主要在于"吉阳"号轮船在触礁时是否已偏离航路。戊通航业公司声称对于此次事故，其并不负有任何责任，因为轮船直至失事那一刻，仍处于正常航路之中，失事之处水深九英尺，然而这只是戊通航业公司的一面之词；而且船长的两份陈述以及引水员的报告中，也多有前后矛盾之处。比如在船长的第一份陈述中，其自称在事发时，正驾驶"吉阳"号轮船从前方的白色方位线（75 号白色立标）驶向红白方位线（74 号白色立标与 74 号红色立标）；但是在其第二份陈述中，却又说当时其并未亲自去确认轮船的位置，位置确认一事是交由副引水员去做的，而其自己仅是负责注意水深变化而已。但船长已承认事发之时其正在当值，如此便可确定其对此事确有责任，因为其于船桥上绝对可以凭肉眼看清轮船是否航行在指定的方位线上。引水员在事发之时并未当班，但根据其陈述，很明显水深 9 英尺的位置是在航路以外的，这恰恰证明了船长与副引水员并未严格地遵守航路标志的指引。

5. 兹认为，商会所持之现行协议已失去存在意义的观点只能反映出其自身的目光狭隘与自怨自艾。在本署看来，如果航路上现有的条件果真不足以保障轮船的航运安全，那么毋庸置疑，应尽快想办法予以改善；当然，如此也就意味着必须要上调江捐税率，向过往商船征收更多的江捐。航务专门顾问一向品德高尚，忠厚正直，但因对俄阿穆尔水道局所提交的账目审查过于严谨，已遭到布拉戈维申斯克（Blagovestchensk）方面的嫉恨。其告知本署，现行协议中所规定的可用于管理与维护航路标志的经费都非常有限，因此只能优先保证最紧要项目的开展。如果航道已经足够宽阔，却还想要继续予以拓展，俄方当然会提出异议。而且俄阿穆尔水道局的职责与义务在中俄双方于 1923 年 10 月 28 日签订的协议中已有明确规定。除非将俄阿穆尔水道局的现有职责（维护边界河道的航路、灯塔与标桩以确保轮船的航运安全）与其他诸如移除航路外障碍物的工作严格做出区分，否则很可能会破坏整个协议的继续实施。而移除航路之外的礁石，无论额外能提升多少安全性，都毕竟不是俄阿穆尔水道局的职责。所以本署提议，如果当真有必要移除航路以外的礁石，应尝试向俄方提出建议，而非蛮横地提出要求。

航务专门顾问告知本署，每移除 1 平方俄丈（1 俄丈等于 7 英尺）的礁石，就需花费200 到 1000 银圆不等。在过去沙皇统治时期，俄国政府每年为黑龙江边界河道航路标志维护工作所划拨的经费多达 200 万到 300 万金卢布，因此，从中支出 5 万到 10 万金卢布用于结雅河、谢列姆贾（Selemdja）河以及布列亚（Bureya）河的礁石移除工作，也并不足怪。至 1922 年，中国开始承担黑龙江航路标志维护工作的部分费用，1922 年、1923 年及 1924

年,总计支出 41477 金卢布。在 1923 年至 1924 年冬季,俄阿穆尔水道局已经支出 200 银圆用于移除索菲斯克（Soyus）航路内的礁石,但并未涉及航路以外的礁石。显然双方的最终目标乃是进一步拓宽航路,使轮船得以更快更安全地航行,但由于俄阿穆尔水道局所能利用的经费数额已今非昔比,因此将整个黑龙江改造成一条可供轮船高速航行之水域的想法显然不切合实际,俄阿穆尔水道局目前所拥有的经费也只够维持原有航路的基本畅通而已。

6. 商会一直将重点放在俄方已承认事故发生地在叶卡捷琳尼斯基浅滩,但却忽视了以下三个非常重要的问题:（1）"吉阳"号轮船所触礁石位于航路外 30–40 俄丈（210–280 英尺）处;（2）该段航路早在战前就已经过疏浚船的疏浚,航路内的礁石均被移除干净,并且俄阿穆尔水道局还在该段航路上树立了信标,以引导过往轮船的航行,轮船在驶过 75 号白色立标而转向 74 号白色立标与红色立标时,对面江岸上仍可见 74 号白色立标,因此轮船若偏离航道,是可以马上意识到的;（3）本署从未接到过关于叶卡捷琳尼斯基浅滩附近因存在礁石而令轮船面临航运危险的投诉。理船厅曾分发给每艘驶入大黑河港口的轮船一本意见簿,希望各位船长能够充分表达他们的意见与建议——这已成为一种惯例。意见簿每有更新,都需一式两份,其中一份会通过理船厅送交航务专门顾问手中,以便航务专门顾问对这些意见进行浏览与筛选,从而对航路现状实施必要的调整。"吉阳"号轮船的船长已在黑龙江上游航行近 15 年,从未向港务课提出任何有关叶卡捷琳尼斯基航路的投诉,由此可推论,其对该段航路上的航路标志现状非常满意,所以从未提出任何意见。既然如此,本署则有理由认为如果"吉阳"号轮船的确一直航行于航路之内,那么绝对可以保证航行之安全——相信船长应该已多次驾驶轮船安全通过叶卡捷琳尼斯基浅滩。

7. 商会于来函结尾处暗称俄方有意使航路危机四伏,从而破坏中国的航运事业。但该想法显然有失偏颇,俄国轮船同样在黑龙江上航行,本署相信俄阿穆尔水道局还不至于做出使己方轮船时时陷于险境的愚蠢行为。

8. 经航务专门顾问与理船厅共同调查,整个事件的真相已基本水落石出,本署兹做出如下结论:此次事故的责任主要在"吉阳"号轮船的船长与副引水员,是由二人的能力有限且粗心大意所致。

9. 兹附道尹来函抄件（附录 1）及本署回函所附各文件抄件:

（1）1924 年 7 月 9 日航务专门顾问报告译本（附录 2a）;

（2）1924 年 8 月 1 日航务专门顾问报告第 1 部分与第 7 部分译文（附录 2b）;

（3）1924 年 7 月 9 日理船厅报告译本（附录 3a）;

（4）1924年7月17日理船厅报告第4部分译文（"应注意……仅提升十分之四"一节）（附录3b）；

（5）船长第一封陈述中"当……触礁"一节的译文（附录4）；

（6）船长第二封陈述中"本人的确一直待在船桥上……但因为当时太过激动未注意到方位线"一节的译文（附录5）；

（7）副引水员陈述中"7月3日……掌舵"一节的译文（附录5）；

（8）引水员陈述中"大概在早上八点，本人感觉……将船引入正确航路"一节（附录5）。

您忠诚的仆人

贺智兰（R. F. C. Hedgeland）

瑗珲关税务司

瑷珲关致海关总税务司署第 180 号呈附件 1

道尹（兼交涉司与海关监督）来函译本

（附商会就戌通行业公司"吉阳"号轮船失事一事向道尹所致信函）

中国商会就"吉阳"号轮船失事一事发来信函，内容如下：

召开于民国十一年（1922）的中俄会议决定，用于维护松花江与黑龙江航路标志的资金应从双方的江捐税收中支出，另表示，鉴于航路标志维护工程乃以改善航路环境为旨归，因此商人亦应为该项工程尽一份力。然而尽管中俄双方已努力对航路环境进行改善，但工程实施以来，松花江下游地区仍时常发生轮船搁浅事件。此类事件的频繁发生，已然为航运带来诸如成本增加、时间延误等一系列不良影响，使商人蒙受了不小的经济损失。若水深不足是因为降水量少，我们自是无可抱怨。但事实却并非如此。7 月 5 日，商会收到戌通航业公司的来信，内容大致如下：

"本公司的"吉阳"号轮船于 7 月 2 日自大黑河驶往漠河，至 7 月 3 日早上 8 时，在经过大阴山（Tayinshan）时意外触礁（是处水深 9 英尺），以致船体严重损毁。船员立即尝试各种办法对轮船进行挽救，努力将轮船驶向河岸，以避免其沉没，但河水早已在轮船触礁之时通过船底的破洞涌入了船体，船员们最终也只能抢救出部分货物而已。轮船仍然沉于水中，大部分货物亦已损毁，实际损失尚无法确定。而我们想要强调的一点是，吉阳号轮船在水深达 9 英尺的航路中仍遭遇这样的不幸，其原因着实不同寻常。本公司对此次事故并不负有任何责任。我们之所以写这封信，就是希望商人们能够理解本公司在此次事件中的态度与立场，我们同样是受害者。"

戌通航业公司大黑河经理陈先生也就此事与商会进行了沟通，其称海关已着手对此次事故的原因展开调查，调查结果若显示此次事故的发生乃由引水员的疏忽所致，即由于引水员的疏忽而使轮船偏离了航路，引水员将受到严厉的处分。不过据陈先生所说，当海关代表到达事发现场后，俄阿穆尔水道局人员也一同参与了调查，最终双方一致认为，"吉阳"号轮船在触礁时并未偏离航路，事故发生的原因乃是由于航路内存在礁石。俄阿穆尔水道局人员还主动提供信息，称此地已发生多起事故，因此引水员并无任何责任。为航运提供必要设施,在水深不足或存在礁石的危险区域安设灯塔或标桩,确保轮船行船安全,乃是俄阿穆尔水道局的职责。如果说俄阿穆尔水道局并不认为大阴山一带存在航运危险,那么对航路中的这一大块礁石又当作何解释。况且俄阿穆尔水道局已经承认过去也曾有数艘轮船相继于此地遇险,因此其理应早对这一问题做出应有的处理,或移除礁石,或竖立危险信号。但事实上,俄阿穆尔水道局从未对这一问题做过任何处理,正因如此,才致使我们中国的轮船频频于此地失事。这不仅浪费了中方所支付的江捐,更严重危及商人的生命及财产安全。

中华民国十一年(1922)至十二年(1923)之间,用于航路标志维护工作的支出多达71000金卢布。然而即使如此,航路中却依然存在多处水位较低或有礁石的危险区域。何况连俄罗斯阿穆尔水运局人员都否定了"吉阳"号引水员的责任。因此我们不得不怀疑,俄方是有意要将中国商人的生命及财产置于危险境地,否则为什么不对大阴山一带的航路予以应有的维护,这本来就是俄阿穆尔水道局的职责,而他们也清楚地知道该处所存在着的危险和已经出现过的事故。他们愿意承认引水员对此次事故并不负有任何的责任,但却不愿意对中国商人所蒙受的巨大损失发表任何言论。须知,向海关缴纳江捐的,正是这些蒙受巨大损失的商人,他们缴纳江捐,原本是为了使航路可以更加安全,然而结果却让他们大失所望,他们交的钱越多,似乎损失的也就越多。如此,又怎能使他们服从海关的管理。俄阿穆尔水道局着实用心险恶。如果我们不向俄方索赔"吉阳"号轮船所蒙受的一切损失,他们则永远不会正视自己的职责,类似的事故也必将继续发生。故希望道尹可以在这方面为我们提供一些帮助。

税务司若能将对此事的立场及意见相告,交涉司(即道尹)将不胜感激。

瑷珲关致海关总税务司署第 180 号呈附录 2a

航务专门顾问关于戊通航业公司"吉阳"号轮船

在叶卡捷琳尼斯基浅滩沉船事的报告译本

（1924 年 7 月 9 日）

1. 兹呈送本人关于 1924 年 7 月 3 日戊通航业公司"吉阳"号轮船在叶卡捷琳尼斯基浅滩（大黑河上游 50 俄里处）沉船一事的报告。

2. 经查，7 月 2 日晚 8 时 45 分，"吉阳"号轮船自大黑河出发，沿黑龙江向上游 800 俄里处的漠河行驶，船上载有 7400 普特货物与 360 名乘客，轮船吃水深度为 4.5 英尺。大部分货物的目的地是呼玛河（黑龙江上游 245 俄里处），而大黑河与呼玛河之间，水位最浅的地方就是卡可夫斯基（Karkovsky）浅滩，水深 6 英尺。然自呼玛河向上至切尔纳耶瓦（Chernayeva）（黑龙江上游 425 俄里处）河段，水位便开始持续下降。切尔纳耶瓦（Chernayeva）上游河段几乎均为浅水域。其中，贝托诺瓦斯基（Beitonovsky）浅滩水深 2.5 英尺，新开辟的"潘葛（Panga）"水道水深 4.5 英尺，其他上游浅滩的水深均在 5 英尺上下。当晚 11 时，由于天色漆黑，且伴有降雨，船长不愿冒险通过别列耶夫斯基（Belayevsky）浅滩（距大黑河 18 俄里），遂将船停下，等待天明。

3. 7 月 3 日早 3 时 30 分，轮船继续向上游航行。4 时，副引水员王德生（Wang Te-sheng）开始值守，但因轮船即将驶入航路狭窄且多沙的马尔科夫斯基（Markovsky）浅滩（距大黑河 35 俄里；实时水深不足 6 英尺），正引水员斯米罗夫（Semeroff）亦留在船桥，直至轮船驶离危险地区；之后斯米罗夫因身体不适返回船舱休息，但其清楚前方已无其他危险浅滩。此后至中午 12 时，船桥上便只剩下船长和副引水员王德生二人。

大约早 8 时左右，轮船逐渐驶入叶卡捷琳尼斯基浅滩。根据副引水员王德生的陈述，其一直按照 75 号方位线的指示航行，当时量水尺所显示的水深在 10 英尺以上。然而在通过 74 号方位线时，轮船却突然遭受到撞击，就在前一刻，测深员还报告说水深尚有 9 英尺，撞击过后，量水尺所显示的水深也还有 7.5 英尺。副引水员王德生立刻将船舵右转。当时轮船的航速较低，船长下令查看货仓情况并开启排水泵。正引水员斯米罗夫也当即行动起来，却发现船身已在航路之外，于是其立刻接管船舵，继续右转，试图重新进入航路。然而,江水很快就渗到了锅炉房,迅速漫过了船底肋板,而锅炉房内又堆满了薪柴,很难找到漏水点,排水泵亦并未起到多大作用。船长随后改变了行船路线,转而向岸边驶进了200到250俄丈,试图将轮船引到岸上。这时,水开始从锅炉房与货仓之间的隔板中涌出,并迅速漫延开去,锅炉中的火遂被湮灭。之后,水手们清空了锅炉房,船长和副引水员终于在锅炉右下方找到了漏水点,然而用尽一切办法也无法将之堵住。涌入锅炉房里的水已有4.5英尺深,整个船身都在渐渐下沉。货仓中的大多数货物都已被浸湿。此时,江水开始退潮。船长明白仅凭一己之力已无法阻止轮船的沉没,于是只好命正引水员乘坐船上的小艇去面见戊通航业公司大黑河代理,向其报告此次意外,并请其派遣一艘轮船前来,接走"吉阳"号轮船上的乘客,并将涌入船中的水用水泵抽掉。

4.7月3日,戊通航业公司将其已结关前往哈尔滨的"瑷珲(Aigun)"号轮船召回,命之前去迎接失事轮船"吉阳"号上的乘客,并将之继续送往漠河。但"瑷珲"号轮船所带去的水泵("瑷珲"号轮船本身并无水泵)和打捞装置却并无用处。7月5日,戊通航业公司又命其原本主要负责大黑河至奇克特(大黑河下游147俄里处)河段邮包及乘客运输工作的"沈阳(Shen-yang)"号轮船前去装载自"吉阳"号轮船卸下之货物。

最初,本人与理船厅博韩(Baukham)先生、戊通航业公司代理陈先生及其助理图索夫(Tusoff)先生同乘"沈阳"号轮船前往上游,途中遇到俄阿穆尔水道局负责黑龙江两岸航路标志维护工作的"先锋(Pioneer)"号测量船后,便改乘该船继续前行,最终抵达叶卡捷琳尼斯基浅滩。

到达浅滩之后,我们严格按照75号方位线与74号方位线行船,并测量了该段航路的水深,结果显示水深在10英尺以上。于是我们又在74号方位线与75号方位线交叉处抛出船锚,固定位置,继而将各个方向的电缆尽数启动,对航路的水深进行全面测量。我们在航路左侧之外探测到一片岩埂(rock bank)地带,其水深为7到9英尺,但此处已用方位线做了标注;我们亦测量了该处航路内的水深,但并未探测到水底。俄阿穆尔水道局测量师对叶卡捷琳尼斯基浅滩的水深进行测量后称,航路内部并无礁石,且各处水深均超过10英尺,失事轮船应该是受到水流冲击,向航道左侧偏移,误入岩埂地带触礁。

抵达现场后,我们于第一时间登上失事轮船,详细查看轮船情况后,一致认为,如果想让该轮船重新浮于水面之上,就必须尽快派遣一艘大型轮船携带超强水泵过来,否则一旦江潮上涨(预计7月5日开始),江水漫过甲板,届时再想将该轮船从水中打捞出来,就必须依靠驳船,而绝非仅凭一个水泵就能做到的。

5. 俄阿穆尔水道局早于1896年至1917年间,便已在黑龙江流域各段航路上建起了航路标志,并进行了移除礁石、疏浚河道等工事,所花经费已超过 3800 万金卢布。叶卡捷琳尼斯基浅滩礁石颇多,但经过此期间的疏浚,移除礁石等工事后,航路环境已得到很大改善,疏浚船在此挖掘的河道状况良好,甚至比其他航段的水位都要深得多,只是该段航道沿线附近有一片岩埂地带,俄阿穆尔水道局当时虽已尽力移除部分礁石,但对于像"吉阳"号轮船所触礁石(位于航路外 30 至 40 俄丈处)这样大的石块,以其在第一次世界大战爆发之前的技术水平根本无法将之移除;尽管如此,俄阿穆尔水道局对叶卡捷琳尼斯基浅滩的航路进行改善后,考虑到轮船在由 75 号方位线驶向 74 号方位线时,很可能会受到侧向水流的冲击误入岩埂地带,产生危险,便在 74 号白色方位线对应的位置竖立了 74 号红色方位线,并在两条方位线之间留出一段距离,以确保引水员可及时发现轮船是否有偏离航路的情况。

6. 根据上述事实,兹得出结论如下:"吉阳"号轮船所触礁石并不在正常航路内,触礁时轮船已严重向左偏离航道。虽然此次轮船失事确与航道本身存在的风险有一定关系,但只要航行无误,亦完全可以避免;此次航行失误主要有两方面原因,一方面是副引水员王德生在黑龙江上的航行经验不足,另一方面是船长谢里帕诺夫(Cherepanoff)先生未能充分考虑水位逐渐下降、船只吃水较深(虽在限度内)以及附近侧向水流流速较快等客观因素。

（签字）易保罗（P.I.Ignatieff）

黑龙江航务专门顾问

此译本内容真实有效,特此证明:

录事:王友燮 三等同文供事后班

瑷珲关致海关总税务司署第180号呈附录2b

航务专门顾问关于戊通航业公司"吉阳"号轮船
在叶卡捷琳尼斯基浅滩沉船事的报告译本
（1924年8月1日）

1. 在中国海关开始建立并维护航路标志之前，松花江上曾频频发生航运事故。而如今，几乎所有专家、船长和引水员都认为，多石的三姓浅滩在经过海关的努力改善之后，其航行难度已大大降低，方位线和灯塔标注都十分完善。虽然松花江上，尤其是三姓浅滩河段如今仍会发生航运事故，但绝大多数都是由于轮船主或轮船代理忽视航路状况、枉顾海关规章、强迫船长超载、不遵水位报告行驶等行为所致。而该地区土匪（红胡子）的出现更是令航运与航路标志维护工作举步维艰，但此非海关之责。

松花江的特点是水位低，航路复杂多变。中国人从俄国人手上买来的轮船，主要依据黑龙江上的航运状况建造的，黑龙江的水位比松花江深得多，这些轮船体积较大，吃水较深，消耗薪柴也较多，不适合在松花江上航行，如吃水超过3英尺的"奉天（Feng-tian）"号轮船和每天需要消耗超过36俄丈薪柴的"镇江（Chen-chiang）"号轮船等。目前中国人还准备将"哈尔滨（Harbin）"号（前"瓦西里 Vasily Alexeeff"号）轮船投入运营，该船长度超过267英尺，是黑龙江流域最大的轮船，一般情况下只适宜在黑龙江下游自布拉戈维申斯克至尼古拉耶夫斯克（Nickolaevsk）一段航行，若航行至松花江浅水区域或者沙洲地带，连转弯都会变得非常困难，恐怕难以避免事故的发生。

2. 自1922年6月17日起，黑龙江上开始征收江捐，整个黑龙江边界河道被划分成两个区段：自（嘎杂克维池至大黑河为一个区段，自大黑河至波克罗夫卡为一个区段。正常情况下，各类货物的总运输量可达300万至500万普特，薪柴的总运输量可达10000至15000立方俄丈，再加上大量的木筏运输，江捐税收足以支付维护边界河道航路标志的费用。但如果出现特殊情况，比如边境关闭或经济抵制，货运量便会骤减（甚至减少50%以上），江捐税收自然也会随之减少。鉴于江捐税收有限，俄阿穆尔水道局也将自己的初始预算削减了60%到75%。削减后的预算仅够维持最关键的工作，比如巡查航路状况、测量航路水深、维护航路标志等。

1923 年至 1924 年冬季，俄阿穆尔水道局支出 200.00 银圆，用于移除索菲斯克（Soyus）浅滩被浮冰带到航路附近的礁石。1922 年，中俄水道委员会所批准的预算金额为 32000.00 金卢布，根据协议，其中 13978.20 金卢布由中方摊付。1923 年获批准的预算金额为 19250.00 金卢布，其中 9623.97 金卢布由中方摊付。1924 年获批准的预算金额为 35750.00 金卢布，其中 17775.00 金卢布由中方摊付。在执行协议的三年间，中方支付给俄阿穆尔水道局的江捐税收共计 41000.00 金卢布。

3. 自 1896 年起，俄阿穆尔水道局便开始在黑龙江流域开展维护航路标志，移除礁石以及疏浚河道等工作，截至 1917 年，共计支出 3800 万金卢布。

众所周知，黑龙江的河床多为石质，因此若想将整条江里的石块全部清理干净，显然是不现实的；而且要保证航运安全亦并非要将所有石块全部移除。俄阿穆尔水道局所开展的建立航路标志、疏浚浅滩、移除部分危险礁石等工作，对于保证航运安全着实非常有效。凡了解航路情况者，只要按照方位线的指示行船，便可安全行驶于水深足够的区域，当然在浅水区域航行仍然较为困难，因此船长、引水员及轮机工程师都应由经验丰富之人担任。很遗憾，中国轮船主所委派的人员常常是资质不足，经验又有限之辈。

4. 由于（叶卡捷琳尼斯基浅滩以前就发生过航运事故，因此俄阿穆尔水道局早已于该浅滩开展过疏浚河道、移除礁石等工作，使其航路条件得到了不小的改善，已可以满足航运的需求。疏浚船当时在此挖掘的河道如今状况依然良好，甚至比其他航段的水位都要深很多，只是该段航道沿线附近有一片岩埂地带，俄阿穆尔水道局当时虽已尽力移除部分礁石，但对于像"吉阳"号轮船所触礁石（位于航路外 30 至 40 俄丈处）这样大的石块却无法在冬季移除；尽管如此，俄阿穆尔水道局对叶卡捷琳尼斯基浅滩的航路进行改善后，考虑到轮船在由 75 号方位线驶向 74 号方位线时，很可能会受到侧向水流的冲击误入 [岩埂 rock bank] 地带，产生危险，便在 74 号白色方位线对应的位置竖立了 74 号红色方位线，并在两条方位线之间留出一段距离，以确保引水员可及时发现轮船是否有偏离航路的情况。

5. 在对此次事件做出调查并对事故现场所有当事人进行询问后，本人得出结论："吉阳"号轮船驶入叶卡捷琳尼斯基浅滩时，值班副引水员王德生未能发现侧方水流变化所带来的潜在危险，忽略了水位逐渐降低以及轮船吃水较深这两个客观因素，因而导致了事故的发生。副引水员年纪尚轻，经验不足，可能并不知道航路沿线附近有一片岩埂地带，因此在听到水深 9 英尺的报告后，便以为前路畅通无阻，继续向前行驶，结果轮船却因受到侧方水流的影响，右侧与航路外的礁石发生撞击，以致锅炉前面的位置受损。

6. 虽然"吉阳"号轮船此次发生事故确与航道本身存在的风险有一定关系，但只要航行无误,亦完全可以避免。出于公正原则,本人认为俄阿穆尔水道局对于此次事故并不负有责任。至于损失方面轮船可向相应投保公司申请赔偿。

7. 自6月19日至7月17日期间,本人与俄国巡江工司乘船至黑龙江边界河段,对俄方的工作成果进行全面检查。由于水位较低,我们得以核准方位线的位置,测量所有浅滩的水深。巡查途中,凡遇有航路标志需进行调改之处,均已立即整改,目前航路状况良好。

您忠诚的仆人

（签字）易保罗（P. I. Ignatieff）

黑龙江航务专门顾问

此译本内容真实有效,特此证明:

录事：王友燮　三等同文供事后班

瑷珲关致海关总税务司署第 180 号呈附录 3

理船厅关于戊通航业公司"吉阳"号轮船
在叶卡捷琳尼斯基浅滩沉船事的报告译本
（1924 年 7 月 9 日）

本人已照贵署指示于 7 月 5 日对 7 月 3 日"吉阳"号轮船于叶卡捷琳尼斯基浅滩沉船事件进行调查，现做出如下汇报。

7 月 5 日下午 12 时 40 分，本人与航务专门顾问易保罗（P.I.Ignatieff）先生及戊通航业公司经理陈先生共同乘坐"沈阳"号轮船前往黑龙江上游。当轮船行至马尔科夫斯基上游浅滩时，恰逢俄国测量船"先锋"号行至于此，双方停船后，"先锋"号轮船船长告知，其奉俄国政府之命前往"吉阳"号轮船失事的叶卡捷琳尼斯基浅滩测量水深。易保罗（P. I. Ignatieff）先生提议换乘船速更快的"先锋"号轮船，以便于测量航道水深。当时天色渐晚（已至下午 6 时），为确保水深测量工作可于天色完全变黑之前完成，"沈阳"号轮船船长对此并无异议。于是我们改乘"先锋"号轮船继续向黑龙江上游方向进发，渐渐领先了"沈阳"号轮船一大段距离。

晚 7 时 30 分，我们抵达叶卡捷琳尼斯基浅滩后，便沿着 75 号方位线和 74 号方位线对航路水深进行测量，结果显示整条航路的水深均超过 11 英尺。于是我们又更改了行船路线，掉头回到 75 号方位线所在的航路内，但并未严格依照 74 号方位线所指示的航路行驶，而是向其偏左一侧行驶，大约行至 74 号方位线下方 60 英尺处，开始试图将轮船向中国一侧的江岸靠近，结果这个位置的水流极强，轮船受到水流冲击，离江岸更近了（"吉阳"号轮船很可能就是因为这样而发生事故的）。我们对该处水位进行测量后，发现水深由 9 英尺渐次下降至 7.5 英尺和 6 英尺，又在水深 6 英尺处的江底探测到一块大礁石，附近的河床上也散落着不少石块。当然，"吉阳"号轮船也可能是在水深 9 英尺处撞到礁石，礁石受到撞击后翻滚到现在的位置。而这块礁石有可能是被春天的浮冰带到航路附近的。但无论如何，也无法改变轮船失事位置是位于航路之外的事实。

据船长报告（存于理船厅办公室）所述，撞击发生时水深记录为 9 英尺；而如果当时轮船是在航路内的话，水深应超过 11 英尺。这已充分说明，该轮船引水员并未严格按照

75 号方位线所标识的航路向 74 号方位线行驶,而是过早地将轮船行驶方向转向了航路左侧(如所附示意图中红色虚线所做标示)。本人推测引水员如此操作是为了节省时间,但因未能考虑到该处水位较低,轮船吃水较深,左侧有强劲水流冲击等因素,导致轮船的行驶路线比其预期的还要更加偏离航路。本人坚信,值班副引水员当时更改了行船路线,过早地偏离了航路,听闻水深测量结果为 9 英尺后,便误以为航路安全,于是不顾方位线的引导继续行驶,最终导致了事故的发生。

尽管副引水员应该对此次事故负上全责,但本人认为船长同样应负有一定责任,因其当时亦在值守,理应监督引水员严格遵照航路标识驾驶轮船。

调查总结

本人与航务专门顾问易保罗先生对"吉阳 Chi Yang]"号轮船失事一事进行了仔细而全面的调查,最终得出如下结论:"吉阳"号轮船于 1924 年 7 月 3 日在叶卡捷琳尼斯基浅滩沉没一事,主要责任在副引水员,其疏忽大意,未能严格按照航路方位线的指示航行,在由 75 号方位线驶向 74 号方位线时,方向变更过早,未考虑到当时水位较低,轮船吃水较深(达 4.5 英尺)等客观因素。因轮船过早在 75 号方位线以内转弯,偏离了航路,再加上强劲的水流不断冲击着轮船,最终致使轮船比引水员所预想的更加偏向中国一侧的江岸,结果与一块或多块礁石相撞,以致轮船受到严重损毁而沉没。

轮船发生事故时船长正在值守,作为整艘轮船的主事人,其理应对轮船的航行严加监督,监督引水员严格按照航路方位线的指引航行。因此船长对事故的发生也应负有一定的责任。其深知该艘轮船已经满载,吃水深度达到 4.5 英尺,而且船上还有 350 名乘客,特别是在水位偏低的情况下,更加不该放任引水员过早驾驶轮船偏离 75 号方位线,偏离既定航路。另外,如果船长心存疑惑,对这条航路不甚熟悉,则应在驶离航路之前要求引水员进行一次细致而全面的说明。

您忠诚的仆人

(签字)博韩(G. E. Baukham)

代理理船厅

11. 为边境关闭后江捐税收不足难抵支出事

海务港务（上）

AMUR AIDS TO NAVIGATION: certain facts re closing of frontier;insufficiency of funds to meet expenditure; no improvement in general
business conditions likely during 1925; Commr.'s three suggestions;
Taoyin's proposal to borrow from Bank of China; Russian Amur
218. Navigation Office's scheme to commence work on river Ussuri rejected by Taoyin.

$\frac{218}{I.G.}$

I.G,   Aigun   24th. April, 1925.

                    Entered in Card-Index.

        Sir,   Replied to in No. 230 .

1.   I have the honour to refer to I.G.

    despatch No. 214/101,722 (in reply to Aigun despatch

    No. 198 and with reference to I.G. despatch No. 205/

    101,122 and Aigun despatch No. 193) :

                        instructing me that I should take an
                        opportunity of pointing out to the
                        Taoyin that a situation into which
                        this district should never have been
                        put has arisen through the action of
                        the Russians in closing the frontier
                        and establishing the tariff barrier
                        at Blagovestchensk; that the local
                        Chinese authorities would be placed
                        in a very difficult position if by
                        reason of the decline in river dues
                        China should be unable to pay her
                        share of expenditure towards the
                        maintenance of Aids to Navigation on
                        the Amur; and that an attempt should
                        be made to settle promptly the question
                        of trade facilities so that the river
                        dues collection may be maintained in
                        such a manner as to insure that the
                        provision of China's share of the expenditure will not be endangered;
The Officiating Inspector General of Customs,
                                              and

        Peking.

and to report that the position in regard to this
matter has been stated by me to the Taoyin again
and again in numerous conversations during the past
few months.   On receipt of your instructions I
called to see him and once more brought the matter
to his notice.   The Taoyin tells me that he has
failed to convince the Russians that they should
yield to the request for the removal of restrictions
upon trans-frontier trade and says that this question
has now grown so big that further effort on his
part would achieve nothing.   He thinks that it was
to meet just such a situation as obtains in this
district that the Sino-Russian Treaty provided for
the creation of a Conference and says that the
solution of the present problem is a question which
the Delegates to the Conference will have to arrange.

2.   The suggestion that the Russians are
responsible for our present misfortunes is absolutely
contradicted by the authorities at Blagovestchensk who
throw back the responsibility on to the Chinese.
They allege that the high-handed course pursued by

the

the Taoyin is the cause of all the difficulties
that have arisen and say that it ill-becomes him to
feign surprise that his unfriendly attitude should
have dissipated good will and provoked retaliation.
For example, the Russians proclaim that the seizure
at Taheiho in July, 1923, by the Chinese Chamber of
Commerce, with the knowledge and consent of the
Taoyin, of machinery and sugar consigned to Blagovestchensk was an act of pure spoliation, and complain
that the sentimental reluctance of the Chinese officials
to deal sternly with the lawlessness of White Rebels
in Heilungkiang has caused Soviet Russia much harm
and enormous expense.   As regards that other cause
contributing to the present deadlock, the controversy
concerning the issue of Frontier Passes by the Taoyin,
they insist that the latter's objection to their
decision to charge a larger fee for a visa than he
himself charges for a pass can not in any way affect
the reasonableness of their claim to be allowed to
charge whatever sum they like for a Russian visa.

3.   The actual closing of the frontier took

place

place in June, 1923, but it was in February of that
year that the Chinese Chamber of Commerce, face to
face with what they believed to be well-grounded
causes of complaint, first informed the Taoyin that
the time was approaching when they would be forced
by the accumulated grievances and uncontrollable
resentment of local merchants to take the war into
the enemy's country.   They complained that Chinese
merchants who proposed to embark upon any line of
business at Blagovestchensk found that the conditions
to which they were required to submit lacked every
element of practicability and urged that some steps
should be taken to make possible the resumption of
business.   The Taoyin's several interviews with
the Soviet consul at this port merely provided for
lengthy talks and it soon became of common knowledge
that the authorities at Blagovestchensk no longer
regarded trans-frontier trade as a legitimate form of
economic intercourse.   Chinese merchants, who were
losing so much from the obstruction and stagnation
of trade, were angrily disappointed.   They decided
to take action of a violent nature and there followed

the

the seizure of machinery and sugar to which reference has been made. The Chamber of Commerce hoped that the detention of Soviet property might have a deterrent and a reformatory effect, but it failed to contribute to that end. The Russians retaliated by acting in the same spirit whereupon the Chamber of Commerce, under authority conferred upon them by the Taoyin, issued an order prohibiting all dealings with Russians in Siberia. The quarrel speedily developed in intensity and the Heiho Citizens Political and Economic Union did all in their power, by appeals for boycotts and other activities, to erect into a national question the somewhat trivial dispute over the issue by the Taoyin of Frontier Passes. There can be no denying the violence of the passions and prejudices aroused by the Citizens Union, but it would be absurd to attribute the original cause of the trouble to the Chinese and the Russians cannot with credit shuffle off their responsibility on to the Taoyin. The truth is that the Soviet authorities have not really wished to trade with this district. They maintain that they can satisfy their principal wants from the products of their

own

own country and seek to convey the impression that they profess great indignation against Chinese merchants in this district for having amassed wealth from activities in connection with war prosecution.   Easier conditions prevail at present, but the Taoyin gives me to understand that the Soviet authorities have never moved from a rigid obstinacy in their attitude towards the frontier question and that they are intolerant of discussion and unable to appreciate any point of view except their own.   He looks for great change and considerable progress as a result of the forthcoming Conference, but insists that there is nothing he can do to help at this end and that things must be allowed to take their course.

4.   Bad trade has so decreased the amount of money available for river dues that we can no longer provide for current expenditure.   We still owe the Russian Amur Navigation Office the sum of Gold Roubles 3,786.18 for work done during 1924 (i.e. during the period from 1st. December, 1923, to 30th. November, 1924) and as we have in hand a balance

only

only of $3,655.42 we shall be unable to pay what we have promised to pay for last year's work without drawing on dues collected during 1925, unless the dollar appreciates and the rate changes from G.R. 1 = $1.03 to G.R. 1 = $0.96. We have also to recognise our present inability to pay anything at all for expenditure to be incurred under the local agreement which the Taoyin, with the consent of the Civil Governor, is proposing to sign for 1925 -i.e. for the period from 1st. December, 1924, to 30th. November, 1925.

5.   The Taoyin acknowledges that if navigation of the Amur by Chinese vessels is to continue, the maintenance of Aids must be in part a charge on Chinese funds and at a recent interview he asked me to suggest a remedy which would get over our present difficulty. He says that it is only by the accident of events that we are so pinched for money and that it will all come right in the end.   I told the Taoyin that in the absence of a prompt recovery of trade there would seem to be three ways of raising the needed money.   My first proposal was to collect River Dues at a full tariff rate.   At present, for the purpose

of

of assessing river dues, the Amur is divided into
two sections, an upper section from Taheiho to Pokrovka
and a lower section from Taheiho to Kasakevitch, and
for each section one half of the tariff only is
paid.   The Russians, on the other hand, collect
a full rate irrespective of distance travelled.   I
submitted that the collection by this office of river
dues at a full rate could be carried out either by
taking the extra half rate from merchants, who at
present bear the whole cost of river dues taxation,
or by collecting it from the steamer companies in
the form of a special fee levied on each vessel at
time of clearance.   The Chairman of the Taheiho
Chinese Chamber of Commerce insists that any extra
charge must be kept off cargo on the ground that an
extra charge on cargo would be a tax upon the poor
trader who has been engaged for several years past
in a desperate struggle with poverty.   He considers
that the proposal that steamer companies should pay a
clearance fee is a fair one.   The Manager of the
local branch of the Wut'ung Company has objected that
the capacity of merchants to pay larger freights, and

of

of passengers to pay larger fares, is just as great
as the capacity of steamer companies to submit to
additional taxation and protests that in these circumstances the collection of a clearance fee from
shipping companies would be an expedient which would
merely shift the burden on to other shoulders equally
unfit to bear it.   He suggests that the money
should be provided out of taxation equitably adjusted
over the whole province.   The Taoyin thinks that
the time has not yet arrived to increase river dues.
He says that an attempt to raise money in this
manner would be bound to offend considerable interests
of one kind or another and he regards this as a
fundamental objection.

6.   My second proposal was to obtain a Grant
from the Provincial Government, the money borrowed to
be repaid from River Dues Account as trade revives
and funds accumulate.   The idea underlying this
suggestion is that money for a project in which the
whole province may be said to be interested being
necessary and unobtainable from the usual source, it
is for the provincial authorities to realise our

difficulty

difficulty and to see that it is got over by
finding the money for us themselves.   The Taoyin
does not like to believe that there is any necessity
for such a step and doubts whether assistance from
the Civil Governor can be expected.   In his opinion,
it is essential that the various problems concerning
navigation should be definitely and finally settled
at the Conference before the Civil Governor is
approached on so difficult and' delicate a subject.

7.   My last proposal was to borrow as occasion
requires from the local branch of the Bank of China
on the security of the River Dues Account.   This
is a suggestion which found much acceptance with
the Taoyin who regards the port as a going concern
and does not believe that the set-back to trade is
of a permanent nature.   He inclines to the view
that the opening of the Frontier, which he thinks
can not be much longer delayed, will be bound to
facilitate the restoration of local commercial prosperity
and professes to believe that processes are already
at work which are tending to bring conditions back

                                             to

to normal.   The Taoyin says that the question
of navigation on the Amur is one of the first
subjects which must engage the attention of the
delegates and that a permanent solution of our
present difficulty will be reached for us by a
common agreement between the two parties at the
Conference.   He therefore proposes to apply for
permission to borrow and thinks that for the moment
there is no need to go further than that, or to
consider in detail the arrangements which may be
necessary some few months hence if the general
unsettlement which has resulted from the closing
of the frontier and the Soviet's restrictions upon
trade should continue.   But, in fact, he considers
there is reason to hope that the present unsettlement
will not continue and that confidence and stability
will be re-established and better conditions all
round prevail as soon as the Conference gets to
work.   The Taoyin thus arrives at the conclusion
that it is only a matter of time when River Dues
will be heaped up again and that a beginning will
soon be made with the clearing off of any debt
we may contract with the Bank.

9.

8.   The Taoyin, in my judgment, is too
sanguine, and it seems to me that even if the
frontier is opened there can be no hope, so
long as the communistic principle on which the
social and economic system of Soviet Russia is
organised is retained, of things taking a turn
for the better.   The years 1917 -when Piece
Goods increased in value from Hk.Tls. 14,111 to
Hk.Tls. 762,872 and Sundries from Hk.Tls. 17,706
to Hk.Tls. 130,729- 1918 -when the increase of
importations amounted to 56% over the figures for
1917 which were already 3 times greater than the
1916 figures, and the value of re-exports abroad
showed an increase of 75% over the 1917 figures-
1919 -when the value of imports, the bulk of
which eventually found their way into Siberia,
rose from 3¼ to 4½ millions in spite of the
fact that depression in the Rouble market and
the low value of Siberian notes debarred Russian
buyers from purchasing freely- and 1920 -the
district's record year- were a period of altogether
abnormal commercial activity during which, owing to

                                                    a

a temporarily stimulated demand in Siberia for certain commodities caused by the cutting off of supplies from Russia, Germany, and other European countries, highly inflated prices ruled in the export market and local merchants transacted a considerable volume of business.   I can see no return of prosperity for this district unless the conditions obtaining at the close of the Great War are re-established in toto.   The conditions are to-day entirely different and it is my opinion that the expectation of better trade during 1925 is wholly illusory and that the present standard of income from river dues is likely to remain practically unchanged for a long time to come.

9.   The Estimates for 1925 amount to Gold Roubles 40,000 as compared with G.R.35,750 in 1924, G.R.19,250 in 1923 (when work commenced only towards the end of the navigation season), and G.R.32,376 in 1922.   I estimate the river dues collection for 1925 at $15,000, as compared with $17,291 in 1924, $23,769 in 1923, and $31,137 in 1922. Granting

the

the accuracy of the above Estimate of Collection for 1925, we shall require a sum of about $33,500 to meet expenditure during the current year. Or to put it in another way, we are likely to be faced with a deficit of $18,500. Thus-

Estimates 1925 : Gold Roubles 40,000.

China's Contribution -50%	G.R.	20,000
Allowance for Loss by Exchange	$	1,500
Allowance for Taoyin's Office	$	2,000
Allowance for Technical Adviser's Office	$	8,500
I.G.'s 1/10th. of Collection	$	1,500
Estimated Sum Required 1925	$	33,500
Estimated River Dues Collection 1925	$	15,000
Estimated Deficit 1925	$	18,500

Where is the money to come from ? This subject has been discussed with the various parties concerned and my three suggestions, so far as I can see, present the only possible alternatives. I venture the opinion that what we really ought to do is to collect dues at a full tariff rate, but it is very doubtful whether this could be accomplished without stronger backing than the Taoyin could give. At any rate the latter tells me that he deems it prudent

not

not to make the attempt at present.   His concern
is the attitude of local opinion and this prejudices
him in his thought towards the proposal.   The
suggestion that the Civil Governor should be requested
to advance the necessary funds has been dropped
because the Taoyin thinks that it is too early to
take such a step.   There remains only the question
of a loan from the Bank of China and I submit that,
to put the case at its lowest, this proposal may
be said to hold the field in the absence of any
other reasonable alternative.

10.   Detailed Estimates for 1925 have been prepared,
but at the last moment Mr. Chebisheff, Director of
the Russian Amur Navigation Office, under instructions
from Moscow, is pressing for the inclusion of a sum
of over $5,000 towards the upkeep of Aids on the
Ussuri, which he insists is a matter of great
urgency.   The Taoyin has replied that the Ussuri
is not in his province and that in any case a
question of this kind could not be settled in a
hasty manner.   He has expressed willingness to conclude
an agreement on last year's lines, but on the

                                        understanding

understanding that what he signs will bind him to nothing if the delegates to the Conference should decide to veto arrangements arrived at locally. Mr. Chebisheff submits that this decision tends to limit the functions of the Russian Amur Navigation Office and he has asked the Taoyin to reconsider the matter. He maintains that his whole object is to diminish inconvenience to shipping and argues that his request does not introduce any new principle because the Ussuri like the Amur is a frontier river. He says that he is quite willing to leave it to the Conference to decide how much China should contribute towards the cost of the undertaking, but invites the Taoyin to agree in principle to the proposal. This is the gist of the argument advanced by the Director of the Russian Amur Navigation Office. The Taoyin has reaffirmed his inability to accede to the request. When submitting the Estimates for 1925 I shall have the honour to hand you a copy of Mr. Chebisheff's letters to the Taoyin.

I have the honour to be,

Sir,

Your obedient Servant,

Commissioner.

呈海关总税务司署 <u>218</u> 号文　　　　　　　　　　瑷珲关 1925 年 4 月 24 日

尊敬的代理海关总税务司（北京）：

1. 根据海关总税务司署第 214/101722 号令（批复瑷珲关第 198 号呈，参阅海关总税务司署第 205/101122 令及瑷珲关第 193 号呈）：

> "请瑷珲关择机向道尹说明，由于俄方关闭边境，并于布拉戈维申斯克（Blagovestchensk）设立关税壁垒，瑷珲关区已陷入前所未有的困境；若因江捐税收减少，而无法支付黑龙江航路标志维修摊款，中国地方政府必会陷入被动；请道尹尽快解决边境贸易问题，以确保海关可征得足够的江捐税收来支付黑龙江航路标志的维修摊款。"

兹报告，在过去数月中，本署已反复向道尹说明这一情况，而且在收到贵署指令后，又再次与其会面重申此事，然道尹却表示，其无力使俄方取消对跨境贸易的限制，况且如今问题已然十分严重，即使再做努力也将无济于事，并认为该情况应由不日即将召开的中俄会议予以解决，与会代表将在会议上提出该问题，并与俄方商定解决办法。

2. 布拉戈维申斯克政府认为，瑷珲关区陷入困境并非俄方之责任，相反，所有的不幸皆是由道尹的肆意妄为所致，并称道尹心中应该十分清楚，正是因为其态度不友好，美好的希望才会烟消云散，中俄双方才会起了冲突。俄方指出，大黑河中国商会于 1923 年 7 月在道尹的授意下没收原本应被运至布拉戈维申斯克的机械设备和糖之行为简直就是赤裸裸的掠夺，还抱怨称，华方官员在面对违法逃至黑龙江省的白色叛军时优柔寡断，使其损失惨重。对于造成当下僵局的另一原因，即道尹签发过境小票引起争议一事，俄方坚持认为，对于俄国为签发签证所收取的费用高于道尹为签发过境小票所收取的费用一事，道尹之反对并不合理，俄国有权制定本国签证收费标准。

3. 边境关闭的实际时间是 1923 年 6 月，但早在同年 2 月，中国商会就已向道尹提出投诉，指责布拉戈维申斯克政府对中国商人的贸易设有太多不必要的限制乃至苛刻的要求，希望道尹可以采取相应措施以使当地贸易尽快恢复正常。道尹遂就此事与苏维埃驻大黑河领事进行多次会谈，却始终也未能取得任何结果。不久之后，布拉戈维申斯克政府便宣称跨境贸易不再是一种合法的经济往来形式。

由于贸易的受阻与停滞，中国商人付出了巨大代价，他们为此悲愤不已，决定以暴力手段扣押本应运往俄岸的机械设备和糖，希望能够起到震慑作用，从而达到改变现状的目的。然而中国商人未能如愿，俄方也采取了同样的暴力扣押行为作为报复。于是，在道尹的的默许下,商会颁布了一则禁令,禁止中国商人与西伯利亚的一切贸易；黑河经济联合会也发起了联合抵制等一系列与俄对抗的活动,遂使矛盾渐次升级,最终演变成了国际性争端。尽管黑河经济联合会采取暴力行为有欠妥当,但因此将中俄纠纷完全归咎于道尹,却实在太过荒唐。事实上,是苏维埃政府有意阻挠布拉戈维申斯克地区的中俄贸易,其声称俄国本土的产品足以满足当地的一切重要需求,并表示对大黑河地区的中国商人依靠武力扣押而积累财富的做法极度不满。

眼下局势虽然有所缓和,但道尹告知本署,苏维埃政府对待边境贸易问题的态度仍十分强硬,始终不肯做出丝毫让步,拒绝一切对其观点的反驳。中俄会议即将到来,道尹表示十分期待这一问题能够早日得到解决,但却坚称自己无能为力,只能静观其变。

4. 贸易的恶化使江捐税收大幅削减,本署已无法负担当前的开支。对于俄阿穆尔水道局 1924 年(即自 1923 年 12 月 1 日至 1924 年 11 月 30 日)所完成的航路标志维护工作,中方仍有 3786.18 金卢布的摊款待付,而目前江捐账户余额仅有 3655.42 银圆,在不动用 1925 年税收的情况下,根本无法付清 1924 年摊款,除非银圆增值,汇率由 1 金卢布 =1.03 银圆跌至 1 金卢布 =0.96 银圆。以目前情况来看,对于道尹经省长批准欲签署的 1925 年(即自 1924 年 12 月 1 日至 1925 年 11 月 30 日)地方协议下的任何开支,海关都将无力支付。

5. 道尹表示,只要中国轮船还要在黑龙江上继续航行,中国就必须承担起航路标志维护工作的部分费用,并于最近一次会谈中提出,希望本署可为摆脱当前困境提供一些建议,其认为经济紧张只是暂时的,待事情解决后,一切都会恢复如常。本署指出,在贸易无法立即复苏的情况下,似乎只有三种办法可以筹集到所需资金。

一是按照全价税率来征收江捐。目前,为征收江捐,黑龙江被分为两段,自大黑河至波克罗夫卡(Pokrovka)为上游河段,自大黑河至嘎杂克维池(Kasakevich)为下游河段,每段仅按半价税率征收江捐；而俄方则不论航行里程,一律按照全价税率征收江捐。海关实现征收全价关税的办法有两种,一是向已承担所有江捐的商人加征另外一半关税,二是以收取特别结关费的方式向航业公司征收另外一半关税。

大黑河中国商会主席坚持认为,不应再向货物加征额外关税,否则会加重这些贫穷商人的负担,他们常年奔波劳碌,始终在与贫穷进行着艰难的斗争,赞成向航业公司收取结关费之提议。然而,戊通航业公司大黑河办事处的经理表示,轮船已无力再缴纳一些特别费用,就如同商人已无力再支付更多运费,乘客也无力再交付更多船票费一样,反对向航业公司收取结关费,认为此种权宜之计只是将负担极不公正地转移给了那些承担不起的人，并建议由整个黑龙江省所征税款平摊所需资金。道尹亦认为目前不宜增加江捐税率，担心若以此等方式筹款很可能会冒犯到某一方的利益，这才是最根本的问题。

6. 二是向省政府申请拨款，待贸易复苏，资金累积起来之后，再由江捐账户偿付。这一做法的深意，就在于让省政府意识到我们的难处，可以说，黑龙江航路标志维护工作是全省关注之事，既然目前资金紧缺又无处筹集，那么也就只能由省政府出面襄助了。然道尹认为无需如此，而且对于能否得到省长的帮助，其亦深表怀疑。在道尹看来，关于航运的各种问题，最好在中俄会议上彻底解决，暂不要劳烦省长。

7. 三是，鉴于形势所迫，可以考虑向中国银行大黑河分行借款，以江捐账户作为担保。道尹对此颇为赞同，认为口岸发展前景依然乐观，贸易受挫只是暂时性的，相信边境开放指日可待，之后大黑河会迎来商业的再次繁荣，一切终将回归常态，并称黑龙江上的航运问题是中俄会议的重要议题之一，与会代表会予以高度关注，中方代表更会极力争取在会议上与俄方达成一个彻底的解决方案。

道尹同意申请借款，但表示于当下而言，暂无需考虑因关闭边境和俄国设立贸易限制而引起的不稳定是否会一直持续下去，亦无需考虑若无好转，接下来几个月应作何安排；其认为有理由相信中俄会议召开后，一切问题都将得以解决，情况亦会有所好转，当前的不稳定终将消失，江捐税收将会逐渐增多，很快便可偿清银行贷款，一切不过是时间的问题罢了。

8. 兹认为，道尹过于乐观，在本署看来，只要苏俄社会的经济体制仍然受共产主义信条的统治，即使边境得以开放，事情亦难有所转机。1917 年，按件货物总值由 14111 海关两增至 762872 海关两，杂货总值由 17706 海关两增至 130729 海关两；1918 年，进口货物总值较 1917 年增长了 56%，较 1916 年增长了 3 倍，出口国外货物总值较 1917 年增长了 75%；1919 年，尽管卢布市场不景气，西伯利亚纸币贬值，俄国人购买力受到限制，进口货物总值（大宗货物最终依然流入西伯利亚）还是由 325 万增长至 450 万；1920 年，西伯利亚市场因俄国、德国和其他欧洲国家暂时中断了某些商品的供给，出现了短时的刺激性需求，大黑河地区的出口市场物价因此飙升，商人的交易量更是大幅提升。然而，对于 1925 年，兹认为大黑河地区的经济很难复苏，除非形势能够恢复到世界大战结束后那般，但今时不同往日，要在 1925 年使贸易转好完全是不切实际的幻想，而且江捐的收入很可能会长期保持在当前的水平。

9. 1925 年黑龙江航路标志维护工作预算总计 40000 金卢布，1924 年为 35750 金卢布，1923 年为 19250 金卢布（仅结算至航运季结束），1922 年为 32376 金卢布。预计 1925 年江捐税收可达 15000 银圆,1924 年为 17291 银圆,1923 年为 23769 银圆,1922 年为 31137 银圆。

1925 年须由江捐税收支付的款项约达 33500 银圆,假设 1925 年江捐税收最终确为 15000 银圆,那么江捐账户最终将面临 18500 银圆的赤字。

具体列下:

1925 年黑龙江航路标志维护工作预算	金卢布	40000
华方摊款:预算 50%	金卢布	20000
汇兑损失津贴	银圆	1500
道尹公署办公经费	银圆	2000
航务专门顾问办事处办公经费	银圆	8500
10% 海关征税佣金	银圆	1500
1925 年预计支出总计	银圆	33500
1925 年预计江捐税收	银圆	15000
1925 年预计赤字	银圆	18500

相关各方已就筹钱办法进行多次讨论,就目前情况来看,唯一可供选择的只有本署的三条建议。兹认为,按照全价税率征税乃为首选,但若无道尹的强力支持,难以确定该计划能否完成。道尹表示,无论如何此时都不应轻举妄动。实际上,其担心的是当地民众的态度,担心民众会因该提议而对其抱有成见。对于向省长申请拨款之建议,道尹认为此举为时过早;至于从中国银行借款,本署认为先不要考虑,该提议可以说是在没有其他合理选择情况下的无奈之举。

10. 1925 年预算报表早已制作完毕,但随后俄国阿穆尔水道局督办切比索夫(Chebisheff)先生接到莫斯科方面的指示,要求在预算中加入乌苏里江航路标志的维护费用 5000 余银圆,并强调此事万分紧急。道尹回复称,乌苏里江不在其管辖范围内,且此类问题不可草率决定,但表示愿意按照 1924 年协议所列各项签署 1925 年协议,只是如果中俄会议的与会代表否决了当地的一些安排,那么该 1925 年协议将不再有任何效力。切比索夫先生认为,道尹若不同意在 1925 年预算中加入乌苏里江航路标志的维护费用,俄阿穆尔水道局的工作势必会受到限制,希望道尹可以重新考虑,并称此举只是为了减少航运的不便,而且乌苏里江与黑龙江同为边境河流,基本原则并未改变。至于中国应摊款项的金额数,切比索夫先生表示愿意交与中俄会议决定,但望道尹可基本同意该提议。道尹已重申其无法同意该要求。呈交 1925 年预算,并附切比索夫先生致道尹信函抄件。

您忠诚的仆人

贺智兰（R. F. C. Hedgeland）

瑷珲关税务司

12. 为督促道尹尽快与俄国地方官员签署拟定协议及向中国银行贷款事

[Δ.—29]

No. 230.   COMMRS.   INSPECTORATE GENERAL OF CUSTOMS,

Aigun   No. 103,232   PEKING,   20th May 1925.

Entered in Card-Index.

Sir,

I have to acknowledge receipt of your

despatch No. 218 :

giving an account of the conditions
engendered by the closing of the
frontier to trade; pointing out that the
consequent diminution of trade has so
decreased the River Dues receipts that
the collection of these Dues is no
longer sufficient to cover expenditure;
stating that the Taoyin, with the consent
of the Civil Governor, now proposes to
sign an Agreement with the local Russian
officials for the period 1st December
1924 to 30th November 1925, on the
same main lines as the former one; and
suggesting, as the merchants and shipowners
are opposed to the increasing of the
River Dues tariff, and as the Taoyin
refuses to obtain a loan from the
Provincial Government, that the local
branch of the Bank of China be requested
to

The Commissioner of Customs,

    AIGUN

to allow an overdraft for the Amur
Aids Account against the security of
the River Dues collection :

and, in reply, to say that, as it is essential

that the Amur Aids organisation be kept in

operation, you are requested to urge the Taoyin

to lose no time in signing the proposed Agreement

for the year 1st December 1924 to 30th November

1925, on the understanding that should the Sino-

Russian conference, about to be held, make other

arrangements for the upkeep of navigation aids

on the Amur, the local Agreement shall not be

considered as binding. It is understood that

the proposed Agreement follows closely the lines

of the previous one, and includes the provisions

that China is not responsible for expenditure

exceeding the actual amount of Dues collected,

and that the amount to be paid by the Chinese

Commission shall in any case not exceed 50% of

the amount of the total estimates (vide Agreement

for 1923-4, Annexe 11; §§ 13 and 15).

As

As soon as the Agreement has been signed you should proceed with the levy of River Dues on the existing scale.

In regard to your suggestion that the local branch of the Bank of China might be requested to advance whatever sums may be required against the security of the River Dues collection, you are authorised to enquire from the Bank whether it would be prepared to allow an overdraft on behalf of the Amur Aids account against the security mentioned, and, if so, on what terms as regards rate of interest, etc. The Bank should be given to understand that you are not as yet negotiating for such an overdraft, but are simply making the necessary preliminary enquiries in case such an overdraft becomes necessary.

I am,

Sir,

Your obedient Servant,

Officiating Inspector General,
ad interim.

致瑷珲关第 230/103232 号令   海关总税务司署（北京）1925 年 5 月 20 日

尊敬的瑷珲关税务司：

第 218 号呈收悉：

"描述因边境贸易关闭引发的状况；指出贸易减少导致江捐收项减少，入不敷出；说明经省长许可，道尹现提议与俄国地方官员依照上一份协议的主要准则签订一份新协议，有效期为 1924 年 12 月 1 日至 1925 年 11 月 30 日；由于商人及船东均反对增加江捐税率，道尹也拒绝向省政府贷款，故建议以江捐收入作为抵押，请中国银行当地分行允许黑龙江航路标志账户可以透支。"

现批复如下：黑龙江航路标志组织至关重要，须保证其正常运转，请贵署督促道尹尽快签署拟定协议，协议生效时间为 1924 年 12 月 1 日至 1925 年 11 月 30 日。但如果即将召开的中俄会议对黑龙江航路标志维护另有安排，则该地方协议不再具备约束力。拟定协议尽可能遵循上一份协议的方法准则，并包含以下规定：凡支出超出实际江捐征收款项，中国不予承担；无论如何，华方委员会所付款项不得超过总估值的 50%（参阅《1923–1924 年协议》附件 11 第 13 条及第 15 条）。

协议一经签订，贵署应当继续以现有比率征收江捐税款。

至于贵署建议以江捐收入作为抵押，请中国银行当地分行预支任意款项，现授权贵署询问该行是否允许黑龙江航路标志账户凭借上述抵押进行透支，如允许，请咨询具体利率等条款。应向该行阐明，贵署并非就此类透支进行谈判，仅做初步询问，以防后续确实需要银行透支。

您忠诚的仆人

泽礼（J. W. Stephenson）

暂代代理海关总税务司

13. 为黑龙江和吉林政府指示由海关命专员执行《中俄边界河道航务条例》事

2 9 APR 1929

MEMORANDUM

Custom House,
Harbin, 20th April, 1929.

To
The Chief Secretary,
Inspectorate General of Customs,
SHANGHAI.

HARBIN Commissioner's comments on Aigun despatch
No.414/I.G. dated 5th April, 1929, docketed,
RULES OF NAVIGATION FOR SINO-SOVIET FRONTIER
RIVERS: instructions, transmitted by Taoyin
from Heilungchiang and Kirin Governments,
that Customs appoint inspector to enforce,
forwarding with comments.

The desirability of enforcing these frontier
rivers navigation rules on the Sungari was
referred to the Harbin Superintendent in letter
No.181 of 6th October, 1928, and met with his
disapproval as expressed in his letter of the
19th of the same month copies of which were
forwarded to the Inspectorate with my Non-urgent
Chinese Correspondence for October, 1928.

(Paragraph 5) As will be seen from the rules
and regulations which form the subject and enclosures
of my despatch No.3635/I.G., the Government of the
Three Eastern Provinces appear to be determined to
rule their own shipping independently of the
Central Government.

Commissioner.

Copies of this Memo are being sent to the Aigun
Commissioner and the Coast Inspector.

1 4 MAY 1929

COAST INSPECTOR'S COMMENTS ON AIGUN DESPATCH
NO.414, I. G., DATED 5TH APRIL 1929, AND DOCKETED:

RULES OF NAVIGATION FOR SINO-SOVIET
FRONTIER RIVERS: instructions, transmitted
by Taoyin from Heilungchiang and Kirin
Governments, that Customs appoint
inspector to enforce, forwarding with
comments.

I do not see how any one individual can
possibly see that the majority of the Rules
of "Navigation for Sino-Soviet Frontier Rivers"
are enforced.

A perusal of these Rules shows that they
relate to the following:-

Part I, Article II, Aids to Navigation
along the channel.

Part II, Article I, Equipment of Vessels
and Rafts.

Part III, Article I, Lighting of Vessels.

Part III, Article II, Use of Search Light.

Part IV, Article I, Navigation of Vessels,
Rafts and Dredges.

Part IV, Article II, Navigation in Fog,
Snow and Rain.

Part IV, Article III, Rules concerning the
meeting or overtaking of Vessels, Rafts
or Dredges.

Part IV, Article IV, Navigation of Vessels
and Rafts through Shallows.

Part V, Article I, Anchorage of Vessels
and Rafts.

Part

Part VI, Article I, Concerning the Use of
  Lights.

Part VI, Article II, Lights on Anchored
  Vessels and Rafts.

Part VI, Article III, Lights of Vessels and
  Rafts under weigh.

Part VI, Article IV, Installation and Use
  of Lights on different Types of Vessels,
  and on Rafts.

Part VI, Article V, Special Lights on
  Vessels.

Part VII, Article I, Signals between
  Vessels before passing.

Part VII, Article II, Signals by Vessels
  and Rafts approaching from opposite
  directions.

Part VII, Article III, Signals by overtaking
  Vessels or Rafts.

Part VII, Article IV, Signals on passing
  Narrow Gorges.

Part VII, Article V, Signals on passing
  Dredges in operation.

Part VII, Article VI, Signals for
  assistance.

Part VII, Article VII, Signals for calling
  out a boat.

Part VII, Article VIII, Signals at a
  landing place.

Part VIII, Article I, Obstructions to
  Navigation.

Part IX, Article I, Regulations in
  Connection with Accidents.

It

It is obvious that the great majority of the above articles are applicable to a vessel when under weigh, and it would be impossible to detect breaches unless we had several Inspectors travelling either in the vessels, rafts, dredges, etc., or instituted a patrol of the river by one or more launches, the duties of the officer-in-charge being to keep a look out on all vessels to see that they conformed to the regulations, and to report to Headquarters ships infringing the rules.

To take a few instances to make my meaning clear:

Part IV, Article I, Navigation of Vessels, Rafts and Dredges. General Rule No.20 reads: "A number of steamers plying in the same direction and keeping the same line must maintain distances from each other sufficient to ensure safe navigation." Now is one individual to detect a breach of this rule? A ship might contravene the rule anywhere along the river. Part IV, Article II, No.25 reads: "Floating vessels and rafts other than passenger steamers are forbidden to ply in dense fog, rain or snow. They must tie up to shore and give warning sound signals every minute." It could only be ascertained that this is done by actual observation along the river.

The great majority of the articles are what I may term a local representation of the International Regulations for Preventing Collisions at Sea, seeing that they have to do with

steering

steering rules, navigation lights, etc. How are
such rules enforced in other countries? What
generally occurs is that when a ship breaks the
Regulations for Preventing Collisions at Sea,
thereby endangering another vessel, the Master of
the latter reports the incident to the proper
authority, who investigates and takes action.
The question is as to whether the Masters of
the vessels plying on the Amur or other rivers
would act in the same way. Personally I am
inclined to think that very few would, and
therefore if we are really to see that these
Regulations are carried out, we must have a
staff to do so, either stationed at points
along the rivers or by means of a launch patrol.

About the only article in these regulations
which an individual Inspector could deal with is
Part II, Article I: Equipment of Vessels and
Rafts. Even this would depend on the number of
vessels requiring attention, and whether the
opportunity occurs of seeing the vessels at a
given port. If not the Inspector would have to
travel from port to port.

My view of the situation is that the
enforcement of the Regulations cannot be carried
out by any one person, and that to do the work
effectively would necessitate a staff. If,
however, we must do the best we can in the
circumstances, I agree with the Commissioner in
recommending Mr. Ignatieff for the post of Inspector.

Another point requiring consideration is as
to what authority an Inspector will have to
enforce the rules in the event of breaches.
As

As explained in my comments on the Harbin Commissioner's Despatch No.3835, here in Shanghai, where we attempt to enforce rules connected with Chinese shipping in the matter of selection of officers, and surveys of vessels and their equipment, we are confronted with great difficulty, and all we can do when owners refuse to carry out our instructions is to withhold clearance, although in practice this is very seldom done. We have no Marine Court, as have other countries, where fines, etc. can be inflicted for failure to carry out regulations.

It is clear from the Heiho Taoyin's letter No.329 (appendix 2 to Aigun despatch No.414, I. G.) that the reason for having a Customs Inspector to enforce the regulations is to prevent diplomatic questions arising. In other words the responsibility is being thrust upon us, and we are expected to accept the burden, and prevent trouble through the medium of an Inspector, when, in my opinion, the work can only effectively be carried out by a staff provided with full powers to enforce the Regulations.

The situation is in many respects similar to that obtaining here in Shanghai, where the Harbour Master is held responsible for certain duties in connection with Chinese shipping, as for instance, the provision of officers for Chinese ships, which it is impossible for him to effect adequately for the reasons outlined in my comments on Harbin Commissioner's despatch No.3835, I. G.

I believe that it is not the function of the

the Customs to be responsible for and to enforce Chinese Shipping Laws. It should be done by and under the authority of the Central Government. If this authority delegates the work to us, then we must be provided with an adequate staff, to carry out the duty effectively, and it is imperative that we be given authority to enforce the Regulations.

                                    (Signed)   H. E. HILLMAN,
                                                        Coast Inspector.

Coast Inspector's Office,
Shanghai, 29th April 1929.

                                                  True Copy:

                                                    Supervisor.

RULES OF NAVIGATION FOR SINO-SOVIET FRONTIER RIVERS;
instructions, transmitted by Taoyin from Heilungchiang
and Kirin Governments, that Customs appoint inspector
to enforce, forwarding with comments.

414.

I. G.   Aigun   5th April, 1929.

Sir,

1.   I have the honour to append copies of
two letters, with translations, from the Heiho
Taoyin, as Chinese President of the Amur Aids
Commission, transmitting, respectively, the
instructions of the Heilungchiang Provincial
Authorities, and their endorsement by the Kirin
Provincial Authorities, that the Aigun Customs
appoint an inspector to insure that Masters of
Chinese vessels (and rafts) plying the Amur,
Argun and Ussuri rivers observe the newly adopted
"Joint Rules of Navigation For Sino-Soviet Frontier
Rivers" and to see that Chinese steamers are in
a fit condition as regards hull, engine and gear
to navigate those waters without raising, if
possible, international incidents with China's
Soviet neighbours. It may be noted that the
Shipping Guild at Harbin (哈爾濱航業公會) has
already been instructed by the Heilungchiang
Government regarding the above.

2.   In Aigun despatch No.377 I give an
account of the earlier negotiations in connection

                                                with

THE INSPECTOR GENERAL OF CUSTOMS,
        SHANGHAI.

with the drawing up of the Rules in question.
Aigun despatch No. 315. from page 13, supplements
the information given in that despatch. S/Os Nos.
54 and 72, with comments by the Harbin Commissioner
also deal exhaustively with the necessity for
Rules of Navigation and the question of their
enforcement.

3.   In Aigun despatch No. 377, just referred to,
I also inform the Inspector General of the
signing of the Agreement by the Amur Aids
Commission on the 11th January, 1928, adopting
"Joint Rules of Navigation for Sino-Soviet Frontier
Rivers" and state that, in accordance with the
instructions of I.G. despatch No. 358/113,628 to
Aigun (and of I.G.'s S/O of 4th July, 1927), the
question of the enforcement of the new Rules
would be left in abeyance until they have been
approved by the Ch'u and instructions issued by
the latter to the Inspector General to give
effect to them.   In paragraph 4 of the same
despatch I state that the Taoyin had already
reported the adoption of the new Rules to the
Wai-Chiao Fu, Chiao-t'ung Fu and Shui-wu Ch'u through
the Tsitsihar Provincial Authorities.

4.   It would appear that the Ch'u never
issued any instructions in the matter - possibly
due to the confusion prevailing in Peking at the
time (I. G.'s S/O of 30th June, 1928).   No effort
was made during 1928 to enforce the Rules on
Chinese steamers navigating the frontier rivers

                                        though

though the Technical Adviser, on his tours of inspection of Aids, found much to criticize and reported his observations to the Taoyin (and myself).

5.   The receipt of the instructions from the Heilungchiang and Kirin Governments that the Customs enforce the Rules raises the question of their authority to issue such a mandate and that of whether the instructions should not have been issued by the Kuan-wu Shu, as well as the delicate point of the relations between the Nanking and Moukden Governments. That the two Provinces should feel they had the right to so instruct the Customs follows on the long term of political autonomy they have enjoyed, especially with regard to the latitude given them in drawing up joint Aids Agreements with the Soviet Authorities through the Amur Aids Commission. The direct interest of the Heilungchiang Government in the question dates from 1920 - _vide_ I. G. despatch No. 2,248/78,057 to Harbin to the effect that a temporary agreement was to be made between the Heilungchiang Tuchün and the Siberian Authorities for the navigation of the Amur by Chinese vessels.

6.   In soliciting your instructions as to what reply I shall make to the appended letters from the Taoyin, I venture to emphasize the growing importance and prosperity of Northern Manchuria which, with the southern part of the

Three

Three Eastern Provinces, has a greater future in many ways than any other part of China and of the favourable opportunity now presented to the Customs, through the friendly efforts of the local Taoyin/Superintendent, to secure firmer control in anticipation of the certain development of commerce and shipping on the Sino-Soviet frontier rivers and the Sungari.

I have the honour to be,

Sir,

Your obedient Servant,

Acting Commissioner.

Appendix

Appendix No. 1. (To Aigun desp. to I.G. to follow)

Translation of Heiho Taoyin's letter No.329 of 15th December, 1928 to the Commissioner of Customs, Aigun.

It has been reported to me that the Joint Rules of Navigation promulgated by the Aids Commission have not been strictly observed by steamers plying on the Amur, Ussuri and Argun frontier rivers. Diplomatic questions will be involved if this carelessness is not corrected. I recommended, therefore, to the Heilungchiang Provincial Authorities that a deputy should be appointed for their inspection and control. Should any violations of these regulations on the part of the steamers and rafts navigating these rivers be reported, the case must be dealt with strictly according to the rules as a warning for the future. I have now received a reply from the Provincial Authorities No. 5.763 to the effect that the proposal to appoint an inspector in this connection is approved and that the Aigun Customs should be directed to carry it into effect. The Shipping Guild at Harbin (哈爾濱航業公會) is also ordered to instruct all steamers to comply with these instructions. As the power of inspecting and controlling steamers has now been conferred on the Customs by Provincial Authority, you are requested to act accordingly and to report to me at your early convenience as to a uniform especially designed for the inspector that steamers may be

duly

duly informed by this office.

A copy of my despatch to the Heilungchiang Authorities in this connection is enclosed as follows:

The Navigation Rules concerning the Amur, Ussuri and Argun frontier rivers drawn up by the local Sino-Soviet Aids Commission in the spring of this year were forwarded to, and approved by, you. Four hundred copies of these Regulations have already been printed and distributed to all steamers (concerned). Now according to a report by Mr. Ignatieff, Technical Adviser, of his inspection trip on the Amur and Ussuri rivers many of the above mentioned Rules were not being observed by (Chinese) steamers; such as an insufficient number of lanterns on various vessels and of lights not being provided in the steering room for use in case the electricity failed. He also noted negligence on the part of ships' crews in transmitting signals when two steamers met each other and of failure to show proper lights when temporarily tied up at night. When at anchor no lights were displayed on occasions. In the transportation of benzine and kerosene oil instances were noted of failure to display the required red light. The S/S "Kwanchow", while towing barges to Hulin, was found to have one white light short. Circumstances such as

as these may give rise to accidents and steamers
navigating frontier rivers, owing to the carelessness
of the pilot, may create serious friction with
Russian steamers and rafts. And, what is worse,
lives would, in all probability, be endangered.
It is, therefore, requested that a deputy be
appointed to inspect and control all steamers
during the navigation season. The newly appointed
Director of the Aigun Mining Bureau, Tu Hsiang
Chun (杜 象 春), reported in person that, when
he was coming to Taheiho by the S/S "Chungwha",
he observed a lack of competence and discipline
on the steamer. When approaching Ti Ta Tsui Tze
(滴 塔 嘴 子) she lost the barges she was towing
as well as the anchors. She sailed without
anchors from the district Pa Yen (巴 彦) to
Fuchin (富 錦). Fire broke out five times
while sailing up the Amur and the whole vessel
was almost burnt down. In view of this information
it is clear that Chinese steamers are in a very
poor condition and if no steps be taken to put
them in order serious incidents may follow. Moreover,
as the Regulations were signed by both parties
(Chinese and Russian) it is feared that diplomatic
questions may be involved. I suggest, therefore,
the appointment of a deputy with full power to
inspect and control the steamers and rafts plying
these waters in order to avoid further confusion.
Any violations of these Regulations should incur

heavy

heavy penalties. If this reform is sanctioned
accidents will be greatly lessened and it will
be of great assistance to navigation and diplomatic
relations. But the question arises of whether the
power of controlling these steamers and rafts is
to be conferred on the Customs or whether a
member of the Sino-Soviet Aids Commission should
be especially deputed for that duty. I dare not
decide arbitrarily. This recommendation is hereby
forwarded for your kind consideration.

Appendix No. 2.

**Translation of letter No. 334 of 19th March, 1929
from Provisional Mayor's Office of Heiho District
(the Taoyin's Office was reorganized as from 15th
February. 1929).**

With reference to my letter No. 329 of
15th December, 1928, stating that a River Inspector
for controlling steamers navigating the Amur and
Ussuri frontier rivers should be appointed and that
this power has been conferred on the Aigun Customs
by the Provincial authorities, I beg now to inform
you that I have also reported this case to the
Kirin Provincial authorities. A reply has since
been received from them stating that the case has
been noted.

通函

由：	致：
哈尔滨关 1929 年 4 月 20 日	海关总税务司署（上海）总务科税务司

1929 年 4 月 5 日瑷珲关致海关总税务司署第 414 号呈收悉：

"呈送由道尹传达的黑龙江政府和吉林政府的相关指示，即由海关命港口巡官执行《中俄边界河道航务条例》，附意见。"

本署已于 1928 年 10 月 5 日第 151 号信函中向哈尔滨关海关监督表明，意欲于松花江实施该《中俄边界河道航务条例》，但 10 月 19 日哈尔滨关海关监督回信表示不予赞成，信函副本已与 1928 年 10 月非紧急中国函件共同呈送至海关总税务司署。

这些条例（第五段）和章程亦为哈尔滨关致海关总税务司署第 3835 号呈的主题及附件，从中可以看出，东三省政府似乎有意脱离中央政府，独立管理船运。

巴闰森（P. G. S. Barentzen）
哈尔滨关税务司

此副本抄送至瑷珲关税务司及海务巡工司

关于由海关命专员执行《中俄边界河道航务条例》的意见

1929 年 4 月 5 日瑷珲关致海关总税务司署第 414 号呈收悉：

"呈送由道尹传达的黑龙江和吉林政府的相关指示，即由海关命专员执行《中俄边界河道航务条例》，附意见。"

兹认为，《中俄边界河道航务条例》中大多条款的执行情况难以查实。

熟读可知相关条例有：

第一部分，第二条——航道沿线的航路标志。

第二部分，第一条——轮船和木筏上的装备。

第三部分，第一条——轮船照明。

第三部分，第二条——探照灯的使用。

第四部分，第一条——轮船、木筏和挖泥船的航运工作。

第四部分，第二条——雾天、雪天和雨天的航运工作。

第四部分，第三条——轮船、木筏或挖泥船回传、超船相关条例。

第四部分，第四条——轮船和木筏穿越浅滩的航运工作。

第五部分，第一条——轮船和木筏的停泊所。

第六部分，第一条——信号灯的使用。

第六部分，第二条——轮船和木筏停泊时的信号灯。

第六部分，第三条——轮船和木筏行进时的信号灯。

第六部分，第四条——各式轮船和木筏上信号灯的安装使用。

第六部分，第五条——轮船上的特殊信号灯。

第七部分，第一条——轮船在超船前应发出的信号。

第七部分，第二条——轮船和木筏从相反方向驶入时应发出的信号。

第七部分，第三条——轮船和木筏超越其他船只时应发出的信号。

第七部分，第四条——轮船和木筏穿越狭窄峡谷时应发出的信号。

第七部分，第五条——轮船和木筏经过正在施工的挖泥船时应发出的信号。

第七部分，第六条——求助信号。

第七部分，第七条——召唤轮船的信号。

第七部分，第八条——码头信号。

第八部分,第一条——航道障碍物。

第九部分,第一条——事故相关条例。

显然,上述条例大多适用于行进中的船只,若要探查违反条例的情况,只能让数名专员同乘这些船只、木筏、挖泥船等,或组建一支航道巡缉队乘一艘或多艘汽艇进行巡查,而当值关员则主要负责监督所有船只遵循章程的情况,发现船只违反条例后向总关汇报。

现举例说明：第四部分,第一条——轮船、木筏和挖泥船的航运工作。第20条规定："为确保安全航行,所有往来于同一方向同一航线上的船只,相互之间必须保持一定的距离。"目前是否有人去探查违反这一条例的情况呢？航道沿线的任何地方都可能发生违反该项条例的情况。第四部分,第二条,第25条规定："若遇浓雾、暴雨、大雪等天气,除客船外,浮船及木筏均禁止出航,必须停泊靠岸,并每分钟发出一次声响信号以警示其他船只。"欲确认该项,则只能在航道沿线实时观察。

鉴于条例大多涉及驾驶规则、航行信号灯等,本署或可称其为《万国航海避碰章程》的地方版本。其他国家如何实施此般条例呢？一般来说,若某船只违反了《万国航海避碰章程》,并因此危及另一船只时,后者的船长需向调查及采取行动的相关当局汇报这一事故。问题在于往返于黑龙江或其他航道的船长是否都能如此行事。兹认为,能够如此行事之船长甚少。因此,便需委派职员专门探查章程的执行情况,或是在航道沿途设立分卡,或使用汽艇巡缉队。

这些章程中,专员个人能够做到的,大约只有一条,即第二部分第一条——轮船和木筏上的装备。即便这一条,亦须视需要检查的船只数量而定,同时也取决于是否能够在一个既定的港口进行检查。如若不能,专员则须穿行于各个港口。

兹认为,若要有效实施章程,必须专人专用,因为此事绝非任何人都可以胜任。然而,如果当下需要海关竭尽所能安排合适的人选,那么本署赞同税务司之提议,由易保罗（Ignatieff）先生出任专员。

另外需要考虑的是,如有违反条例的情况,专员应有何授权方能执行条例。正如本署在关于哈尔滨关税务司第3835号呈的意见中所释,当江海关试图实施中国船运的相关条例时,曾在挑选关员、调查船只及船只设备等方面遭遇巨大困难。如遇船主拒不执行命令时,海关也只能不予发放结关单照,但实际上亦很少如此操作。其他国家设有海事法庭,可对未能执行章程的行为处以罚款等,但中国没有。

黑河道尹第329号信函（瑷珲关致海关总税务司署第414号呈2号附录）中已经说明,正是为了避免产生外交问题,才需委派一名海关专员来实施章程。换言之,这一重担已落到海关的肩上，海关需要通过专员来防止纠纷。兹认为，唯有委派一名职员全权实施这些章程，方能行之有效。

该情况与江海关多有相似——江海关港务长的职责虽涉及中国船运工作，但其却无法为中国船只提供足够的关员，本署已于《关于哈尔滨关税务司致海关总税务司署第 3835 号呈的意见》中概述其原因。

兹认为，中国《海运法》的实施并不在海关的职能范围之内，应由中央政府授权执行。若将该项工作授权给本署，则需向本署提供一名合适的职员，以便有效行使职责。当务之急是唯有得到授权，方能施行章程。

（签字）奚理满（H. E. Hillman）

海务巡工司

1929 年 4 月 29 日，上海巡工事务局

该抄件内容真实有效，特此证明

签字：劳德迷（Lowder. E. G.）监理员

呈海关总税务司署 <u>414</u> 号文　　　　　　　　瑷珲关 1929 年 4 月 5 日

尊敬的海关总税务司（上海）：

兹附黑河道尹兼黑龙江水道委员会华委员长的两封函件副本及其翻译，分别为黑龙江省政府之指示及吉林省政府之签署，命瑷珲关委派一名专员稽查管理，一方面确保中国轮船（及木筏）在黑龙江、额尔古纳河及乌苏里江航道上航行时，其船长能够遵循新采用的《中俄边界河道联合航务条例》，另一方面监察中国轮船的状况是否良好，包括船体、发动机及机械装置，以避免在这些海域航行时与俄方发生国际冲突。另黑龙江省政府已向哈尔滨航业公会下达上述指示。

本署于瑷珲关第 377 号呈中汇报了与草拟条例相关的前期谈判情况。瑷珲关第 315 号呈亦详尽说明《航务条例》的必要性及其实施问题。

本署于瑷珲关第 377 号呈中告知总税务司黑龙江水道委员会已于 1928 年 1 月 11 日签署协议，采用《中俄边界河道联合航务条例》，并按照海关总税务司署致瑷珲关第 358/113628 号令（及 1927 年 7 月 4 日海关总税务司署机要文件）之指示，在税务处批准新条例并指示总税务司予以实施之前，将暂且搁置新条例的实施问题。瑷珲关第 377 号呈（第四段）中说明道尹已通过齐齐哈尔政府向外交部、交通部以及税务处报告采用新条例。

但税务处并未对此事下达过任何指示——或因北京方面当时对此事尚未明晰（根据 1928 年 6 月 30 日海关总税务司署机要文件）。1928 年并未竭力要求边界河道上的中国轮船遵守《航务条例》，但黑龙江航务专门顾问在巡查航路标志时发现可批之处甚多，已将其所查汇报给道尹（与本署）。

关于黑龙江政府及吉林省政府命海关实施《航务条例》一事，有几点问题，黑龙江省政府及吉林省政府是否有权颁布此令，关务署是否有权下达指示，南京政府与奉天政府的微妙关系也是问题之一。黑龙江省政府及吉林省政府自觉有权向海关下达指令，是因为两省长期享有政治自制，特别是在通过黑龙江水道委员会，起草与苏维埃政府的《联合航路标志协议》一事上被给予了一定的自由度。黑龙江省政府与此事的直接关系可追溯至 1920 年——参阅海关总税务司署致哈尔滨关第 2248/78057 号令，即黑龙江督军与西伯利亚当局签订关于中国轮船在黑龙江上航行的临时协议。

请指示本署应如何回复道尹函件。此外，北满洲接邻东三省南部，发展势头超越中国其他任何城市，日益重要，也日渐繁荣。而今海关也迎来有利契机，可以通过当地道尹或海关监督的帮助,加强管制中俄边界河道和松花江上的商务及船运发展。

您忠诚的仆人

铎博赉（R. M. Talbot）

瑷珲关署理税务司

附件 1

1928 年 12 月 15 日黑河道尹致瑷珲关税务司

第 329 号函件的译本

本署收到汇报称黑龙江、乌苏里江及额尔古纳河等边界河道之轮船对于公布之《联合航务条例》竟有并未严格遵守者。若不严加整顿,难免发生外交问题。遂向黑龙江省政府提议派一名专员稽查管理。凡航行于边界河道之轮船或木筏,如查有不遵守章程之行为,即予照章处理,以示警戒。省政府第 5763 号回函批准委派一名专员之提议,请瑷珲关遵照办理。哈尔滨航业公会已收到指示命所有轮船遵守章程。省政府现已将稽查管理轮船之权力授予海关,请贵署查照核办并尽早告知此等稽查员服制之进展,以便本署通告各轮船。

兹附本署致黑龙江省政府的呈文副本:

地方中俄水道委员会于今春起草与黑龙江、乌苏里江、额尔古纳河相关的《航务条例》,已呈送并得本署批准。已印制 400 份《航务条例》分发各轮船(相关)遵照办理。黑龙江航务专门顾问易保罗(Ignatieff)先生汇报称,此次巡查黑龙江及乌苏里江航道时发现(中国)轮船未能严格遵守《航务条例》:如各轮船之号灯数目不足,舵楼中亦无预藏之灯烛以备电灯断绝时所用;发现船员之疏忽如传达信号于两船相遇或追赶时及轮船靠岸时,往往忘将行船号灯打开,而于轮船落锚时又忘将停船号灯打开,并于运输石油和轻汽油时未燃点红色号灯;"广州"号轮船拖带拖船开往虎林时,缺少第二盏白色号灯。上述情形颇能引起意外之损失,且在边界河道航行时,往往因船员之不谨慎易与俄船及木筏发生重大事端,甚至牺牲人命。应请派一名专员于航运季期间担任稽查轮船之责。瑷珲金矿监察局新任局长杜象春称,在乘坐"中华(Chungwha)"号轮船来大黑河的途中,目击该轮船腐败情状,如轮船驶至滴答嘴子(Ti Ta Tsui Tze)时,丢失所带拖船和船锚,由巴彦到富锦期间无锚行驶,又在黑龙江中共失火五次,险些全船烧毁。由此可见中国轮船情状之不良,若无人整顿,一旦发生危险,前途不堪设想,况且该条例既经中俄两国签字,如不遵照恐会引起外交问题。遂建议委派一名专员全权稽查管理边境航道上的轮船及木筏,以免后患。如查有不遵章程之行为,即予照章处办,以示警戒。如蒙批准,事故可望大幅减少,航运及外交关系亦会大受裨益。唯可否将此稽查管理轮船及木筏之权完全授予海关,抑或于中俄水道委员会华方委员中指派一员专司其事。本署未敢擅自决定,遂呈请指示。

附件 2

1929 年 3 月 19 日黑河地区暂代黑河市政筹备处处长办公室(1929 年 2 月 15 日起公认为道尹公署)第 334 号函件译本

1928 年 12 月 15 日本署第 329 号函件中说明需要委派一名专员来负责黑龙江及乌苏里江边界河道上的轮船管理工作,且省政府已将该权力授予瑷珲关。省政府已告知收悉此事。

此副本抄送至海务巡工司及哈尔滨关税务司
录事：黎彭寿 四等二级帮办

14. 为报告免除航务专门顾问职务及已按道尹要求移交航路标志账户余额事

Regd

451

I. G.   Aigun (Harbin) 29th November, 1929.

AMUR AIDS COMMISSION: Technical Adviser to, dispensing
with services of, reporting. Balance in Aids account,
action taken in connection with request by Taoyin that
it be handed over, informing.

Sir,

I have the honour to append copies of
correspondence exchanged between the Provisional
Mayor (Taoyin) and myself on the subjects of
dispensing with the Services of the Technical
Adviser to the Amur Aids Commission, Mr. P. I.
Ignatieff, and of handing over the balance in
Aids account.   The three letters concerned may
be summarized as follows:

A letter from the Taoyin dated the 9th
November to the effect that as Aids
activities had ceased the services of the
Technical Adviser to the Amur Aids Commission
were no longer required and he should be
given three months pay, in lieu of notice,
from the 1st November; also as the Aids
Commission was no longer functioning and as
its future was uncertain the balance in
Aids account should be handed over before
the evacuation of the Customs from Taheiho.

My reply, dated the 9th November, stating
that Mr. Ignatieff's three months' pay would
be issued on my arrival at Harbin he having
                                                    just

The Inspector General of Customs,
     S H A N G H A I.

just left for there; as regards the
balance in Aids account I suggested that
this matter be allowed to rest until my
arrival at Harbin - accounts had been
packed and there were still certain payments
to be made.

The Taoyin's reply, of the 10th instant,
that he had already reported to the
Provincial Authorities that he was taking
over the Aids balance, which he regarded
as local moneys, but that, as it was
difficult to close the account now, he
would accept a round sum from the balance.

The above questions were brought up by the
Taoyin when I was on the point of leaving Taheiho.
In the interview which he requested he stated that
as the Aids Commission was not likely to function
for some time and as its status might be entirely
changed in the negotiations for the settlement of
the present crisis he considered that the services
of Mr. Ignatieff as Technical Adviser should be
dispensed with and that he should be given three
months pay in lieu of notice. He went on to
say that if the former activities of the Commission
were renewed or if an Adviser to the Chinese was
required on the question of Sino-Soviet frontier
rivers in the conference which would eventually be
called he would be glad to avail himself again of
Mr. Ignatieff's services. I was not surprised at
this decision of the Taoyin's as Aids activities
had ceased last July and told him that I would
issue

issue the three months pay as requested and would refer the matter to you.   I consider, however, that as the notice was not given until the 9th November the three months pay should be issued from that date and have acted accordingly.

The Taoyin's request that I pay over to him the balance in Aids account I did not approve of. It seemed to me the severing of all connections between Customs and Aids was a step that would require your approval.   I took the occasion to inquire as to the prospects for the repayment of the $15,000 loan made to the Amur Aids Commission by the Sungari Aids.   He said that if Aids could not repay this that the Heilungchiang Government would.   I am not so sure about this.   The interview ended by my asking him to address me officially about the matters we had discussed which he did (Appendix No.1).   He was not pleased with my reply (Appendix No.2) that I considered the question of paying over the balance of Aids account might rest until I got to Harbin.   In a stormy interview which followed I adhered to my point, however, that the account should be kept open and in Customs hands until all outstanding questions were settled, but I agreed to let him have a round sum of $4,500, from the balance of some $6,600, to carry on with, which amount was duly paid over.

Mr. Ignatieff was originally engaged by the Customs as Adviser to the Amur Aids Commission on a contract that his services might be dispensed

with

with after three months notice (<u>vide</u> I.G. despatch
No.75/90,949 to Aigun). As far as the Aids
Commission is concerned there is no need of his
services at present and it may be said that they
have been dispensed with. It would appear to me,
however, that one with his expert knowledge of
navigation conditions on Sino-Soviet frontier rivers
and of Aids matters in general should not be
lost to China and it is to be hoped that, in
view of his excellent record over the last 7
years as Technical Adviser to the Amur Aids
Commission, his services can be availed of in some
other capacity.

Mr. Ignatieff brought the Aids archives to
Harbin when he came and they have been turned over
to the Harbin Commissioner. He has reported to
the latter and now awaits your instructions.

I have the honour to be,

Sir,

Your obedient Servant,

Acting Commissioner.

Appendix

呈海关总税务司署 <u>451</u> 号文　　　　　　　　瑷珲关 1929 年 11 月 29 日

尊敬的海关总税务司（上海）：

　　兹附暂代黑河市政筹备处处长（道尹）与本署关于免除易保罗（P. I. Ignatieff）先生黑龙江航务专门顾问一职，以及移交航路标志账户余额相关事宜的往来函件。相关三封函件总结如下：

　　　　"道尹于 11 月 9 日来函说明航路标志活动既已停止，则不再需要黑龙江航务专门顾问一职，应直接支付其 3 个月薪俸，自 11 月 1 日起结算；另因水道委员会已停止运行，且前途未卜，航路标志账户余额应于海关撤离大黑河之前移交。"

　　　　"本署于 11 月 9 日回复说明当本署抵达滨江关时，将发放易保罗（P. I. Ignatieff）先生三个月的薪俸，其已前往滨江关；另建议本署抵达滨江关后，再移交航路标志账户余额——账簿已封装，且仍有待付款项。"

　　　　"道尹于 10 日即刻回复称已向省政府汇报航路标志账户余额（道尹认为此为地方公款）移交事宜，但鉴于目前关闭账户不妥，可以接收账户余额中的整数金额。"

　　道尹于本署离开大黑河之际提议与本署会谈，并提出上述问题。道尹在会上说明鉴于水道委员会可能要停运一段时间，届时委员会在解决当下危机之谈判中的地位会彻底改变，遂认为应免除易保罗（P. I. Ignatieff）先生航务专门顾问的职务，并直接发放其三个月的薪俸。道尹还表示若将来水道委员会之前的工作需要重新开始，或者将来召开大会解决中俄边界河道问题时，中国水道委员会需要一位顾问，其愿意亲自提出恢复易保罗先生之职务。去年 7 月航路标志活动就已停止，道尹有此决定亦在意料之中。本署回复道尹将依照其要求向易保罗先生发放三个月的薪俸，并将此事汇报海关总税务司署。但本署认为鉴于通知发于 11 月 9 日，故三个月的薪俸也应于此日开始发放，已照此办理。

　　本署未同意道尹提出的移交航路标志账户余额之要求。兹认为，海关与水道委员会切断关系需经海关总税务司署批准。本署趁机询问道尹，黑龙江水道委员会从松花江航路标志账户所借的 15000 银圆应如何偿还。道尹表示若黑龙江水道委员会不能偿还该借款，黑龙江政府将代之还款，本署对此并不确定。道尹已按会谈结束时之要求发送有关会谈讨论事项的正式公文（附录 1）。本署回复（附录 2），将于抵达滨江关后，再行移交航路标志账户余额，道尹对此不甚满意。接下来的会谈非常激烈，本署坚持在所有问题解决之前，航路标志账户不应关闭并由海关负责管理，但同意从 6600 银圆的余额中向道尹移交

4500 银圆，剩余金额也会按时移交。

易保罗先生最初由海关任命为黑龙江航务专门顾问，根据合同规定，应提前三个月下发免除职务通知（参阅海关总税务司总署致瑷珲关第 75/90949 号令）。就水道委员会而言，目前已不再需要易保罗先生之职务。但本署认为，中国不应失去像易保罗先生这样对中俄边界河道航路环境及航路标志事宜有全面的了解和专业知识之人，希望鉴于易保罗先生担任黑龙江航务专门顾问 7 年以来的优秀业绩，可以让其担任其他职位。

易保罗先生抵达滨江关后，已向滨江关税务司报告，并移交所带的航路标志档案，现等待指示。

您忠诚的仆人

铎博赉（R. M. Talbot）

瑷珲关署理税务司

15. 为松花江航路标志委员向黑龙江水道委员会划拨协济款事

[A.—29]

No. 253   COMMRS.

Aigun   No. 104,793

INSPECTORATE GENERAL OF CUSTOMS,

PEKING, 21st September, 1925.

Sir,

With reference to your despatch No. 230:

reporting, inter alia, the difficulty caused by lack of funds in the Amur River Dues Account;

I am directed by the Officiating Inspector General to append hereto for your information copy of his despatch No. 3,480/104,776 to Harbin, authorising the Harbin Commissioner to make arrangements for an advance of, say, $ 20,000.00 to the Amur Aids Account from the Sungari Aids Account.

On receipt of such advance from the Harbin Customs as may be arranged, you are requested to credit the amount received to your Amur River Dues Account, from which account refund is to be made as soon as funds allow.

You are requested to inform the Superintendent

of

The Commissioner of Customs,

AIGUN.

of the receipt of this advance.   Copies of

Shui-wu Ch'u despatch No. 1,096 and of the

Officiating Inspector General's reply (despatch No.306)

in connection with this question are appended for

your information.

I am,

Sir,

Your obedient Servant,

Chief Secretary Officiating.

Appendix.

<u>Appendix</u>.

I. G. despatch No. 253/104,793 to Aigun

Copy: I. G. despatch No. 3480/104,776 to Harbin.

                                    Peking, 18th September 1925.
Sir,

        With reference to the Officiating Inspector
General's semi-official letter of the 20th May, 1925:
                suggesting that as the Amur Aids Account
                was urgently in need of funds the
                Sungari Aids Account might be in a
                position to advance to the Amur Aids
                Account from its surplus funds, say,
                $20,000.00 to be paid in two instalments
                and to be refunded as soon as the Amur
                River Dues collection permitted:
and to your semi-official letter of 23rd May
1925, in reply:
                stating that there would be no
                difficulty in making the proposed advance,
                particularly if interest thereon could
                be obtained:
I am directed by the Officiating Inspector General
to request you to make arrangements with the
Aigun Commissioner for an advance from your
Account <u>D</u>, Local Moneys, Aids to Navigation
Account, to the Aigun Customs Amur River Dues
                                                Account

Account of $20,000.00, to be paid in two instalments as required and to be refunded as soon as the Amur River Dues collection permits. Until repaid, a note concerning this advance is to be borne on your quarterly "Local Moneys Expenditure" vouchers.

I am to add that if interest charges be contemplated the question should be referred to the Inspectorate for decision.

I am,

Sir,

Your obedient Servant,

(Signed) J. H. SCHNUYER

Chief Secretary Officiating.

True copy:

Assistant Secretary.

536

AMUR AIDS COMMISSION: Heilungkiang Government's
proposal that Commission's present indebtedness($25,000)
to Sungari Commission be cancelled and that latter make
further advance of $30,000 in aid of former: result of
discussion with Sungari Commission through Harbin
Commissioner in re, reporting.

I. G.   A I G U N   6th February, 1931.

536
I. G

RECEIVED

Sir,

1.   With reference to Aigun despatch No. 492 :
            reporting, inter alia, that the Provisional
            Mayor - who also acts as Superintendent -
            had requested that the River Dues
            Collection, less 1/10th for Customs cost
            of collection, be turned over to him
            monthly; explaining that, as the
            Commissioner's control of Aids funds was
            inadequate, such a request would receive
            full support if it were not for the
            outstanding indebtedness of the Amur Aids
            Commission to the Sungari Aids Commission;
            quoting the Harbin Commissioner's suggestion
            that the Sungari Aids be given a lien on
            the Amur and Ussuri River Dues collected
            on behalf of the Amur Commission by
            Harbin's sub-port of Lahasusu; pointing out
            that no effort at repayment would be
            seriously considered or allowed by the
            Mayor so long as a measure of supported
            pressure were not brought to bear by the
            Commissioner, and that, with the funds in
            the hands of the Mayor, the last vestige
            of hope of recovery would disappear; and,
                                                      finally,

The Inspector General of Customs,

     S H A N G H A I.

finally, requesting your instructions on
the points at issue :

and to your despatch No. 132,077 :

stating that you had laid before the Kwan-
wu Shu a statement of the case, and while
requesting their decision on the Mayor's
proposal, pointed out at the same time
the extent of the indebtedness of the Amur
Aids Commission to the Sungari Aids
Commission, and suggested that the Aigun
Commissioner be authorised to deduct from
each month's River Dues Collection one-tenth
- in addition to the one-tenth cost of
collection, - in order to repay the
outstanding debt to the Sungari Aids
Commission: remarking that the Heilungkiang
Government contended that, on account of
insufficiency of River Dues revenue, the
proposal to deduct one-tenth from the
annual revenue to repay the debt to the
Sungari Aids Commission was not acceptable,
and asked that the latter should not only
cancel the outstanding indebtedness of the
Amur Commission but should also make a
further appropriation from its funds of
$50,000.00 for the benefit of the Amur
Aids: and instructing me to hand over to
the Mayor at the close of each month the
Dues collected, minus one-tenth for Customs
cost of collection; to approach the Sungari
Aids Commission, through the Harbin
Commissioner, to see whether arrangements
could be made in regard to the proposals
of

of the Heilungkiang Government; and, on reaching an understanding with the Sungari Aids Commission, to report the result by despatch, with Chinese version in duplicate:

I have the honour to report that, in accordance with your instructions, I duly approached the Sungari Aids Commission, through the Harbin Commissioner, in regard to the proposals of the Heilungkiang Government that the outstanding indebtedness of the Amur Commission to the Sungari Commission be cancelled, and that the latter Commission extend further financial help of $30,000.00 to the Amur Commission.

2.   In his comments on your despatch No. 132,077, and in his despatch No. 103/1222 to me, the Harbin Commissioner makes no reference to the outstanding indebtedness of the Amur Commission to the Sungari Commission. I understand his silence on this subject to denote that in his opinion the chances of repayment are so remote that he regards with indifference any decision in this connection. It would therefore seem possible to settle this proposal of the Heilungkiang Government without further discussion by cancellation of the outstanding debt.

3.   From a perusal of the correspondence appended to your despatch under reply, it occurred to me that the Heilungkiang Government was attempting to relegate to the Sungari Aids Commission the full responsibility for financial assistance to the Amur Commission and, with this in view, I suggested to the former that it would, perhaps, be wise to forestall such action by offering to assume full responsibility in exchange for complete control by the Customs of Amur Aids funds. However, in his comments on your despatch

No.

No. 132,077, and in his despatch No. 103/Aigun, the Harbin Commissioner has affirmed his conviction that the Sungari Aids Commission will in the near future be taken over by the provincial authorities, when the question of paying off the Sungari Aids staff - who are contributors to the Pension Scheme - will arise. As the funds at present at its disposal would only suffice to meet these liabilities, the Sungari Aids Commission has expressed unqualified opposition to any further advances in aid of the Amur Commission, especially as further demands on the resources of the Sungari Commission would necessarily entail deterioration in the aids to navigation on the Sungari.

4.   I beg to forward, appended hereto, copy of Aigun despatch No. 125/243 to Harbin, of Harbin despatch No. 103/1222 in reply, of my S/O letter of the 13th January, 1931, and of part of the Harbin Commissioner's S/O letter of the 22nd January, 1931. It will be seen from these documents that the Harbin Commissioner has suggested that the Heilungkiang and Kirin Governments assume complete responsibility over the funds of the Amur and Ussuri Aids service and advance the necessary sums against a lien on the collection of River Dues.   The above is, in fact, the position to-day, but the Heilungkiang Government is evidently of the opinion that, both Commissions being engaged in similar work for the welfare of China, their funds should be used for mutual assistance.   The sum of $30,000.00 now applied for is for the repayment of a loan of $15,000.00 from the Kuang Hsin Company （廣信公司） for Amur Aids purposes, and for funds wherewith to pay the last

instalment

Appendices
1 - 4

instalment of $11,300.00 due to Russia under the Joint Aids Agreement signed in August 1930.

5.   A Chinese version, in duplicate, of part of paragraph one and of paragraphs two and three of this despatch is forwarded, enclosed herewith.

           I have the honour to be,

              Sir,

        Your obedient Servant,

        (Signed) C. B. Joly

            (C. H. B. Joly)

          Acting Commissioner.

Appendix No. 1

APPENDIX No. 1

Copy of Aigun despatch No. 125/243 to Harbin dated the 12th January, 1931.

Sir,

1. With reference to I. G. despatch No. 132,077 (copy of which was supplied to you) :

> calling for a report from me, after approaching the Sungari Aids Commission through the Harbin Commissioner, regarding the suggested cancellation of the outstanding indebtedness of $25,000.00 of the Amur Aids to the Sungari Commission; and the proposal that the latter extend further financial help of $30,000.00 to the Amur Commission :

I now beg to request that you will be so good as to provide me with your views in regard to these two recommendations so as to enable me to prepare the report called for by the Inspector General.

2. The Amur Aids Commission at present lacks the funds wherewith to pay the last instalment of $11,300.00 for 1930 due to the Russian Amur Navigation Bureau under the joint Aids Agreement, and it will also be unable to issue the salary and allowances of the Technical Adviser from next February until the opening of the navigation season. Owing to the greatly diminished value of silver, the Chinese share of the cost of upkeep of the joint aids to navigation on the Amur, Argun and Ussuri Rivers was increased by about 70% under the agreement concluded in August 1930 to cover the work of that year and of 1931. The Heiho Mayor is now contemplating a general increase of the River

Dues

Dues Tariff from the beginning of next navigation season
so as to make shipping and trade provide the additional
funds required during the present year, but, it is
estimated, the increase will only suffice to meet
current expenses and no provision for the repayment of
loans or for the building up of a reserve will be
possible. Should the price of silver remain at its
present low level, a further rise in the amount of
China's contribution for the upkeep of aids will have
to be considered when a new agreement has to be
negotiated.

3.   Trade in this district has, as the result of
various political circumstances, declined seriously since
the Amur Aids Commission was first inaugurated, but,
although traffic on the three frontier rivers is
comparatively small, the political importance of
maintaining and assisting Chinese shipping on these
waterways cannot be over-stressed, especially as there
is a marked tendency on the part of the Russian
authorities to claim that various islands and channels,
whose ownership is disputed, are within the Russian
border.

4.   The system of joint aids agreements between
China and Russia is, undoubtedly, the most economical
manner in which the former can participate in the
upkeep of aids on the frontier rivers as her share of
the cost is based only on actual upkeep and makes no
contribution towards the extensive equipment necessary for
such work and supplied gratis by the Russians. China's
payments for 1931 towards the work on the Amur, Argun
and Ussuri Rivers, a stretch of over 2,500 versts, will
aggregate $38,200.00 .

                                                          5.

5.   Until shipping and trade on the three frontier rivers increase, financial assistance to the Amur Aids Commission will be necessary. The point of primary importance, and the one which should be settled once for all, is, therefore, from what source such assistance should emanate. As the Amur Commission is maintaining China's political and territorial rights in these regions, it might be argued that the requisite funds should be subscribed by the Central Government. On the other hand, the benefit of increased trade and of frontier stability accrues to the provinces of Heilungkiang and Kirin and the view may be taken that some contribution should be made from their exchequers. Again, the Central and Provincial Governments might contend that the shipping benefited by the aids is the same as that plying on the Sungari; that it has already contributed towards the upkeep of aids to navigation; and that it can, in consequence, rightly claim that any balance in the hands of the Sungari Commission be used to assist it on the frontier waterways. The last is evidently the view now taken by the Manchurian authorities. Moreover, the analogy of the collection and disposal of Tonnage Dues in China proper could be quoted in support of this argument.

6.   I am of the opinion that we must now look beyond the question of an immediate advance of $30,000.00 from Sungari Aids' funds to the Amur Commission. I see an attempt in embryo on the part of the Heilungkiang Government to relegate to the Sungari Commission the full responsibility for financial assistance to the Amur Aids and, from this standpoint,

I

I would now advocate the following measures to safeguard our mutual interests.

7.   Many of the questions with which the Amur Commission has to deal are of a political and international character and it would be inadvisable for the Customs to attempt to obtain complete control of the Commission. I would recommend that the local Mayor and the Aigun Commissioner constitute the Amur Commission, the former to be solely in charge of political and international questions and the latter to be in complete control of the financial side of the work; all future Aids agreements to be concluded by these two representatives with the expert assistance of the Technical Adviser; and any increase or changes in the River Dues Tariff to be drawn up by the Mayor and the Commissioner and to be enforced after approval by the Ministry of Finance. As explained above, these recommendations are made on the assumption that the tendency will be to call on the Sungari Commission for financial assistance to the Amur Commission, and it would therefore be preferable to forestall such a course by offering to assume responsibility if, in exchange, the Customs were granted complete control of the funds of the Amur Commission. My principal reason for this recommendation is that there is no guarantee that, the precedent having once been established, in the future frequent requests for assistance from the Sungari Commission will not be made. An appropriation of $30,000.00 would, instead of satisfying present requirements, act as a stimulant for further demands and more lavish expenditure. There would also be no means of ensuring that it would be used for the purpose for which it was intended.

8.

8.　　　　If you can see your way to support my
recommendations, an appropriation of $50,000.00 would not
be required now.　The question of the payment of the
last instalment of $11,300.00 due to the Russian Amur
Navigation Bureau is now under consideration by the
Heilungkiang Government and the Heiho Mayor.　If they
arrange to pay this sum in the near future, financial
assistance to the Amur Aids may not be necessary this
year if the increase of the River Dues Tariff is
authorised, but failure to settle this debt would
compel an application for an appropriation of funds for
this purpose.

9.　　　　I am convinced that my proposal for the
solution of points at issue would in the long run be
by far the most economical for both Commissions.　By
forestalling development along the lines foreshadowed in
the request of the Heilungkiang Government, and by
having complete control of Amur 'Aids' funds vested in
the Aigun Customs, we should be safeguarding the
interests of both the Sungari and Amur Commissions.

　　　　　　　　I am,

　　　　　　　　　　Sir,

　　　　　　　　　Your obedient Servant,

　　　　　　　　　(Signed) C. H. B. Joly,

　　　　　　　　　　Acting Commissioner.

True copy:

3rd Clerk B.

　　　　　　　　　　　　　　Appendix No. 2.

APPENDIX No. 2

Copy of Harbin despatch No. 103/1222 to Aigun dated the
20th January 1931 (in reply to Aigun despatch No. 125/243)

Sir,

      I beg to acknowledge receipt of your despatch
No. 125/243 :

           concerning the Heilungchiang Government's request
           for financial assistance from the Sungari Aids
           in aid of the Amur and Ussuri Aids; and
           your recommendations for the complete financial
           control by the Aigun Customs of the Amur
           Aids as a means of preventing constant
           encroachment on the Sungari Aids.

My comments on I. G. despatch No. 132,077 to Aigun must
have crossed your despatch. The suggestions put forward
in my comments are to the effect that the Heilungchiang
and Kirin Governments assume complete responsibility over
the funds of the Amur and Ussuri Aids service and
advance the necessary sums against a lien on the
collection of river dues on these two rivers. As, in
my opinion, it is only a question of months before the
Sungari Aids Service is taken over by the Provincial
Authorities, my principal preoccupation is, as explained
in my comments, to have sufficient funds in reserve to
pay off the Sungari Aids staff, who are contributors to
the Superannuation scheme.

      For the Aigun Customs to assume complete
financial control of the Amur Aids appears to me a
very great responsibility and outside of our province.
The tendencies of the Central and Provincial Governments
as they gradually wake up to a sence of affranchisement

                              are

are to take over control from the Customs of all
services that do not pertain exclusively to the
collection of Revenue on cargoes. It is a very
natural desire on their part. Your recommendations
being in the opposite direction, would, I feel certain,
meet with a curt negative and I think that we would
be exceeding our own - already very great - responsibilities
by assuming such financial control.

                    I am,

                         Sir,

                    Your obedient Servant,

                    (Signed) René d'Anjou,

                         Commissioner.

True copy:

     3rd Clerk B.

                                   Appendix No. 3.

APPENDIX No. 3

Copy of Aigun Commissioner's S/O letter of the 13th January, 1931, to the Harbin Commissioner.

Dear Mr. d'Anjou,

I hope you will not think that my despatch No. 125 to you was inspired by any desire to add to the importance of this office. The contents represent my real fears regarding the future and I feel strongly that the only safe course is to take the bull by the horns and to offer to assume responisbility for Amur deficits, on the terms explained in my despatch. From what I know of local conditions, and from what the new Mayor has mentioned, it is evident that the Heilungkiang authorities are after the balance of $15,000.00 remaining from the sum of $40,000.00 authorised by the Inspector General in his despatches Nos. 253/104,793 of 21st September 1925, and 300/108,242, of 29th June 1926, (Aigun numbers) as a loan to the Amur Aids. The authorities have, so the Mayor informs me, already borrowed $15,000.00 from the Kwang Hsin Company and they want the same amount from the Sungari to repay this loan; the additional $15,000.00 asked for in the petition to the Ministry are for the payment of the last 1930 instalment of $11,300.00 to Russia. What would become of the extra $3,700.00, I cannot say! You will see from the above that the question of repaying the former loan of $25,000.00 from the Sungari Aids does not enter into their calculations at all and I am positive that their intention is to establish the Sungari's responsibility for Amur deficits. With the funds out of our control and with the Sungari balances to draw on, it would probably be

found

found that provincial requirements would result in
frequent demands on your funds. In the past we
controlled Amur Aids' moneys to some extent, but with
the handing over each month of River Dues collections
to the local Mayor, all vestige of control disappears.
Another aspect of the case, which strengthens my
conviction that the only thing to do is to assume
responsibility for Amur deficits in exchange for complete
financial control, is that I foresee that Nanking will,
if you have any available balance, overrule any
objections and support the request of the Heilungkiang
Government which has already been recommended by the
North Eastern Executive Council.

A solution on the lines suggested by me would
do away with the necessity for an immediate appropriation
of $30,000.00 for the Amur, although one would be
necessary if the local authorities make no provision
for paying the $11,300.00 already overdue to the Russians,
but we should certainly not require more than $15,000.00
at the utmost. Furthermore, under present arrangements
it will make little difference whether the outstanding
indebtedness of $25,000.00 is cancelled or not as,
undoubtedly, care would be exercised to ensure that no
balance remained at the end of each year. With
Customs control of Amur funds, it might be possible
ultimately to repay this loan.

Yours sincerely,

(Signed) C. H. B. Joly.

True copy:

3rd Clerk B.

Appendix No. 4.

APPENDIX No. 4

Copy of part of Harbin Commissioner's S/O letter of the 22nd January, 1931, to the Aigun Commissioner (in reply to Aigun Commissioner's S/O letter of the 13th January, 1931)

Dear Joly,

*　　*　　*　　*　　*　　*

On the question of financial assistance from the Sungari Aids to the Amur Aids, I do not doubt for a moment that we shall have to give in, in spite of all our arguments for the separation of the two services. The Provincial Authorities are well aware of the sound financial condition of the Sungari Service and I expect that it will be taken over in the immediate future. All I am concerned about is the paying off of the foreign Aids Staff. They have done their work bravely and loyally, sometimes at great personal risk and they thoroughly deserve not to be left stranded. As to the Amur Aids it would be folly to assume financial responsibility; there are too many political strings attached to it, and I doubt very much that the Provincial Authorities would agree.

*　　*　　*　　*　　*　　*

Yours sincerely,
(Signed) René d'Anjou.

True copy:

3rd Clerk B.

AMUR AIDS COMMISSION: advance of $40,000 from the
Sungari Aids Account authorised by the I.G. in aid
of: payment of balance of $15,000 made through the
Harbin Commissioner, reporting.

539   539
                                                           I.G

I.G.   A I G U N,   10th February, 1931.

Sir,

1.   With reference to Aigun despatch No. 492 :

            explaining the financial position of the

            Amur Aids Commission and its outstanding

            indebtedness of $25,000.00 to the Sungari

            Aids Commission; and pointing out probable

            effects if the Provisional Mayor's proposal,

            - that the River Dues collection, less 1/10th

            for Customs cost of collection, be turned

            over to him monthly, - be accepted, especially

            as regards the continued employment of Mr.

            P. I. Ignatieff, the Technical Adviser :

    to I. G. despatch No. 132,077 :

            instructing me to approach the Sungari Aids

            Commission, through the Harbin Commissioner,

            to see whether arrangements could be made in

            regard to the proposals of the Heilungkiang

            Government that the outstanding indebtedness

            of the Amur Aids Commission to the Sungari

            Aids Commission be cancelled, and that the

            latter should make a further appropriation from

            its funds of $30,000.00 for the benefit of

            the Amur Aids; to report by despatch on

            reaching an understanding with the Sungari

            Aids Commission; to hand over to the Mayor

            at the close of each month the River Dues

                                                collected.

The Inspector General of Customs,

    S H A N G H A I.

collected, minus one-tenth for Customs cost
of collection; and to note that Mr.
Ignatieff is to continue to be employed and
that his salary and allowances are to be
paid from the net collections of River Dues:

to Aigun despatch No. 532 :

reporting that the funds in the Amur River
Dues Account would suffice to pay Mr.
Ignatieff's salary and allowances for the
month of January only; and requesting
authority to issue these, when necessary,
from my Account D, Suspense Account, and to
recover such advances from future collections
of River Dues :

and to Aigun despatch No. 536 :

reporting the results of the negotiations
with the Sungari Aids Commission, conducted
through the Harbin Commissioner, in regard to
the two proposals of the Heilungkiang
Government :

I have the honour to report that the Sungari Aids
Commission has now advanced, through the Harbin Commissioner,
a further sum of $15,000.00 to the Amur Aids
Commission, in compliance with the recent request of
the Taheiho Mayor transmitted through the Harbin
Superintendent.   This represents the fourth and final
instalment of the amount originally authorised in I. G.
despatches Nos. 104,776 and 108,241 to Harbin as an
advance from the Sungari Aids Commission to the Amur
Aids Commission, and increases the outstanding
indebtedness of the latter from $25,000.00 to
$40,000.00.

2.

2.　　　　The actual amount received by me for the credit of the Amur River Dues Account is $14,925.37 = $15,000.00 less $74.63 remittance fee.　This money will enable the Amur Commission to pay the final instalment of $11,300.00 due to the Soviet authorities for the year 1930 under the Joint Aids Agreement, and to pay Mr. Ignatieff's salary and allowances to the end of April, 1931.

I have the honour to be,

Sir,

Your obedient Servant,

(Signed) C. B. Joly

(C. H. B. Joly)

Acting Commissioner.

致瑷珲关第 253/104793 号令　　　　海关总税务司署（北京）1925 年 9 月 21 日

尊敬的瑷珲关税务司：

根据第 230 号呈：

"专门汇报黑龙江航路标志账户资金短缺造成的难题"

奉代理总税务司命令，兹附海关总税务司署致哈尔滨关第 3480/104776 令号副本，以供参考。此令授权哈尔滨关税务司安排自松花江航路标志账户拨款 20000 银圆至黑龙江航路标志账户。

按照安排一旦收到这笔哈尔滨关的借款，请贵署将收到的款项计入黑龙江航路标志账户贷方。如果资金充足，尽快从黑龙江航路标志账户偿还借款。

请转告海关监督已收到此笔借款。兹附有关此问题的税务处第 1096 号令副本及代理海关总税务司呈函（第 306 号呈）副本，以供参考。

您忠诚的仆人

贝乐业（J. H. Berruyer）

代理总务科税务司

海关总税务司署至瑷珲关第 253/104793 号令附件

尊敬的哈尔滨关税务司：

根据代理总税务司 1925 年 5 月 20 日半官方信函：

"黑龙江航路标志账户资金紧缺，建议将松花江航路标志账户盈余资金暂借黑龙江航路标志账户，共计 20000 银圆，分两次转账。只要黑龙江江捐征收金额充足，立即还款。"

及 1925 年 5 月 23 日半官方信函回复：

"借款没什么问题，尤其是如果可以收取利息的话。"

奉代理总税务司命令，请贵署会同瑷珲关税务司协商，安排从贵署 D 账户地方公款航路标志账项下分两次借款 20000 银圆至瑷珲关黑龙江江捐账户，并且只要黑龙江江捐征收金额充足，立即还款。直至还款，贵署季度"地方公款支出"传票上均需附有有关此借款的备注。

此外，如需计议利息问题，则应提交至海关总税务司署决定。

您忠诚的仆人

（签字）贝乐业（J. H. Berruyer）

代理总务科税务司

此副本内容真实有效，特此证明。

福贝士（A. H. Forbes）

襄办总务科副税务司

呈海关总税务司署 536 号文 瑷珲关 1931 年 2 月 6 日

尊敬的海关总税务司（上海）：

1. 根据瑷珲关第 492 号呈：

"兹汇报，暂代黑河市政筹备处处长兼海关监督要求瑷珲关扣除 10% 海关征税佣金后，按月上交江捐税收。然因黑龙江水道委员会尚未付清从松花江水道委员会所贷之款，而税务司对航路标志资金又无充分管理之权，故目前难照暂代黑河市政筹备处处长要求行事。滨江关税务司建议，允许松花江水道委员会扣留由滨江关拉哈苏苏分关代表黑龙江水道委员会征收的黑龙江和乌苏里江江捐。但无论如何，税务司若无法获得支持向暂代黑河市政筹备处处长施压，其便不会认真考虑偿还松花江航路标志债款一事，而今航路标志资金又由其管理，可以说归还债款的最后一丝希望亦将破灭；还望贵署予以指示；"

及海关总税务司署第 132077 号令：

"谨告知，已向关务署说明黑龙江水道委员会对松花江水道委员会的债务情况，并向其建议批准瑷珲关税务司每月除从江捐税收中扣除 10% 海关征税佣金以外，额外再提扣十分之一用以偿还松花江水道委员会的债款，关于黑河市政筹备处处长之要求，亦已提请其定夺。但黑龙江省政府提出，由于江捐税收本不充足，无法接受再从每年的税收中扣除十分之一来支付松花江水道委员会的债款，并认为松花江水道委员会不仅应将未结清的欠款一笔勾销，还应从其资金中划拨 30000 银圆协济黑龙江水道委员会。鉴于此，请瑷珲关每月扣除 10% 海关征税佣金后，将江捐税收移交给黑河市政筹备处处长，并通过滨江关税务司与松花江水道委员会进行洽谈，以确定是否可照黑龙江省政府之建议办理，待与松花江水道委员会达成协定后，再呈文汇报，并附汉文译本，一式两份。"

兹汇报，本署已照海关总税务司署指示通过滨江关税务司与松花江水道委员会进行商议，松花江水道委员会同意将黑龙江水道委员会所欠债款一笔勾销，并同意再向黑龙江水道委员会预支 30000 银圆协济之款。

2. 滨江关税务司在其关于海关总税务司署第 132077 号令的意见以及滨江关致瑷珲关第 103/1222 号文中，均未提及黑龙江水道委员会尚未付清从松花江水道委员会所贷之款一事。兹认为，滨江关税务司之所以对此事保持缄默，意在表明，于其而言，还款之事既已无望，此事最终如何决定亦无关紧要。由此看来，或可直接照黑龙江省政府之提议办理，无须再议勾销欠款一事。

3.详阅贵署令文所附函件后,本署认为黑龙江省政府意在令松花江水道委员会承担资助黑龙江水道委员会的全部责任,并已据此向松花江水道委员会提议,由其主动提出承担协济黑龙江水道委员会的全部责任,但前提条件是由海关全权管理黑龙江航路标志资金。然滨江关税务司已在其关于海关总税务司署第132077号令的意见以及滨江关致瑷珲关第103/1222号文中确认,松花江水道委员会不日将由省政府接管。而松花江水道委员会的职员均为养老储金计划参保人员,届时还需应对退还养老储金一事。鉴于松花江航路标志资金仅够支付职员养老储金,松花江水道委员会已表示,坚决反对今后再向黑龙江水道委员会提供资金援助,否则松花江航路标志亦会受到影响。

4.兹附瑷珲关致滨江关第125/243号文抄件,滨江关致瑷珲关第103/1222号文抄件,瑷珲关1931年1月13日半官函抄件,以及滨江关1931年1月22日半官函部分内容抄件。从中可知,滨江关税务司建议由黑龙江和吉林省政府全权负责黑龙江及乌苏里江航路标志所需资金的筹备事宜,并预支相关款项,最后再以江捐税收抵之。但黑龙江省政府显然认为,黑龙江和松花江水道委员会所谋之事大抵相同,皆是在为中国谋福祉,故双方在资金方面亦应相互扶持。目前所申请之30000银圆资金,一则用以偿还为开展黑龙江航路标志工事从广信公司所贷之款,二则用以向俄方支付1930年8月中俄联合航路标志协议所定金额的最后一笔分期款项,即11300银圆。

5.兹附该呈第一、二、三段部分内容的汉文版本,一式两份。

您忠诚的仆人

周骊（C. B. Joly）

瑷珲关署理税务司

附录1

1931 年 1 月 12 日瑷珲关致滨江关第 125/243 号文抄件

尊敬的滨江关税务司：

1. 根据海关总税务司署第 132077 号令：

"请通过滨江关税务司与松花江水道委员会商议将黑龙江航路标志委员所欠之 25000 银圆债款勾销，并另行划拨 30000 银圆协济黑龙江水道委员会；达成协定后，再行呈文汇报；"

望贵署可对该两条提议给出意见，以便本署向海关总税务司汇报。

2. 目前，黑龙江水道委员会资金短缺，已无力向俄阿穆尔水道局支付 1930 年中俄联合航路标志协议所定金额的最后一笔分期款项 11300 银圆，且从明年 2 月到航运季开始前亦无力向航务专门顾问支付薪俸和津贴。此外，由于银价暴跌，1930 年中俄联合航路标志协议（协定 1931 年黑龙江、乌苏里江及额尔古纳河航路标志的联合维护工事）所定之华方摊款金额将上涨 70%。黑河市政筹备处处长现已开始考虑从下一个航运季开始全面提高江捐税率，以期通过船运和贸易税收的增加，解决今年资金短缺问题。但据估算，增加的税收仅够支付目前各项费用，依然无法偿还债款，亦无法留有储备金。因此，银价若持续低迷，待中俄双方商定新协议时，或将需要考虑增加华方摊款之金额数。

3. 自黑龙江水道委员会成立以来，大黑河地区的贸易因受政治环境的影响已严重衰退，然而，尽管中国船运在三条边境河流上的货运量相对较小，但与之相关的维护及辅助工作于政治而言却极为重要，尤其如今，俄国政府又有意将归属权仍有争议的小岛及水道划入俄国境内。

4. 毫无疑问，于中国而言，中俄联合航路标志协议是其实现参与边界河道航路标志维护工作最为经济之法，其仅需支付航路标志维护工作的实际支出，相关设备均由俄方无偿提供。华方将为 1931 年黑龙江、额尔古纳河以及乌苏里江航路标志维护工作（共计约 2500 俄里）支付摊款 38200 银圆。

5. 然在三条边境河流的航运量和贸易量有所增加之前，黑龙江水道委员会依然会需要经济援助。因此，最重要，亦是最需要彻底解决的便是资金来源问题。若从黑龙江水道委员会是在维护中国边境地区的政治和领土主权的角度考虑，资金则应由中央政府提供；若从黑龙江和吉林省政府因贸易增加和边境稳定而受益的角度考虑，资金则应由两省政府提供。但中央政府及黑龙江和吉林两省政府可能会认为，松花江上的往来船只与边境河流上的一样，均受益于航路标志的建立，且已为航路标志维护工作贡献份额，因此若松花江水道委员会仍有结余,则应协济边界河道水道委员会;满洲政府显然亦是持此意见。此外,中国内地关于船钞的征收及处置办法亦可支撑该观点。

6.兹认为,从黑龙江省政府要求松花江水道委员会向黑龙江水道委员会预支30000银圆一事中可以看出,黑龙江省政府有意将资助黑龙江水道委员会之责任施加于松花江水道委员会。鉴于此,为保护哈尔滨关和瑷珲关之利益,兹提出如下建议。

7.鉴于黑龙江水道委员会需解决的问题大多涉及政治和国际事务,因此于海关而言,争得黑龙江水道委员会的全部管理权绝非明智之举。兹建议,黑龙江水道委员会的政治及国际事务由黑河市政筹备处处长负责,财务相关事项则由瑷珲关税务司全权管理;日后中俄联合航路标志协议均由黑河市政筹备处处长和瑷珲关税务司共同出面签署,并由航务专门顾问协助,另外,江捐税率的调整亦须由二者共同拟订,再呈交至财政部进行审批。如上所述,这些建议都是基于松花江水道委员会将被迫承担协济黑龙江水道委员会之责任这一前提进行考虑的,因此,兹认为,若欲阻止此等情况的发生,松花江水道委员会最好主动提出承担协济之责,并以由海关来全权管理黑龙江水道委员会资金作为交换条件。本署有此建议,主要考虑此先例一开,日后松花江水道委员会难免会频繁收到援助请求,也就是说,拨发30000银圆的协济款后,将会收到更多的拨款请求,数额亦会愈来愈大,且无法保证经费是否皆能花得其所。

8.若贵署认为上述建议可行,30000银圆的拨款将暂无需求。至于应向俄罗斯阿穆尔水道局支付的最后一笔分期款项11300银圆,黑龙江省政府和黑河市政筹备处处长已开始予以考虑。若该笔欠款可于近日还清,同时提高江捐税率一事又能获得批准,黑龙江水道委员会今年将不再需要资助;但若该笔欠款未能得以偿付,黑龙江水道委员会还将需要申请拨款。

9.兹坚信,从长远来看,上述建议于松花江和黑龙江水道委员会而言皆为最经济的解决方案。通过预先阻止黑龙江省政府请求背后的意图,并让海关完全掌控黑龙江航路标志资金等举措,松花江和黑龙江水道委员会的利益必会得到保护。

您忠诚的仆人

周骊（C. H. B. Joly）

瑷珲关署理税务司

该抄件内容真实有效,特此证明:

录事：陈培因 三等二级税务员

附录2

1931年1月20日滨江关致瑷珲关第103/1222号文抄件

（回复瑷珲关第125/243号文）

尊敬的瑷珲关税务司：

根据瑷珲关第125/243号文：

"关于黑龙江省政府要求松花江水道委员会协济黑龙江水道委员会一事；建议由瑷珲关全权管理黑龙江水道委员会资金，以免松花江航路标志资金受到侵害。"

本署已在关于海关总税务司署致瑷珲关第132077号令的意见中提出，应由黑龙江和吉林省政府全权负责黑龙江和乌苏里江航路标志所需资金的筹备事宜，并预支相关款项，最后再以两江江捐税收抵之。兹认为，松花江水道委员会迟早将由省政府接管，因此需要留有足够资金来支付相关职员的养老储金。

至于由瑷珲关全权管理黑龙江水道委员会资金一事，兹认为，此事责任重大，已超出海关职权范围。此外，中央政府和省政府的最终目的绝不仅仅是干涉货物税收的相关事宜，而是要接管海关的一切事务。而贵署之建议恰与政府意图相悖，势必遭到反驳；且海关已身负重担，若再承担管理资金之责，恐会过于繁重。

您忠诚的仆人

覃书（Rened' Anjou）

滨江关税务司

该抄件内容真实有效，特此证明：

录事：陈培因 三级二等税务员

附录 3

1931 年 1 月 13 日瑷珲关税务司致滨江关税务司半官函抄件

尊敬的覃书（Rened'Anjou）先生：

万望勿对瑷珲关第 125 号文有何误解，本人并非意图凸显瑷珲关的重要性，而是为表达对未来之担忧。兹认为，唯有迎难而上，按照瑷珲关第 125 文中所述之办法，主动承担协济黑龙江水道委员会的责任，方为可靠之策。

根据本人对大黑河地区实际情况的了解，以及从新任黑河市政筹备处处长处了解的信息，可以推测出黑龙江省政府已有意占用黑龙江水道委员会账户上的 15000 银圆余额（1925 年 9 月 21 日海关总税务司署致瑷珲关第 253/104793 号令和 1926 年 6 月 29 日海关总税务司署致瑷珲关第 300/108242 号令共批准松花江水道委员会借给黑龙江水道委员会40000 银圆）。

黑河市政筹备处处长告知，黑龙江省政府已从广信公司借款 15000 银圆，并欲由松花江水道委员会偿付该笔债款；另已向财政部申请拨款 15000 银圆用于向俄方支付 1930年中俄联合航路标志协议所定金额的最后一笔分期款项。然该笔款项仅为 11300 银圆，实不知余下之 3700 银圆将作何用途！

由此可知，黑龙江省政府从未考虑过向松花江水道委员会偿还此前的 25000 银圆欠款，而是意图将资助黑龙江水道委员会之责强加给松花江水道委员会。目前，海关并无管理航路标志资金之权，而黑龙江省政府又可动用松花江水道委员会的资金余额，恐怕将来省政府会频繁占用松花江航路标志的经费。

海关此前对黑龙江航路标志资金尚有一定的管理权限，但按月向黑河市政筹备处处长上交江捐税收后，便消失殆尽。此外，兹认为，举凡松花江航路标志资金存有余额，南京方面必会驳回所有反对意见，按照东北政务委员会的建议，支持黑龙江省政府的拨款要求。由此本人更加确信，以由松花江水道委员会承担协济黑龙江水道委员会的责任换取海关对航路标志资金的完全管理权乃为唯一的解决办法。

若按照本人之建议，松花江水道委员会将无需立即向黑龙江水道委员会拨发 30000 银圆的协济款。当然若地方政府最终无力向俄方支付 11300 银圆的尾款，依然会需要援助，但最多不超过 15000 银圆。此外，依据现有安排，是否将未结清的 25000 银圆欠款勾销，结果并无不同，毕竟确保每年年末航路标志账户中无结余方为要紧之事。海关最终若可获得黑龙江航路标志资金的管理权，或还有偿还该笔欠款之可能。

周骊（C. H. B. Joly）

瑷珲关署理税务司

该抄件内容真实有效，特此证明：

录事：陈培因 三级二等税务员

附录4

1931 年 1 月 22 日滨江关税务司致瑷珲关税务司半官函抄件

（回复 1931 年 1 月 13 日瑷珲关税务司半官函）

尊敬的周骊（C. H. B. Joly）先生：

　　关于黑龙江省政府要求松花江水道委员会资助黑龙江水道委员会一事，本人一直深信，无论海关如何强调两个委员会的独立性，最终仍需做出让步。黑龙江省政府深知松花江水道委员会财务状况良好，相信很快就会将之接管。本人所关心的是遣散洋籍航路标志职员一事，他们在工作中忠于职守，英勇无畏，有时为完成工作，甚至不顾生命危险，理应得到合理安置。但承担协济黑龙江水道委员会的责任绝非明智之举，此事牵扯众多政治势力，相信黑龙江省政府亦未必会予以同意。

覃书（Rened' Anjou）

滨江关税务司

该抄件内容真实有效，特此证明：

录事：陈培因 三等二级税务员

呈海关总税务司署 <u>539</u> 号文　　　　　　　　瑷珲关 1931 年 2 月 10 日

尊敬的海关总税务司（上海）：

　　1. 根据瑷珲关第 492 号呈：

　　　　"说明黑龙江水道委员会的财务状况及其拖欠松花江水道委员会 25000 银圆债款一事；汇报接受暂代黑河市政筹备处处长之提议，按月向其上交江捐税收（扣除 10% 海关征税佣金）后，会造成之影响，尤其对航务专门顾问易保罗（P. I. Ignatieff）先生继续任职一事之影响。"

及海关总税务司署第 132077 号令：

　　　　"请通过滨江关税务司与松花江水道委员会进行洽谈，以确定是否可照黑龙江省政府之提议，将黑龙江水道委员会未结清的欠款一笔勾销，并另行划拨 30000 银圆协济黑龙江水道委员会，待与松花江水道委员会达成协定后，再呈文汇报；请瑷珲关每月扣除 10% 海关征税佣金后，将江捐税收移交给暂代黑河市政筹备处处长；继续雇用易保罗（P. I. Ignatieff）先生，其薪俸及津贴将由江捐税收净额支付。"

及瑷珲关第 532 号呈：

　　　　"汇报黑龙江江捐账户资金仅够支付易保罗（P. I. Ignatieff）先生一月份薪俸及津贴事；申请批准在必要时自瑷珲关 D 账户暂付款账下支取款额为其发放薪俸及津贴，日后由江捐税收偿付。"

及瑷珲关第 536 号呈：

　　　　"汇报通过滨江关税务司与松花江水道委员会就黑龙江省政府两项提议进行谈判之结果。"

　　兹汇报，按照滨江关海关监督传达之黑河市政筹备处处长的最新要求，松花江水道委员会已通过滨江关税务司再次向黑龙江水道委员会预支 15000 银圆。此为海关总税务司署至滨江关第 104776 号令和 108241 号令批准松花江水道委员会预支给黑龙江水道委员会协济之款的第四笔，亦是最后一笔款项。由此，黑龙江水道委员会的未结欠款已由 25000 银圆增至 40000 银圆。

　　2. 松花江水道委员会预支的 15000 银圆已记入黑龙江江捐账户项下，扣除 74.63 银圆银行手续费后，实际到账金额为 14925.37 银圆。该笔款项可供黑龙江水道委员会向俄方支付 1930 年中俄联合航路标志协议所定金额的最后一笔分期款项 11300 银圆；同时还可支付 1931 年 5 月 1 日前易保罗（P. I. Ignatieff）先生的薪俸及津贴。

您忠诚的仆人

周骊（C. H. B. Joly）

瑷珲关署理税务司

专题二

年度航务报告

1. 为 1922 年及 1923 年黑龙江航务年度报告事

ENCLOSURE.

AIDS TO NAVIGATION ON THE AMUR.

REPORT WRITTEN BY MR. P.I.IGNATIEFF, TECHNICAL ADVISER ON
AMUR AIDS TO NAVIGATION OF WORK DONE BY HIS DEPARTMENT
DURING 1922 AND 1923.

CUSTOM HOUSE,
Aigun/Taheiho, 27th. March, 1924.

Sir,

1.   When preparing an account of the work done
by the Chinese Maritime Customs at Taheiho from
the time the Sino-Russian Technical Agreement on
Aids to Navigation of the Amur was signed, viz.
from the 27th June 1922, I would stress the great
advantage which China has gained and will still
gain, by this Agreement.

Enclosure .2.   The river Amur with its tributaries is one
Chart.   of the mightiest navigable rivers, and its Aids to
Navigation erected by Russia were thought to be
the best. Before the out-break of the revolution
this river was navigated exclusively by Russian
steamers. In the year 1897 the Russian Amur
Navigation Office was established, to attend to all
water-ways in the Amur basis. This Office was
subject to the Central Government in St. Petersburg.
During the period 1895 to 1917, 36,857,000 Gold
Roubles were expended on the improvement of
Navigation conditions on the rivers in the Amur
basis. For the maintenance of the Amur Navigation
Office the Government assigned over 3,000,000 Gold
Roubles

The Inspector General of Customs,
      PEKING.

Roubles yearly. By this means the Bay Aids to
Navigation, over 7,000 versts, were maintained; and
the entire water-way from Stretensk to Nikolaevsk,
a distance of 3,028 versts, and from Blagoveschensk
to the Zeya, a distance of 610 versts, was lighted
during the Navigation Season. The total navigable
length of the Amur and its large tributaries is
roughly 10,000 versts. For the maintenance of the
channel 5 dredges were constantly at work. Surveys
of rivers and shallows were carried out; the shores
cleared and stones removed. A few steamers, steam
launches and barges were employed to attend to Aids
to Navigation and dredge-works.

3.   The Amur River Fleet consisted until 1917 of
208 steamers, (not counting 71 vessels, such as:
steamboats, motor-boats and barges in the charge of
Amur Navigation Office and the Amur River Navy), 44
motor-launches, and 269 barges, on which during the
Navigation in 1911 over 80,000,000 poods of transitory
and local cargo as well as about 621,000 passengers
were carried. Owing to the revolution in Russia
and the consequent general state-collapse the entire
Russian State Transport has been ruined; 40% of the
private Fleet went over into Chinese hands, and the
remaining Amur Steamship and Trading Co. was
nationalised. From that time, owing to the lack of
transitory and local cargo, the Russian Transport
gradually began to decrease, and if a small part
of the Transport still exists until now, it is only
thanks to an excellent former state of the machinery
and hull-construction and the left reserve-parts.

4.   From the beginning of the revolution the

state

state of the Amur Navigation Office also gradually grew worse; the sums assigned for the maintenance and upkeep of Aids to Navigation became less and less, and in 1922 the Amur Navigation Office received instructions to merge with the Water Transport into one body, and it was decided that for its upkeep a certain percentage on goods carried should be levied. But as there was little cargo to carry, the means for the repairs of Aids to Navigation and lighting of same did not suffice, and it was in that period of monetary crisis that the idea of carrying on the repairs and upkeep of Aids to Navigation on the frontier section of the Amur together with China has germinated. It was after the Russo-Chinese war, as far back as 1907, that the question of elaborating mutual rules for the Navigation on the frontier waters of the Amur was raised, and in the winter of 1908-09 this matter was discussed by a Sino-Russian commission, but a mutual agreement was not arrived at and the question remained unsolved.

4. As a result of the revolution in Russia, and the transfer of a part of the Russian fleet into Chinese hands, Chinese steamers began to navigate the rivers in the frontier section of the Amur basis for the first time.

5. The first Sino-Russian Agreement, concerning a mutual upkeep and repairs of Aids to Navigation on the frontier section of the Amur, was concluded and signed on 27th. June 1922, for the period from 1st. June to 31st. December, 1922. In view of the deficiency and the general character of

some

some articles of the Agreement and Regulations, a few changes and supplements were introduced afterwards. The estimate, presented by the Amur Navigation Office for 1922 was also revised and changed.

7.   Before the expiration of the term of the Agreement of 1922, the question of its extension was discussed, but the Representatives of the Russian Water Transport, in connection with the arrival in China of Mr. Karakhan, Russian Diplomatic Representative received instructions to refrain from further parleys and consequently the latter were interrupted; but it was proposed by the local Chinese Authorities to accelerate and submit the accounts for work done in 1922. In the beginning of April 1923 the Representatives of the Russian Water Transport proposed to discuss the extension of the 1922 Agreement to the years 1923 - 24 and as the Taoyin consented a meeting was held in April. At this meeting the wording of the Agreement and Regulations was mutually worked out and afew changes made in that of 1922; but the inclusion in the Agreement of the 4th part though requested by the Chinese Authorities, was objected to by the Russian Representatives, as it had reference to the question of Navigation as far as Habarovsk and Nikolsevsk. The Russian Representatives not having full powers, refrained from giving any definite reply, arguing that this question was beyond the lines of a Technical Agreement and that as it had a political character, it should be submitted to the consideration of the Sino-Russian Conference, which was to take place at an early date in Peking. In June 1923 the Hei-ho Taoyin sent a letter to the

Russian

Russian Water Transport proposing not to include the
4th part in the Technical Agreement, but to add
it as a supplement, and to send it for decision to
the Conference at Pekin. From the Russian
Representatives, owing to the departure of and change
in, the Chief Directors, no reply was received, and
it was only in September 1923, after the return
of the member of the Administration of the Water
Transport, Mr. Legutin, Engineer, from a tour of
inspection that the question of concluding an
Agreement for 1923 was finally gone into with the
consent of the Hei Ho Taoyin.

8.   In view of the high water which prevailed
during the navigation season 1923 no repairs to
Aids to navigation were undertaken. For the purpose
of examining the channel after such high water and
performing small repairs, I requested the Russian
Amur Navigation Office to despatch immediately two
steam-launches, one up-and the other down-stream.
The Russian side, having approved of it, the steamboats
were sent and the work performed.

        Owing to the decision to make a few alterations
both in the wording of the Agreement, and in the
Regulations, the signing of the Agreement took place
only on the 28th October 1923, and that of the
Additional Rules on the 30th November 1923.
Simultaneously the Amur Navigation Office submitted
their Estimates for 1923, i.e. from 1st January to
30th November 1923, the end of their financial year,
amounting to 19,250 Gold Roubles. After the Agreement
for 1923 was signed, the final examination of the
Accounts of 1922 was made. These were then found
                          to

to be quite correct; within the limits of the
Estimate; with all receipts, documents affixed.

9.   As soon as the Technical Agreement for a
mutual upkeep and repairs of Aids to Navigation in
the frontier section of the Amur for 1922 was
signed, the collection of River Dues was begun:
the Russian side from May, according to the Law
of the Far Eastern Republic of 17th May, and the
Chinese Side from June, according to the Annex
to the Agreement.

          At the end of June 1922, for the purpose
of performing repairs to Aids to Navigation, the
first advance was issued by the Chinese Customs
to the Russians. Accordingly the Russian side
started to examine the channel and to repair old
and erect new Signals.

          In September 1922 the Acting Commissioner of
Aigun Customs, Mr. Boezi, undertook a voyage from
Taheiho to Lokuho (Lokrovka) with a view to
examining all really working Traffic and Depth-Signal
Stations; all repaired and newly erected Signals.
In August the Senior Outdoor Staff Officer, Mr. Baukham,
started down-stream and made an examination of the
repairs of Aids to Navigation from Taheiho to the
mouth of the Sungari. From the mouth of the
Sungari to Habarovsk the Aids to Navigation which
were destroyed by Russian military detachments in
1920 were re-erected after his trip. These
investigations proved that the upkeep and repairs
of Aids to Navigation were satisfactory, and
consequently it was resolved to accept the expenditure
incurred

incurred within the limits of the Estimate.

At the same time as the question of concluding a Technical Agreement was raised, the Acting Commissioner of the Aigun Customs, Mr. Boezi, sent in a suggestion to the Inspector General of Customs to engage a specialist, in the capacity of Technical Adviser on Aids to Navigation from 16th September 1922. As I had been in the employ of the Russian Amur Navigation Office over 13 years as River Inspector in the Amur basis, I was invited by the Harbin Commissioner to take up the appointment. I arrived at Taheiho on 4th October and reported for duty.

10.   Consideration of Estimate for 1922. While perusing the wording of the Agreement, and considering the Estimate for 1922, submitted by the Amur Navigation Office, I found it necessary to make a few additions to the Agreement, as well as a few alterations in the Estimate. For instance, I disallowed expenditure on removal of stones, but sanctioned a small sum for the maintenance of the Amur Navigation Office (formerly Blagovestchensk Technical Section).

The General Estimate amounting to Gold Roubles 32,475.50 for the upkeep of Aids to Navigation and works in the frontier section of the Amur for the period 1st May to 31st December 1922 was confirmed.

Besides, the Sino-Russian Commission accepted the estimates for the maintenance of the Taoyin's Office amounting to $ 2,057.50 and that for the Custom House, amounting to $ 2,145.76.

11.   Removal of break-water. After having acquainted
                                                        myself

myself with the local conditions under which steamers
came into port and went along side the wharves,
I carried out a survey of the Taheiho Harbour and
proved the great harm done by the break-water, which
was built by the Wu-tung S.S. Co. in 1919 to
accommodate their steamers in the winter. In April
1923 a part of the break-water had to be removed
in order to allow the current an unimpeded access
into the Harbour. The Harbour had silted up during
the past few years, and the sand-bank, which had
already existed before, rose considerably and thereby
became dangerous for plying steamers. To obviate
this danger, a red beacon with a red light was
placed on the upper end of the spit during 1923.

12.   Erection of Water-gauge. To have a more regular
observation of the fluctuation of water in the Amur,
a Water-gauge was set-up in Taheiho. This station
was opened on 1st February 1923, and the respective
sea-level was connected through Blagovestchensk with
that of the Pacific Ocean.

13.   Removal of stones from channel. The great
water-fall in winter and subsequent thawing of snow
on the shore of the Taheiho Harbour revealed many
stones, and 4.25 cubic sajens were removed at the
end of April, at a cost of $38.42.

14.   Improvement of Quay. Owing to the spring
drift-ice; to summer floods; and particularly to
the waves caused by the prevailing strong north
winds, the river shore at Taheiho Port was to a
great extent washed away and gradually destroyed,
so that the Custom House, being situated on the
Quay, was this year (1923) only 50 feet from the

edge

edge of the bank. Taking into consideration that the further washing and dashing of the waves against the bank would greatly diminish the size of the Quay, where the Customs Administration examines cargo in summer, and the more so in winter; and also considering that from a technical point of view there was risk of danger to the Custom House by the sinking of foundations and the cracking of walls, it was decided to strengthen the bank by means of fascines and stone-layers, 240 feet long and 34 feet broad. A total space of 7,066 square feet was strengthened at the expense $ 313.38. As the shore in this place is yearly washed away (in the Navigation Season of 1923 over 14 feet) I recommend that some 214 feet more up the river be similarly strengthened so that the Water-gauge, which is a little way up-stream, may be included in the improved space. A proposal to this effect was already made by me in 1923, but not all private house-owners consented to assign the required sum, and thus the question was left unsolved. It would be desirable to carry out this improvement even from the balance of River Dues Collections, assigned for the maintenance of the Technical Adviser's Office.

15.   Water-gauge records. To notify the steamship owners of the state of water in the Amur and the Sungari during the Navigation Season 1923, the Custom House arranged for the receipt of telegraphic information which it displayed in the Office. The steamship owners were guided by this informations when freighting ships.

16.   Navigation 1923. The great mass of snow that fell

fell in the winter 1922-23, owing to a cold spring
thawed away gradually, and therefore there was no
simultaneous drift-ice in the entire basis. The ice
off Taheiho stirred for the first time on 27th and
29th April; then on the Beliaevsky shallows, 18
versts up the Amur, and on the Zeya shallows, 4
versts down-stream the ice was heaped up, and the
current off Taheiho became clear of ice. On 7th
May when the water rose to over 14 feet the ice
broke up entirely and the floe lasted 3 days.
On 10th May the ferry steamboat "Daur" began to
operate on the Amur, and on 13th May the first
S.S. Hsiking and Chinglan having left Harbin on
25th and 28th April, arrived here in Port.

The dredge belonging to the Tsitsihar Bank,
which remained during winter behind the break-water,
did not suffer any damage at first while the ice
was stirring and breaking up, but as it was not
drawn nearer to the shore in time, on the 8th May
it was cut into by the floe and sunk. Eventually the dredge was lifted and repaired at the
local works of Mr. Chepurin. On 9th May the
steam-boiler of the Russian S.S. "Moscow", which
hibernated in Taheiho Port, burst when undergoing
a hydraulic trial by a Russian expert, but it was
eventually repaired in Taheiho by Mr. Chepurin.

During the Navigation Season 1923 particularly
high water prevailed. The highest water-level was
observed on 16th June - 420.5 feet by the Pacific
sea-level; the lowest water-level was observed on
11th November - 399.3 feet. Thus the fluctuation of
water was over 21 feet. There were three great
floods in the Zeya: the 1st at the end of May;
the

the 2nd and greatest, in the middle of July; and
the 3rd in September. The fluctuation of the winter
and summer water-level was about 28 feet. All
low-lying villages, gardens, cultivated land, and
meadows were inundated, and all vegetables, products,
and hay were destroyed. Famine dominates now in
those districts.

On the Sungari no shallow water was observed
even at the very end of the Navigation Season.
The depth on Sansing Shallows was not under 3 feet
during the whole season. It was above the average,
and at the end of August and September the water
was particularly high, even over 8.75 feet. The
high water in the entire Amur basis throughout the
whole Navigation Season had in many places, particularly
where the river-bed was sandy, both in the Sungari
as well as the lower Zeya, washed away and changed
the channel. In the Amur, as having a more solid
bottom (gravel) no great channel-changes were
discovered during the October investigations.

Thanks to high water the traffic-depth in
the Sungari as well as the Amur was great and
exceeded that required: besides there was little
cargo to be carried, and therefore the conditions
of plying in the Navigation Season 1923 may be
regarded as having been facile, in spite of the
fact that Aids to Navigation had not been repaired
and new Signals erected to take the place of those
that were rotten, burned, or carried away.

On the Amur the bandits did not molest the
steamers, as was the case on the Sungari.

Thanks to high water the plying of Chinese
Steamers in the frontier section of the Amur, Argun
and

and Ussuri was done under favourable conditions, and during the Navigation Season there were only two accidents - 1st the rudder of the barge Sheli, freighted with fire-wood and towed by S.S. Yang Hu was broken when passing the Bussevsky shallows (100 versts above Taheiho); and 2nd: the barge Ta Ming, freighted with fire-wood and towed by the S.S. San Shui, ran aground on the Upper-Sichevsky shallows (100 versts below Taheiho). The comparatively early drift-ice that began on the 24th October in the Taheiho-Pashkovo (Paohsingshan) section did not allow the stern-wheel wooden S.S. I Hsing belonging to the Wut'ung Co. to arrive in this Port, and 10 versts from Taheiho, having been cut by the ice, she was forced to make for the Chinese shore. There she sank, having damaged about 30 % of her cargo. The two wheeled S.S. Yang Hu, having in tow the barge She Li, could not, owing to dense drift-ice, pass the Zeya-Shallows, and therefore was forced to leave the barge 7 versts below Taheiho near the village Ch'angfat'un. The S.S. Yang Hu, however, managed to reach Taheiho where she tied up for the winter. Three Russian steam-tugs with barges also failed to reach Blagovestchensk and were forced to remain 100 versts from Blagovestchensk.

17.   Hibernation of steamers. In the winter 1923-24 the following steamers remained in Taheiho-Harbour: S.S. Aigun, Shao Hsing, Chi Yang, Shun Tien, Moscow and the two-wheeled S.S. Yang Hu, the iron barge Fu Hsien and the Tsitsihar Bank dredge.

18.   Repairs to Aids to Navigation in 1923. By means of the steam launches Hin-gan and Komsomolets the fairway was examined in the whole frontier section of the Amur from Blagovestchensk to Kasakevich, and as

the

the course of the channel had changed, the position of the Signals had to be altered; all Signals that stood too near the banks were removed farther in and the grass was cut, and ditches dug, to preserve them from autumn and spring fires; trees that were hiding from view the Signals in the sight-line were felled; shields repaired and new ones erected; signals, both those that had been cut down maliciously and those that fell from other causes, were raised and re-erected. A description of the state of the Signals was made, and the extent of repairs to old ones and the number of new Signals to be erected in the Navigation Season 1924, was decided. Likewise all water-depth, Traffice, and Water-gauge Stations were inspected, and enquiry made as to the number of the personnel and the time of their being engaged. The books kept at the respective stations, and the inventories and materials were also examined. All housing accommodation was inspected, and the necessary repairs for 1924 estimated. Likewise the five Offices of the District-surveyors were inspected, viz: that at Jalinda, Chernayevo, Blagovestchensk, Innokentieva and Ekaterino-Nikolsk, and at the same time all accounts, salaries and pay-lists were verified. The inventories and rowing-boats were also inspected. The latter owing to the lack of any repairs during more than 4 years, are rather ruined. The Signals in the Amur section from the mouth of the Sungari to Kasakevich, which were erected during the Navigation Season of 1922 in place of those cut down by Russian military detachments, do not answer by far the requirements of navigation in this section; they do not correspond with the conventional type. For the

the width of the Amur and the long reaches in that
section, the Signals are too small and their props
too short; moreover there are no wedges, and therefore
the Signals do not stand steady. I have therefore
proposed a more simplified type of the former River-
and Sea-type Signals, which are much cheaper, and
this type will be erected in the Navigation Season
of 1924.

The cost of river-type Signals has been too
high, i.e. 20 roubles with another 8 roubles for a
shield. A sea-type pyramid has cost about 22 roubles
with 15 roubles for a shield. The price varied in
different places. I am of the opinion that in future
new river-type Signals with shields should cost no
more than from 8 - 10 roubles; and a pyramid from
15 - 20 roubles. The cost of reparation work should
be diminished by one-half 2 - 3 roubles for a
river-type Signal, and 4 - 5 roubles for a pyramid.
The estimates of April 1923 submitted by the Amur
Navigation Office for the repairs and upkeep of Aids
to Navigation, in which cost of Signals was placed
at far too high a figure, amounted to 60,800 gold
roubles, whereas the estimate prepared by the Customs
amounted to 40,000 gold roubles only.

While re-examining the estimates in autumn it
was found possible to diminish them further so as to make
them agree with the actual expenditure incurred by
the Amur Navigation Office. The diminished estimate
amounting to 19,250 gold roubles was confirmed on
16th January 1924, by the mixed provisional local
Technical Commission, and in conformity with Article
15 of the Regulations added to the Agreement, 50%
of the confirmed estimate have to be issued by the
Chinese side. So far only a part, i.e. 5,000 gold

roubles

roubles have been paid on account, the remainder
being kept until the annual account for 1923 has
been submitted and verified.

In the Navigation Season of 1923 only 4
shallows were lighted, i.e. the Zeya, Konstantinova,
Soyus and Ekaterino-Nikolsk, likewise the Taheiho -
Lahasusu section, as having a most lively navigation.
In the upper section, Taheiho - Moho, two Traffic -
Stations were opened, viz: the Beketovsky and
Tsagayansky, and only two most dangerous shallows:
the Chernayavsky and Permikinsky were attended to.

During my expedition up-stream I examined the
charts of the entire frontier section of the Amur,
and from Poyarkovo new charts were made on a smaller
scale, the latter being more convenient. At the
same time lists indicating places with fire-wood on
the Chinese side were drawn up. These lists showed
the quantity of fire-wood stacked and left at the
end of the Navigation Season.

It must be remarked that the greatest care
in former times was given to the Signals on the
Russian as well as Chinese sides, whereas at present
many accidents take place - e.g. the shields of Signals
and pyramids are torn off; the props and even the
Signals cut down. The Director of the Amur Navigation
Office had issued a notification warning thereby the
population that severe punishment will follow the
destruction of Signals, and this order will be sent
to all Russian settlements in the frontier section.

When the Amur Navigation Office was started,
i.e. 1897, the frontier region from Pokrovka to
Habarovsk, 1769 versts long, was divided into 5
Districts, each of which was over 300 versts long,
and at night all signals were lighted. Now, when
the

the Aids to Navigation are used only by day, it was by some inexplicable reason found necessary to divide the region into 6 Districts. I find this entirely superfluous, and in the estimates for 1924 I propose to allow for only 5 Districts which is what I did in 1923.

I consider as quite rational, that the annual personnel for a District should consist of: I District Surveyor, I Foreman, and I Watchman. The above was included by me into the estimates. The Offices, as well as living houses of the District Surveyor, Foreman and Watchman, and of the watchmen of Depth-Signal and Traffic Stations will be in the houses built by the Amur Navigation Office and as no rent is paid, I propose to put into the estimate 5 % as one year's Depreciation of the houses. For the use of the equipment and the rowing boats - 10% of the cost-price will be written off as Depreciation of that property.

19.   Plying of Russian steamers on Chinese side.
In the Navigation Season 1922, when the Chinese steamers were permitted to proceed as far as Habarovsk, Russian steamers enjoyed the right of navigating the Sungari and attended to the needs of the Chinese side along the Amur and Argun. Out of the total 612 steamers that came to Taheiho Port, 190 were Chinese, and 422 were Russian. Two Russian steam launches, "Hingan" and "Komsomoletz" that plyed between Taheiho and Chikete every other day, are included in the above number. The following quantity of cargo was carried: 1,900,000 poods by Chinese, and 1,100,000 poods by Russian, steamers. The number of passengers carried by Chinese steamers
was

was 14,000 by Russian steamers 17,000. 1,000,000 poods of cargo were exported from Taheiho to Blagovestchensk by steamers and ferry-boat. From Blagovestchensk to Taheiho 100,000 poods of cargo were imported, and 4,000 cubic sajens of fire-wood were exported from China to Russia.

In the Navigation Season 1923, when the Chinese steamers were deprived of the privilege of navigating the Amur as far as Harbarovsk, and Soviet Russian steamers the privilege of navigating the Sungari, the Russian steamers continued to attend to the Chinese side along the Amur and Argun. In the Taheiho - Moho section plied S.S."Bistry" and others; in the Taheiho - Chikete section plied two steam launches: "Hingan" and "Komsomosletz". The latter made 55 cruises and derived good profit before the frontier was closed and a boycott unanimously carried out by all Chinese against Russians. With the closing of the frontier these steam launches had to return to Russia, and then two steamers of Wut'ung Co., viz: S.S."Chi Yang"up-stream, and S.S. "Shen Yang" down-stream , began to ply in these sections.

In 1923, 164 Chinese steamers arrived in Taheiho Port, and 1,085,000 poods of cargo and 21,000 passengers were carried on same. The fire-wood exported to Russia is not included here. The above named Russian steam launches carried 45,000 poods of cargo and 2,000 passengers during their short-term navigation.

2,000 cubic sajens of fire-wood were carried over to Blagovestchensk. From the above stated data we see that the work of Russian Steamers on the Chinese side is considerable, but no Chinese Steamers are privileged to ply on the Russian side. This circumstance does not seem to correspond with the
time

time and it should be necessary to solve it somehow.

20.   Turnover of cargo of Chinese steamers in the frontier section of the Amur. When the results of the harvest of 1922 were known, a most acute speculation began to dominate the Harbin mart, and the prices of wheat and flour sprang suddenly high. The Taheiho and Aigun merchants availed themselves of this opportunity and forwarded their stock of wheat and flour to Harbin. From statistics we draw the conclusion that the boycott and the closing of the frontier affected the turnover of cargo carried on Chinese steamers most unfavourably.

In 1922 over 600 steamers arrived in Taheiho, and over 3,000,000 poods of sundry cargo; 2,500,000 poods of fire-wood and timber, and about 31,000 passengers were carried on same. In the Navigation Season 1923 only about 200 steamers came to Taheiho, and 1,150,000 poods of cargo, 2,100,000 poods of timber and fire-wood, and about 23,000 passengers were carried on same.

21.   Timber and Fire-wood. Until 1915, felling and rafting was carried out chiefly by Russians, but now the same is done by Chinese exclusively, and there are over 20 wood-cutter settlements. As regards places with fire-wood for sale between Taheiho and Pokrovka, there are over 90 where there are more than 17,000 cubic sajens in stock, 80% of this fire-wood being old stock. When navigation was more brisk a large quantity, i.e. from 5,000 - 10,000 cubic sajens a year, was exported by Russian steamers to Blagoveschensk, but now that the frontier is closed to trade, the merchants are left with this enormous stock of fire-wood in their hands and they cannot

find

find a market for it close by, and the price of fire-wood has dropped to the lowest minimum. Furthermore several steamers, both Russian and Chinese, have been taken off the up river run, and this has helped to reduce the consumption of fire-wood considerably.

Birch fire-wood from Taheiho to Chernayeva district, a distance of 425 versts, 1 arshine in length, costs from $ 1.40. to 1.80; and from Chernaeva up river from $ 1.00 to 1.40 per square sajens, whereas the cost price of it, together with taxes, is $ 1.60.

Between Taheiho and Kasakevich there are over 50 places with fire-wood for sale where there were over 6,000 cubic sajens in stock. Only the great quantity, 5,000 cubic sajens, of fire-wood sold here at the price $ 9.00 - 10.50 a cubic sajen for carriage to Harbin by steamers and barges has saved the wood-merchants from utter ruin.

Owing to the very small number of Russian steamers plying and the heavy taxes imposed upon wood-merchants, the Russian settlers along the Amur found it impossible to keep a large quantity of fire-wood in stock, and in the Navigation Season of 1923 fire-wood was supplied to take the place of taxes, with the result that fire-wood remaining was not sufficient to meet the demand of Mail steamers.

Owing to the prohibitive tariff introduced by the Russian Customs in February, it was not found possible to export any great quantity of wood rafted by Chinese in 1922, and as a consequence the rafting of wood in 1923 decreased 75 % when compared with that of 1922. Prices also fell very much. The price of timber, 8 inches thick, is from $ 1.20 to 1.50; that of beams 6 - 7 inches thick, from $ 0.70 - 0.80-1.00.
These

These facts affect small woodcutting companies and
may ruin them ultimately. It must be remarked that
some of these raftsmen produce pitch which they
forward to Harbin. This trade is gradually increasing.

22.   Investigation of the Chinese Amur Region. Having
investigated the water-way on the frontier section of
the Amur in the Navigation Season 1923, I have to
submit the following statement. From the out-break
of the revolution in Russia, the Chinese side of
the Amur from Lokuho to Wenhochen (Innokentieva)
began obviously to populate not only with separate
houses, where the inhabitants chiefly trade with
spirits carried in a large quantity to the Russian
side, but also in large villages, the people of
which occupy themselves not only with felling trees,
floating rafts, cutting and stacking of fire-wood,
but also with agriculture and cattle-breeding. Moreover
new auriferous districts have been found which
likewise favour the founding of new settlements.

        The Chinese river region in the Wenhochen
(Innokentieva) - Irga (Kasakevich) section, during the
time the Amur Railway was built, began to be
populated by many Chinese settlers, mostly merchants,
but now that the frontier is closed and a boycott
declared, trade has entirely ceased and this section
is becoming depopulated, though some settlements are
still prominent, e.g. "Hsing-tung-tao" situated opposite
the Russian Cossack settlement "Soyus", and "Chao-hsing-
chen" and "Tai-ping-kou".

23.   Agriculture and cattle-breeding. Along the right
side of the Amur the mountains recede in many
                                                    places,

places, and between them and the shore there are excellent plains, fit for sowing corn as well as for starting ranches. On over 20 such plains, where settlers have formed pretty large villages consisting of from 30 - 50 houses, the arable land, as well as cattle-breeding, accumulates rapidly. Large herds of horses (200 head) and cattle (150) are grazing on these pastures and the export of corn, horses and cattle is considerable.

24. Hunting. Vast tracts southward between the rivers Amur, Argun, Albasiha and Kumara abound with all kind of wild beasts, but owing to the lack of roads these places are visited only by ~~indigenous Mongols.~~ the natives. The chief occupation of these people is hunting the elk for the sake of its horns, also deer, squirrel, fox and wolf.

25. Gold. A considerable role in the development of this district has been played by gold which is dug by the Government as well as private companies in the neighbourhood surroundings of Hu-ma-ho, Mo-ho, Tai-ping-kou and on the newly discovered mines, 9 versts from the mouth of the Argun on a brook, where shaft-mining in winter only can be undertaken, as in summer the place is flooded. In the winter 1922 and 1923 there were about 2,000 persons at work and the village situated on the Argun, where over 30 new solid block houses have been built became during 1923 a large settlement. The private gold mines near Hsin-li-t'un are also working with such. But the chief or most important mining centre at present is 70 versts from Taheiho, where over 6,000 workmen are digging and extracting gold of

high quality. Over 30 new gold mining companies
have applied for permission to prospect.

26.   <u>Junks</u>: Competitors of steamers are the junks,
which owing to the lack of regular steamship service
and the consequent high freight tariff, carry goods
and fire-wood anywhere, going up the stream as far
as Hu-ma-ho, 250 versts, down to Chikete, and even
200 versts below this place. There are about 60
junks in Taheiho Port, and their capacity is from
400 up to 5,000 poods. Likewise about 10 junks,
capacity 500 poods, operate in Mo-ho - Argun district
where they are going 400 versts up river, supplying
the settlers with all requirements. To these remote
places steamers do not ply and junks charge for
freight up to $ 0.50 - 0.60 a pood.

      The boycott and the closed frontier have
likewise affected most unfavourably the movement of
junks, which, if compared with 1922, has fallen by
50 %.

27.   <u>Post and Telegraph</u>. There are Post and
Telegraph Offices in Taheiho, Aigun, Hu-ma-ho, Mo-ho,
Tai-ping-kou and Hsing-tung-tao, and these render in
a great measure assistance to the coast service
strategically as well as commercially.

28.   <u>Roads</u>: As the ways of communication are the
most important factors in the development of the
colonisation, the greatest care should be bestowed on
this subject.

29.   <u>Organisation of regular S.S. Service</u>. As there
are not overland routes in the entire river region,
                           the

the water-way is the only means of communication, and therefore the development of Steamship Service should receive the most careful consideration.

Ever since the appearence of the Russians on the Amur, a regular Mail and Passenger steamship service has been thought to be the greatest factor in the development of the country, and accordingly a steamship service was started on the Shilka and Amur in 1872, and on the Zeya in 1910.

In the Navigation Season of 1923 the steamship communication between Taheiho and Mo-ho was not a regular one, but had a rather casual character.

The S.S. Chi-Yang of the Wut'ung Co. plied during the whole Navigation Season in the section, making in 14-20 days time one trip. Only 8 trips were made up-stream during the season. Owing to the boycott and closed frontier the only S.S."Chi-yang" was not able to supply the Taheiho - Moho section with the requisite goods and other steamers belonging to the Wut'ung and other Companies availed themselves of this circumstance.

During the Navigation Season in 1923, 18 cruises were made up-stream and approximately 150,000 poods of cargo were carried up, and 36,000 poods of sundry cargo, and 4,000 cubic sajens of fire-wood, down. Before the closing of the frontier 2,000 cubic sajens were exported to Russia (Blagovastchensk) and 2,000 to Harbin.

During the Navigation Season of 1922 over 300,000 poods of cargo were carried up-stream in the Taheiho-Moho section, and the quantity of cargo carried down stream was less than in 1923 by 20,000 poods. Besides in 1922 1,500 cubic sajens of fire-wood were shipped to Taheiho; 2,000 cubic sajens

to

to Blagovestchensk, and 2,000 cubic sajens to Harbin. Thanks to flourishing gold-mining places such as Hu-ma-ho, Hsin-li-t'un, Mo-ho and Elohe, and the general development in the colonisation of the Amur region from Taheiho to Mo-ho and Elohe, (the latter lying 4 versts from the mouth of the Argun) the number of passengers was comparatively large, being 5,400 in 1922 and 5,150 in 1923.

Both the freight rate and the fare had been comparatively high in the Taheiho-Moho section in the Navigation Season of 1922 and 1923 and steamers plying in that section derived good profit.

The freight rate which was rather high in the Harbin-Taheiho section in 1922 ($0.12 - 0.15) fell enormously in 1923. There were occasions when goods were shipped from Taheiho to Harbin for from $0.05-0.06 per pood.

The S.S."Shen-yang" of the Wut'ung Co. which plied between Taheiho and Chikete (147 versts) every 3 days, operated most favourably in one of the most populated Amur regions.

The question of offering the population a regular S.S. communication can be solved only by organising a regular Mail and Passengers S.S. Service in the Taheiho-Lokuho and Taheiho-Chikete sections. The preference should be granted by an agreement to either the Wut'ung or Tung Ya (Wang Yu-ching) steamship Co, and the conditions should require the S.S. Co. to detail two steamers for the Taheiho-Moho-Lokuho section with 10,000 poods of tonnage to leave the Port on a fixed day. A small steamer like the "ShenYang" should ply in the Taheiho-Chikete section. Such a regular Navigation should evoke a more lively traffic of passengers and cargo, for until now, owing to the

irregularity

irregularity and indefiniteness of the departure of steamers up-stream, a great deal of cargo and passengers is carried some 250 versts by junks.

30. **Plying of Chinese steamers as far as Harbarovsk** At out-break of the revolution in Russia, and the transfer of 40% of Russian shipping to Chinese hands, and the organisation of the large Wut'ung Steamship Company, Chinese Steamers began to navigate the Amur as far as Habarovsk. In the latter town, during the Kolchak regime in 1919, and Agency of the Wut'ung Co. was opened, but since the occupation of the Maritime Province by the "Reds" and their consolidation of power, Chinese Steamers plying to Habarovsk and Nikolaevsk began to experience various difficulties and in the winter 1922-23 the Russian Authorities decided to close the Wut'ung Agency in Habarovsk, and withdraw from Chinese Steamers the privilege of plying as far as Habarovsk. In return the Chinese Authorities forbade entry into the Sungari of steamers plying under Soviet colours.

In the Navigation Season 1922 a Russian gun-boat was stationed at the mouth of the Sungari. This gun-boat stopped all Chinese Steamers in order to examine the passports of Russian passengers, but in 1923, about the middle of the Navigation Season, this order was cancelled and all Chinese Steamers now pass unmolested, approaching only the Chinese gun-boat stationed in the mouth of the Sungari for the examination of documents.

31. **Aids to Navigation in the Kasakevich water course stretch:** Now that the plying of Chinese Steamers to Harbarovsk is forbidden the Kasakevich

water

water course necessarily calls for careful consideration, for there are no Aids to Navigation, and even in mid channel it is hardly navigable on account of its many meanderings. Also the Chinese living in the Ussuri region need some means of communication, to obtain supplies by water, as this route is the cheaper. In the Navigation Season of 1923, with the help of the high water which prevailed almost during the whole season, some steamers with barges negotiated the Kasakevich water course and entered the Ussuri, proceeding as far as the Chinese village Ima-kousa, situated opposite the Russian settlement Iman.

Arguing that the plying of Chinese Steamers along the Ussuri is indispensable, I propose to improve the passage for steamers proceeding to the Ussuri by erecting Aids to Navigation along the Kasakevich water course by Signals of a small type.

32.　　River Dues collection. As the Agreement for 1922 was signed so very late, the Chinese side commenced to collect River Dues only in the middle of June 1922. In 1923 the collection was begun from the beginning of the Navigation Season and the following table illustrates the figures of Dues collected on the Chinese side:

Landing places	1922.	1923.
Taheiho	$ 23,932.45	$ 15,068.64
Aigun	$ 1,450.43	$ 2,458.12
Lahasusu	$ 5,754.31	$ 6,243.14
Total	$ 31,137.19	$ 23,769.90

The decreased collection of Dues is to be attributed to the closing of the frontier and the export from Harbin having entirely ceased. While the turnover

of

of goods exported and imported in the Navigation Season of 1922 was 3,000,000 poods, that of 1923 was only 1,130,000. The number of passengers fell from 31,000 to 23,000, and the rafting of wood also decreased by 75 per cent.

On the Russian side, where both in 1922 and 1923 the River Dues Collection was begun from the very beginning of the Navigation Season, the collection was as follows:-

Landing places.		1922.	1923.
Blagovestchensk.......Gold Roubles		8,763.90	13,366.06
Harbarovsk............. " "		28,245.42	12,265.35
Stretensk............. " "		417.64	1,375.00
Nikolaevsk............ " "		...	9,446.02
Upper-Zeya............ " "		442.55	1,310.78
Administration of " " State fleet.		11,823.58	13,539.74
Total " "		49,693.09	51,302.95

The slight increase of River Dues collected in 1923 on the Russian side has not to be attributed to improved import or export generally, but to unusual circumstances. 1st: a great quantity of fish was caught and carried from Nikolaevsk to Blagovestchensk; and 2nd: about 400,000 poods of beans were carried from the Sungari, (instead of the contracted 2,000,000poods) the export of which has ceased with the beginning of the boycott. In the autumn a great lot of wood was rafted because of the high prices of fire-wood in Blagovestchensk. The latter circumstance was due to the boycott and closed frontier, when the Russian Water Transport was deprived of the possibility of carrying fire-wood from the Chinese side. But in the main the large sums collected on the Russian side are due to the

increased

increased rate of River Dues which are collected in accordance with the Law of the Far Eastern Republic of 17th May 1922. These Dues are levied in full, irrespective of the distance and section. On the Chinese side, however, the frontier district is divided into 2 sections: (1) Kasakevich - Taheiho, (2) Taheiho - Moho, and in each section only a half of the rate is charged.

The River Dues collections on inland rivers in the Amur basis are very small owing to the lack of any transit goods from Nikolaevsk to Stretensk, and to the decreased gold-mining business on the Zeya, Selemdja, Bureya and Argun.

33.   Verification of Accounts for 1922. In December 1923 I made an examination of the accounts presented by Amur Navigation Office in connection with the expenses on the repairs and upkeep of Aids to Navigation in the frontier section of the Amur, during the Navigation Season of 1922. I found that expenses did not exceed, but were made according to, the sum assigned as per estimates, and though some separate items exceeded the estimated amounts, other items showed a saving. The expense on the personnel exceeded the estimate by 757.13 Gold Roubles as the salary of some employees was increased during the Navigation Season. A saving in expenditure of 3,295.75 Gold Roubles was got because many Traffic and Depth-Signal Stations did not work at all, and others were operated only temporarily. 1,009.13 Gold Roubles were saved in connection with the despatching of information re water depth of shallows, as some of the latter stations were not opened. The telegraph accounts were granted credit by the Telegraph

Department

these

Department and as were presented too late to be included in the annual Accounts of the Amur Navigation Office, the latter debited the inland rivers with this account. The sum expended on the lighting of shallows and travelling allowances, exceeded the estimates by Gold Roubles 453.97 and 356.03 respectively and the original estimates were too small.

The Property Depreciation Account (buildings and boats) was diminished by me from 3,270.47 to 2,444.21 Gold Roubles. The original figure was cut down because I found out that some living houses, store houses and rowing boats could be excluded. The above Depreciation expenses had not been foreseen in the Estimates, but District Surveyors, Foremen and Traffic and Shallows Watchers have to be supplied with living accommodation and but for existing quarters it would be necessary to rent houses. This would be more expensive and it might be difficult to secure quarters in unpopulated places. I therefore considered it fair to accept this Account, especially as the total expenses were less than allowed for by the Estimate.

The total estimated amount for 1922 was **32,376.20** Gold Roubles, and expenditure, as per presented documents, 31,766.05 Gold Roubles. I considered it indispensable to draw the attention of Amur Navigation Office to the fact that in future years care should be taken to foresee all considerable expenses in the Estimates in order to avoid non-estimated expenditure. Besides I advised them not to deviate from, but strictly to keep to the amount actually authorised by the Estimate, and on no

account

account to exceed the salary estimates without first obtaining permission.

According to the resolutions of the Sino-Russian Joint Commission passed at the session of 24th October 1922, all expenses on the upkeep and repairs of Aids to Navigation during the year in the frontier part of the Amur were to be covered proportionately out of the sums of River Dues collected:

The Chinese side will pay 100% of all Dues collected;

The Russian side will pay 2/3rds of the total collection.

34. Collection on the Chinese side 1922: In accordance with the information of the Aigun Customs, communicated by the Acting Commissioner of Customs on the 21st January, 1923, the total amount of Dues collected on the Chinese side in 1922 was 33,929.47 Gold Roubles and deducting 10% in favour of the Customs, according to Article 5 of the Regulations of the Agreement of 27th May, 1922, the sum of ....Gold.Roubles 30,536.47 was handed over as net proceeds in favour of the Commission.

Collection on the Russian side 1922: According to the Account List of River Dues collected by the Amur Navigation Office, the total amount of Dues collected was 49,693.13 Gold Roubles. Deducting 10% in accordance with Article 5 of the "Regulations" the amount of Dues collected amounted to 44,723.13 Gold Roubles, and of this sum 2/3rds equals .... Gold Roubles 29,815.33 which amount was handed over to the disposition of the Joint Commission.

The Grand total received by the Commission was Gold Roubles 60,351.80

35. The

35. <u>The total amount of expenses to be covered by the</u>

<u>Sino-Russian Commission 1922:</u>

The Russian side expended on the upkeep
of the frontier water sections as per
Account List of the Amur Navigation
Office .... Gold Roubles   31,766.05

The same on the Chinese side, according
to a confirmed Estimate..... Gold Roubles   4,241.54

                                    "   "   36,007.59

The above expenditure will be covered proportionately
as follows:-

The Russian side pays 49.4% ... Gold Roubles   17,787.85

The Chinese side pays 50.6% ...   "   "   18,219.74

                                    "   "   36,007.59

According to the Annexed receipts of the
Financial Department of the Amur Navigation
Office the Chinese Government paid to the
Amur Navigation Office for the execution of
works in cash during 1922 the sum of Gold Rbls. 13,978.20
In accordance with the Estimate of the
Chinese side the amount spent by China
was .... "   "   4,241.54
Thus the total paid by China in 1922 was "   "   18,219.74

36.   <u>Turnover of cargo of Russian Water Transport.</u>
The turnover of cargo on the Russian side in 1923 has
to be recognised as extremely small. Cargo carried
by State steamers in the entire basis was about
3,000,000 poods; that by private steamship owners over
1,000,000 poods of sundry cargo, and about 3,000,000
poods of firewood, the total being 7,000,000 poods
against 80,000,000 poods in 1911. The passenger
traffic has entirely fallen now that no Chinese are
flowing in large masses, as was the case once, to
work on Russian gold-mines.

                                        37.

37.   General review of economic conditions in the
Amur Province.   laying down a general synopsis on
the navigation of Chinese and Russian steamers in the
Navigation Season 1923, it must be observed that
inspite of the fact that the Russian Transport had
in its control a good and large fleet, yet owing to
the lack of cargo results were excessively unfavourable
and a loss of about 200,000 Gold Roubles was
sustained.   Chinese shipping, though the boycott and
closed frontier affected it unfavourably, had a turnover of cargo by Chinese steamers on the Amur and
Sungari, which much exceeded the Russian.

Though the Russian State Floating Transport tried
by all means to suppress or repress the private fleet,
of which some ten steamers remained, yet the operation
of the latter were more favourable; but the enormous
taxes, the agreement between the employés and
proprietors according to which the owners of vessels
were bound to keep a much larger crew than before
and, in addition to pay wages of crews for the
whole season, and defray all kind of extras such as
medical assistance, annuity and social maintenance,
combined to paralyse the whole work.   These conditions
and the lack of cargo and low freight-rate allowed
no profit at all.

The private steamship owners have got their
last blow from the crew already after the end of
1923 Navigation Season by their demand for payment
a bonus for extra work done in holiday, as decreed
by the Navigation Union, inspite of there being three
watches, each working only 8 hours a day. The above
contingency   had not been foreseen at the signing
of the agreement with the crews at the beginning of
the Navigation and the steamship owners have refused

to

to pay. The sum due to the crews were then claimed by litigation and criminal prosecution, and in addition to the amount decreed by the court, exceeding in all 50,000 Gold Roubles, fines were imposed on the various owners from 2,000 to 3,000 Gold Roubles. The steamship owners not possessing, any funds, refused to pay and offered their steamers instead, but the authorities declined the offer and liened their house and other property, which is now subject to sale. The private steamship owners are now completely ruined. Thus comes to an end the existence of the private steamship companies and none of the owners who have been thus robbed can hope to repair their steamers. Merchants have not fared much better, since owners of houses and shops are compelled to buy War-bonds for a sum equal to what they pay in taxes. These War-bonds are nowhere accepted as legal tender.

Mention must be made of the work of the only Far-Eastern Bank in Blagovestchensk which until November, when a second State-Bank was established, granted credit at high rates on short term (3 months). If the term was extended for another 3 months, the rate was increased almost twice as much, and if the credit was granted for a year, the interest to be paid was almost equal to the credit granted. Moreover every debtor was obliged to buy War-bonds for the same sum. The Far-Eastern Bank accepted gold from debtor gold-miners at 5.05 Roubles a Zolotnik, whereas the market price was not under 5.25 - 5.50 Roubles, thereby as a matter of course lowering the hall-mark.

The aforesaid facts completely paralysed the gold mining business and the rich Amur district from which

which once were extracted about 1,000 poods of gold
a year yields now less than 80 poods which includes
the gold washed by dredges owned by two foreign
companies.   The Anglo-American Mining Company, working
on the Rivers Selemdja and Semertak, obtains about
5 poods of gold a year with a small dredge.   The
private company formerly styled "Mordin's Dredge
Operations", which had once in its management two
dredges, works now with one, but as no extensive
repairs have been done to it, partly owing to the
lack of reserve parts and trained workmen, it is
constantly breaking down and the amount of gold obtained by this company has fallen from 50 - 100 poods
to 8-10 poods a year.

In a still more difficult position are the
peasants on whose shoulders the whole burden of
taxes is put, the government demanding from them
taxes exceeding 10 times those of pre-war times.
The poor crops and bad quality of wheat harvested
in 1923 was not taken into consideration by the
Government.   The city workmen are almost free of
taxes.   To pay the taxes even the well-to-do
farmers are forced to dispose of a part of their
live stock (horses, cows) or agricultural implements.
The realisation of the above-named is seen by the
peasants driving in masses their horses and cattle to
the Chinese side and selling all for a trifle.

The inhabitants of Blagovestchensk, as well as
the frontier villages, occupy themselves with smuggling
merchandise (which is 4 times dearer on the Russian
side), local produce and large quantities of spirits,
the latter being double the price on the Russian
side.   To counteract this state of affairs the
Government is taking measures to free Russian spirit
from

from excise and thus make it cheaper. A rough calculation makes it seem that 150,000 - 200,000 vedros (3 gallons to a vedro) of spirit are smuggled over to the Russian side during any one year.

The position of the local Russian Government is very difficult. The collection of taxes from the peasantry is a question of doubtful result; the harvest in 1923 was so poor that the farmers have absolutely no stocks; on the contrary they have not corn enough for the maintenance of their families, and reserve- corn for sowing. The gross total of corn required in the three Eastern provinces, the Transbaikalian, the Amur and the Maritime provinces, amounts to 50,000,000 poods annually. This year's crop was only 25,000,000 poods.

Newspapers have announced that private Corn merchants will supply this country with cereals from West-Siberia and that more will be furnished by the Government by water from Odessa to Vladivostok. It is very much doubted whether this good intention will be justified, and most people regard these rumours as an expedient to quiet the population.

Owing to the exceedingly high rise of taxation and poor receipts, both the private trading houses and Government Offices have diminished their personnel, and the number of unemployed in Blagovestchensk (where there is a population of 45,000 inhabitants) amounts to over 15,000. The outlook is gloomy. The Amur State Water Transport has discharged all its crews. Examination of the statistics of the Amur Navigation Office for the period from 1900 until the revolution shows that supplies for the Amur District have exclusively come from Manchuria, and abroad via Nikolaevsk or Vladivostok. The

prohibitive

prohibitive duty established by the Russian Government on all imports with a view to open a mart for their home-made goods (in European Russia) will hardly justify their hopes, as inspite of the numerous cordons huge masses of all kinds of goods are smuggled into the Amur District. The disadvantage of such a procedure is that far too much is being paid for the simplest necessaries.

38.   **Conclusion**.   A general review of the conditions in the River region of the Amur and generally the whole Heilungchiang Province leaves a most cheerful impression with regard to the colonisation and development which in this country is going fast ahead.   Cultivated soil likewise increases every year.   Almost all well-to-do farmers have ploughs, grass-mowing and harvesting machines. The distillery of Mr. Hsü Peng-yuan, built up 4 versts from Taheiho, facilitates the realisation of local field produce.   The main factor in the development of this country is the discovery of some rich gold containing areas, some 70 - 100 versts from Taheiho; a great lot of produce finds there a ready market.   Two flour-mills in Taheiho and one in Aigun also effect great sales by sending their produce to the gold mines.

In connection with the above remarks I call the attention of the local Authorities who are interested in the development and prosperity of this country, to render every assistance in effectuating the following measures:

1. To maintain, if feasible, friendly and neighbourly relations with the local Russian Authorities, as the boycott and closed frontier inflict only losses to both sides.

2.

2. To extend to 1925 and following years the term of the local Technical Agreement concluded for mutual upkeep and repairs of Aids to Navigation in the frontier section of the Amur.

3. To organise a regular Mail and Passenger Steamship Service in the Taheiho - Moho and Taheiho - Chikete sections.

4. To regulate the question of Russian steamers plying on the Chinese side and Chinese steamers on the Russian side, both to enjoy equal rights.

5. To set up Aids to Navigation in the Kasakevich water-course region, so that Chinese steamers proceeding to the Ussuri, with a view to attending to the needs of the Chinese settlements, can proceed under less dangerous conditions.

6. To forbid categorically the Russian gunboat at the mouth of the Sungari to stop Chinese steamers.

7. The question of Chinese steamers navigating the Amur as far as Harbarovsk and Nikolaevsk, and Russian steamers the Sungari to be solved mutually.

8. To settle the question of selling and exporting firewood from the Chinese to the Russian side, thus developing the wood-trade in the Chinese frontier section of the Amur.

9. The Provisional Local Agreement to be mutually elaborated and concluded, introducing proper

Regulations

Regulations for the guidance of Chinese and Russian steamers, junks, and rafts plying in the frontier section of the Amur.

        I have the honour to be,

             Sir,

        Your obedient Servant,

P. Ignatieff.

        Technical Adviser on Amur Aids to Navigation.

1922 年及 1923 年黑龙江航务年度报告

（由黑龙江航务专门顾问易保罗（P. I. Ignatieff）先生编制）

瑷珲关/大黑河 1924 年 3 月 27 日

尊敬的海关总税务司（北京）：

1. 本报告谨对瑷珲关（大黑河）自《中俄黑龙江航路标志工程协议》于 1922 年 6 月 27 日签订之日起所完成之工作做出总结，值得强调的是，中国通过签订该协议已然受益匪浅，未来亦将继续获益。

2. 黑龙江及其支流乃为最大的适航流域之一，俄方于此所建立的航路标志可以说非常完善。在大革命爆发之前，航行于黑龙江上的只有俄国轮船。1897 年，俄阿穆尔水道局成立，负责对黑龙江流域的航路进行管理，该部门隶属位于圣彼得堡的俄国中央政府。1895 年至 1917 年间，俄国政府共耗资 3885.7 万金卢布用于黑龙江流域的航路维护工程。为维持俄阿穆尔水道局的正常运作，俄国政府每年都会拨发超过 300 万金卢布的拨款。时至今日，俄国所安设的航路标志已覆盖超过 7000 俄里的航路；其中，自斯列坚斯克（Stretensk）至尼古拉耶夫斯克（Nickolaevsk）全长 3028 俄里的航路及自布拉戈维申斯克（Blagovestchensk）至结雅河全长 610 俄里的航路在航运季期间均会装灯，以为引航之用。黑龙江及其支流可供航行之水道共计 10000 俄里，为保证航路畅通，俄国共安置五艘疏浚船长期于河道上作业，定期勘测航道及浅滩，清理河岸，移除礁石；此外，为有效管理航路标志维护工作及疏浚工作，俄国还分派了一些轮船、汽艇和驳船。

3. 至 1917 年，俄阿穆尔河船队共有轮船 208 艘、汽艇 44 艘、驳船 269 艘（另有 71 艘船只未列于此，包括俄阿穆尔水道局与俄阿穆尔河海军所拥有的汽艇、摩托艇以及驳船）。1911 年航运季期间，俄阿穆尔河船队的货运量总计高达 8000 万普特，客运量总计多达 621000 人次。然而随着俄国大革命的爆发，航运形势濒临崩溃，俄国整个航运业均受到重创，私营船队中有 40% 落入中国人手中，俄阿穆尔河航运与贸易公司剩余的船队则被收归国有。此后，因货物稀缺，俄国运输业逐渐衰败，如今尚存的少数运输船队能够得以维系，全赖轮船本身的机械设备和船体结构坚固耐用，备用零件数量充足。

4. 自大革命爆发伊始，俄阿穆尔水道局便开始走下坡路，用于航路标志维护工作的拨款也在逐年减少。1922 年，俄国政府指示俄阿穆尔水道局与俄阿穆尔国家水运局合并，同时为了保持运转,决定对往来货物征收一定比例的税款。然而由于当时的货运量极低,所征税款远不足以承担维护航路标志及为航路标志装灯所需之费用,又因俄国当时正值货币危机,俄国政府遂萌生出与中国共同管理黑龙江边界河道的想法。1907 年中俄战争结束后,俄方提出要制定一份中俄双方共同遵守的黑龙江边界河道航务条例。1908/1909 年冬季,中俄双方成立委员会就此事展开了协商,但最终未能达成协议,该问题就此搁置。

5. 如上所述,俄国大革命爆发后,俄国船队有一部分船只落入中国人手中,此后,中国轮船便开始航行于黑龙江边界河道之上。

6. 1922 年 6 月 27 日,中俄双方首次就共同维护黑龙江边界河道航路标志一事签署了协议,协议有效期自 1922 年 6 月 1 日起至 12 月 31 日止。但因部分条款存在一定缺陷,中俄双方之后又对协议做出一些修改与补充;俄阿穆尔水道局所制定的 1922 年预算也几经调整。

7. 在 1922 年协议期满之前,中俄双方就是否续签该协议一事展开了协商,但随后俄国外交代表加拉罕(Karakhan)先生访华,俄阿穆尔国家水运局代表接到了中止协商之指示,协议续签一事就此中断;当地中国政府随后提出请俄方尽快提交 1922 年已完成工作的报告。1923 年 4 月初,俄阿穆尔国家水运局代表提出希望将 1922 年协议延期至 1923 年和 1924 年,征得道尹同意后,于同月召开了一次会议。会上,中俄双方共同商定了协议条款内容,对 1922 年协议内容做了一些修改;然而中国政府所提出的协议第四部分内容遭到俄国代表的拒绝,因该部分内容涉及哈巴罗夫斯克(Habarovsk)至尼古拉耶夫斯克河段的航路,俄国代表表示其权限不足,无法给出确切答复,认为该问题带有一定的政治性,已超出工程协议的范畴,应交由即将于北京召开的中俄会议决定。1923 年 6 月,黑河道尹向俄阿穆尔国家水运局致函,提出第四部分内容可暂不列入工程协议正文之中,仅作为补充内容附于其后,交由北京中俄会议裁决。但俄阿穆尔国家水运局总督办当时因职位调动已离开布拉戈维申斯克,俄国代表方面未能及时给出回复。直到 1923 年 9 月,俄阿穆尔国家水运局督办工程师拉古丁(Lagutin)先生考察归来后,方就签订 1923 年协议一事与黑河道尹达成共识。

8. 1923 年航运季期间水位较高,无法开展航路标志维护工作。水位下降后,本人向俄阿穆尔水道局提出,应即刻派遣两艘汽艇,分别检查航道上游和下游的航路状况,以便进行必要的维修。俄方同意后,已派遣汽艇前去完成相关工作。

新协议因条款内容及措辞均有需要修改之处,故至 1923 年 10 月 28 日方得以签署,附加条款则于 1923 年 11 月 30 日签署。与此同时,俄阿穆尔水道局提交了 1923 年预算(1923

年1月1日至11月30日），总计19250金卢布。1923年协议签署之后，中方对俄阿穆尔水道局1922年账簿进行了最终检查；经检查，各项账目正确无误，均未超出预算；随呈附上一应发票及相关文件。

9. 1922年，中俄双方为联合维护黑龙江边界河道航路标志签署《临时地方工程协议》后，便立即开始江捐征收工作：俄方于5月11日开始遵照远东共和国法律征收江捐；中方于6月开始照协议附录之规定征收江捐。

1922年6月底，中国海关向俄方支付了第一笔预付款，用于航路标志维护工作；俄方亦相继开始进行河道检查以及航路标志的安设与维修工作。

1922年9月，瑷珲关署理税务司包安济（G. Boezi）先生乘船自大黑河前往洛古河（波克罗夫卡），对黑龙江上游已开放的通行信号站和水深信号站以及新立和修理完毕的标桩进行检查。8月，超等外班关员博韩（G. E. Baukham）先生乘船前往黑龙江下游，对大黑河至松花江口河段的航路标志维护情况进行了全面检查。自松花江口至哈巴罗夫斯克河段的航路标志于1920年被俄国军队分遣队破坏，但已于超等外班关员博韩（G. E. Baukham）先生巡查后得以重新建立。根据调查显示，航路标志维护工作已圆满完成，因此只要航路标志维护工作的实际支出未超过预算限额，便可予以接受。

商讨签署《工程协议》的同时，瑷珲关署理税务司包安济（G. Boezi）先生向海关总税务司署提议，自1922年9月16起任命一名专业人士担任黑龙江航务专门顾问一职，负责与黑龙江航务有关的一应事宜。本人曾于俄阿穆尔水道局担任黑龙江流域巡江工司一职13年之久，此次经哈尔滨关税务司推荐被任命为黑龙江航务专门顾问，于1922年10月4日至大黑河报到上任。

10. 关于1922年预算：本人详阅协议内容及俄阿穆尔水道局所提交的1922年预算后，发现均有需要修改之处。预算方面，本人已驳回俄方提出的礁石清理费用，但已同意摊付俄阿穆尔水道局（原布拉戈维申斯克技术部）的办公经费（数额较小）。

最终确定，1922年5月1日至12月31日期间计划用于黑龙江边界河道航路标志维护工作的支出预算共计32375.50金卢布。

此外，中俄黑龙江水道委员会已批准，1922年道尹公署办公经费预算总计2057.50银圆，海关办公经费预算总计2145.76银圆。

11. 关于拆除戊通航业公司码头事：在对大黑河港口轮船入港、停靠码头等情况有所了解之后，本人便进行了一次港口测量，结果发现戊通航业公司于1919年为船只过冬所建码头已对港口造成严重影响。1923年4月，为使水流流入港口时畅通无阻，部分码头已被拆除。然而过去数年间,港口已被淤泥堵塞,此前形成的沙洲业已日渐升高,港口内的行船安全已然受到威胁。为规避风险,已于1923年在沙洲最高处竖立起一个红色标桩,并于夜间悬挂红灯,以作警示之用。

12. 关于建立水位观测站事:为定期监测黑龙江的水位变化,已于1923年2月1日在大黑河设立一处水位观测站,测量数据将与布拉戈维申斯克方面发来的太平洋海平面数据进行对比。

13. 关于清理河道礁石事:随着冬季水位的大幅降低,大黑河港口岸边冰雪的日渐融化,许多潜藏于水中的礁石纷纷显露。至4月底,共计清理礁石4.25立方俄丈,花费38.42银圆。

14. 为修缮码头事:黑龙江春有浮冰、夏有洪水,平时还有强劲的北风搅动水浪,此番种种,皆使得大黑河港口的堤岸遭到大面积的冲刷,几乎已损坏殆尽。而海关办公楼就位于码头之上,今年(1923年)距离江堤边缘仅有50英尺(15.24米)。若置之不理,任由江水继续冲刷堤岸,码头面积势必会逐渐变小,而冬、夏两季海关均会在码头上进行验货,如此难免会受到影响;而且从技术角度来看,海关办公楼亦有地基沉陷、墙体破裂之风险。有鉴于此,海关决定使用柴捆和石头对长240英尺(73米)、宽34英尺(10.36米)的堤岸进行加固,最终加固面积共计7066平方英尺(657平方米),费用共计313.38银圆。

鉴于大黑河港口的堤岸已被逐年冲毁(1923年航运季损毁长度超过14英尺),兹提议向上游方向额外加固214英尺堤岸,将位于上游的水位观测站也包含在加固范围内。实际上,本人早于1923年便有此提议,但因私营业主中有人不同意摊付加固堤岸所需款项,故未能实现;然而在本人看来,即使要从航务专门顾问的办公经费之中支出这笔费用,那也是值得的。

15. 关于水位监测记录:1923年航运季期间,为告知各船主黑龙江与松花江的水位情况,海关决定在收到有关水位信息的电报后,将之公示于海关关署,以便轮船船主依此安排货运工作。

16. 关于1923年航运:1922/1923年冬季降雪量较大,而1923年春季的气温又一度较低,冰雪消融速度缓慢,因此黑龙江整个江面上并未同时出现浮冰。4月27日至29日期间,大黑河的冰面开始活动;随后,黑龙江上游18俄里处的别列耶夫斯基(Beliaevsky)浅滩以及下游4俄里处的结雅河浅滩均开始有浮冰堆积,大黑河江面冰层下的江水亦开始流动。5月7日,黑龙江水位已上涨至14英尺之多,江面冰层全部开始破裂,3天后浮冰彻底消融。5月10日,"达翰尔(Daur)"号汽艇渡船开始在黑龙江上航行;5月13日,大黑河迎来首批抵港的轮船"西京（Hsiking）"号和"镜兰（Chinglan）"号，两艘轮船分别于4月25日及28日由哈尔滨关出发。

江面冰层开始移动破裂时，一直停靠于戊通码头后面的齐齐哈尔银行疏浚船并未受损，但由于未能及时转移至江岸附近，5月8日受到大片浮冰撞击后沉没，打捞起来后，已由查普林（Chepurin）先生于当地修理妥善。5月9日，在大黑河口岸过冬的俄国轮船"莫斯科"号在接受一名俄国专家的水压检测时，蒸汽炉突然爆炸，后由查普林（Chepurin）先生在大黑河对之进行了修复。

1923年航运季期间，黑龙江水位极高，至6月16日达到最高点，高于太平洋海平面420.5英尺；至11月11日降至最低点，高于太平洋海平面399.3英尺；水位波动总体超过21英尺。此间，结雅河共发生三次大洪水，分别于5月底、7月中旬和9月，其中第二次灾情最为严重。冬、夏两季水位波动约28英尺，举凡地势较低的村庄、园圃、田地及牧场均被淹没，蔬菜等农作物以及草料亦损失殆尽。这些地区目前正陷于饥荒之中。

整个航运季期间乃至航运季结束，松花江上均未出现浅水域；三姓浅滩的水位始终未低于3英尺，已高于历史平均值，自8月底至9月水位一度上涨，最高时甚至超过了8.75英尺。航运季期间，黑龙江水域的水位整体都很高，很多区域的河床都遭到严重的冲刷，特别是松花江和结雅河下游地区那些河床多沙之处，航路亦随之改变。黑龙江干流水底则较为坚实，主要为砂砾层，在10月勘测时并未发现航路有明显的改变。

因水位普遍较高，黑龙江与松花江流域均十分利于航运，但可运之货物却寥寥无几，因此尽管航路标志的维修与安设工作未能如常开展，1923年航运季期间的航运条件依然未受影响。

黑龙江和松花江上均未出现海盗劫船情况。

黑龙江、额尔古纳河以及乌苏里江边界河道的水位十分利于航行，整个航运季期间，中国轮船仅发生了两起航运事故。

第一起是"猞猁（Sheli）"号驳船，在由"扬湖（Yang Hu）"号轮船拖拽运载薪柴经由大黑河上游100俄里处的布塞斯基（Bussevsky）浅滩时，船舵受损；第二起是"大明（Ta Ming）"号驳船，在由"三水（San Shui）"号轮船拖拽运载薪柴经由大黑河下游100俄里处的西切夫斯基上游（Upper-Sichevsky）浅滩时，搁浅。

大黑河至巴斯科沃（Pashkovo，保兴山）河段的江面于10月24日便已出现浮冰，比往年更早，戊通航业公司的木制船尾明轮"宜兴（I Hsing）"号在距离大黑河10俄里处被浮冰击中，无法行至大黑河港口，只得前往附近华岸停靠，结果还未抵达便已沉没，约有三成货物受损。双叶轮船"扬湖"号在拖拽"猱狋"号驳船经由结雅河浅滩时，因浮冰过于密集，不得已将驳船暂留于大黑河下游 7 俄里处长发屯附近，独自前往大黑河，最终得以于大黑河港口停泊过冬。三艘拖有驳船的俄国拖轮因未能在浮冰出现之前抵达布拉戈维申斯克，只得暂时停泊于距离布拉戈维申斯克 100 俄里之处。

17. 关于轮船过冬：1923/1924 年冬季，停泊于大黑河港口的轮船如下："瑷珲（Aigun）"号轮船，"绍兴（Shao Hsing）"号轮船，"吉阳（Chi Yang）"号轮船，"顺天（Shun Tien）"号轮船，"莫斯科"号轮船，"扬湖"号双叶轮船，"普贤（PuHsien）"号铁制驳船，以及齐齐哈尔银行的疏浚船。

18. 关于 1923 年航路标志维护工作：本人乘"兴安（Hin-gan）"号和"共青（Komsomoletz）"号汽艇对黑龙江边界河道自布拉戈维申斯克至嘎杂克维池河段进行了全面勘查。

因航路发生变化，信标位置已重新调整；凡过于靠近江堤的信标，均已迁移至更远处，岸边荒草已铲除干净，沟渠业已挖掘完毕，由此可保护信标免受春、秋两季野火的侵袭；影响信标能见度的树木俱已伐除；盾形标桩的维修及安设业已完成；因恶意毁坏或其他原因而折损的信标亦已重新竖立。本人已将信标现状及 1924 年航运季期间需要进行维修和新立的信标数量统计成文。

此外，水深信号站、通行信号站以及水位观测站的状况业已检查完毕，包括统计各站职员的人数及入职时间；检查各站账簿、库存、材料的使用情况、职员宿舍情况以及 1924 年需要进行维修之处。

同样，加林达（Jalinda）、切尔纳耶瓦（Chernayevo）、布拉戈维申斯克、因诺肯季瓦（Innokentieva）和叶卡捷琳堡 – 尼科利斯克（Ekaterino-Nikolsk）五个地区的测量师办事处亦已检查完毕，包括检查一应账簿、职员薪俸和支付清单、库存以及划艇。其中，划艇因超过四年未曾修理，现已基本报废。

黑龙江航道自松花江口至嘎杂克维池河段的航路标志此前被俄国军方分遣队破坏，后于 1922 年航运季期间得以修复，但现已无法满足该段航路之需求，且与传统信标多有不符之处。黑龙江江面较宽，江段较长，上述信标在江中就显得过于短小，又因无三角支撑而不甚牢靠。有鉴于此，本人已提议对旧有的江式与海式信标进行简化，以节约成本，新型信标将于 1924 年航运季投入使用。

过去使用的江式信标成本过高，单价一般为 20 卢布，若安装防护罩还需额外增加 8 卢布；海式角锥形信标的单价一般为 22 卢布，若安装防护罩还需额外增加 15 卢布；但各地区价格略有不同。兹认为，新型江式信标（包括防护罩）的单价不会超过 8-10 卢布，角锥形信标的单价不会超过 15-20 卢布。由此，信标的维护费用亦将相应减少，江式信标每个将仅需 2-3 卢布，角锥形信标每个将仅需 4-5 卢布。

俄阿穆尔水道局于 1923 年 4 月所提交的航路标志维护工作预算中，信标的安设与维护费用十分高昂，以致预算总额高达 60800 金卢布；而中国海关制定的预算仅有 40000 金卢布。

本人秋季重新检查预算时，将之与俄阿穆尔水道局的实际支出进行了对比，发现仍有缩减的余地。1924 年 1 月 16 日，中俄临时地方工程委员会商定将预算缩减至 19250 金卢布，根据协议附加条款中的第 15 项，华方将摊付预算的 50%。截至目前，中方已支付 5000 金卢布，余者将待俄方提交 1923 年年度报表并由中方审核通过后再行结付。

1923 年航运季期间，装灯浅滩仅有 4 处，分别为结雅河浅滩、康斯坦丁诺瓦（Konstantinova）浅滩、索菲斯克（Soyus）浅滩和叶卡捷琳堡 – 尼科利斯克浅滩。此外，大黑河至拉哈苏苏河段往来船只较多，沿线亦安有灯桩。黑龙江上游自大黑河至漠河河段，通行信号站仅开设两处，分别为贝克托夫斯基（Beketovsky）通行信号站和察尔岩斯基（Tsagayansky）通行信号站，被看顾的浅滩亦仅有两处，分别为切尔纳耶夫斯基（Chernaysvsky）浅滩和派米津斯基（Permikinsky）浅滩。

在前往上游巡查途中，本人通过比照校订整个黑龙江边界河道的航图，重新绘制了一份更便于携带的小比例航图，并将黑龙江华岸一侧能够提供薪柴的地点统计列明，包括各地点的薪柴储存量以及航运季结束时的存余数量。

另需强调的是，此前，华俄两岸对信标一直精心看护，但近来却发生了多起恶意破坏信标的事件，有些信标的防护罩被撞掉，有些更是连同支柱一并被撞倒。俄阿穆尔水道局督办已向俄国边境居民下达严令，凡当地民众有恶意破坏信标者，一律严惩不贷。

早在 1897 年，俄阿穆尔水道局设立伊始，自波克罗夫卡至哈巴罗夫斯克之间长达 1769 俄里的边界河道便已被划分为 5 个地区，每一地区的里程均在 300 俄里以上，夜间皆有灯桩引航。然而如今，航路标志仅供日间使用，俄方又不知为何竟将原来的 5 个地区重新划分成了 6 个地区。本人认为实不必如此，故于 1923 年和 1924 年的预算报告中，提出按照 5 个地区来划分。

人员配置方面，兹认为，各地区每年派驻一名地区测量师、一名工头及一名更夫足矣，遂已照此制作预算。各地区的测量师、工头及更夫，以及水深信号站与通行信号站的更夫均可于俄阿穆尔水道局所建楼宇内居住办公，如此一来便无需支付租金，鉴于此，兹提议将房屋一年的折旧费（5%）列入预算中。至于设备与划艇的使用,亦可将其一年的折旧费（10%）列入预算之中。

19. 关于航行于黑龙江中国一侧的俄国轮船:1922 年航运季期间,中国轮船获准自黑龙江航行至哈巴罗夫斯克,俄国轮船可于松花江及黑龙江和额尔古纳河的中国一侧航行。此间,抵达大黑河口岸的轮船共有 612 艘,其中 190 艘为中国轮船,422 艘为俄国轮船。其中两艘俄国汽艇"兴安"号和"共青"号定期（每隔一日）往返于大黑河与奇克特之间。1922 年,中国轮船的货运总量为 190 万普特,客运总量为 14000 人次;俄国轮船的货运总量为 110 万普特,客运总量为 17000 人次。由轮船及渡船自大黑河运至布拉戈维申斯克的货物总量为 100 万普特,自布拉戈维申斯克运至大黑河的货物总量为 100 普特;中国向俄国出口的薪柴总量为 4000 立方俄丈。

1923 年航运季期间,中国轮船不再享有自黑龙江航行至哈巴罗夫斯克的权利,俄国轮船亦不再享有于松花江上自由航行的权利,但仍可于黑龙江与额尔古纳河的中国一侧航行。俄国"比斯特里（Bistry）"号等轮船定期往返于大黑河至漠河河段;"兴安"号和"共青"号两艘汽艇定期往返于大黑河至奇克特河段。在中国一致抵制俄国并封锁边境之前,"共青"号汽艇已航行多达 55 次,获利颇丰。边境封锁后,该两艘汽艇只得返回俄国,自此,戊通航业公司的两艘轮船"吉阳"号和"沈阳"号便开始分别往返于黑龙江上游和下游河段。

1923 年间,共有 164 艘中国轮船抵达大黑河口岸,货运总量达 1085 普特（不包括出口至俄国的薪柴）,客运总量达 21000 人次;上述两艘俄国汽艇"兴安"号和"共青"号在短途航行中共运输货物 45000 普特,乘客 2000 名;自大黑河向布拉戈维申斯克运输的薪柴总量达 2000 立方俄丈。

由上述数据可知,俄国轮船于中国一侧的运输量十分可观,而中国轮船却无权在俄国一侧航行,此形势与时局不符,应采取措施予以解决。

20. 关于中国轮船在黑龙江边界河道上的货物运输量:1923 年庄稼欠收的消息传出后,哈尔滨市场上便出现了大量的投机倒把行为,小麦与面粉的价格突然暴涨。大黑河与瑷珲地区的商人抓住这一机会,趁势将储备的小麦和面粉运往哈尔滨。据相关数据显示,因抵制俄国封锁边境后,中国轮船在黑龙江边界河道上的货物运输量已受到严重影响。

1922 年航运季期间,抵达大黑河口岸的轮船超过 600 艘,各种货物的运输总量超过 300 万普特,乘客运输量多达 31000 人次;薪柴和木料的总运输量也达到 250 万普特。而

1923 年航运季期间,抵达大黑河口岸的轮船仅有 200 艘左右,货物运输总量仅达 113 万普特,乘客运输量仅约 23000 人次; 薪柴和木料的运输总量仅 210 万普特。

21. 关于木料与薪柴:1915 年以前,伐木与造筏主要由俄国人完成,而今却已完全被中国人垄断,目前黑龙江华岸的伐木工居留地已超过 20 处。大黑河与波克罗夫卡之间贩卖薪柴之地众多,总计超过 90 处,薪柴的总库存量超过 17000 立方俄丈,其中有 80% 为旧存。 在航运业比较兴盛的时期,俄国轮船每年要运载大量薪柴（大概 5000 到 10000 立方俄丈）出口至布拉戈维申斯克,如今边境封锁,贸易受阻,木料商人手上所积压的巨量薪柴已难以出售,薪柴价格亦随之降至最低。此外,曾于黑龙江上游航行的中俄两国轮船中,已有数艘停止运行,此亦为薪柴需求量减少之原因。

桦木薪柴自大黑河运至切尔纳耶瓦地区（距离 425 俄里）,每平方俄丈需要花费 1.40 银圆到 1.80 银圆; 自上游运至切尔纳耶瓦地区,每平方俄丈需要花费 1.00 银圆到 1.40 银圆; 桦木薪柴的成本加上税费,每平方俄丈约合 1.60 银圆。

大黑河与嘎杂克维池之间售卖薪柴的地点已超过 50 处,薪柴的存储量总计超过 6000 立方俄丈。 只有将不少于 5000 立方俄丈的薪柴通过轮船或驳船运至哈尔滨,并以每立方俄丈 9.00 银圆到 10.50 银圆的价格卖掉,这些木商才可能免于破产。

俄国方面,由于黑龙江上往来的俄国轮船较少,而加诸于木料商身上的税赋又颇重,黑龙江沿岸的俄国居民难以囤积大量薪柴,1923 年航运季期间,木料商大多以薪柴折抵税款,以致剩余薪柴无法满足俄国游轮所需。

1923 年 2 月,俄国海关开始征收高昂关税,中国的木料出口严重受限,以致 1923 年木料的运输量比 1922 年下跌了 75%。 木料价格亦随之大幅下降。8 英寸厚的木料为 1.20 银圆到 1.50 银圆不等,6 到 7 英寸厚的方木为 0.70 银圆到 1.00 银圆不等。 如此一来,小型伐木公司受到严重的影响,倒闭者众多。 随后,部分撑筏者开始生产柏油,运往哈尔滨售卖,此项贸易现已有上涨趋势。

22. 黑龙江华岸地区调查:本人于 1923 年航运季期间对黑龙江边界河道进行了全面调查,情况如下。 自俄国爆发大革命以来,黑龙江华岸自洛古河至温和镇（因诺肯季瓦（Innokentieva））一带人口骤增,有以酿酒贩酒（主要向俄国一侧居民贩卖酒水）为生的独户居民,也有于大型村落居住的居民,谋生方式更是多种多样,有伐木、撑筏、砍伐薪柴、耕种、放牧,等等。 此外,随着金矿的出现,新的居留地又相继建立。

黑龙江华岸自温和镇（因诺肯季瓦）至伊力嘎（嘎杂克维池）河段沿线,早在阿穆尔铁路修建时期就已有许多中国人移居至此,其中多数为商人。 而如今由于边境封锁,中俄贸易中断，当地的商业发展已完全处于停滞状态，人口正在逐渐外流，只剩下少数区域仍有一定的百姓居住，比如俄国哥萨克居留地"索菲斯克"对岸的兴东道，以及肇兴镇和太平沟。

23.农业、畜牧业和养殖业：黑龙江右岸有很多地方的山林与江岸相隔较远，中间形成大片平原，非常适宜种植谷物和发展畜牧业。这样的平原地带共有20多处，随着定居者增多，村落亦逐渐扩大，一个村落通常会有30到50所房屋，农业和畜牧业发展迅速。牧场上，牛（超过150头）马（超过200匹）成群，出口之数非常可观，谷物亦是如此。

24.狩猎：黑龙江、额尔古纳河、阿尔巴西哈（Albasiha）[①]河以及库马拉（Kumara）河南岸的大片区域土地肥沃，野生动物种类繁多，但由于这些地方尚未开辟道路，因此只有当地人知晓出入之路。这些人多以打猎为生，主要是捕杀麋鹿，以取得鹿茸；此外也捕捉普通的鹿、松鼠、狐狸以及狼等。

25.黄金：黄金对本地区的发展至关重要。政府与呼玛河、漠河及太平沟附近的私营企业均可开采黄金。最新发现的金矿位于额尔古纳河河口9俄里外的一条小溪处，但因夏季该地会被河水淹没，唯有冬季方可使用竖井开采黄金。1922/1923年冬季，约有2000人到这里开采黄金。额尔古纳河沿岸的村落，新建有超过30栋砖房，至1923年已成为大型居留地。新立屯附近的私营金矿，情形也是这般。目前的主矿地（或者说是最重要的金矿）距离大黑河70俄里，总计有6000余名矿工正在那里开采并冶炼高品质的黄金。有超过30家新成立的金矿开采公司已经正式提出申请，有意对金矿进行勘探。

26.民船：民船是轮船的主要竞争对手，因班轮数量较少，运费又颇高，所以人们在运输货物及薪柴时往往会选择民船；民船向黑龙江上游可行至距离大黑河250俄里的呼玛河，向黑龙江下游可行至奇克特，甚至奇克特下游200俄里处。大黑河口岸共有60条民船，载重量从400普特到500普特不等。漠河至额尔古纳河河段共有10艘载重500普特的民船往来，为当地居民提供各种物资，里程约400俄里。对于此等无轮船往来之偏僻地区，民船通常收取每普特0.50银圆到0.60银圆的运费。

不过民船的运输量也受到抵制俄国和封锁边境的不利影响，相比1922年降低了50%。

27.邮政及电报：大黑河、瑷珲、呼玛河、漠河、太平沟以及兴东道等地区均设有邮政局和电报局，对海关事务和沿岸贸易均有极大助益。

---

① Albasiha一词经查应为今额木尔河。据资料记载额木尔河又作"额穆尔河"，原名阿巴昔河或阿尔巴西哈河，1980年地名普查改为兴安河，为方便记述，现代水文仍称额木尔河。此处因阿尔巴西哈与Albasiha发音最为接近，故取之为其中文译名。

28.公路：人口的迁移,居民区的发展与交通密不可分,应对公路建设予以更多关注。

29.组织定期船运服务：黑龙江沿线地区陆路不可通行,只能通过水路进行运输,因此应对船运服务的发展予以极度重视。

自俄国人开始在黑龙江上航行起,定期往返的邮轮与客轮服务便成为俄国发展的支柱产业,石勒喀河与黑龙江上的船运服务始于1872年,结雅河上的船运服务始于1910年。

1923年航运季期间,大黑河与漠河之间并无定期的船运服务,轮船往来时间极不固定。

戊通航业公司的"吉阳"号轮船整个航运季期间一直往来于大黑河与漠河之间,但每次往返约需14到20天,且其间仅向上游航行过8次。但随后因抵制俄国,封锁边境,往来于该河段的轮船仅剩下"吉阳"号一艘,已然无法满足大黑河至漠河段居民的生活所需,戊通航业公司的其他轮船以及其他航运公司的轮船便纷纷来至该河段。

1923年航运季期间,轮船共向大黑河上游河段航行了18次,运往上游的货物约达15万普特,自上游运回的杂货约达36万普特,薪柴约达4000立方俄丈。在边境封锁前,由大黑河向俄国（布拉戈维申斯克）出口的薪柴总计2000立方俄丈,向哈尔滨输出的薪柴亦为2000立方俄丈。

1922年航运季期间,大黑河至漠河河段,运往上游的货物总计超过30万普特,自上游运回的货物量比1923年少2万普特。此外,1922年运至大黑河的薪柴仅有1500立方俄丈;自大黑河运至俄国布拉戈维申斯克和哈尔滨的薪柴均为2000立方俄丈。另因呼玛河、新立屯、漠河以及额勒河（Elohe）等地的矿业发展颇为繁荣,愈来愈多的民众迁移至黑龙江自大黑河至漠河以及额勒河（额勒河距离额尔古纳河河口仅4俄里）之间各地,该区间的客运量亦相对较大,1922年总计5400人次,1923年总计5150人次。

1922年及1923年航运季期间,大黑河至漠河之间的货物运费与乘客票价同比较高,往返于该区域的轮船获利颇丰。

1922年哈尔滨至大黑河一段的货物运费相对较高,每普特达到0.12银圆到0.15银圆,但1923年开始迅速下跌,有时甚至会低至每普特0.05银圆到0.06银圆。

戊通航业公司的"沈阳"号轮船每隔三天往返于大黑河与奇克特之间一次,航程147俄里,该区域为黑龙江沿岸地区人口最多的区域之一。

大黑河至洛古河及大黑河至奇克特河段需要有定期的邮轮与客轮往来方能保证当地居民的生活所需,因此最好同戊通航业公司或东亚（王玉京（Wang Yu-ching））航业公司签署一份协议,协定由航业公司派遣两艘载货量可达10000普特的轮船定期往返于大黑河至漠河乃至洛古河河段。而像"沈阳"号这样的小型轮船则可派遣至大黑河至奇克特河河段。由于目前轮船向上游区域航行的时间极不稳定，以致大批货物和大量乘客均需乘坐民船航行长达 250 俄里，因此上述定期航运对于增加乘客与货物的运输量来说就显得格外重要。

30. 中国轮船自黑龙江航行至哈巴罗夫斯克（Habarovsk）：由于俄国大革命的爆发令俄国 40% 的轮船落入中国人手中，再加上像戊通航业公司这类大型航运公司的积极组织，中国的轮船开始在黑龙江上航行，最远可航行至哈巴罗夫斯克；1919 年高尔察克政府当权时，哈巴罗夫斯克镇上还成立了戊通航业公司办事处。但是后来"红色政权"掌控了整个沿海地区，高尔察克政府与"红色政权"合二为一，于是中国轮船在哈巴罗夫斯克和尼古拉耶夫斯克地区的航行开始举步维艰。1922 至 1923 年冬季，俄国政府决定关闭哈巴罗夫斯克的戊通航业公司办事处，撤销中国轮船在黑龙江上远航至哈巴罗夫斯克地区的权利。而中国政府亦从此禁止悬挂苏维埃旗帜的轮船驶入松花江。

1922 年航运季期间，俄国政府在松花江口驻扎了一艘炮艇。该炮艇对所有往来的中国轮船都加以阻拦，以便检查船上的俄国乘客护照。直到 1923 年航运季中期，俄国政府方撤回该炮艇，自此，凡中国轮船通过松花江口时，均不再受到俄方阻扰，只须接受驻扎于此的中国炮艇对其船舶证件进行检查。

31. 关于嘎杂克维池水道的航路标志：目前中国轮船已无法远航至哈巴罗夫斯克，而嘎杂克维池水道上却完全没有航路标志，且水道过于曲折，即使是航路中心也几乎无法正常航行，因此着实有必要尽快于嘎杂克维池水道上建立航路标志。住在乌苏里江地区的中国人也需要一些水上的交通途径，以便通过水路获取一定的生活补给，而嘎杂克维池水道无疑正是成本较低的一条途径。1923 年航运季期间，黑龙江流域整体水位都很高，因此有几艘拖着驳船的轮船得以成功通过嘎杂克维池水道驶入乌苏里江，最远到达名为"依玛口撒（Ima-kousa）"的中国村庄（位于俄国伊曼对岸）。

本人认为有必要让中国轮船获得在乌苏里江自由航行的权利，提议在嘎杂克维池水道建立小型信标作为航路标志，以改善乌苏里江航路状况，使之能够满足轮船的航行需求。

32.1922 年及 1923 年江捐征收（附录 2 和附录 3）：因 1922 年协议签署时间较晚，中方已先于 1922 年 6 月中旬开始了江捐征收工作。1923 年的江捐征收工作则是于当年航运季伊始着手进行的；下表即为中方的江捐征收明细。

口岸	货币	1922 年	1923 年
大黑河	银圆	23932.45	15068.64
瑷珲	银圆	1450.43	2458.12
拉哈苏苏	银圆	5754.31	6243.14
总计	银圆	31137.19	23769.90

江捐税收的减少，主要因为边境封锁后，哈尔滨关无法出口货物。1922 年航运季期间，进出口货物的运输总量为 300 万普特，而 1923 年航运季期间，却只有 11.3 万普特；乘客运输总量也从 1922 年的 31000 人次降至 23000 人次；木料运输总量比 1922 年同期减少 75%。

俄方 1922 年及 1923 年的江捐征收工作均在航运季伊始开始进行，税收金额如下：

口岸	货币	1922 年	1923 年
布拉戈维申斯克	金卢布	8763.90	13366.06
哈巴罗夫斯克	金卢布	28245.42	12265.35
斯列坚斯克	金卢布	417.64	1375.00
尼古拉耶夫斯克	金卢布		9446.02
结雅河上游	金卢布	442.55	1310.78
国家船队管理局	金卢布	11823.58	13539.74
总计	金卢布	49693.09	51302.95

1923 年俄方江捐税收的增长并不是因为进出口货物的增加，而是因为一些特殊的情况：（1）俄方当年所捕获的鱼类数量巨大，皆由尼古拉耶夫斯克船运至布拉戈维申斯克；（2）自松花江运输出口的豆类多达 40 万普特（并非合同上所写的 200 万普特），但该项出口自抵制俄国的活动开始后便被迫中止。秋季，因受到抵制俄国活动和边境封锁的影响，俄阿穆尔水道局无法从中国一侧运输薪柴，以致布拉戈维申斯克地区的薪柴价格暴涨，木筏运输薪柴之量亦随之骤增。不过俄国之所以能够在自己一侧征得如此多的税款，主要还是因为俄方自 1922 年 5 月 17 日起提高了其依照远东共和国法律征收之江捐的税率，且无论运输里程与始讫地点，均全价征收江捐。而中国一侧是将边境地区划分为两段：自嘎杂克维池至大黑河为一段，自大黑河至漠河为另一段；每段仅征收半价江捐。

由于自尼古拉耶夫斯克至斯列坚斯克河段基本无货可运，结雅河、谢列姆贾（Selemdja）河、布列亚（Bureya）河以及额尔古纳河一带的金矿生意也颇不景气，黑龙江流域的内陆河道江捐税收金额已是相当之微薄。

33. 1922 年账目核对：本人于 1923 年 12 月对俄阿穆尔水道局所提交之 1922 年航运季期间黑龙江边界河道航路标志维护费用支出报表进行了核对，其中实际支出虽未超出预算金额，但亦未完全遵照预算所定之分配比例，有些个别项目的实际支出超出了预算金额，有些项目则有所结余。因航运季期间部分雇员的薪俸有所上调，故用于职员薪俸的支出超出了预算金额 757.13 金卢布；因不少通行信号站与水深信号站并未投入运营，其他很多站点也只是临时工作，故在这方面的实际支出较预算金额有 3295.75 金卢布的节余；因某些浅滩处的水深信号站并未工作，故在发送浅滩水深信息方面节约 1009.13 金卢布。此外，因电报账单已来不及添加到俄阿穆尔水道局的年度账单中，故电报部门同意将电报款账暂时赊欠在内陆水域账单上。用于标注浅滩之灯桩的实际支出超出预算 45397 金卢布，旅费超出预算 356.03 金卢布，皆因原本的预算金额太低所致。

资产折旧账单（包括房屋与船艇）之金额原为 3270.47 金卢布，但本人核查后发现，其中一些宿舍、库房和划艇不必计算在内，故将之削减到 2444.21 金卢布。最初的预算中虽未含上述折旧费用，但考虑地区测量师、工头及通行信号站和浅滩的巡役都需要相应的膳宿供应，而现有的宿舍又无法容纳所有雇员，租赁宿舍十分必要，唯如此一来开支更大，而且荒无人烟之地又难以租到房屋，故此，本人认为应该对该笔开支予以报销，特别是在实际支出尚未达到预算金额，且预算仍有结余的情况之下。

1922 年的总预算额为 32376.20 金卢布，实际支出如呈送文件（附录 4）所示，即 31766.05 金卢布。本人认为有必要提醒俄阿穆尔水道局，以后制订预算时应尽量考虑到所有可能的支出，避免在实际工作中出现原本未列入预算的必要支出。此外，本人已请俄阿穆尔水道局注意严格遵守预算的获批金额，若有实际支出不得不超出预算金额之情况，则应先向有关部门报备并申请批准。

根据 1922 年 10 月 24 日中俄水道委员会通过之议决，1922 年黑龙江边界河道航路标志的维护费用均从双方所征得的江捐税收中支出。中方支出所征江捐的全部，俄方支出所征江捐的三分之二。

34. 1922 年中方江捐税收：根据瑷珲关署理税务司 1923 年 1 月 21 日提供之信息，中方 1922 年的江捐税收总额为 33929.47 金卢布，根据 1922 年 5 月 27 日所签协议第 5 项之规定扣除 10% 海关征税佣金后，净税收值为 30536.47 金卢布，已如数转交中俄水道委员会。

1922 年俄方江捐税收：根据俄阿穆尔水道局所提供之江捐税收报表，俄方 1922 年的江捐税收总额为 49693.13 金卢布，根据 1922 年 5 月 27 日所签协议第 5 项之规定扣除 10% 征税佣金后，净税收值为 44723.13 金卢布，其三分之二即为 29815.33 金卢布，业已如数转交至中俄水道委员会。

中俄水道委员会共计收到 60351.80 金卢布税款。

35. 1922 年中俄水道委员会支出总计：

	货币	金额
俄方维护边界河道航路标志的相关支出（根据俄阿穆尔水道局所提交之账目）	金卢布	31766.05
中方维护边界河道航路标志的相关支出（根据既定预算）	金卢布	4241.54
总计：	金卢布	36007.59
上述支出分配比例如下：		
俄方支付 49.4%	金卢布	17787.85
中方支付 50.6%	金卢布	18219.74
总计：	金卢布	36007.59

中方摊款明细：

	货币	金额
1922 年中国政府为边界河道航路标志维护工作向俄阿穆尔水道局支付之款（根据俄阿穆尔水道局财务科所附收据）	金卢布	13978.20
中方支出金额（根据既定预算）	金卢布	4241.54
华方 1922 年摊付总额：	金卢布	18219.74

36. 俄方水上货运量：1923 年俄方货物运输量极少，整个黑龙江流域，由国营轮船所运之货物约为 300 万普特；由私营轮船所运之杂货超过 100 万普特，薪柴运输量约为 300 万普特，水上总运输量为 700 万普特；而 1911 年的总运输量高达 8000 万普特。乘客运输量亦大跌，今时不同往日，已经没有大批中国人因在俄国金矿工作而往来流动了。

37. 阿穆尔省经济形势总览：从 1923 年航运季期间中俄两国整体航运形势来看，俄国虽有大批高质量的船队，但因无货可运，损失了近 20 万金卢布；而中国方面，虽受到抵制俄国与封锁边境的影响,但中国轮船在黑龙江与松花江上的货物运输量却远高于俄国。

尽管俄国国家浮运局（Russian State Floating Transport）极力打压尚存十余艘轮船的私营船队,但民众还是更喜欢通过私营船队进行运输。然私营船队的船主不仅须缴纳高昂的税款,还须遵照雇主与雇员之协议规定供养比以往更多的船员,此外还要在整个航运季期间支付船员薪俸以及各种额外费用（如医疗护理费、养老金、社保等）,这些重担加在一起,船主的运营可谓举步维艰。更何况目前无货可运,运费又极低,航运业对俄国轮船船主来说几乎已完全无利可图。

压垮私营轮船船主的最后一根稻草,是在 1923 年航运季结束之后,船员要求船主为他们在假日期间所付出的劳动支付额外奖金。尽管每位船员每天的工作时间仅为 8 小时,且三班轮换,但航业工会（Navigation Union）还是批准了船员的要求。在与船员于航运季初期签署协议的时候,轮船船主并未预见有此意外支出,因此拒绝支付奖金。船员们遂提起民事诉讼与刑事诉讼。最终,法院判决轮船船主必须向船员支付全额奖金,共计 50000 金卢布,并向各轮船船主处以 2000 到 3000 金卢布的罚款。然而轮船船主确实已无资金可用,于是只得提出用轮船来偿抵债务。但政府却表示反对,并指示轮船船主可以考虑用房屋或其他资产抵债,目前用以抵债的资产正在拍卖中。随着私营轮船船主宣告破产和私营航业公司日渐衰败,轮船的维修工作已是无人问津。商人的情况亦不甚乐观,他们被迫购买了战时公债,公债金额与所纳税额相同,然而这些战时公债在任何地区都是无法作为合法货币使用的。

值得一提的是,布拉戈维申斯克唯一的一所远东银行在 11 月第二所国资银行成立之前,主要的工作就是以高昂的利率发放短期贷款（3 个月）。若要将贷款时间延期 3 个月,利率则几乎翻倍,若要延期至一年,利息则几乎与所贷金额相同。此外,借贷人还必须购买同样金额的战时公债。远东银行接受金矿抵债,价格为每索拉尼 5.05 卢布,然而金矿的市场价却不低于 5.25-5.30 卢布,远东银行给出的价格显然偏低。

上述这些情况令阿穆尔地区的金矿业彻底瘫痪,原本黄金的年产量约为 1000 普特,而现在却只有 80 普特,其中还包括了两家外国公司的疏浚船所淘得的金砂。一家公司为英美矿业公司（Anglo-American Mining company）,主要负责谢列姆贾河与赛美塔克河的疏浚工作,其一艘小型疏浚船每年可淘得 5 普特的黄金。另一家公司为私营公司,此前名为莫汀疏浚营运公司（Mordin's Dredge Operation）,旗下曾拥有两艘疏浚船,但目前仅余一艘,且未经大修（因缺少备用零件及熟练的修理工）,时常出现故障,因此该企业每年的淘金量也就从昔日的 50-100 普特下降至每年 8-10 普特。

最困难的还是农民,他们几乎承担了所有赋税,政府要求他们缴纳的税款接近战前时期的 10 倍。1923 年谷物收成极差,小麦的质量也很低,但政府对于这一切却似乎完全没有加以考虑。城市里的工人几乎无需纳税;而农民若想要交上这些税,则只能卖掉牛马一类的牲畜或者农业用具。农民将牛马驱赶到中国一侧贱卖,便恰好印证了上述的情况。

布拉戈维申斯克以及边境村庄均有部分居民从事违禁品(这些违禁品进入俄国之后,价格将翻 4 倍)、土货以及大量烈酒(烈酒在俄国也能卖到两倍价钱)的走私活动。为了抑制这一状况,俄国政府决定对本国烈酒免征消费税,以降低烈酒价格。粗略估计,平均每年大约有 15 万到 20 万俄桶(3 加仑为 1 俄桶)烈酒走私至俄国。

当地俄国政府所面临的形势相当严峻。能否从农民手中征得税款,依然存疑。1923 年的收成量实在太低,农民根本没有多余的收入,甚至连维持家庭温饱,购买明年播种所需的种子都很困难。东三省以及黑龙江沿江各地每年需要总计 5000 万普特的谷物,而当年的谷物产量仅有 2500 万普特。

据报纸报道,即将有私营谷商从西西伯利亚为当地提供谷物,而政府也已决定从敖德萨地区征调更多的谷物经由水路运送至符拉迪沃斯托克(Vladivostok)。这无疑是振奋人心的消息,但能否顺利实现尚难以确定,很多人都认为这些只是政府为稳定人心而放出的假消息。

因赋税过高,盈利又偏低,私营贸易公司和政府机关纷纷开始裁员。布拉戈维申斯克居民大约有 45000 人,目前失业人口已超过 15000 人,该地区的前景可谓一片渺茫。俄阿穆尔州水道局已遣散所有员工。据俄阿穆尔水道局自 1900 年至大革命爆发之间的统计资料显示,阿穆尔地区所需补给皆由满洲所提供,出口运输则通过尼古拉耶夫斯克或符拉迪沃斯托克实现。俄国政府对一切进口货物均施加高额关税,主要是为了让本国货物能够拥有充足的市场,但恐怕难以实现,毕竟即使俄国拉起了许多"警戒线",但依然有大量货物以走私方式进入阿穆尔地区。而且如此高额之关税亦会导致日常必需品价格之暴涨。

38. 总结：黑龙江沿岸地区以及黑龙江全省之情况整体上非常乐观,地区经济飞速发展,定居人口大幅增加,耕地面积亦在逐年增长。富农几乎家家都有耕犁、除草机以及收割机。徐鹏远(Hsu Peng-yuan)先生的酿酒厂距离大黑河仅 4 俄里,可大量收购当地农产品。大黑河附近 70-100 俄里范围内已发现数个金矿区,黄金市场较好,已然成为本地区发展的主要力量。大黑河两家磨坊以及瑷珲一家磨坊均向这些金矿地区售卖大量产品。

鉴于上述情况,本人希望当地政府为了地区的发展与繁荣,可以同意并尽量推动下列措施的实施：

（1）如果可以的话，尽可能与俄国地方政府保持友好睦邻关系；互相抵制、封锁边境等行为于双方而言，均无益处。

（2）将中俄双方所签署的关于联合维护黑龙江边界河道航路标志的《地方工程协议》续约至1925年，乃至1925年之后。

（3）在大黑河至漠河河段以及大黑河至奇克特河段组织定期的邮轮与客轮服务。

（4）针对俄国轮船航行于中国一侧以及中国轮船航行于俄国一侧之一应事宜制定规章，保证中俄双方轮船享有平等权利。

（5）在嘎杂克维池水道竖立航路标志，以确保轮船为乌苏里江沿线中国居民提供补给品时，能够安全航行。

（6）严禁俄国炮艇在松花江口以任何理由拦截中国轮船。

（7）中国轮船在黑龙江上航行至哈巴罗夫斯克及尼古拉耶夫斯克的问题，以及俄国轮船在松花江上的航行问题，均应由中俄双方共同解决。

（8）解决自中国一侧向俄国一侧出口薪柴之问题，以发展中国在黑龙江边境地区的木料贸易。

（9）《临时地方工程协议》应由中俄双方共同制定并签署，从而为航行在黑龙江边界河道上的中俄两国轮船、民船及木筏提供合理的指引，以供其遵循。

您忠诚的仆人

易保罗（P. I. Ignatieff）

黑龙江航务专门顾问

2. 为 1924 年黑龙江航务年度报告事

Enclosure(Separate).

AMUR AIDS TO NAVIGATION: Technical Adviser's Report
for 1924; Summary of River Dues Collection, 1924;
enclosing.

216.

216.

I.G.

I.G.

Aigun   28th. March, 1925.

Entered in Card-Index.

Sir,
Replied to in No. 228.

I beg leave to refer to my despatch

No. 155:
Amur Aids to Navigation: Technical

Adviser's Report for 1922 and 1923;

Appendix 1.
and to hand you herewith a Report written by

Mr. Ignatieff on the work done by his department

during 1924.   An album of photographs to

supplement this Report is being forwarded to your

Appendix 2.
address under separate cover.   A Summary of

Amur River Dues Collection during 1924 is also

enclosed.   Detailed Estimates for the year

1925 will be submitted at an early date.

I have the honour to be,

Sir,

Your obedient Servant,

Commissioner.

The Inspector General of Customs,

Peking.

DESPATCHES		
From I.G.	To I.G.	
Commrs. No.	Port No.	
58/90,054	44 47 54	
74/90,942	67 77 91	
85/91,680	101 110 119	
93/92,051	144 155 156	
107/93,376	179 180 185	
108/93,388	193 198 215	
(Tel.10/6/'23)		
163/97,625		
188/99,953		
205/101,122		
214/101,722		

AIGUN NO. 216 TO I.G.

APPENDIX 1.

AIDS TO NAVIGATION ON THE AMUR.

REPORT WRITTEN BY MR. P. I. IGNATIEFF, TECHNICAL ADVISER ON AMUR AIDS TO NAVIGATION, ON THE WORK DONE BY HIS DEPARTMENT DURING THE YEAR 1924.

Custom House,

Aigun/Taheiho, 24th. March, 1925.

1.   The Provisional Technical Agreement for the year 1923-1924 was signed on the 28th October and the Regulations on the 30th November, 1923. The General Estimate of expenditure on upkeep of Aids to Navigation for the navigation season of 1923-1924, as foreseen by this Agreement, amounted to 55,000 Gold Roubles.

The estimate for the year 1923, i. e. from the 1st January, to the 30th November, 1923, amounted to the sum of 19,250 Gold Roubles, this being the sum approved by the Joint Technical Commission. When I was verifying the account of expenses for the year 1923 submitted by the Russian Amur Navigation Office, I found that the sum authorised to be spent was exceeded, therefore the expenditure was reduced and a final sum amounting to 19,247.94 Gold Roubles decided on.

Having finished the Annual Accounts for 1922 and 1923, I began to work out the Estimates for 1924.

2.   The closing of the frontier strongly affected the turnover of cargo, and the collection of River Dues on both Chinese and Russian sides considerably diminished. As a result of the above, a general decrease of navigation took place, and the C. M. Customs submitted a project to erect a new type

of

of Signal of a reduced size, which lessened the price by 50%. This project was approved and accepted.

The estimate for the year 1924, i. e. from the 1st December 1923 to the 30th of November 1924, submitted by the Amur Navigation Office was examined and reduced to the sum of 35,750 Gold Roubles by the C. M. Customs, and then approved by the Joint Technical Commission.

3.   The spare time before the opening of the Navigation season of 1924 was utilized by me in compiling a "Brief description of the Amur Province", and drawing charts of a reduced scale.

4.   At the beginning of the Navigation season, several questions concerning Aids to Navigation were mutually discussed with the representatives of the Amur Navigation Office. In June, availing myself of the shallow water, I proceeded together with the Russian River Inspector on board a Russian surveying launch on a tour of inspection. We carried out the sounding of the channel in the whole frontier section; corrected all defects in Aids to Navigation; and gave necessary directions and orders to the District Surveyors. The successful achievement of repairs to Aids to Navigation in due time was hampered by the G. P. U. (Governmental Political Office) which hesitated to give permission to the crew of the launch and to the District employees and workmen to cross the frontier. Moreover, the frequent transfer of district employees

employees irrespective of their experience and knowledge, carried out under the pressure of the dominant party, also affected the above operations. There were also several mistakes made by the Amur Navigation Office, which failed to give sufficient information to the District Surveyors. All these omissions were gradually corrected by us, when passing each separate District.

By the middle of August the repairs of Aids to Navigation were completed.

Towards the end of August and during September the Inspection Commission, consisting of representatives from the Russian side and myself, took over the work, and examined and verified the equipment of Districts. It must be mentioned that the boats in the various districts, which have not been repaired for many years, are now in a state of dilapidation, and that instruments necessary for carrying out repairs should be replaced by new ones.

5. Captains and Pilots on the Chinese vessels consider the repairs of Aids done by the Amur Navigation Office in the present year as quite complete, and the erection of Signals as correct.

6. There are 1,285 Signals of river-type, and 171 Signals of sea-type (Pyramid) in the whole frontier section (1,703 versts): of these, 162 old Signals of river-type and 5 old pyramids were replaced by new ones; over 50% of the shields and over 25% of posts were painted, and the Signals were all

perfectly

perfectly visible after the trees and vegetation surrounding them had been cut down.

7. During the present Navigation season the following Stations were opened and work done:-

  a/ Depth-Signal-Stations on 6 shallows where water was exceptionally low, for the purpose of indicating the change in depth. As the water on Beitonovsky shallows was very low, a Depth-Signal-Station was opened on the waterway "Panga" which was provided with Aids to Navigation.

  b/ 2 Traffic-Stations in 2 narrow passages.

  c/ Lighting on 8 shallows.

  d/ Water-gauge records kept on 6 Water-gauge Stations.

8. Information concerning the water level in the shallows on the Sungari, as well as on the Amur, were received by the C. M. Customs and were communicated to Captains of steamers.

9. During the present Navigation season the Harbour Master of the Taheiho Port, Mr. Baukham, kept a complaint book, in which Captains and Pilots of the Chinese vessels were invited to enter their remarks concerning defects in Aids to Navigation and any desirable alterations in, or addition to, Signals and lighting. All requests made by Captains were carried out by the Amur Navigation Office whenever possible.

10. The steam-launch used for work in connection with

with the upkeep of Aids to Navigation on the frontier section accelerated the work.

11.   At the beginning of the Navigation season the Taoyin and the Amur Navigation Office informed the population along the frontier of the severe punishment which would be imposed by Law upon persons damaging the Signals, and during the whole Navigation season no Signal was damaged.

12.   According to the local Technical Agreement and to the Estimates approved for 1924, the C. M. Customs, from time to time, advanced sums to the Amur Navigation Office, a total of 13,881.25 Gold Roubles being paid.
The balance on account of the actual expenditure incurred, will be paid on presentation and verification of the necessary documents. The Estimate will not be exceeded.

13.   At the end of the Navigation season the following statements were prepared:

a/ Table showing Commercial vessels and the turnover of cargo;

b/ Table of junks and the quantity of cargo carried;

c/ Statement concerning rafts;

d/ Statement of work done by the District Surveyors in general; erection of new Signals; painting of shields and posts; and repairs to Signals and quarters; and

e/ Estimates for upkeep of Aids to Navigation for the year 1925.

14.

14. The activities of the Russian Amur Navigation Office.

From 1896 to 1920, the Amur Navigation Office was an Independent Office, but in 1921 it became a part of the Amur Government Water Transport. On the 1st of January 1924, in accordance with orders received from the Central Government in Moscow, the Amur Navigation Office was again separated from the Amur Water Transport, and this has considerably improved its activity. The Amur Navigation Office has since received from the Amur Water Transport, dredges, steamers and launches for the upkeep of Aids to Navigation. In 1924, 100,000 Gold Roubles were assigned by the Russian Central Government for the use of the Amur Navigation Office and this enabled the latter to provide itself before the Navigation season with timber, paint, etc. for the repairs of Aids to Navigation.

At the opening of the Navigation season, the Amur Navigation Office commenced work in connection with repairs to Aids to Navigation.

To accelerate this work, two launches started from Blagovestchensk, one up and the other down the Amur. Temporary Signals to replace those destroyed were erected by District Surveyors, and Depth-Signal and Traffic-Stations were opened. Groups of workmen were organized by District Surveyors, and the repairs to Aids began between the 20th and 25th of June.

The surveying launch used for the transportation of materials was subsequently used by myself and the Russian River Inspector during the Navigation season

season for examining the channel and Aids to
Navigation on the frontier section. In the middle
of August, when the repairs to Aids has been
completed, a Commission was sent to take over
the work and check the equipment, and the
inspection was completed towards the end of
September.

Before the end of the Navigation season, Foremen
were sent to every district to cut the grass
and shrubbery around the Signals with the purpose
of protecting them against autumn and spring fires.
In addition to work in connection with the upkeep
of Aids to Navigation in the frontier section,
the Amur Navigation Office re-erected the Aids in
the section between Habarovsk and the Verhny-
Tambovsk, and a part of Aids as far as Nikolaevsk;
also those on the Zeya. Further, it took in hand
the construction of a jetty in the Blagovestchensk
winter-port, and also carried out dredging operations in the Muravevsky and Stretensky winter-ports.
After the termination of the 1924 Navigation
season, the Amur Navigation Office prepared accounts
showing sums spent on upkeep of Aids to Navigation
in the frontier section, as well as Estimates for
the year 1925, the latter being drawn up on the
basis of a grant of 400,000 Gold Roubles, which
the Central Government (in Moscow) has promised to
assign.

The above sum will be spent on the following
operations:

Dredging the channels and repairing the winter-
harbour; maintaining 2 steamers for River Inspection
work; keeping launches for use in the various
                              districts;

districts; increasing lighting Signals on dangerous
shallows; re-erecting Aids to Navigation on the
Ussuri and the Selemdja, and on the Amur as far
as Nikolaevsk; and removing rocks and obstructions.
Sums received as River Dues over and above the
grant will be available to cover cost of expenses
incurred in other directions.

15.   Navigation during 1924. Notwithstanding the
abundance of rain in April 1924, the water-level
during the ice-drift was fair only. In the
Taheiho harbour the ice started to break up on
the 29th of April; on the 2nd of May the ice-
drift began in a number of places; and it was
only on the 16th of May that the ice-drift
became general.

On the 11th of May the s/s "Aigun" left Taheiho,
on the 12th of May the s/s "Yang-hu" sailed with
a barge in tow; and on the 13th of May s/s
"Shanghai" and s/s "Shun-tien" left the port.
On the 15th of May the s/s "Tai-hsing" and the
s/s "Ching-lan" arrived, these having started from
Harbin on the 4th and 5th May. The s/s "I-hsing",
which went into winter quarters 10 versts below
Taheiho, safely arrived on the 12th of May.
In 1924, the water level in the Amur during the
Navigation season was above the average, but on
the Sungari a lasting lowness of water was
observed, a circumstance which strongly affected the
export of the autumn crop of beans and wheat.
A great innundation took place on the Selemdja,
which destroyed the stacks of hay, the corn
fields and vegetables, and carried away many

houses

houses and cattle. Several people lost their lives. An unexpected storm with snow, which broke out on the 19th of October impeded navigation; the next day the ice-drift began, and many vessels could not reach port.

16. **Mail & Passenger Steamship Service on the Amur:** As the result of the suggestion made by the C. M. Customs, the Heiho Taoyin proposed to the steamship Co. Wu-tung the organisation of a Regular Mail & Passenger Steamship Service which was affected at the beginning of the Navigation Season. The Wu-tung Co. selected 2 steamers: s/s "Chi-yang" and s/s "Tung-shan" to sail between Tahsiho and Moho (830 versts), and these two steamers sailed at the opening of the Navigation season. It was intended that there should be a sailing once a week. The s/s "Shen-yang" plying between Tahsiho and Chicote (147 versts) left the Port twice a week.

The 2 accidents to the s/s "Chi-yang", which took place on the 2nd of July and the 27th of August, interfered with the original plan, but the Wu-tung Co. replaced this vessel with another one.

17. **Turnover of cargo carried by Chinese steamers on the frontier section of the Amur.** The figures given below plainly indicate the yearly decrease of the turnover of cargo, as well as of the number of passengers. This decrease is due to the following causes:

  a/ The closing of the frontier;

  b/ The low economic condition of the Russians;

  c/

c/ The increase of the frontier guard along
the Russian shore on the Amur;

d/ The decline of trade and mining
business in the Amur region, due in
part to constant raids by bandits;

e/ Construction of a large distillery
(4 versts from Taheiho) which is now
supplying the nearest markets with about
200,000 vedros (1 vedro = 20 bottles)
yearly, this taking the place of spirit
formerly imported from Harbin; and

f/ The considerable yearly increase in the
ground under cultivation, this enabling
the local market to dispense with wheat
imported from Harbin.

A further decrease in the turnover of cargo is
prevented by the import of goods from Harbin for
the rich mining areas discovered in the neighbourhood of Taheiho. In summer 1924 on the above
mines over 15,000 workmen were employed; in winter
time this number fell to 10,000.

Arrival of steamers at Taheiho.

Flag.	1922.	1923.	1924.
Chinese	190	164	152
Russian	422	55	18
Total	612	219	170

Arrival of barges at Taheiho.

1922.	1923.	1924.
168	90	41

Amount

Amount of cargo carried.

Poods.

Flag.	1922	1923.	1924
Chinese	 1,900,000	 1,085,000	 812,575
Russian	 1,100,000	 45,000	 1,500
Total	3,000,000	1,130,000	814,075

Passenger traffic.

Flag.	1922	1923	1924
Chinese	 14,000	 21,000	 19,000
Russian	 17,000	 2,000	 15
Total	31,000	23,000	19,015

Amount of cargo carried by Russian vessels.

Poods.

	1922.	1923.	1924.
From Taheiho to Blagovestchensk	... 1,000,000	... 5,986	... nil.
From Blagovestchensk to Taheiho	....	100,000	...15,925 ... 1,500

Amount of firewood carried by vessels from the Chinese side.

To Blagovestchensk on Russian vessels:

Sajens:

1922.	1923.	1924
3,407	 3,139	.... nil.

To Harbin on Chinese vessels:

7,479	 5,650	 5,628

To Taheiho:

3,782	 172	 348

Arrival of Rafts at Taheiho.

Pieces of Timber.

529,015	 85,417	 66,846

Passenger traffic by junks:

918	 639	 667

Amount of cargo carried by junks.

Poods.

573,000	 400,000	 403,000

MOHO

MOHO - TAHEIHO TRAFFIC.

Number of Trips:

1922.   *1923.*   *1924.*
22 .... 14 17

Cargo carried.

1922.   1923.   1924.

Poods:

Up river:

300,000 .... 150,000 83,000

Down river:

20,000 .... 36,000 33,550

Passenger Traffic.

Up and down river:

5,400 .... 5,150 4,170

18.   River Dues: The sum collected as River Dues Collection was as follows:-

	1922.	1923.	1924.
Taheiho	$ 23,932.45	$ 15,068.64	$ 13,811.97
Aigun	$ 1,450.43	$ 2,458.12	$ 960.30
Lahasusu	$ 5,754.31	$ 6,243.14	$ 2,518.98
Total	$ 31,137.19	$ 23,769.90	$ 17,291.25

The sum of $ 17,291.25 will not suffice to cover expenditure on upkeep of Aids to Navigation in the frontier section of the Amur during 1924. The estimates prepared for 1924, amounting to the sum of 35,750 Gold Roubles were reduced to as low a figure as possible and it will not be possible to reduce them further during 1925. If an Agreement for 1925 is to be prepared on the basis of those of the past two years, i. e. if 50% of the cost of upkeep is to be paid by China, the following sums will have to be found:-

For

```
                                        Gold Roubles.
For  the  Amur  Navigation  Office ...  17,500
For  the  Taoyin's  Office ..........$ 2,000
For  the  Technical  Adviser's  Office$ 8,250
For  the  Collecting  Office (Customs)$ 2,000
                                 Total   29,750
```

Thus China must find a sum of approximatly $ 30,000 to meet her obligations during 1925. An increase in the River Dues Collection can be attained only by levying dues not as is done now, by dividing the Amur into 2 Sections and charging ½ tariff for each section, but by collecting at full rate, irrespective of distance and destination, as is done on the Russian side. This would double our collection and no additional grant from the Government would be needed.

19.   Freights.

                    Cost of passenger tickets:

	1922.	1923.	1924.
Harbin-Taheiho and Taheiho-Harbin 2nd.Cl.	$20.60	$21.60	$26.00
3rd.Cl.	$10.80	$10.80	$13.00
Moho-Taheiho and Taheiho-Moho 2nd.Cl.	$13.20	$13.20	$13.20
3rd.Cl.	$ 6.60	$ 6.60	$ 6.60

                    Freight on cargo per pood.

	1922	1923	1924
Harbin-Taheiho and Taheiho-Harbin	$0.06-$0.70	$0.06-$0.70	$0.08-$0.80
Moho-Taheiho and Taheiho-Moho	$0.08-$0.25	$0.08-$0.25	$0.08-$0.25

                    Freight on firewood per sajen (length).

	1923.	1924.
From the upper Amur..	$4.00-$5.00	$7.00-$8.00

20. Accidents to shipping. 1/ Fire broke out on the s/s "Chi-yang" when she was in her winter-berth on

on the 18th of May at 12 a.m., but fortunately there was no wind blowing and the flames were soon extinguished with assistance of the pumps of the s/s "Yang-hu".

2/ The s/s "Chi-yang" proceeding up the Amur with Mail and Passengers, on the 2nd of July, sprang a leak through striking a stone and was beached; she sank on the Ekaterininsky Shallows, 60 versts above Taheiho. The passengers were taken off by the s/s "Aigun", sent from Taheiho for the purpose. A part of the cargo was damaged by water.

As all attempts to raise the "Chi-yang" with the aid of barges were unsuccessful, the Russian Salvage steamer "Ivan Butin" with efficient pumps was engaged by the Wu-tung Co. and pumped out the water from her holds. The Wu-tung Co. paid to the Amur Water Transport Office $ 4,500 for this work. On the 8th of August the s/s "Chi-yang" safely returned to Taheiho. The cause of the accident was as follows. The steamer, having a 4½ feet draught, proceeded without paying due attention to the bearing-line Signals. The depth of water in the shallow was 9 feet.

3/ The s/s "Chi-yang", proceeding down the Amur from Moho with Mail and Passengers, on the 27th of August at 8 p.m. sank near the shore, when turning in Kuznetsovsky Shallows (40 versts below Chernayeva, and 390 versts above Taheiho). The cause of the accident could not be discovered, but it may be that, owing to the weak state of the hull, a stern plank was torn out when the steamer was making a quick turn. Attempts to

raise

raise the steamer were not successful, and she remained for the winter at the place of the accident. The Wu-tung Co. intend to cut her out of the ice and to make thorough repairs.

4/ Barges "Wên-chu" and "Fan-yin", towed by s/s "Nan-hsiang" and loaded with firewood, ran ashore on the Konstantinovsky Shallows. This accident was due in part to the great weight of the barges, which were being towed and which were more than the steamer could control, and in part to insufficient experience on the part of the Captain. After a portion of the firewood had been unloaded, the barges were got afloat again and towed into the Sungari.

5/ The s/s "Shanghai", proceeding with Mail and Passengers up the Amur to Moho, ran ashore on the Beitonovsky Shallows. The accident was due to the attempt made by the pilot to take the steamer through the old channel which was too shallow. This accident could have been avoided as the steamer companies were aware that a new passage through the waterway "Panga" had been provided with Aids to Navigation. The steamer got afloat by her own means.

6/ The s/s "Chung-hwa", which cleared for Harbin shortly before the end of the Navigation season, ran ashore on the 19th October, at 8 p.m. on the Konstantinovsky Shallows, and not being able to get afloat by her own means, she was frozen in by the ice and forced to winter there. The situation of the steamer is dangerous and it will be necessary to haul her to a safer place nearer to the shore. A snow storm and faulty steering caused the accident.

7/

7/ The s/s "Shanghai", which cleared for Harbin at the end of the Navigation Season, lost her anchor when shifting her berth opposite the village Sagibova. The anchor has not yet been found.

The accident was caused by a severe storm and insufficient strength of the anchor-chain.

The above mentioned accidents confirm the necessity of making the most careful examination of steamers and their boilers.

All the Chinese steamers purchased from Russians have had very little done to them since they changed hands, and the fact that they are still serviceable is to be explained by their originally solid construction and careful upkeep. If, however, owners continue to disregard the necessity of undertaking repairs, accidents will be likely to increase in number, and losses incurred by owners to become heavier. It would seem that when complete freedom of navigation is granted to Russian and Chinese vessels, on the frontier waterways, a still stricter examination of vessels should be undertaken every year by a Joint-Commission, as a single accident due to neglect, may have consequences entailing considerable expense. Inspection of this kind will be all the more important when Chinese vessels are allowed to navigate as far as Nikolaevsk, because vessels must be in a thoroughly sound condition to stand the severe storms frequently occurring in the lower Amur.

The

The Chinese owners of vessels are entirely
ignorant of the steamship navigation business
and do not appreciate the danger which menaces
vessels which have worn out hulls and boilers
and are generally in need of repairs.

21.　Vessels wintering at Taheiho.　In the winter
of 1923/24, repairs to vessels and boilers were
carried out in the Taheiho Port.
On the s/s "Chi-yang" one third of the foot-
walling was renewed and many planks were replaced
by new ones; on other steamers, planks, etc.
were also replaced. On the s/s "Shun-tien" a
patch was put upon the boiler which had developed
a hole, as a result of neglect.
The dredge belonging to the provincial government
was repaired.
After the vessels had been examined and their
boilers tested by the Harbour Master, they were
permitted to sail.
None of the vessels which wintered at Taheiho
were injured by the drift ice.
The following shipping remained in the harbour
during the winter: the government dredge; the
s/s "Hung-tai" (previously s/s "Moskwa"); the s/s
"Kwang-chi"; and the barge "Chi-pu".
The following vessels which had been caught by
the ice wintered on the Amur: the s/s "Aigun",
65 versts below Taheiho; s/s "Teh-hui", near
Chicote, 147 versts below Taheiho; s/s "I-hsing"
at Wen Ho Chen, 281 versts below Taheiho;
s/s "Chung-hua" on the Konstantinovsky Shallows,
90 versts below Taheiho; and the s/s "Chi-yang",
sunk

sunk on the upper Kuznetsovsky Shallows, 390 versts above Taheiho.

22. Work done in the Port: In the Taheiho Harbour before the opening of the Navigation season, many stones which were washed out and carried by the drifting ice, were removed from the foreshore.

In June the strengthening of the bund with fascines and stones, which was begun in 1923, was continued for a distance of some 6,410 square feet up the river, The water-gauge was also strengthened.

The sum spent on this work, $ 510.12, was taken from the unexpended portion of the sum assigned for the upkeep of the Technical Adviser's Office for 1923 and 1924.

The bund has been strengthened during the past 2 years for a distance of 417 feet, i. e. 13,476 square feet, at a total cost of $ 823.50.

It would be well, for the preservation of the foreshore and the bund at Taheiho to continue the strengthening of the shore every year by degrees, the cost to be defrayed from sums collected from vessels arriving in the Port.

23. The s/s "Hung-tai" (formerly the Russian s/s "Moskwa") belonging to Wang Yü-yün, a Chinese subject, who had taken previously Russian nationality, sailed under the Chinese flag on the 8th of October from Taheiho to Moho, under special authority received from the Taoyin.

Twelve

Twelve versts above Taheiho she was compelled
by a Russian gunboat, to return to Blagovestchensk,
but was subsequently released and proceeded on
the 10th up river with passengers and cargo
under the Chinese flag. The vessel returned to
Taheiho on the 20th October still flying the
Chinese flag, and remained in harbour for the
winter.

24. <u>Activity of Chinese Shipping</u>. The refusal of
the Chinese Authorities to allow vessels belonging to the Chinese Eastern Railway, and private
Russian vessels, to navigate the Sungari in 1924,
enabled Chinese S. S. Cos. to increase freights
and navigate without competition. The Wu-tung
Co., not foreseeing this state of affairs leased
a number of their cargo and passenger steamers
last autumn at low prices and sustained heavy
losses. The Wu-tung Co.'s vessels towing boats
in the early part of the Navigation season, made
a profit, because they were almost the only
such vessels in the district, but towards the
end of the Navigation season, partly owing to
the low water in the Sungari, and partly to
the fact that many barges and steamers were
engaged for transportation of firewood from the
Amur, their tow steamers on the Sungari were
insufficient to import the new crops to Harbin,
and as a result the Wu-tung Co., farmers, and ex-
porters, all sustained heavy losses. According to
information received, passenger and cargo steamers
belonging to the Wu-tung Co. have been chartered
for the Navigation season of 1925, at considerably
higher prices.

25.

25. **Activity of the Russian Water Transport**: The Russian Amur Government Water Transport closed their 1923 Accounts with a deficit, and the situation was critical. Before the Navigation season of 1924 commenced, the Amur Water Transport raised a loan of 250,000 Gold Roubles, and after having paid their debts, carried out repairs to shipping, and Mail and Passenger steamers began to sail in due time.

Private S. S. Cos. were overburdened with heavy taxes, and were unable to sail their vessels. The vessels of the Amur Government Water Transport, though they had no competition to face, had seldom passengers or cargo, and as a rule sailed in ballast.

The decrease that has taken place in shipping can be instanced by navigation on the Selemdja, where previously 16 steamers were plying during any one season. Last summer only one steamer was plying and she ran at a loss.

Owing to the large quantity of fish found in the Amur, about 1,000,000 poods of fish were available for transport, and the high freight (over $ 0.50 per pood from Nikolaevsk to Blago-vestchensk) should have helped to improve the shipping business. Owing, however, to inexperience on the part of those administrating the Russian Water Transport, who were entirely ignorant of navigation and commercial business, all the profits will be wasted through vessels being forced to winter far from their harbours and workshops, the necessity of doing so being due to wilful negligence on the part of crews in the execution

of

of their duties. The vessels loaded with fish
from Nikolaevsk lost an enormous amount of time
by stopping unnecessarily en route, no thought
being paid to dangers of navigation in the
autumn and the possibility of an early appearance
of drift ice. On the 20th of October, after
the snow storm of the previous day, drift ice
appeared and since the vessels were in a bad
state of repairs in many case paddles were
much damaged and 7 steamers, 1 sea motor boat,
and 9 barges with 250,000 poods of fish, were
forced to remain for the winter at places where
they had been caught in the ice.

Owing to the fact that private vessels did not
sail, and that the number of the vessels belonging to the Amur Government Water Transport was
insufficient, there was a good deal of unemployment among the employees. The Government to ease
the situation, decided to permit private Companies
to take vessels on lease on slightly easier
terms than usual. Five companies were formed, and
5 steamers taken on lease, but the Government
placed all kinds of obstacles in the way of
these companies; steamers were constantly stopped
for examination; fines were levied on every
conceivable pretext, and private persons were
prosecuted for giving cargo to the steamers and
the ventures came to an end.

Lack of experience is further shown by the manner
in which arrangements were made to supply firewood.
Firewood was stacked during 1924 in great quantity
on the whole frontier section of the Amur because
the

the countrymen, having no money, were paying their taxes with firewood, which they stacked along the river. The Administration of the Water Transport at the beginning of the navigation season proceeded to transport firewood from the mountainous district of the river Burea, which made it necessary to discharge and reload the firewood twice, and to convey it against the current, whereas it would have been a simple matter to bring it down stream from the upper part of the Amur. The firewood stacked in the upper part of the Amur had to remain where it was because all available barges had been sent in the autumn to Nikolaevsk to transport fish. As a consequence, there was a considerable shortage of firewood and an increase in price at Blagovestchensk.

Employees on government vessels were discharged in greater number than ever before and unemployment is now general.

These facts are stated to illustrate the lack of experience of the Bolshvist Authorities, as well as the gradual decay of vessels belonging to the Amur Water Transport, all of which were previously in an excellent state.

26. Economic survey of the Russian Amur province:

a/ The bad harvest of 1923 and the rising which took place in February of 1924, adversely affected the economic state of the province. A great many farms were totally ruined, because when the farmers were imprisoned their families were forced to sell horses and cattle at exceedingly low prices in order to pay the taxes. This prevented

the

the peasants from carrying out sowing on the
usual scale. Again, seed promised by the
Government was not given, and the total area
of land under cultivation considerably decreased.
The crop of 1924 in the Amur province was fair
only, whereas taxes were trebled. Such a state
of things is highly oppressive for the people
and tends to ruin those engaged in agriculture.
The price of flour fell to $1.20 per pood,
whereas the prices of the agricultural machines,
leather, tea and sugar remained high.

b/ The speculation in silver (old roubles)
undertaken by the government adversely affected
trade and caused lack of confidence on the part
of every one. The fall in the value of paper
-money caused people to hoard silver coins, and
this resulted in the disappearance of silver
from the market. A silver rouble was equal to
90 kopeks gold; 1 rouble 60 kopeks in small
silver coins was equal to 1 Gold Rouble. When
the time for the payment of taxes arrived, the
government banks unexpectedly declared that 1 silver
rouble was equal to 75 kopeks gold; and 2 roubles
50 kopeks small silver coins equal to 1 Gold
Rouble. Silver money of the new coinage is now
beginning to circulate. The size of the new coins
is equal to that of old coins, and 1 silver
rouble equal to 1 gold rouble. A decree has been
issued announcing that commencing from the 1st
January 1925 all silver and gold money of the
old coinage will cease to be legal tender and
that banks and government offices will be forbidden
to accept it.

c/

c/ Owing to heavy taxation and stiff terms
demanded by Labour of holders of concessions,
work in connection with gold mining in the Amur
province has been suspended. The English Gold
Mining Co. which was working with a dredge on
the Selemdja, succeeded in winning only a small
quantity of gold, and suspended its operations.
The workmen were discharged and returned to
Blagovestchensk at the expense of the Company.
Another rich English Gold Mining Co. which
undertook the prospecting of mines on the
Selemdja, which formerly belonged to Mordin, after
a short time quitted the mines, owing to never-
ending complications with workmen. This Company
has refused to continue work under present
conditions.

d/ In 1924, in the Yakutsk province in the Talmot,
a brook 1700 versts from Blagovestchensk, rich
deposits of gold were discovered, but the absence
of roads and the great difficulty with which
provisions are supplied, impede regular operations.
According to calculations made by the Mining
Department about 9,000 poods of gold can be
worked in this brook.

27. Economic state of the Heilung-kiang province
and of the frontier section of the Amur. The
welfare of the province depends entirely upon
the quantity of gold won. Discovery of rich
gold-bearing areas in the neighbourhood of Taheiho
with an annual output which has varied from
250 poods in 1923 to 300 in 1924 has added
to the welfare of the neighbourhood, and now
that land under cultivation has greatly increased,
                                                    the

the mines are being more and more supplied with
local products, which are much cheaper than
those imported from Harbin. Locally grown wheat
costs from 80 to 90 cents and oats from 60 to
65 cents per pood. Local farmers recognise the
importance of ploughs and other agricultural
machines, and these are in great demand.
Two steam flour mills in Taheiho, and one in
Aigun, have been working without intermission
and tens of thousands of poods of flour have
been sent to the mines every month. A considerable quantity of grain and potatoes is absorbed
by the distillery of Hsü Peng-yuan which is
equipped to supply yearly about 200,000 vedros
of spirit. Formerly this quantity of spirit was
sold to the Russian side every year, but now,
owing to the closed frontier, to the poverty of
the Russian population, and to the severe punishment for smugling, the quantity of spirit sold
to the Russian side has fallen to about 40% of
this amount.
Taheiho is the centre of the buying and exporting
of furs at a cost of about $ 200,000 yearly.
The passenger communication between Taheiho and
Tsitsihar in winter time is done by 12 autocars,
the price of a ticket being $ 50.00.

28. I should like to emphasize the fact that at the
time of the discovery of rich gold-bearing areas
in the Heilung-kiang province, there has been an
increase in population and in the amount of land
under cultivation, this tending to improve the
economic

economic state of the province.

There are a number of matters to which the local Authorities who are interested in the welfare of the province should give their attention.

They should endeavour:-

    1/ To open the frontier and secure reduction of the high Russian Customs Tariff;

    2/ To settle the question about the navigation of Chinese vessels to Habarovsk and to Nikolaevsk, and of Russian vessels on the Sungari to Harbin;

    3/ To determine the frontier line between the Chinese and the Russian Republics;

    4/ To elaborate mutual Rules of Navigation;

    5/ To carry out a still more careful examinations of vessels;

    6/ To increase River Dues Collection;

    7/ To levy dues from steamers for anchoring in the Taheiho Port, such dues to be used for carrying repairs to the bund; and

    8/ To come to a decision: 1/ whether there should be a mutual Administration of all the waterways in the Amur basin, and, if so, how funds are to be obtained; or 2/ whether the upkeep of Aids to Navigation should be continued as at present under a local technical Agreement with funds derived from collection of River Dues.

                          29.

29. For use in the forthcoming Sino-Russian
Conference, the Customs prepared Information
and data concerning the frontier line, and
the navigation of vessels on the Amur,
Sungari, Ussuri and Argun. This includes:-

1/ Information concerning the Russian Amur
Navigation Office;

2/ Information concerning Aids to Navigation
in the Amur basin;

3/ Information concerning the method of
controling the Waterways by the C. M.
Customs in the frontier section of
the Amur;

4/ Notes on a proposed new Agreement for
the ^year 1925;

5/ Memorandum of indispensable questions to
be discussed at this Conference;

6/ A re-statement of the 4th part of the
Annex to the Agreement of 1923 and 1924;

7/ Brief information concerning the mutual
maintenance of the Water Ways in the
Amur basin;

8/ Note on the frontier line between the
Chinese and the Russian Republics; with
chart of the Amur;

9/ Remarks on the right of military and
commercial vessels to navigate the rivers
in the Amur basin;

10/ Criticism of the proposed organisation of
a Joint Amur Water Ways Administration;

11/ Notes on the mutual maintenance of the
frontier rivers in the Amur basin with
estimate of cost;

12/

12/ Levying of River Dues;

13/ Notes on River Dues Tariff;

14/ Remarks on River Dues Collection
procedure;

15/ Memorandum on the navigation of vessels
on frontier and inland rivers, and on
the observation of Customs Rules;

16/ Proposed supplementary Rules to govern
the navigation of Chinese and Russian
vessels on frontier and inland waterways,
i. e.

    a/ Technical Rules concerning fire-fighting
      and life saving appliances;

    b/ Sanitary Rules for vessels and rafts;

    c/ Rules concerning the construction,
      adjustment, care and examination of
      boilers on steamers;

    d/ Rules concerning the examination of
      vessels;

    e/ Technical Rules concerning installation
      of electric light on vessels;

    f/ Rules concerning construction and
      equipment of motor-boats;

    g/ Rules concerning transportation of
      dangerous cargo;

    h/ Rules to govern conduct of passengers;

    i/ Rules to be attended to by vessels
      and rafts passing under rail bridges;
      and

    j/ Rules to be attended to by vessels
      passing the places where the telegraph
      cables are lying on the river bottom.

S. Ignatieff.

Technical Adviser on Amur
Aids to Navigation.

appendix . 2.

呈海关总税务司署 <u>216</u> 号文　　　　　　　　瑷珲关 1925 年 3 月 28 日

尊敬的海关总税务司：

根据瑷珲关第 155 号呈：

"黑龙江航务：呈送航务专门顾问 1922 年及 1923 年《黑龙江航务年度报告》。"

兹附黑龙江航务专门顾问易保罗（P.I.Ignatieff）先生编制的 1924 年《黑龙江航务年度报告》（附件 1）。另函附寄该报告相关照片集。

另附上 1924 年江捐税收分配图表（附件 2）。1925 年预算明细亦会尽快呈上。

您忠诚的仆人

贺智兰（R.F.C.Hedgeland）

瑷珲关税务司

1924 年黑龙江航务年度报告

（由黑龙江航务专门顾问易保罗（P.I.Ignatieff）先生编制）

瑷珲关 / 大黑河 1925 年 3 月 24 日

1. 根据中俄双方于 1923 年 10 月 28 日签署之 1923/1924 年《临时地方工程协议》以及于 1923 年 11 月 30 日签署之附加条款规定，1923 年及 1924 年航路标志维护费用预算总计 55000 金卢布。

中俄水道委员会批准之 1923 年（即 1923 年 1 月 1 日至 11 月 30 日）预算为 19050 金卢布，但本人核对俄阿穆尔水道局 1923 年费用报表时发现实际支出超出了预算金额，因此做出了适当的调降，费用支出最终定为 19247.94 金卢布。

1922 年和 1923 年的年度财务报表已编制完成，1924 年的预算核对工作即将开始。

2. 边境关闭后，黑龙江华俄两岸的货物贸易和江捐税收均受到严重影响，船运往来亦因此而大幅减少。有鉴于此，中国海关提出采用新式小型信标，如此可节省 50% 的费用；该方案已获批准。

俄阿穆尔水道局提交的 1924 年（即 1923 年 12 月 1 日至 1924 年 11 月 30 日）预算，经中国海关审核后，被削减至 35750 金卢布，中俄水道委员会业已批准。

3. 本人于 1924 年航运季到来之前完成了《黑龙江省简介》和小比例航图的汇编工作。

4. 另于航运季伊始与俄阿穆尔水道局代表就与航路标志有关的几个问题进行了讨论；6 月又与俄巡江工司共乘一艘俄国测量船，对边境地区的航路进行巡查与勘测，将航路标志有误之处一一改正，并对地区测量师进行了指导。

此前，本可在预计时间内顺利完成的航路标志维修工作却意外遭到俄国政府政治部的阻挠，政治部迟迟不允许船员、地区职员及工人过境工作；此外，俄国执政党不顾职员的经验和能力而对其进行频繁调动，也对航路标志维修工作进度造成了不小的影响。与此同时，俄阿穆尔水道局方面也出现了一些失误，未能给地区测量师提供足够的信息，幸而此等疏漏已于 6 月巡查期间得到纠正。

航路标志维修工作最终得以于 8 月中旬完成。

8 月末及 9 月间，本人与俄阿穆尔水道局代表对航路标志工作进行视察，对各地区的设备进行了检查核验。需要一提的是,各地区均有一些多年未曾修缮的轮船,如今已无法使用,用以维修轮船的工具亦须予以更新。

5. 中国轮船的船长和引水员也认为,俄阿穆尔水道局 1924 年的航路标志维修工作完成度较高,信标的竖立也达到了要求的标准。

6. 整个边界河道（计 1703 俄里）共有 1285 座江式信标和 171 座海式（角锥形）信标；其中有 162 座旧江式信标和 5 座旧海式（角锥形）信标都已换新,一半以上的盾形标桩和四分之一以上的标杆均已重漆,信标周围的树木等植被业已伐去,所有信标皆已清晰可见。

7. 1924 年航运季期间各站的开设及完成工作情况如下：

（1）有六处水位极低的浅滩设立水深信号站,以示水位变化；因贝托诺瓦斯基（Beitonovsky）浅滩水位极低,已于竖有航路标志的"潘葛（Panga）"水道设立水深信号站；

（2）有两段狭窄水路设立通行信号站；

（3）有 8 处浅滩设立灯塔；

（4）有 6 处水位观测站保留水位监测记录。

8. 松花江与黑龙江各浅滩的水位信息均已由中国海关实时传达给各轮船船主。

9. 大黑河口岸理船厅博韩（Baukham）先生于 1924 年航运季期间准备了一份意见簿,以供船长和引水员记录航行过程中所发现的航路标志问题,以及对信标、灯标乃至其他相关事宜的改进意见。对于船长所提各项,俄阿穆尔水道局已尽量予以解决。

10. 边界河道航路标志维修工作因使用了汽艇得以加快完成。

11. 航运季伊始,道尹和俄阿穆尔水道局便向黑龙江中俄两岸民众发出通告,凡有蓄意损坏信标者,一律严惩不贷,因此整个航运季期间,均无信标受到破坏。

12. 中国海关已根据《临时地方工程协议》和已通过的 1924 年预算向俄阿穆尔水道局分期支付摊款,总计 13881.25 金卢布。

尾款将于俄阿穆尔水道局呈交实际支出报表并通过审核后再行支付,总支出将不会超出预算。

13. 1924 年航运季结束后,下列报表业已开始编制：

（1）商船及其货物运输量统计表

（2）民船及其货物运输量统计表

（3）木筏相关统计表

（4）各地区测量师工作统计表（包括新式信标的竖立、盾形标桩和标杆的涂漆以及信标和宿舍的维修工作）

（5）1925 年航路标志维护工作费用预算表

14. 俄阿穆尔水道局

自 1896 年至 1920 年，俄阿穆尔水道局一直是一个独立的部门，直到 1921 年，才开始并入俄阿穆尔国家水运局。1924 年 1 月 1 日，根据莫斯科中央政府下达的命令，俄阿穆尔水道局又从俄阿穆尔国家水运局重新分离出来，这对此次航路标志的维修工作大有裨益。俄阿穆尔水道局不仅得到了俄阿穆尔国家水运局提供之用于航路标志维护工作的疏浚船、轮船和汽艇，还获得了俄国中央政府为之拨发的 10 万金卢布，由此得以于航运季开始之前购入用于航路标志维修工作的木料、油漆等材料。

刚一进入航运季，俄阿穆尔水道局便开始着手处理航路标志维护工作的相关事宜。

为加快进程，俄阿穆尔水道局派遣两艘汽艇自布拉戈维申斯克（Blagovestchensk）出发，分别前往黑龙江上游和下游各地开展维护工作。凡有必要之处，均设立了水深信号站和通行信号站；各地区测量师在有信标损毁之处竖立了临时信标，并组织工人维修队于 6 月 20 日至 6 月 25 日期间进行了航路标志维修工作。

用于运输材料的测量船后来为本人及俄国巡江工司在巡查边界河道的航路及航路标志时所征用。8 月中旬，航路标志维修工作得以完成，视查工作相继开始，并于 9 月末完成。

航运季结束之前，工头们被派往各地区清理信标周围的杂草和灌木，以防春秋两季发生火灾。除边界河道的航路标志维护工作外，俄阿穆尔水道局还对自哈巴罗夫斯克（Habarovsk）至外 – 坦波夫斯科（Verhny–Tambovsk）河段，至尼古拉耶夫斯克（Nickolaevsk）河段，以及结雅河上的航路标志进行更换。此外，俄阿穆尔水道局还承担了布拉戈维申斯克冬季口岸码头的维修建设工程，以及穆拉维夫斯基（Muravevsky）和斯列坚斯克（Stretensk）冬季口岸的疏浚项目。

1924 年航运季结束后，俄阿穆尔水道局编制了 1924 年边界河道航路标志维护工作实际支出报表，并照莫斯科中央政府承诺拨款之数（40 万金卢布）制定了 1925 年预算。

该预算将用于：疏浚河道和维修冬季停泊处；维修两艘轮船以供巡视河道之用；确保各地区汽艇可正常使用；增加危险浅滩的灯标数量；重建乌苏里江、谢列姆贾（Selemdja）河和黑龙江（远至尼古拉耶夫斯克）上的航路标志；清除石块和障碍物。江捐税收最终若超出上述拨款,还可用于支付其他方面的开支。

15. 1924 年航运

尽管 1924 年 4 月的降雨量不小,但浮冰期的水位仍保持正常。在大黑河港口,4 月 29 日冰块开始消融,5 月 2 日浮冰开始四处漂流,至 5 月 16 日,浮冰已是随处可见。

"瑷珲"号轮船、"扬湖"号轮船(拖带一条驳船)以及"上海"号和"顺天"号轮船分别于 5 月 11 日、5 月 12 日以及 5 月 13 日驶离大黑河口岸;"大兴"号轮船和"镜兰"号轮船分别于 5 月 4 日和 5 月 5 日自哈尔滨出发,共同于 5 月 15 日抵达大黑河口岸;冬季停泊于大黑河下游 10 俄里处的"宜兴"号轮船于 5 月 12 日安全抵港。

1924 年航运季期间,黑龙江的水位线一直保持在平均值以上,而松花江的水位却始终较低,严重影响了秋季大豆和小麦的出口。谢列姆贾河遭遇特大洪水,干草垛、农田及蔬菜均被冲毁,房屋和牲畜也损失了不少,还有几人不幸在洪水中遇难。10 月 19 日,一场始料未及的暴风雪骤然席卷而至,航运被迫中断,次日浮冰开始漂流,许多轮船都被困于江中,无法抵达口岸。

16. 黑龙江上的邮包与乘客运输

黑河道尹根据中国海关的建议向戊通航业公司提议由其负责组织航运季期间黑龙江上的班轮服务,以便定期运送邮包和乘客。戊通航业公司遂于航运季初派遣"吉阳"号和"东山"号两艘轮船前往黑龙江上游负责大黑河与漠河之间的航运(计 830 俄里),计划每周至少航行一次;同时派遣"沈阳"号轮船前往黑龙江下游负责大黑河与奇克特之间的航运(计 147 俄里),计划每周航行两次。

由于"吉阳"号轮船曾在 7 月 2 日和 8 月 27 日发生过两次事故,打乱了原来的航行计划,戊通航业公司遂派遣另一艘轮船予以替代。

17. 中国轮船在黑龙江边界河道上的货物运输量

1924 年的客货运输量均有明显下降,原因如下:

(1)边境关闭;

(2)俄国经济状况不佳;

(3)黑龙江俄岸守卫加强;

(4)黑龙江沿岸地区土匪猖獗,贸易和矿业受到重创;

(5)距大黑河 4 俄里处新建了一家大型酿酒厂,一年向附近各贸易市场供应的酒量可达 20 万俄桶(1 俄桶 =20 瓶),如此各贸易市场便不再如从前一样自哈尔滨进口酒;

（6）耕种面积逐年扩大,当地市场不再需要从哈尔滨进口小麦。

不过由于大黑河附近发现了丰富的矿区,需要从哈尔滨进口大量的供给品,货物运输量不断减少的趋势暂时得到遏制。1924年夏季,有15000多名工人在大黑河附近的矿区工作,冬季也还有10000人左右。

各项数据统计如下:

抵达大黑河的轮船数量			
轮船悬挂旗帜	1922 年	1923 年	1924 年
中国旗帜	190	164	152
俄国旗帜	422	55	18
总计	612	219	170

抵达大黑河的驳船数量			
	1922 年	1923 年	1924 年
	168	90	41

货物运输量（万普特）			
轮船悬挂旗帜	1922 年	1923 年	1924 年
中国旗帜	1900000	1085000	812575
俄国旗帜	1100000	45000	1500
总计	3000000	1130000	814075

乘客运输量（人次）			
轮船悬挂旗帜	1922 年	1923 年	1924 年
中国旗帜	14000	21000	19000
俄国旗帜	17000	2000	15
总计	31000	23000	19015

俄国轮船载运货物量（万普特）			
	1922 年	1923 年	1924 年
自大黑河至布拉戈维申斯克	1000000	5986	无
自布拉戈维申斯克至大黑河	100000	15925	1500

黑龙江华岸木枰运输量(俄丈)

(1)由俄国轮船运往布拉戈维申斯克的木枰量

1922 年	1923 年	1924 年
3407	3139	无

(2)由中国轮船运往哈尔滨的木枰量

7749	5650	5628

(3)运至大黑河的木枰量

3782	172	348

由木筏运至大黑河的木料数量

1922 年	1923 年	1924 年
629015	85417	66846

民船载运乘客量(人次)

1922 年	1923 年	1924 年
918	639	667

民船载运货物量(普特)

573000	400000	403000

自漠河至大黑河河段的运输

(1)航运次数

1922 年	1923 年	1924 年
22	14	17

(2)载运货物量(普特)

1922 年	1923 年	1924 年
上游		
300000	150000	83000
下游		
20000	36000	33550

(3)载运乘客量(人次)

上游和下游		
5400	5150	4170

18. 江捐征收：

	1922 年	1923 年	1924 年
	银圆	银圆	银圆
大黑河口岸	23932.45	15068.64	13811.97
瑷珲口岸	1450.43	2458.12	960.30
拉哈苏苏口岸	5754.31	6243.14	2518.98
总计：	31137.19	23769.90	17291.25

中方 17291.25 银圆的税收不足以摊付 1924 年边界河道航路标志维护工作的实际支出，而且 1924 年 35750 金卢布的预算业已为最低数值，1925 年预算的下调空间有限。因此如果 1925 年的协议仍以过去两年的协议为基础，规定由中方承担半数摊款，那么华方须支付的费用将包括：

	金卢布
俄阿穆尔水道局办公经费	17500
道尹公署办公经费	2000
航务专门顾问办事处办公经费	8250
征税部门（海关）办公经费	2000
总计：	29700

由此可见，中方 1925 年的应付摊款数额约达 30000 银圆。若要江捐税收有所提高，就必须提高江捐税率，且不宜再将黑龙江边界河段分成两段，每段按照半价税率征税，而应当像俄国那样，不管距离远近与目的地在何处，都按照全价税率征税，如此将多得一倍的税款，无需再依赖政府的额外拨款。

19. 运费

客票费				
		1922 年	1923 年	1924 年
		银圆	银圆	银圆
哈尔滨至大黑河	二等舱船票	20.60	21.60	26.00
大黑河至哈尔滨	三等舱船票	10.80	10.80	13.00

续表

客票费				
		1922 年	1923 年	1924 年
		银圆	银圆	银圆
哈尔滨至大黑河	二等舱船票	13.20	13.20	13.20
大黑河至哈尔滨	三等舱船票	6.60	6.60	6.60

每普特货物的运费				
哈尔滨至大黑河				
大黑河至哈尔滨		0.06—0.70	0.06—0.70	0.08—0.80
漠河至大黑河				
大黑河至漠河		0.08—0.25	0.08—0.25	0.08—0.25

每俄丈（长度）木桴的运费				
自黑龙江上游			4.00—5.00	7.00—8.00

20. 航运事故

（1）"吉阳"号轮船于 5 月 18 日中午 12 时在冬季停泊处不慎起火，所幸当日无风，火很快就在"扬湖"号轮船水泵的帮助下被扑灭。

（2）"吉阳"号轮船于 7 月 2 日载运邮包和乘客自大黑河前往黑龙江上游，行至"叶卡捷琳尼斯基"浅滩（大黑河上游 60 俄里处）时不幸触礁沉船；随后，船上的乘客转乘"瑷珲"号轮船继续向上游进发，但部分货物因落水而损毁。

戊通航业公司使用驳船打捞"吉阳"号轮船多次未果，最终不得不租用拥有高效水泵的俄国打捞船"伊万布廷（IvanButin）"号将船舱中的积水抽出，并为此向俄阿穆尔水运局支付 4500 银圆。至 8 月 8 日，"吉阳"号轮船终于得以安全返回大黑河。叶卡捷琳尼斯基浅滩的水深有 9 英尺，"吉阳"号轮船的吃水深度为 4.5 英尺，此次事故的主要原因是轮船在行进过程中未能严格按照方位线指示行船。

（3）"吉阳"号轮船于 8 月 27 日上午 8 时载运邮包和乘客自漠河前往黑龙江下游，在库茨涅佐夫斯基（Kuznestsovsky）浅滩（大黑河上游 390 俄里处；切尔纳耶瓦（Chernayeva）下游 40 俄里处）转弯时不慎沉船。

事故原因尚未查明，但很可能是因为船身脆弱，以致急转弯时船尾木板开裂。戊通航业公司使用各种办法进行打捞均不得其果，只能将轮船留在事发地，待冬季将之从冰层中移出，再进行修复。

（4）装载木桩的"文储（Wen-chu）"号和"梵音（Fan-yin）"号驳船在由"南乡（Nan-hsiang）"号轮船牵引途中，于康斯坦丁诺夫斯基浅滩搁浅。此次事故的部分原因是驳船重量超过了轮船所能控制的范围，且船主经验不足。船上的木桩卸下部分后，驳船再次漂浮起来，得以被牵引至松花江。

（5）"上海"号轮船在载运邮包和乘客沿黑龙江向漠河行进途中，于贝托诺瓦斯基浅滩搁浅。此次事故是由于引水员试图驾驶轮船从水位已经变浅的旧航路通过而造成的，但实际上各轮船公司早已知道新航路"潘葛"水道设有航路标志，此次事故本可避免。该轮船已自行重新漂浮起来。

（6）航运季濒临结束之际，"中华"号轮船于大黑河办理结关前往哈尔滨，不幸于10月19日上午8时在康斯坦丁诺夫斯基浅滩搁浅，无法自行漂浮起来，随后江面结冰，又被困于冰中，只得在原地过冬。该轮船目前的处境不妙，必须拖至岸边的安全地带。本次事故是由于雪暴以及驾驶失误所致。

（7）航运季结束之际，"上海"号轮船于大黑河办理结关前往哈尔滨，在行至俄村（萨吉博沃）对面转换锚位时不慎将船锚丢失，至今仍未找到。此次事故主要是由于特大暴风雪以及锚链的长度不足所致。

上述事故充分证明了对轮船及其发动机进行仔细检修的必要性。中国人从俄国人手中购入轮船后几乎未对之进行过检修，这些轮船之所以尚能使用，主要是因轮船本身结构坚固且养护得当，船主若继续漠视检修之必要性，事故发生的频率还将继续攀升，所酿成的损失也将越来越大。

如此看来，日后若中俄两国轮船获准于边界河道上自由航行，中俄两国有必要成立联合委员会对轮船进行更为严苛的年检，因为每一次由于疏忽而酿成的事故，都有可能造成巨大的开支。待中国轮船获准于黑龙江上行至尼古拉耶夫斯克时，此等检查则更有必要，因为轮船只有在完全稳定的状况下才能抵挡黑龙江下游频繁发生的暴风雪。

中国船主完全忽视了航运安全问题，他们没有察觉到那些船身及发动机已经受损的轮船所存在的安全隐患。

21. 在大黑河口岸过冬的船只

1923年/1924年冬季，大黑河口岸对停泊于此的轮船及其发动机进行了维修。

"吉阳"号轮船三分之一的底板均已换新，许多厚木板业已更换；其它轮船上的厚木板等部件也已置换。"顺天"号轮船的发动机因长期未检修出现破洞，已修补完毕。

省政府的疏浚船业已修理妥当。

凡于大黑河口岸过冬的船只，均由理船厅检验完毕后放行；过冬期间无被浮冰损坏者。

在大黑河口岸过冬的船只有：省政府的疏浚船、"鸿泰"号轮船（原俄国"莫斯科"号）、"广吉"号轮船以及"吉普"号驳船。

因江面结冰困于黑龙江上过冬的船只有："瑷珲"号轮船，泊于大黑河下游 65 俄里处；"德辉"号轮船，泊于大黑河下游 147 俄里靠近奇克特处；"宜兴"号轮船，泊于大黑河下游 281 俄里的温和镇；"中华"号轮船，泊于大黑河下游 90 俄里处的康斯坦丁诺夫斯基浅滩；"吉阳"号轮船，泊于大黑河上游 390 俄里处的库茨涅佐夫斯基浅滩。

22. 大黑河口岸已完成工作

航运季开始前，大黑河港口随水流和浮冰而来的石块均已清除干净。

自 1923 年起，大黑河口岸便开始使用梢捆和石块加固堤坝，1924 年 6 月，又向上游加筑 6410 平方英尺的堤坝；沿岸的水位标尺业已加固。

该项工程共花费 510.12 银圆，已由 1923 年和 1924 年拨予航务专门顾问办事处的办公经费支付。

过去两年间，筑堤总长达 417 英尺，面积共计 13476 平方英尺，总计花费 823.50 银圆。

为保护港口前滩和堤岸，最好每年都对河岸进行加固，相关费用可出江捐税收支付。

23. "鸿泰"号轮船（原俄国"莫斯科"号）为中国人王有云（本为俄国国籍）所有，10 月 8 日奉道尹特批，悬挂中国旗帜由大黑河驶往漠河；不料却于大黑河上游 12 俄里处被一艘俄国炮艇扣押并带回布拉戈维申斯克，但不日即被释放，并于 10 月 10 日继续悬挂中国旗帜载运客货向上游进发；最后于 10 月 20 日安全返回大黑河并于此过冬。

24. 中国航运业

1924 年中国政府拒绝属于中东铁路的轮船和俄国私人轮船在松花江上航行，中国航业公司的货运量因此而得以增加，面对的航运竞争压力亦得到缓解。然而戊通航业公司未能料及此事，已于前一年秋季低价租出了大量货船和客船，因而蒙受了巨大损失，好在其带拖船的轮船因是该地区唯一可用者而得以在航运季初期获利。然而，在航运季末期，由于松花江水位较低，大多驳船和轮船又均至黑龙江上运输木桄，戊通航业公司带拖船的轮船数量有限，未能完成自松花江沿岸各地运输新谷物至哈尔滨的工作，以致公司自身、农民以及出口商都蒙受了巨大损失。有消息称，对于 1925 年航运季，戊通航业公司已高价租出其货船与客船。

25. 俄阿穆尔国家水运局

俄阿穆尔国家水运局 1923 年财务亏损，形势不太乐观，幸而在 1924 年航运季开始之前,筹集到 25 万金卢布贷款,付清债务之后,便开始对轮船进行维修,最后邮轮和客轮均得以按照预期的时间航行。然私营轮船公司因不堪沉重的税赋,已无法再开展航运。

俄阿穆尔国家水运局的轮船虽已无竞争对手,但因乘客和货物量极少,往往是空载而行。

关于航运业的衰退,可以以谢列姆贾河的航运情况为例。以前该地区每年航运季都有 16 艘轮船往来不断,而去年夏季却只有一艘轮船定期往返,且属于亏本运营。

黑龙江中有大量鱼货,可供运输之量约达 100 万普特,再加上高昂的运费(自尼古拉耶夫斯克至布拉戈维申斯克的运费每普特约达 0.05 银圆),俄国航运业本应有所改善,然因俄阿穆尔国家水运局管理人员经验不足,对航海与商业一无所知,船员玩忽职守,往往将轮船泊于远离港口之地过冬,以致既得利益损耗殆尽。

轮船自尼古拉耶夫斯克载运鱼货后,航行途中经常会有不必要的停留,以致浪费了大量时间,而且从不考虑秋季航运期间可能遇到的危险,从不考虑浮冰是否会提前出现。10 月 19 日暴风雪骤然来袭,10 月 20 日开始有浮冰出现,而轮船因状况不佳,多数船桨受损;7 艘轮船、1 艘航海摩托艇和 9 艘载有 25 万普特鱼货的驳船均因浮冰出现而困于江中过冬。

由于私营轮船均未投入运营,而俄阿穆尔国家水运局的轮船数量又十分有限,大量职员惨遭失业。为缓解颓势,俄国政府决定准许私营公司以比以往更加优惠的条款租用轮船;随后五家公司顺势成立,租用了五艘轮船,然而摆在这五家公司面前的是政府设下的种种阻碍,轮船不断受到阻拦接受检查,因各种理由受到罚款,凡个人将货物交与轮船者均会受到检举,此番种种致使五家公司最终接连倒闭。

俄阿穆尔国家水运局的管理不善亦体现在木桴运输一事上。1924 年,农民因无钱纳税均以木桴相抵,以致整个黑龙江边界河道沿岸堆积了大量木桴。航运开通后,俄阿穆尔国家水运局的管理人员便前往黑龙江下游的山区运输木桴,但如此运输须装卸两次,运回时还须逆流而行,其实更简单的办法是从上游开始运输。但由于秋季所有可用的驳船均被派遣至尼古拉耶夫斯克运输鱼货,黑龙江上游沿岸囤积的木桴只能留于原地,结果导致布拉戈维申斯克地区木桴紧缺,价格飙升。

由此可见,布尔什维克政府经验匮乏,俄阿穆尔国家水运局的轮船状况亦已日渐衰败,不再如从前一般优良。

26. 俄阿穆尔省经济调查

(1)俄阿穆尔省 1923 年谷物歉收,1924 年 2 月又发生暴乱,经济受到重创。暴乱期间,农民被捕,家人们迫于无奈只能以极低的价格将牛马卖掉,以换得钱银缴纳税款。农民缺少牛马便无法如常播种,而俄国政府又未按照承诺下发谷种,以致耕种面积大幅减少。虽然俄阿穆尔省 1924 年的谷物收成还算可以,但税赋却增长了三倍,农民所受压力过大,濒临破产。面粉价格已降至每普特 1.20 银圆,但农用工具、皮革、茶叶和糖的价格却一直居高不下。

（2）政府对银币（旧卢布）进行投机买卖的行为不仅使贸易发展受到了影响,亦使民众失去了信心。纸币贬值后,人们纷纷开始储藏银币,以致市面上再无银币流通。当时 1 银卢布合 90 金戈比,小银币 1 卢布 60 戈比合 1 金卢布。然而,当民众缴纳税款时,政府银行却宣称 1 银卢布合 75 金戈比,小银币 2 卢布 50 戈比合 1 金卢布。目前新银币已开始流通,大小与旧银币相同,1 银卢布合 1 金卢布。政府已颁布法令宣布,旧式金银制币自 1925 年 1 月 1 日起不再为合法货币,银行和政府机构均不得再予以接受。

（3）俄阿穆尔省的金矿开采工作因税赋过重以及相应条款太过严苛等因素已被迫中止。此前一直在谢列姆贾矿山采金的英国金矿公司仅采到少量金子,无奈停工,业已将工人遣散并送回布拉戈维申斯克。另外一家英国金矿公司在谢列姆贾矿山勘测一段时间后,因工人问题太过复杂,断然离去,并表示情况若无好转,将不会重新开工。

（4）1924 年,雅库茨克省的塔莫特（Talmot）河（距布拉戈维申斯克 1700 俄里）一带经勘查发现存有大量黄金,然因无运输供给之路,开采之事受阻。据金矿部门估算,该地黄金开采量可达约 9000 普特。

27. 中国黑龙江省及黑龙江边境地区经济调查

黑龙江省的经济发展主要依赖于黄金产量,大黑河附近发现的金矿地区（1923 年年产量达 250 普特,1930 年年产量达 300 普特）已然推动了相邻各地的经济发展。目前,当地耕种面积逐年扩大,日益成为矿区所需供给的主要供应来源,与自哈尔滨进口的产品相比,当地产品的价格更为低廉。当地小麦每普特售价 80 到 90 分不等,燕麦每普特 60 到 65 分不等。当地农民开始意识到耕犁和其他农用工具的重要性,由此大大增加了农用工具的需求。大黑河的两家面粉厂和瑷珲的一家面粉厂昼夜生产,每月为金矿地区输送上万普特的面粉。徐鹏远的酿酒厂每年收购大量谷物和马铃薯,可产 20 万桶酒,此前均售予俄岸各地,而如今由于边境封锁,俄国经济萧条,走私又会受到严惩,其向俄方售卖的酒量已下降了六成左右。

大黑河是皮货的收购和出口中心,每年交易额约达 20 万银圆。冬季,大黑河与齐齐哈尔之间有 12 辆汽车往来运输乘客,每张票价 50 银圆。

28. 值得强调的是,黑龙江省发现大量金矿地区后,人口一度增长,耕地面积逐年扩大,全省经济状况得以改善。

为保证黑龙江省的经济繁荣，省政府应当：

（1）开放边境，设法让俄国海关降低其高额的关税；

（2）解决中国船只在黑龙江上自哈巴罗夫斯克行至尼古拉耶夫斯克以及俄国船只在松花江上行至哈尔滨一事；

（3）确定中俄两国边境线；

（4）制定中俄两国共同的《航务条例》；

（5）对船只进行更加彻底的检查；

（6）提高江捐税率；

（7）向泊于大黑河口岸的轮船征税，以此税款支付堤岸维护所需费用；

（8）决定：①中俄双方是否需要成立专门机构来管理黑龙江流域的所有水道，如有此需要，须决定筹集运营资金的渠道；②是否继续按照当前办法通过签署地方工程协议并使用江捐税收来完成航路标志的维护工作。

29.瑷珲关已将与黑龙江、松花江、乌苏里江和额尔古纳河上的船只航行以及中俄两国边境线有关的各类信息数据汇编成文，以供不日即将召开的中俄会议使用，具体内容包括：

（1）俄阿穆尔水道局相关信息；

（2）黑龙江流域航路标志相关信息；

（3）中国海关对黑龙江边界河道管理办法的相关信息；

（4）说明拟订 1925 年新协议事；

（5）中俄会议必谈议题的备忘录；

（6）1923/1924 年《地方工程协议》附录第四部分摘录；

（7）黑龙江边界河道联合维护相关信息概要；

（8）说明中俄两国边境线事（附黑龙江航图）；

（9）关于军队及商船在黑龙江流域各河道上航行权利事的意见；

（10）关于拟建黑龙江流域联合管理机构事的意见；

（11）说明黑龙江边界河道联合维护费用预算事；

（12）关于江捐征收事；

（13）说明江捐税率事；

（14）关于江捐征收办法的意见；

（15）关于边界及内陆河道上的船只航行及《海关章程》遵守情况的备忘录；

（16）关于管理中俄两国轮船在边界及内陆河道上行船的拟议补充条例：

① 消防及救生设备相关技术条例；

② 船只及木筏相关卫生条例；

③ 轮船锅炉的建造、调试、护理及检验相关条例；

④ 船只检验条例；

⑤ 船只上安装电灯相关条例；

⑥ 摩托艇的建造及设备相关条例；

⑦ 危险货物运输相关条例；

⑧ 乘客行为管理条例；

⑨ 船只及木筏通过铁路桥时须遵守之条例；

⑩ 船只通过江底铺有电报线处应遵守之条例。

易保罗（P. I. Ignatieff）

黑龙江航务专门顾问

3. 为 1925 年黑龙江航务年度报告事

AIDS TO NAVIGATION ON THE AMUR.

Annual Report for 1925.

Joint upkeep of Aids to Navigation on the Frontier Waterways in the Amur Basin mutually maintained in 1925 by Russia and China under the direction of the Sino-Russian Amur Aids Commission* may be summarised as follows:

1. GENERAL. The Chinese members of the Commission wishing to conclude as early as possible the 1925 Local Technical Agreement began negotiations with the Russian Members of the Commission early in the autumn of 1924 before the

Agreement for that year had expired. At this time, the opening of the Sino-Russian Conference seemed likely to take place and in consequence the Russian members of the Commission declined for a time to consider the proposal of a new yearly agreement arguing that the question concerning joint navigation on the Rivers Amur, Ussuri, Argun and Sungari, and the joint upkeep of Aids on them would be decided on a general comprehensive scale at this conference. The Conference, however, was postponed and the need for Aids work in 1925 being urgent, the Russian and Chinese members of the Commission finally by mutual agreement on 18th May, 1925, renewed the Provisional Local Technical Agreement for the period from 1st December, 1924, to the 30th November, 1925.

The original general estimate submitted by the Amur Navigation Office for work to be done during 1925 amounted to 65,000 Roubles : 55,000 Roubles for Amur Aids and 10,000
for

* Members of 1925 Amur Aids Commission.

Mr. Sung-Wen-Yu, Heiho Taoyin and Superintendent of Foreign Affairs
Mr. Ch'e-Hsi-chen, Adviser on Foreign Affairs.
Mr.R.F.C.Hedgeland, Aigun Commissioner of Customs.
Mr.P.I.Ignatieff, Technical Adviser on Amur Aids to Navigation.
Mr.G.D.Toropoff, Consul of U.S.S.R. at Taheiho.
Mr.P.P.Chebisheff, Director of Amur Navigation Office.
Mr.A.P.Sidoroff, President of Russian Government Amur Water Transportation Bureau.

For Ussuri Aids which the Amur Navigation Office hoped
would be begun during the year. A careful scrutiny of
this estimate found it excessive and it was at first
reduced to Roubles 44.000 : 40,000 Roubles being thought
sufficient for Amur Aids and 4,000 Roubles for Ussuri
Aids. The question of maintaining Aids on the Ussuri River
was eventually postponed because of the political difficulties involved; this river being under the jurisdiction of
Kirin Province, the approval of the Kirin authorities was
essential before any programme could be started and this
approval the Heiho Taoyin failed to receive, merely a
hope that for 1926 the way would be clearer for such
Aids work. The 1925 Agreement was finally concluded, the
final cost agreed to by both sides for Aids work to be
carried out by the Amur Navigation Office being fixed
at 44,268 Roubles, of which China was liable for payment
of half.

2. INSPECTION TOUR.

In March, 1925, the Amur Navigation Office forwarded
to the Chinese members of the Commission their proposals
for Aids work to be done in 1926, the estimated cost
of this work amounting to not less than 100,000 Roubles.
The following operation were proposed:

(a) Aids on Kasakevich Waterway between the Amur and Ussuri
Rivers.
(b) Aids on the Ussuri as far as Hulin.
(c) Aids on the Ussuri beyond Hulin, on Sungacha River, and
Lake Hanka.
(d) Dredgework on the Uper Amur above Taheiho.
(e) Rock removal on the Argun River.
(f) The usual Aids work on the Amur as per 1925 Agreement.

I started at the end of September, 1925, on the Russian
s.s. "Amur" on a tour of inspection down the Amur, through
the Kasakevich Waterway and up the Ussuri as far as
Hulin. From the information gathered it was clear that
(a) Aids on the Kasakevich Waterway and (b) Aids on the
Ussuri as far as Hulin was welltimed and necessary.

Chinese

Chinese shipping and trade between the Sungari and Ussuri had noticeably increased, the Ussuri valley was more cultivated, and there were more inhabitants and settlers. The Kasakevich Waterway is winding, full of shoals and often alters its channel and is the only way by which Chinese ships at present can navigate between the Amur and Ussuri; this is the former boundary line between Russia and China and the erection of Aids on it is likely to raise boundary questions, as China desires that the land between this Waterway and the real mouth of the Ussuri be regarded as Chinese soil, Chinese steamers to have the right to navigate to Habarovsk on both the Amur and Ussuri Rivers, a right which up to this time has been denied them by Russia.

As far as the technical side of Aids upkeep on this Waterway is concerned, at least 50 beacons will be necessary and the cost of erection, repairs etc., for the first season should not be beyond 2000 Roubles. Should politics complicate the question on the ground that the Aids Commission doing joint work thereon might prejudice China's future claims for a readjustment of boundaries - a fear that is entertained in some quarters - it might be possible to find a way whereby the work could be done either by the Chinese authorities alone or by the Amur Navigation Office, the entire cost to be paid by China. I found on the Ussuri stretch to Hulin about 100 beacons still remaining from the former Aids, and that in order to reestablish Aids, it would be necessary to erect from 130 - 140 new beacons, repair the old ones, and shift many of them because of changes in the channel. The cost of such work it was estimated should not cost more than 8,000 Roubles the first year. With reference to

(c) Aids on the Ussuri beyond Hulin, on Sungacha River,

and

and Lake Hanka, the need at the present time was found
not to be urgent. The land bordering this upper section
of the Ussuri is low, is sparsely populated, poor in
soil, the river is shallow, no Chinese ships ply thereon,
and only one Russian steamer with two barges navigated
this stretch to Lake Hanka during the 1925 season, return-
ing empty as the Chinese authorities refused her permission
to export beans from China. Moreover the likelihood of
increased steamer traffic is remote at present as steam
navigation on Lake Hanka, Sungacha, and Ussuri is opposed
by the Ussuri Railway which in 1925 transported 1,253,000
poods of beans by rail from the surrounding regions.
With reference to (d) Dredgework on the Upper Amur above
Taheiho, this project was also regarded as unnecessary for
the present. With a closed frontier and trade on the
Amur practically at a stand-still, during the summer of
1925 only one Chinese steamer plied above Taheiho and
only 3 Russian mail and passengers steamers above Blagovestchensk and occasionally a towing steamer for firewood.
For such limited shipping, extensive dredging operations
were regarded as premature and, with the shortage of funds
at the disposal of the Chinese members of the Commission,
out of question should the work be jointly undertaken.
(e) Rock removal on the Argun I reported to the Commission
as also unnecessary for the time being. Lower Argun is
stony and rocky with mountainous shores: Upper Argun is
shallow with lowlying shores easily inundated: navigation
on both reaches is difficult and there is little trade
because of the sparse population. There are no Chinese
steamers on the Argun and only one Russian Government
steamer making one or two trips each summer frequently
wrecked and working under great difficulties. Eight small
junks sailing on the Argun are proving sufficient for the
                                                    needs

needs of the Chinese settlers. The project for joint removal of rock under the present circumstances failed to have the approval of the Chinese members of the Commission and the matter was dropped, as was also Aids on the Ussuri above Hulin, on Sungacha, and Lake Hanka, dredging on the Amur being left unsettled dependent on whether China would grant Russia permission to do this work on her own account, and the Commission mutually agreeing favourably to consider when the time came for signing the 1926 Agreement, Aids on Kasakevich Waterway and on the Ussuri as far as Hulin.

(f) The Aids work on the Amur as agreed to the 1925 Agreement, I found was very satisfactory and I brought back a very favourable impression. The channel had been accurately marked, beacons had been well placed, were in good repair, and conspicuously placed, the most important shallows and dangerous places were being lighted at night thus enabling steamers to sail safely during favourable water and clear weather, and watchmen were on duty on the various shallows. In large measure, the good state of the Aids in 1925 was due to better organisation of the Supervisory Staff, duties of the District Surveyors being more clearly defined, and to the fact that workmen were hired locally in each sub-district whereas in 1924 the workmen sent from Blagovestchensk by the labour unions caused much trouble and did their work carelessly. During the season of 1925, there were 1303 river-type beacons and 171 pyramids; of these, 115 river-type beacons, 20 pyramids, and 2 signal masts were renewed during the season. From 1st January, 1925, signals on the shallows were changed in accordance with new U.S.S.R. Rules governing weights, measures, etc,, depths now being measured by centimeters and meters instead of by feet.

3 . SINO-RUSSIAN

3. SINO-RUSSIAN CONFERENCE AT MUKDEN. Having been invited
by the Chinese Authorities and with the consent of the
Inspector General, I attended this conference which took
place at the end of March, 1925, in the role of Technical
Adviser on Frontier River Questions. Information compiled
at Taheiho - (1) Amur Navigation Office, (2) Aids in the
Amur Basin, (3) Steam Navigation on the Frontier Rivers together with Charts and plans, (4) Suggested Navigation
Rules for Chinese and Russian ships on Frontier Rivers, -
were handed over to Admiral Shen, President of the Conference. Later, in accordance with his request, I prepared
four projects for joint upkeep of rivers mutually used
by Russia and China, and a project regarding a River
Inspectorate Staff, and placed at his disposal all information considered of value in understanding the conditions
on these rivers. One of the contentions of the Russian
representatives at the Conference was that the purchase
of Russian ships by China had been unlawful and that
this question must be solved before others were taken
up; another was that Russian ships be allowed on the
Sungari. The Chinese on their side wished (1) a re-
determination of the Frontier: (2) the islands between
Kasakevich Waterway, Amur, and Ussuri, to be given back to
China: (3) Chinese ships to have the right to navigate
to Habarovsk on both Amur and Ussuri Rivers: (4) the
land on the River Zeya formerly belonging to Chinese to
be given back to China: (5) Chinese ships to have the
right to ply on the Amur as far as Nikolaevsk. With
reference to the last request, the Russian representatives
submitted that (a) Chinese ships must first conform to
"Lloyd's" the same as Russian ships: (b) they must follow
Russian Navigation Regulations and submit to Russian
Customs, River, and G.P.O. Inspections: (c) must have profes-
sional Certificates and pay the same taxes as Russian
ships

ships: (d) the Chinese crews must become members of the Russian Workers Union of Water Transport and conform to its regulations: (e) Chinese ships owners must agree to all clauses of the "Collective Contract" as well as pay wages according to the Union Regulations and all levies in favour of various kinds of Russian Government activities for the welfare of workmen in the way of medical aid, social betterment, and public instruction. All these stipulations obviously being so impossible for Chinese ships, it proved an unprofitable undertaking for the Chinese authorities to get permission for Chinese ships to navigate to Nikolaevsk. The Conference subsequently failed, and I left for Taheiho toward the end of June.

4. RUSSIAN AMUR NAVIGATION OFFICE. After the Amur Navigation Office was separated from the Russian Government Amur Water Transportation Bureau, and became an independent organisation, River Dues collected on Russian ships was discontinued from the summer of 1925, and funds for the carrying on of Aids work on Russian Inland Waters and Frontier Waters were obtained from Moskow, work being planned without much regard for immediate needs of trade, number of vessels plying on the waters concerned, and navigation in general. In 1924, the Amur Navigation Office sent to Moskow estimates for work contemplated amounting to 280,000 Roubles; Moskow appropriated 170,000 Roubles. In 1925, an estimate for 478,000 Roubles was submitted: Moskow granted 395,000 Roubles. For work planned in 1926 the Office submitted an estimate for 1,200,000 Roubles: it is understood that Moskow has appropriated 780,000 Roubles. The situation in which the Chinese Members of the Aids Commission find themselves is now different from that of previous years. Russia is

is now apparently not so eager to obtain money from
China for Aids work and is making plans quite out of
proportion to the Chinese funds obtained from River Dues.
This financial situation of the Amur Navigation Office
will explain the extensive Ussuri Aids projects, dredging
plans and rock removal on the Argun which the Russian
Members of the Commission hoped to carry through this
year. A great deal of the money obtained from Moskow
is of course being spent in improving navigation on
Russian Inland Waters, but the Amur Navigation Office is
especially eager to bring back the Amur and Ussuri Aids
to the former high state of efficiency of the Czarist
Czarist Regime. Toward the end of the 1925 season, the
Navigation Office got back from the Transportation Bureau
all its working steamers, barges, several workshops and
stores, and is now an independent organisation. The
Director of the Office is a newly appointed communist
from Moskow, Mr. Dianoff; the former Director, Mr.Chebisheff,
Engineer, having been appointed Assistant Director.

5. RUSSIAN GOVERNMENT AMUR WATER TRANSPORTATION BUREAU.
The expected Sino-Russian Conference in the spring of
1925 and the undisguised hopes of the Representatives of
the above Bureau for a favourable result of negotiations
were the motives for big plans for the transportation
of beans and wheat from the Sungari - above 3,000,000
poods - to Habarovsk and Nikolaevsk, - and from Lake
Hanka - 1,000,000 poods and more - to the Railway Station
at Iman. With the unsuccessful termination of the Mukden
Conference, all these plans had to be dropped. The
Russian Authorities then started to solicit Mukden
permission for ships belonging to the C.E.R. to navigate and exchange loaded barges at the mouth of the
Sungari, but this also was not allowed. Consequently the
                                                    whole

whole plan of the Transportation Bureau broke down, and
owing to the absence of local and transit cargo, the
small number of passengers, and the poor catch of salmon,
its **ships** were practically without work and at the end of the
year there was a deficit of 400,000 Roubles. 17 steamers
run by this Bureau which started sailing at the beginning
of the navigation season were laid up in Blagovestchensk,
and the crews were discharged. Toward the end of the
season, only 3 mail steamers sailed between Stretensk and
Blagovestchensk: four between the latter place and Nikolaevsk:
two on the Zeya River and there were two towing steamers.
In view of the many unemployed crews, five private companies were organised and tried to run 5 private steamers, but the Bureau wishing entirely to kill competition
kept its own steamers running on lowered freight rates
and passenger fares, thus depriving these private companies
of any profits because they had to pay burdensome taxes
placed on private enterprises. The experiment of this
Bureau in running government steamers on the Rivers Argun,
Selemdja, Upper Zeya, Burea, and Amgun, was a failure
because of the lack of cargo, stagnant mining and industry
and also because of low water prevailing on these rivers
during the summer. The new dry dock constructed at
Blagovestchensk proved too small for the bigger steamers
owing to mistakes in project and also in calculations.
The lack of technical **know**ledge and commercial ability
are the main causes of the Bureau's failure in every
transport and trade business. On the Ussuri there were
2 steamers navigating with barges: one made 8 trips, the
other which traded on behalf of the co-operative stores
made 5 trips, but both ran at a loss. The Bureau also
tried to heat steamers with charcoal, but this trial as
on previous occasions was not successful, and the accounts
showed that the charcoal, having been purchased at existing

high prices together with cost of constructing storehouses, was 2½ times more expensive than firewood. No Russian steamers traded with the Chinese side, four Russian vessels entering Taheiho Harbour in ballast during the season.

6. CHINESE SHIPPING. The Chinese steamer traffic on the Amur and Ussuri is largely linked with that on the Sungari and practically all steamer traffic at Taheiho is between this port and Harbin. The fact that the C.E.R. boats and private Russian steamers were not allowed to sail on the Sungari enabled Chinese shipping to work without foreign competition and with increased freightage. For a time, freight on grain from Chiamussu to Harbin was as high as 22 cents per pood and from Fuchin 33 cents per pood. Freight between Harbin and Taheiho was quoted as high as $0.80 per pood for general cargo and between Taheiho and Moho as high as $0.40 per pood. The advantage of absence of foreign competition was plainly appreciated by Chinese shipowners and merchants who during the Mukden Conference sent many solicitations to prohibit Russian vessels from the Sungari. Further protests were also sent against allowing Russian vessels permission to transport grain and beans from the Sungari to Habarovsk and Nilolaevsk. The Chinese merchants and shipowners understood clearly that the compensation the Russians proposed to give for such rights, namely that Chinese vessels would also be allowed to ply on Russian Inland Waters to Nikolaevsk, would tell heavily against them because of the restrictions, regulations imposed, high standard to be maintained by Chinese steamers, and the endless possibilities of misunderstandings. Due to the prohibition against Russian vessels on the Sungari, Soskin **Bros.** of Harbin sold 4 of their steamers and 10 barges to various Chinese firms. The end of a very favourable navigation

navigation season saw practically all grain and beans transported to Harbin. On the 1st September, the Wutung Steam Navigation Company transferred its working plant to the North East Navigation Bureau operating under the auspices of the Government of the Three Eastern Provinces. The above company plans to sail during 1926 independently of other steamer companies and is placing the big steamer "Haicheng" on the Harbin - Taheiho run for mail and passengers, but this steamer as well as the s.s. "Harbin" are too big for navigation on the Sungari, and accidents may be expected. Although steamer traffic on the Sungari was so profitable, the same cannot be said with reference to traffic on the Amur. There was a clear decrease in turnover of cargo and passengers and number of entrances and clearances of vessels largely due to the closed frontier, low economic condition of the Russian and Chinese sides, decline in Chinese trading enterprises and mining, more land under cultivation in the Taheiho regions making it unnecessary to import wheat from Harbin, and the small amount of firewood transported to Harbin.

Vessels Entered and Cleared at the Taheiho Customs.

Year.	River Steamers. (including Towed Barges)		Native Craft.		Total.	
	NO.	Tons.	NO.	Tons.	NO.	Tons.
1922.	1,543	436,500	1,796	25,144	3,339	461,644
1923.	605	192,768	1,315	36,820	1,920	229,588
1924.	407	113,952	1,352	20,617	1,759	134,569
1925.	263	59,846	1,490	25,225	1,753	85,071

Gross Value of the Maritime Customs Trade at Taheiho.

1922	1923	1924	1925
6,727,105 Hk.Tls.	5,324,035Hk.Tls.	4,617,175Hk.Tls.	3,108,210Hk.Tls

Passenger Traffic to and from Taheiho.

1922	1923	1924	1925
30,255	21,800	19,530	15,083

7.

7. AMUR RIVER DUES COLLECTION. The effect of such a marked decrease in trade of the port, had a disastrous effect on the River Dues Collection, as it proved insufficient to meet the expenses for 1924 and 1925, and the Mukden authorities although they found it highly necessary to continue the present arrangment for mutual Aids work, maintained that the money for the undertaking must continue to be found locally. Early in the season, anticipating a shortage, it was finally decided by the Chinese Commission Members and approved by the Taheiho Chamber of Commerce that River Dues should be levied at double rates. This measure although it increased the 1925 collection nevertheless did not suffice to bring in sufficient money to cover expenses.

Amur River Dues Collection (Collected at Taheiho, Aigun, Lahasusu)

1922	1923	1924	1925
$31,137.19	$23,769.90	$17,291.25	$28,819.61

Expenditures on behalf of Amur Aids.

1922	1923	1924	1925
$20,168.99	$22,156.86	$30,097.90	$36,408.96

The balances carried forward in 1922 and 1923 plus the 1924 collection were sufficient to meet the 1924 payments with the exception of $225,41 which were paid out of the 1925 collection. In order to meet the 1925 obligations, it was necessary to negotiate a loan authorised by the Inspector General from Sungari River Dues Account kept by the Harbin Customs totalling $20,000 of which a 1st instalment of $10,000 was applied for to balance the 1925 Account. The collection for 1926 seems destined also to be too little to cover the programme outlined for that year

year, and the question of putting Amur Aids on a proper
financial basis is urgent.

8. CONDITIONS OF NAVIGATION DURING 1925. The season was
very long and the depth of the water as a whole very
low. On the 1st May, the river was free of ice at
Taheiho, and on the 2nd May two steamers arrived from
Aigun where they had spent the winter. Because of the
early spring, there was little ice drift, most of it
melting away. On the river Shilka, water remained low -
2 feet - until the middle of July. On the Upper Amur
there was low water during May, but later on high water
on the Argun raised it to heights above the average.
On the Middle Amur, owing to the lack of water on the
Zeya and Selemdja Rivers, the water was extremely low
until the first days of August: on the Konstantinovski
and Poyarkovski Shallows the level of water was constantly
changing, falling to two feet and less, obliging steamers
to pass by deeper side - channels. The Sungari had
sufficient water at the beginning of the season, but
became very shallow during June, remained so throughout
July and August and then with big rains had very
favourable water during September and October. In October
ice at Taheiho began to form and started to drift after
a snowstorm on the 20th October. The last steamer left
Taheiho for Harbin on the 23rd October, whereupon the
weather became warm again and the river did not close
until the 17th November, the latest date since 1903. Such
a long navigation season enabled all ships to reach
their winter ports.

9. ACCIDENTS TO SHIPPING. In my Annual Report for 1924
I stated that Chinese steamers were in bad condition,
the wooden hulls of many were rotten, the machinery and
boilers were getting too old, that serious attention must
be given to the raising of standards under which these
vessels

vessels were to be allowed to run, and that the aging of these vessels without replacement or most thorough repairs would lead to an increase in accidents. The steamer accidents during the season of 1925 were mainly due to the above causes. The s.s. "Chiang" and s.s. "Hsiching" had their stern planks torn out because the beams were rotten and crutches could not stand: the s.s. " Shanghai" sank on the Sungari after scraping over a mud shallow in an overloaded condition, her bottom planks having sprung through strain on rotten parts: the s.s. "Shuntien" on Sansing Shallows sprang a leak through striking a stone. The steamers "Shaohsing" and "Harbin" collided in trying to pass each other in a narrow channel above Fuchin on the Sungari, and the s.s. "Shaohsing" sank with a broken hull. An accident of this kind emphasises the need for an official code of "Rules for Navigation on the Sungari" and also for "Rules for Navigation on the Frontier Rivers". The s.s. "Chunghua" in landing on the beach on the Upper Amur near the village Sandoka sprung a leak by striking a stone with resulting damage to cargo. The Aids must consider in the near future the removal of stones near Chinese landing places.

10. **TAHEIHO HARBOUR**. All changes in channel, alterations to beacons, depths and lights were reported by the Amur Navigation Office to the Chinese Customs which posted such information for the use of the Public. Telegrams were also received from Sansing reporting the depths on the Shallows for steamer information. In order to guide steamers entering the Taheiho Harbour, a red floating beacon was again moored at the upper end of the gravel spit and kept lighted at night. Large stones carried down near the bund by drifting ice or washed out from the shore during high water were removed. In order to strengthen the embankment opposite the Custom House and

watergauge

watergauge, willows were planted. The foreshore and bund are in need of further improvement and the gravel spit threatens to silt up the entire harbour. Sums of money are required for these works which it is impossible at the present time to consider collecting because of the stagnant condition of shipping and trade in general.

11. CONCLUSION.

There are a number of matters to which the Chinese Authorities who are interested in the welfare of Kirin and Heilungkiang Provinces should give their attention.

1) To draw up the Technical Agreement on Aids for 1926.

2) To include in it arrangments for maintaining Aids on the Ussuri as far as Hulin and on the Kasakevich Waterway.

3) To take up the question of "Rules for Navigation on Chinese Inland Waters in North Manchuria".

4) To issue "Rules for Navigation on Frontier Rivers" with the concurrence of Russia.

5) To raise the standard of Chinese vessels, lay down "Sanitary Rules", and prohibit overcrowding of passengers.

6) To effect a stricter control of Officer's Certificates.

7) To strengthen the power of ships Captains and prevent Compradores from interfering with the running of vessels.

8) To obtain for working vessels of the Amur Navigation Office the right to enter the Sungari as far as the Lahasusu Custom House which gives the Amur Aids a great deal of assistance.

9) To remove stones from Chinese landing places along the Amur.

10) To consider Taheiho Harbour Conservancy.

11) To raise funds for Amur Aids as the River Dues Collection are insufficient.

P. Ignatieff

Custom House,

Aigun /Taheiho,1st May,1926.

Technical Adviser on Amur Aids

to Navigation.

1925 年黑龙江航务年度报告

1925 年，在中俄黑龙江水道委员会①的指导下，中俄双方再一次对黑龙江流域边界河道航路标志展开了联合维护工作，总结如下：

1. 概览

1924 年初秋，即 1924 年《临时地方工程协议》期满前，中俄黑龙江水道委员会双方委员开始就续签该协议一事进行协商。中方委员希望可以尽早签订 1925 年《临时地方工程协议》，而俄方委员则以中俄会议即将召开为由，拒绝就签署该协议一事进行协商。原本黑龙江、乌苏里江、额尔古纳河及松花江上的航运问题，以及联合维护上述河道航路标志的各项事宜，都将在中俄会议上进行协商，但会议意外延期，而边界河道航路标志维护工作却迫在眉睫。最终，中俄黑龙江水道委员会双方委员于 1925 年 5 月 18 日续签《临时地方工程协议》，有效期自 1924 年 12 月 1 日起，至 1925 年 11 月 30 日止。

俄阿穆尔水道局提交之 1925 年初始预算总计 65000 金卢布，其中 55000 金卢布用于黑龙江航路标志维护工作，10000 金卢布用于乌苏里江航路标志维护工作（俄阿穆尔水道局希望该项工作可于 1925 年开展）。本人仔细审核后发现该预算过高，并将之削减至 44000 金卢布，其中 40000 金卢布用于黑龙江航路标志维护工作，4000 金卢布用于乌苏里江航路标志维护工作。然因乌苏里江属于吉林省管辖，维护工作须有吉林省政府之批准方可开展，而黑河道尹最终亦未能获得该项批准，故该项航路标志维护工作最终因涉及政治性问题而遭到搁置，希望该问题可于 1926 年得到进一步的解决。1925 年《临时地方工程协议》最终顺利签订，中俄双方将预算定为 44268 金卢布，由中国摊付一半。

2. 巡查

1925 年 3 月，俄阿穆尔水道局向中俄黑龙江水道委员会中方委员递交了 1926 年航路

---

① 1925 年中俄黑龙江水道委员会委员：

黑河道尹兼海关监督兼瑷珲交涉员宋文郁先生

道尹公署外交顾问车席珍先生

瑷珲关税务司贺智兰（R.F.C.Hedgeland）先生

黑龙江航务专门顾问易保罗（P.I.Ignatieff）先生

驻大黑河苏俄领事多罗波夫（G.D.Toropoff）先生

俄阿穆尔水道局督办切比索夫（Chebisheff）先生

俄阿穆尔国家水运局局长西多霍夫（A.P.Sidoroff）先生

标志维护工作计划,预计至少需要支出 100000 金卢布。计划主要内容如下:

（1）嘎杂克维池水道（连接黑龙江与乌苏里江）上的航路标志重建工作;

（2）乌苏里江至虎林河段的航路标志重建工作;

（3）乌苏里江至虎林以外河段、松阿察河及兴凯湖的航路标志维护工作;

（4）黑龙江上游（大黑河以上）的河道疏浚工作;

（5）额尔古纳河的石块清理工作;

（6）1925 年协议所规定的黑龙江航路标志维护工作。

本人于 1925 年 9 月末乘俄国"阿穆尔"号轮船前往黑龙江下游进行巡查,后经嘎杂克维池水道行至乌苏里江上游至虎林河段。从已掌握的信息来看:①嘎杂克维池水道与②乌苏里江至虎林河段的航路标志重建工作已是迫在眉睫。

中国轮船在松花江与乌苏里江之间的航运及贸易情况已明显好转,随着乌苏里江流域的土地日益肥沃,定居和移居于此的人也越来越多。而作为目前中国轮船在黑龙江与乌苏里江之间航行的唯一通道嘎杂克维池水道,却是蜿蜒迂回,浅滩众多,航路经常发生改变。若要于此重建航路标志,从技术方面而言,至少需要竖立 50 座标桩,第一期的建造费、维护费等应不会超出 2000 卢布;从政治方面而言,该水道此前虽曾为中俄边界线,但中国一直希望将该水道与乌苏里江和黑龙江交汇处之间的土地划为己有,从而使中国轮船拥有自黑龙江出发,经乌苏里江而远航至哈巴罗夫斯克（Habarovsk）的权利,然俄方对此却始终持反对态度,因此若在此开展航路标志重建工作,很可能会引起边境争端。考虑到若由中俄双方联合维护该水道,中国将来重新规划边界线之要求或将受到阻碍,故建议由中国政府或俄阿穆尔水道局单独完成该项工作,费用则由中国全权承担。

据勘察,乌苏里江至虎林河段大约有 100 座标桩仍为旧时所建,因此除修建 130 至 140 座新标桩之外,还要对旧有标桩进行维修;此外,因航路发生变化,还需对一些标桩进行转移。预计该项工作第一年所需费用不会超出 8000 卢布。

③乌苏里江至虎林以外河段、松阿察河以及兴凯湖的航路标志维护工作,尚不算紧急。乌苏里江上游土地地势较低,土壤贫瘠,人烟稀少,河谷亦甚浅,因此中国轮船大多不会在该区域停靠,此前仅有一艘拖带两只驳船的俄国轮船曾在 1925 年航运季期间航行于这一区域,不过因中国政府禁止其出口中国大豆,所以该轮船每次航行至兴凯湖后,都是空手而归。此外,轮船运输量增加的可能性也是微乎其微的,因为乌苏里铁路一向反对轮船在兴凯湖、松阿察河以及乌苏里江上航行,更曾于 1925 年用火车向周边地区运输了

1253000普特大豆。

④黑龙江上游（大黑河以上）的河道疏浚工作，同样不算紧急。随着边境的关闭，黑龙江上的贸易可谓一片死寂。整个1925年夏天，仅有一艘中国轮船往来于大黑河上游，三艘俄国轮船往来于布拉戈维申斯克（Blagovestchensk）上游，偶尔还会有一艘载着木样的拖船出现在该河段。因此，对黑龙江上游进行大规模的疏浚工作未免为时过早，而且中国水道委员会目前资金不足，根本无法与俄方联合开展此项工作。

至于⑤额尔古纳河的石块清理工作，本人业已向中俄黑龙江水道委员会说明，此事绝非当务之急。额尔古纳河下游两岸山峦叠嶂，河底多有礁石，而上游水位较浅，河岸颇低，极易淹没，均不利于轮船航行。而且，额尔古纳河两岸人烟稀少，几乎没有什么贸易往来，更无中国轮船在此航行，仅有一艘俄国政府轮船会在每年夏季航行一到两次，但却频繁失事，每每承担着巨大的航运风险。至于当地中国居民的日常需要，经常往来于此的八艘小型民船已足可满足。

由此，额尔古纳河的石块清理工作和乌苏里江至虎林以外河段、松阿察河以及兴凯湖的航路标志维护工作均未获得中俄黑龙江水道委员会中方委员的批准，而黑龙江上游（大黑河以上）的河道疏浚工作尚须等待中国对俄国自费开展该项工作一事表态之后方会有所定论，至于嘎杂克维池水道与乌苏里江至虎林河段的航路标志重建工作，双方委员已商定在签署1926年协议时再议。

⑥1925年协议所规定的黑龙江航路标志维护工作，完成情况极好。航路均已标示妥当，标桩位置准确醒目，状况良好，各处浅滩均有巡役值守，凡重要浅滩和危险区域业已安设灯塔，以确保轮船可于水位有利的晴好天气安全航行。1925年的航路标志状况较好，主要是因各地的测量师职责明确，组织有序，所雇工人皆为当地居民；而1924年所雇工人大多来自布拉戈维申斯克地区，由此造成了很多麻烦，工人们的工作态度也都十分消极。1925年航运季期间，共设有1303座江式标桩和171座海式角锥形标桩，其中115座江式标桩、20座海式角锥形标桩以及2座标杆皆为新立。自1925年1月1日起，随着苏联最新修订的度量衡规定的出台，浅滩上的信标亦做了相应调整，水深一律按厘米和米测量而不再按英尺测量。

3. 中俄奉天会议

应中国政府之邀，经总税务司批准，本人以边界河道航务专门顾问的身份出席了1925年3月末于奉天召开的中俄会议，并向大会主席沈将军呈交了与大黑河有关的信息汇编，内容包括（1）俄阿穆尔水道局，（2）黑龙江流域的航路标志、（3）边界河道的轮船航运状况及航图以及（4）边界河道上中俄轮船航行拟定章程；随后又应沈将军要求，为中俄共用的边界河道联合维护工作草拟了四套方案，为巡江事务所职员配置草拟了一套方案，另将所有与边界河道相关的有价值的信息悉数呈报，供其审度。

会议上，俄方代表提出，中国购买俄国轮船之行为并不合法，此事若不解决，其他问题免谈，另要求中国允许俄国船只在松花江上航行。中方代表则提出：（1）重新划定中俄边界线；（2）将嘎杂克维池水道、黑龙江与乌苏里江之间的岛屿归还中国；（3）准许中国船只自黑龙江和乌苏里江航行至哈巴罗夫斯克；（4）将之前结雅河流域属于中国的土地归还中国；（5）准许中国船只自黑龙江航行至尼古拉耶夫斯克。对于中国的第五项要求，俄方代表提出：①中国轮船必须与俄国轮船一样，遵守劳埃德规定；②中国轮船必须遵循俄国航行章程，积极配合俄国海关、水运局和政府政治部的检查；③中国轮船必须备有航行执照，并缴纳与俄国轮船一样的税款；④中国船员必须加入俄国水运联合工会，并遵守该组织的规定；⑤中国船主必须遵守"共同合约"的所有条款，并遵照工会规定为其船员发放薪俸，缴纳俄国政府所征收的一切福利费用，用于医疗救助、社会改良和公共指示等方面。然而于中国轮船而言，俄方所提种种规定显然难以遵守，中国政府即使为中国轮船争得航行至尼古拉耶夫斯克之权利，亦是毫无利处可得。会议就此以失败告终，本人亦于6月末动身返回大黑河。

4. 俄阿穆尔水道局

俄阿穆尔水道局从俄阿穆尔国家水运局分离出来，成为一个独立的部门后，对俄国轮船的江捐征收也就于1925年夏天中断了，之后用于俄国内陆水域航路标志维护工作的经费均由莫斯科政府所拨给，俄阿穆尔水道局计划工作时便不会过多考虑航运总体状况如何，计划的工事是否为贸易切实所需，工程所涉水道上的轮船往来数量是否足够多等实际情况。1924年，俄阿穆尔水道局向莫斯科呈交的预算为280000卢布，莫斯科政府予以拨款100000卢布；1925年呈交的预算为478000卢布，莫斯科政府予以拨款395000卢布；1926年，俄阿穆尔水道局呈交了总计1200000卢布的预算，据悉莫斯科政府已予以拨款780000卢布。

中俄黑龙江水道委员会的中方委员已感觉到现下形势大不同于往年。此时，俄方显然已不再寄希望于中方对航路标志维护经费有所分担，各项工作计划的所需经费与中国江捐税收数目严重不成比例。俄阿穆尔水道局也正是因为当前经济状况良好，才希望于今年开展乌苏里江航路标志重建工程、黑龙江上游河道疏浚工程以及额尔古纳河的石块清理工程。莫斯科政府所拨资金自然应主要用于改善俄国内陆水域的航运状况，但俄阿穆尔水道局仍希望可使黑龙江和乌苏里江上的航路标志恢复到沙俄政权时期的高效状态。截至 1925 年航运季末,俄阿穆尔水道局已从俄阿穆尔国家水运局取回所有工作艇和驳船,又分得数间作坊和仓库,现已成为独立的组织机构,并由莫斯科任命了新督办,即共产党人托阿诺夫(Dianoff)先生,前任督办工程师切比索夫(Chebisheff)先生担任副督办一职。

5. 俄阿穆尔国家水运局

俄阿穆尔国家水运局代表们此前一直希望预期召开于 1925 年春的中俄会议能够顺利进行并圆满完成,从而实现自中国运输大豆和小麦的计划——自松花江运输 300 万普特至哈巴罗夫斯克和尼古拉耶夫斯克,自兴凯湖运输 100 万普特甚至更多至伊曼铁路站。然而奉天会议以失败告终,上述计划亦被迫搁置。之后,俄国政府又向奉天方面提出,希望可以准许俄国轮船航行至松花江口,并于此承接载有货物的驳船,但遭到拒绝。至此,俄阿穆尔国家水运局的中国运输计划彻底失败,而俄国本地并无货物运输,乘客数量也是寥寥,就连鲑鱼的捕捞量都是少之又少,轮船几乎无生意可做,截至 1925 年年底,俄阿穆尔国家水运局总计赤字达 40 万卢布。

1925 年航运季伊始,俄阿穆尔国家水运局的 17 艘轮船出航后不久便搁置于布拉戈维申斯克,停止使用,船员也随之被解雇。至航运季末,俄阿穆尔国家水运局仅有 3 艘邮轮往来于斯列坚斯克和布拉戈维申斯克之间,4 艘往来于布拉戈维申斯克和尼古拉耶夫斯克之间,2 艘往来于结雅河上,此外还有两艘牵引船。

为解决船员失业问题,五家私营公司顺势而立,尝试运营 5 艘私人轮船,但俄阿穆尔国家水运局希望垄断航运业,让自己的轮船一直以低廉的运费和便宜的船票抢占市场,私营公司又须缴纳沉重的税款,终是无利可得。俄阿穆尔国家水运局还试图于额尔古纳河、谢列姆贾河、结雅河上游、布列亚河以及阿姆贡河上运营政府轮船,但最终因去年夏季水位普遍较低、货物短缺、矿工业停滞等不利因素而以失败告终。布拉戈维申斯克新建的干船坞由于在规划和计量时出现失误,最后建成的面积过小,无法容纳大型轮船。俄阿穆尔国家水运局正是由于专业知识和商业能力的匮乏,才会在运输和贸易方面屡遭失败。

1925 年航运季期间,俄阿穆尔国家水运局还有 2 艘带有驳船的轮船往来于乌苏里江上,其中一艘共计航行 8 次,另一艘与商铺合作,进行贸易,共计航行 5 次,但这两艘轮船都处于亏本运营的状况;此间,只有 4 艘俄国轮船进入大黑河港口,但皆是空载而至,并无对华贸易。俄阿穆尔国家水运局还曾尝试用木炭为轮船加热,但屡试屡败,据账目显示,木炭购入价格高昂,还需为之修建仓库,总费用是购买木桦做燃料所需经费的 2.5 倍。

6. 中国航运业

中国轮船于黑龙江和乌苏里江上的运输主要与松花江相连,大黑河口岸往来的轮船几乎均往返于该口岸与哈尔滨之间。由于俄国轮船未获准于松花江上航行,中国轮船便再无竞争对手,运费亦因此而得以提高。1925 年,谷物从佳木斯到哈尔滨的运费曾一度达到每普特 22 分,从富锦运送更是高达每普特 33 分。哈尔滨与大黑河之间的普通货物运费报价高达每普特 0.80 银圆,大黑河与漠河之间的运费为每普特 0.40 银圆。

中国船主和商人均因无俄国轮船竞争而受益,他们曾在奉天会议期间竭力要求务必阻止俄国船只在松花江上航行,亦对俄国船只自松花江运输谷物和大豆至哈巴罗夫斯克和尼古拉耶夫斯克的计划提出过抗议,因为他们深知,俄国为换取此等航行运输的权利,虽然会准许中国船只来往于黑龙江至尼古拉耶夫斯克河段,但亦会设定种种规定限制,为中国船只制定极高的标准,甚至会引来无休止的误解。

由于俄国船只被禁止于松花江上航行,哈尔滨索斯金(Soskin Bros.)洋行售予中国航业公司 4 艘轮船和 10 艘驳船。截至 1925 年航运季末,几乎所有的谷物和大豆都成功运至哈尔滨。9 月 1 日,戊通航业公司在东三省政府的大力支持下,将工厂移至东北航务局,并计划于 1926 年不再与其他航业公司一起出航,决定安排大型轮船"海澄(Haicheng)"号负责哈尔滨与大黑河之间的邮件和乘客运输,但"海澄"号和"哈尔滨"号两艘轮船的体积过大,不适合在松花江上航行,很有可能会发生事故。

虽然松花江上的轮船运输获利颇丰,但黑龙江上的情况却未能如此。由于边境关闭,黑龙江中俄两岸经济状况不景气,中国的贸易公司和矿业明显衰落,大黑河地区的耕地面积逐年扩大,已无需再自哈尔滨进口小麦,而运往哈尔滨的木样量亦是微乎其微,因此大黑河口岸无论是客货运输量,还是船只进港结关的数量,均已大幅减少。

大黑河海关入港和结关船只数量

年份	轮船（包括牵引驳船）		民船		总计	
	数量	运输量（吨）	数量	运输量（吨）	数量	运输量（吨）
1922 年	1534	436500	1796	25144	3330	461644
1923 年	605	192768	1315	36820	1920	229588
1924 年	407	113952	1352	20617	1759	134569
1925 年	263	59846	1490	25225	1753	85071

大黑河海关贸易总值

1922 年	1923 年	1924 年	1925 年
海关两	海关两	海关两	海关两
6727105	5324035	4617175	3108210
大黑河口岸往来客运量（人次）			
1922 年	1923 年	1924 年	1925 年
30255	21800	19530	15083

7. 黑龙江江捐征收

1925 年的江捐税收因受到贸易减少的影响，无法与 1924 年和 1925 年的开支相抵，奉天政府虽认同联合维护航路标志工作的必要性，但依然坚持由地方解决资金问题。航运季初期，因考虑到会有资金短缺情况，中国黑龙江水道委员会已决定提高江捐税率，大黑河商会亦已同意，然 1925 年的江捐税收虽因此而有所提高，但依然不足以应对各项支出。

黑龙江江捐税收
（于大黑河口岸、瑷珲口岸及拉哈苏苏口岸所征）

1922 年	1923 年	1924 年	1925 年
银圆	银圆	银圆	银圆
31137.19	23769.9	17291.25	28819.61
黑龙江航路标志支出			
1922 年	1923 年	1924 年	1925 年
银圆	银圆	银圆	银圆
20168.99	22156.86	30097.90	36408.96

1924 年所征税收连同 1922 年和 1923 年的税收余额可以应对 1924 年的大部分支出，但仍余 225.41 银圆须由 1925 年所征税款支付。为向俄方支付 1925 年摊款，瑷珲关已向总税务司申请从由哈尔滨关管理的松花江江捐账户预支 20000 银圆借款以协济黑龙江江捐账户，并已从中提取 10000 银圆用以结平 1925 年账目。目前看来，1926 年的税收又将难以应对所规划的各项工事支出，因此当务之急便是将 1926 年黑龙江航路标志工程的预算控制在地方经济可承受的范围之内。

8. 1925 年航运状况

1925 年航运季的时间虽然很长,但水位普遍较低。大黑河地区春季到来的时间较早,5 月 1 日附近的江面上便已无浮冰漂流,5 月 2 日两艘在瑷珲口岸过冬的轮船抵达大黑河。然而,石勒喀河的水位直到 7 月中旬还是很低,只有 2 英尺左右。黑龙江上游的水位在 5 月期间一直很低,随后受到额尔古纳河上高水位的影响,方涨至平均值以上。而黑龙江中游则因结雅河和谢列姆贾河的水量持续不足,水位一直极低,直到 8 月初方有所好转,期间波亚尔科沃浅滩和康斯坦丁诺瓦浅滩的水位持续偏低,有时甚至连 2 英尺都达不到,轮船只得绕至水位较深的航道通过。航运季初期,松花江的水量尚算充足,但进入 6 月之后,水位就开始逐渐变浅,这种情况一直持续到 7 月、8 月。所幸,9 月、10 月松花江迎来了大雨。10 月,大黑河附近的江面开始结冰。10 月 20 日一场暴风雪之后,河上的冰块开始漂流,随后天气再次回暖,河道直至 11 月 17 日才关闭,此亦为自 1903 年以来河道关闭最晚的一次。10 月 23 日,最后一艘轮船驶离大黑河前往哈尔滨,最终所有轮船皆得益于航运季时间的延长,而抵达各自的冬季停泊处。

9. 航运事故

本人曾于 1924 年黑龙江航务年度报告中指出,中国轮船状况不佳,许多船只的木质外壳已经腐烂,机器和发动机业已老化,急需予以置换或进行彻底维修,否则必会增加事故发生的风险,同时亦应提高轮船出航检验标准。1925 年航运季的轮船事故大多出于以上原因。"蒋（Chiang）"号轮船和"西京"号轮船的船尾木板因木梁腐烂,支架失去支撑能力而断裂;"上海"号轮船因负载过重在松花江上一处泥潭搁浅,船底厚木板由于张力已被冲到腐烂部件之上;"顺天"号轮船于三姓浅滩触礁后,船体出现裂缝;"绍兴"号轮船和"哈尔滨"号轮船在通过松花江富锦上游河段的狭窄航路时相撞,"绍兴"号轮船因船身损毁而沉没。由此可见,现急需出台《松花江航务条例》和《边界河道航务条例》的官方准则。此外,"中华"号轮船在向黑龙江上游三道卡（Sandoka）村附近的沙滩停靠过程中触礁,致使船体出现裂缝,货物受损。有鉴于此,黑龙江水道委员会实有必要尽快将黑龙江华岸泊地附近的礁石清除。

10. 大黑河港口

凡涉及航道、标桩、灯桩和水深变化等信息,俄阿穆尔水道局皆会适时告知大黑河中国海关,三姓浅滩水深电报亦会定期而至,大黑河海关收到各项信息后,会将之公示以便各轮船船主知悉。为引导轮船驶入大黑河港口,港口沙嘴上游处已安设一座红色浮标,夜间常亮;堤岸附近那些随浮冰和水流而来的巨石,业已被悉数移除;另已于海关办公楼和水位表对面的堤岸上种植大量柳树，以起到加固作用。然而，浅滩和堤岸仍有待改善，沙嘴处亦有扩大之势，恐怕会堵塞整个港口，但由于航运和经济状况不景气，此等工程所需金额目前无法筹齐。

11. 总结

为保证吉林省和黑龙江省的繁荣发展，中国政府应关注：

（1）1926年《航路标志工程协议》之草拟事；

（2）于协议中增加乌苏里江至虎林河段以及嘎杂克维池水道的航路标志维护工作事；

（3）解决北满洲内陆水域航务条例统一事；

（4）与俄方联合颁布《中俄边界河道联合航务条例》事；

（5）提高中国船只质量标准，制定《卫生条例》，禁止轮船超载事；

（6）严格把控关员资质事；

（7）加强船长权力，阻止买办插手船只运营事；

（8）授予俄阿穆尔水道局工作艇进入松花江至拉哈苏苏分关河段的权利事（拉哈苏苏分关已为黑龙江航路标志工作给予了极大的帮助）；

（9）于黑龙江华岸泊地清理石块事；

（10）考虑大黑河港口的管理事；

（11）为黑龙江航路标志筹集资金，以弥补江捐不足事。

易保罗（P. I. Ignatieff）

黑龙江航务专门顾问

4. 为 1926 年黑龙江航务年度报告事

AMUR AIDS TO NAVIGATION: Technical Adviser's Annual
Report for 1926 together with Accounts Statement,
forwarding.

313/I.G.

313.

Registered.

I.G.

Aigun   22nd April, 1927.

Sir,

      I have the honour to forward, enclosed

herewith,

      The "Annual Report on Aids to

Navigation for 1926", prepared by

Mr. P. I. Ignatieff, Technical Adviser

on Amur Aids to Navigation.

      The "Amur Aids Accounts Statement for

1926" which includes

    1. Statement of Receipts and
      Payments for fiscal year of 1926

    2. Summary of Receipts and Payments
      for fiscal year of 1926.

    3. Summary of Expenditures by the
      Amur Navigation Office on behalf
      of Joint Upkeep of Amur Aids
      (Pokrovka-Kasakevich) for fiscal
      year of 1926.

    4. Summary of Expenditure for
      Technical Adviser's Office for
               1926.

Officiating Inspector General of Customs,

    Peking.

sure No.1.

sure No.2.

1926.

5. Statement of Advances to date, from
Harbin Sungari Aids Account,
authorized by the I.G. in Aid of
Aigun Amur River Dues Account.

6. Schedule of Advances made from
Harbin Sungari Aids Account to
assist Amur Aids.

It will be noted that "3. Summary of
Expenditures by the Amur Navigation Office on behalf
of Joint Upkeep of Amur Aids (Pokrovka-Kasakevich)
for fiscal year of 1926" shows a total expenditure
of Gold Roubles 59,800 whereas the detailed estimates
submitted in Aigun despatch No. 263, Appendix No. 2,
allowed for an expenditure of Gold Roubles 60,031.

Enclosures Nos. 5 and 6 to the "Amur Aids
Accounts Statement for 1926" are additional to those
of previous years and show the amount of advances
authorized from Sungari Aids and the amount actually
drawn to date. In this connection I should be glad
to receive your instructions as to whether the loans
received from the Sungari Aids Account should be
carried forward as advances in A/c. D in the future.

The

The balance available as authorized to be drawn from Sungari Aids Account is shown to be $20,000 at the end of the year. Since then $5,000 has been requesitioned. With the increase in the River Dues Tariff foreshadowed in my despatch No.311 it is hoped that the repayment of these advances may commence during the coming navigation season - always provided there is no political upheaval in Manchuria.

I have the honour to be

Sir,

Your obedient Servant,

Acting Commissioner.

REFERENCE.

From I. G.   To I. G.

For previous references see docket of Aigun No.262/I.G.

294/107,936	262
300/108,242	263
308/109,068	275
323/110,666	276
	286
	297
	309
	311

AIGUN NO. 313 OF 1927.

ENCLOSURE NO.1.

AIDS TO NAVIGATION ON THE AMUR.

ANNUAL REPORT FOR 1926.

AIDS TO NAVIGATION ON THE AMUR.

Annual Report for 1926.

The joint upkeep of Aids to Navigation on the frontier Waterways in the Amur basin, mutually maintained in 1926, by U.S.S.R. and China under the direction of the Sino-Russian Amur Aids Commission may be summarised as follows:

GENERAL. The Chinese members of the Commission wishing to conclude as early as possible the 1926 Local Technical Agreement began negotiations with the Russian Members of the Joint Commission early in the Autumn of 1925, before the Agreement for that year expired. The Soviet representatives insisted on signing the Agreement for the Amur and the Ussuri simultaneously, but some difficulties arose in discussing the question concerning the establishment of new Aids on the Ussuri. According to the old treaty between China and Russia, of 1858, the right side of the Amur, on the stretch from the mouth of the Argun down the Amur to the Ussuri, was regarded as belonging to China, but the Sino-Russian Boundary Commission in 1911 recognised the Kasakevich Waterway to be the boundary line; and the islands between the Amur, Kasakevich Waterway and Ussuri as belonging to Russia: A stone as a boundary sign was erected on the Chinese shore, at the confluence of the Kasakevich Waterway and the Ussuri; this stone has recently been removed. When it was understood that U.S.S.R. had denounced the former unequal Treaties between China and Russia, the Kirin Taoyin considered the rivers Amur and Ussuri to Habarovsk as being natural boundary-lines between China and U.S.S.R. and the Kasakevich Waterway to be be a Chinese inland waterway.

In Article 7 of the Sino-Russian Agreement
signed on the 31st of May, 1924, it was stated:
"The Governments of the two contracting countries have
agreed to readjust their national Boundaries at a
conference to be convened for that purpose, as provided
in Article 2 of the present Agreement, but, until such
Agreement is made, to keep to the present Boundary-lines".

The Heiho Taoyin not having the right of
drawing up an agreement for the Ussuri Aids, waited for
authorisation from the Kirin authorities or the arrival
of a representative appointed by them. As neither came
from Kirin and the Taoyin himself left for Mukden, an
Agreement to include the Ussuri Aids was out of the
question, and the Soviet representatives, in view of the
approaching navigation season, hurried to draw up the
Agreement for the Amur Aids only, which was signed on
the 21st of April, 1926. The estimate submitted by the
Amur Navigation Office for Amur Aids work amounting to
a sum of Gold Roubles 75,000, could have been cut down
to Gold Roubles 50,000, if the Agreement had been signed
in the Autumn of 1925, but as the document was not
signed until late in the Spring of 1926, the estimate
had to be fixed at the sum of Gold Roubles 60,031,
because of an increase in salaries to employees and
workmen of the Amur Navigation Office in February, 1926.
50% of this general estimate, i.e. Gold Roubles 30,000
was agreed to as the contribution of China.

At the same time the Soviet representatives
took

took up the question of dredging operations on the Upper Amur and submitted an estimate for this work amounting to Gold Roubles 81,000, as well as plans of shallows with marked directions of cuts to be made, but this question being a very complicated one and quite unnecessary for Chinese shipping, was left undecided.

INSPECTION TOURS. I started at the beginning of the navigation season on a tour of inspection up and down the Amur, to examine the preliminary state of the Aids; on the way I gave necessary directions and advice to the District Surveyors.

At the end of August, together with the Russian Commission, I examined the Amur Aids work done, and checked the correctness of beacons along the channel. I found everything very satisfactory, so I approved the work that had been done and the statement of expenditure in connection therewith.

THE PAYMENT TO THE AMUR NAVIGATION OFFICE FOR THE WORK DONE DURING THE SUMMER, 1926. During the year advances were made to the Amur Navigation Office from time to time and the final payment was made on the 12th of January, 1927, after a full Account was submitted by that office, checked by me and sanctioned by the Joint Commission. The total sum paid to the Amur Navigation Office amounted to Gold Roubles 29,900, which at various rates, amounted to $29,931.53.

At the beginning of the year 1926 the Soviet Rouble was higher than the Chinese Dollar, but by the end of the year it was lower, so that for the year the

dollar

dollar and rouble averaged about the same in value.

THE SIGNING OF THE AGREEMENT FOR THE YEAR 1927.　In the Spring of 1926 the Amur Navigation Office submitted to the Chinese Commission the estimate for the year 1927, planning the following operations:

```
          1. On Aids work:  a) on the Amur      G.Rls.180,000
                            b) on the Argun      ..   12,000
                            c) on the Ussuri     ..   18,000
          2. Removal of rocks in the Argun       ..    8,000
          3. Dredging work on the Upper Amur     ..  120,000
                              TOTAL:.........G.Rls.338,000
```

After many difficulties I got them to agree to an estimate for the Amur Aids at G.Rls.60,000 instead of 18o,000, and on the 10th of January, 1927, the Local Provisional Technical Agreement was signed for one year, for the period from the 1st December, 1926, to the 30th of November, 1927. The question of erecting Aids on the Ussuri still remains unsettled, as it has been impossible to agree with Russians as to the mutual Aids work to be done on the lower Ussuri owing to the dispute over the boundary between Kasakevich Waterway and Habarovsk.

The question of dredging work in the Upper Amur which the Amur Navigation Office had planned during the navigation season of 1927, is also under negotiation.

The Taoyin has agreed to the request of the Amur Navigation Office for permission to remove rocks from the Argun, during the winter 1926/27, at their own expense, and Huchao has been issued.

5.

THE RUSSIAN AMUR NAVIGATION OFFICE: is planning Aids work
without much regard for the immediate needs of trade,
the yearly decrease in turnover of cargo and steamer
traffic in general. They are anxious only to enlarge
operations to a scale comparable to that of the Czarist
Regime; consequently every year more funds are requested
by this Office from the Central Government in Moscow.
For the year 1926 the Amur Navigation Office asked Gold
Roubles 1,200,000, but got from Moscow only 780,000.
Such a large credit enabled the Office to plan large
operations, whereas China, having at its disposal River
Dues Collection only, could not share works most of
which were quite unnecessary for the present.

As the question concerning dredging work in the
Upper Amur failed to be agreed to with the Chinese
Commission the Amur Navigation Office undertook dredging
work on the river Zeya, on the stretch from the Railroad
bridge down the river, during the summer of 1926.

Having had funds enough for erecting Aids on
the Ussuri the Amur Navigation Office, during summer,
1926, used part of them and established Aids on the
stretch between Habarovsk and the village Kasakevich, on
both sides of the river, 36 versts long; and above that
village, as far as 20 versts, on the Russian side only.

The advantage of very low water in the Argun,
lasting to the end of August, 1926, was not availed of
by the Russians at that time to mark rocks for removal
during the coming winter by stakes along the shore.
Workmen sent for this work at the end of October, owing

to

to high water and the lateness of the season, could
only approximately indicate the most dangerous rocks on
the maps, which is not sufficient, while increasing the
cost of the work and reducing the productiveness
thereof.

Great attention was paid by the Amur
Navigation Office to the betterment of their own
inland waterways.

For the year 1927 the Amur Navigation Office
requested from Moscow Gold Roubles 2,200,000, but
received 1,000,000 only. Later on Rls. 90,000 more was
received especially for the purchase of starting the
arrangement of a new winter port and workshops in
Habarovsk because the old winter port in the Ussuri
side-channel, 12 versts from Habarovsk, is obstructed
now and needs considerable dredging. Moreover the
ownership of the islands, between the rivers Amur,
Ussuri and Kasakevich Waterway, where the port now
lies, is in dispute as indicated above. For these
reasons and due to many other inconveniences, it has
been decided to arrange a new winter port.

Such a great credit granted by Moscow
enabled the Amur Navigation Office to plan operations
for the year 1927 on a much larger scale than ever.

RUSSIAN GOVERNMENT AMUR WATER TRANSPORTATION BUREAU: with
the unsuccessful termination of the Mukden Conference,
and the persistent protests of Chinese merchants
against Russian ships being allowed on the Sungari, all
large plans of this Bureau for transportation of lots
of

of cargoes from the Sungari had to be dropped. Also the whole plan intended to be carried out through the summer of 1926, and based on the transportation of cargoes on the tributaries of the Amur, failed owing to many circumstances, as follows: a) As there were no rains in the whole North Manchuria, and very low water in the Argun up to the first days of September, the Amur Water Transportation Bureau could not export from the village Olochi (on the Upper Argun) about 200,000 poods of wheat desired by the Soviet cooperative store; when high water eventually came the export of wheat was refused because of a very poor crop in the whole Argun region; b) the Government Mines Bureau provided the Selemdja and Bureya mines with all provisions by land during the winter time, finding it more profitable, because of the very high freight rates on steamers; c) on the Ussuri during the whole navigation season only 3 steamers and 7 barges plyed for the transportation of 313,000 poods of beans from Lake Hanka to the Railroad station Iman; such an insignificant amount of cargo made the work of steamers unprofitable; d) the Mail and Passenger steamers running between Blagovestchensk and Stretensk sailed the whole summer in ballast, whereas in autumn when they got salt for transport from Stretensk to Nikolaevsk fisheries, and sugar from Nikolaevsk to Stretensk several accidents happened to the steamers, so that the Bureau failed in this business too.

The work of steamers on the river Zeya has been a little more profitable.

The Amur Transportation Bureau has only been secured

secured from great losses by the work of some mail and
towing steamers running on the stretch between
Blagovestchensk and Nikolaevsk when the rich catch of
Salmon near Nikolaevsk (about 600,000 poods during summer
and 1,000,000 poods in autumn) provided a large amount
of cargo for transportation. Only 2 steamers remaining
in private hands plyed during the Navigation season of
1926.

CHINESE SHIPPING: The newly formed North East Navigation
Bureau which, from the 1st September, 1925, took over
all steamers of Wu-tung Co., partly repaired these ships
in the winter and commenced running them in the spring
of 1926, trying to meet all needs of settlers along the
rivers Amur, Ussuri and Sungari.

As the result of sound conditions, regular trips,
sanitary and technical betterments, increased salaries to
employees, and welltimed payment of such, there was a
large increase in cargo and passenger traffic. The whole
shipping started to work intensively, and with very
favourable water during the autumn in the Sungari,
transported a great deal of cargo to Harbin.

Owing to the increased freight rates fixed by
the North East Navigation Bureau, obligatory also for
private steamers, and to the improved conditions mentioned
in the preceding paragraph, all Chinese shipping showed
a gain of about $4,000,000. The profit of the North
East Navigation Bureau enabled the company to grant to
their employees five months salary, to let many of them
remain in service for the winter, and to undertake more
solid repairs. The good example was followed by many

private

private shipowners. As Chinese shipping had too few
barges, two wooden barges are to be built at Taheiho,
one of 220 feet long and 38 feet broad, the other of
160 feet long and 28 feet broad.

Towards the end of navigation season, ships of
China-East Railroad, by an order from Mukden, have been
transferred to the North East Navigation Bureau, which
put some of them into immediate use to transport cargo.

Chinese shipping on the Amur was not so
profitable as it was on the Sungari and Ussuri. The
closed frontier and the resulting decrease in trade
reduced the steamer traffic on the Amur, whereas on the
Ussuri it almost doubled compared with the year 1925.

The number of rafts carrying firewood from the
Upper Amur was very small, but the junks transported a
good deal of it to Taheiho. The Taoyin has in view
the imposition of a lighter tax on timber in order to
promote the export of this commodity to Harbin.

Vessels Entered and Cleared at the Taheiho Customs.

Year.	River Steamers. (including Towed barges)		Junks.		Total.	
	No.	Tons.	No.	Tons.	No.	Tons.
1922	1,543	436,500	1,796	25,144	3,339	461,644
1923	605	192,768	1,315	36,820	1,920	229,588
1924	407	113,952	1,352	20,617	1,759	134,569
1925	263	59,846	1,490	25,225	1,753	85,071
1926	354	107,130	1,240	21,643	1,574	128,773

Gross value of the Maritime Customs Trade at Taheiho.

Hk.Tls. 1922.	Hk.Tls. 1923.	Hk.Tls. 1924.	Hk.Tls. 1925.	Hk.Tls. 1926.
6,727,105.	5,324,035.	4,617,175.	3,108,210.	3,095,322.

Passenger

Passenger Traffic to and from Taheiho.

1922.	1923.	1924.	1925.	1926.
30,255.	21,800.	19,530.	15,083.	15,232.

AMUR RIVER DUES COLLECTION: At the beginning of the navigation season of 1926, the Chinese Maritime Customs issued a specially printed tariff of "Amur River Dues Collection", thanks to which the control is much easier now.

The small amount of River Dues collected, insufficient to cover the cost of expenses on the Joint Amur Aids work done by the Amur Navigation Office, forced the Chinese Commission to ask the Harbin Commissioner of Customs to collect in Lahasusu, towards the end of navigation season, River Dues on passengers sailing to the Ussuri.

The levying of double River Dues on cargo from the very beginning of navigation season, the collecting of River Dues on Ussuri passengers, and the increased amount of cargo carried through the Ussuri, (almost double that of the year 1925) as well as the fact that much timber was exported from Taheiho, increased a little the Collection of River Dues of 1926, compared with 1925.

The sum of $35,469.42 of Amur River Dues Collection of the year 1926, plus the loan of $20,000 from Harbin Sungari River Dues Account, has been sufficient to cover a part of the obligations of 1925 and to meet the 1926 payments. The credit balance at the end of the season of 1926 amounted to $3,687.58.

Amur

Amur   River   Dues   Collection   (collected   at
Taheiho,   Aigun   &   Lahasusu)

1922.	1923.	1924.	1925.	1926.
$31,137.19	$23,769.90	$17,291.25	$28,819.61	$35,469.42

Expenditures on behalf of Amur Aids.

1922.	1923.	1924.	1925.	1926.
$20,168.99	$22,156.86	$30,097.90	$36,408.96	$43,967.06

Amur River Dues collected at Lahasusu on steamers and
junks plying on the Ussuri.

1923.	1924.	1925.	1926.
$1,371.32	$1,598.78	$3,496.50	$10,272.14*

* Including $3,202.47 collected on passenger tickets
beginning from August, 1926.

The   expenses   estimated   to   be   met   from   River   Dues
Collection   of   the   year   1927   are   estimated   at   some $44,600,
not   including   the   expenditure   of   about $5,000   for
installation   of   Aids   on   the   Ussuri.

To   offset   this   the   income   from   the   collection
of   River   Dues   in   1927   is   expected   to   be   some $30,000,
plus $20,000   balance   of   the   loan   authorised   by   the
Inspector   General   from   Sungari   River   Dues   Account.

CONDITIONS OF NAVIGATION DURING 1926:   The   snow   melted   very
slowly   during   the   spring   and   did   not   give   much   water   to
the   rivers,   and   the   ice   on   the   Amur   and   its   tributaries
drifted   in   very   low   water.   The   icedrift   at   Taheiho   began
on   the   30th   of   April,   and   lasted   without   stoppage   until
the   10th   of   May.   The   first   steamer   "Ta-hsing"   arrived
from   Harbin   on   the   11th   of   May.   It   is   interestingly   to
note   that   in   1925   all   left   tributaries   of   the   Amur,   and
in   1926   all   the   right   ones   of   the   Argun,   Sungari   and

Ussuri

Ussuri had a very low depth of Water. As all the left tributaries are larger than the right ones in the Amur basin, the Amur in 1926 had sufficient water and steam navigation has been favourable.

There were no Chinese steamers sailing on the Argun. One Russian steamer, with a barge, after having proceeded 140 versts up the river, turned back because of a very low water.

On the Sungari, during June and July the water was excessively low - 2 feet on Sansing Shallows - which prevented passenger traffic. Toward the end of August the water in Sungari increased in depth and continued favourable to the close of the navigation season, which enabled steamers to transport, during August, September and October, a good deal of grain from the lower Sungari region to Harbin.

In spite also of very low water in the Ussuri, Chinese small crafts plyed busily with cargo and passengers.

The first ice appeared on the river Zeya on the 17th of October and on the Amur on the 20th, and the last steamer "Puchiang" left Taheiho on the 20th October.

ACCIDENTS TO SHIPPING: Many repairs, if not very extensive, yet thorough enough were made to Chinese ships; the Officers paid more serious attention to their duties, resulting in a much smaller number of steamer accidents in 1926.

1) One of the most serious accidents happened on the
                                                    Ussuri

Ussuri to the steamer "Shengyang" belonging to the North East Navigation Bureau. The steamer was of very small draft, but as the Ussuri is not provided with Aids, she proceeded out of the channel too much to the right, struck an obstruction and sank in the Verhne-Kniajevski shallows; later on she was lifted with aid of barges.

2) The shaft of the stern-wheeled S/S "Aigun" broke two times.

3) On the S/S "Puchiang" the cover of the cylinder was blown off.

4) The S/S "Shaohsing" struck stones on two occasions during the low water.

In every way, the condition of hulls, machinery and boilers of Chinese steamers should be much better, and those who are administering them must give more serious attention to the raising of the standard under which their ships are navigating, as well as to the betterment of the sanitary conditions of vessels.

Due attention must also be given to the appointment of Captains and Engineers, who must have satisfactory certificates and must really know their business. For example, it happened last summer that two Chinese steamers, in meeting one another, did not exchange passing signals; moreover the steamer proceeding down the river had no regulation white lights.

On another occasion, thanks only to the experience of the Captain of the Russian S/S "Amur", an accident was avoided, in passing the Czagaian narrow gorge, which the Chinese S/S "Ta-hsing" entered, in

proceeding

proceeding up the river, without paying any attention to the hoisted signal.

As the old experienced Russian Captains and Engineers are now being replaced gradually by Chinese of very little experience, the occasions of infringement of "Russian Rules to Navigation" become more frequent, and the drawing up of simple "Mutual Rules of Navigation for Chinese and Russian steamers on Rivers the Amur, Argun and Ussuri" is imperative.

ECONOMICAL SURVEY OF AMUR PROVINCE: The crops in the Amur Province, in 1926, were above the average owing to periodical rains. The taxes on peasants having been lowered, it would seem that their welfare would have been improved, but the high prices of goods needed by them, as well as bad conditions of sale of their grain products, greatly reduced their purchasing power.

All gold miners are now almost ruined; credit at banks which was formerly extended to them is now being withdrawn and is very difficult to get owing to the reduced output of gold which is almost nothing now.

Burdensome taxes and stiff conditions in getting timber concessions caused a reduced amount of floated timber and firewood to arrive from the Upper Amur and Zeya to Blagovestchensk, and greatly increased the prices on that which did arrive.

The Russian Government commercial shipping runs at a loss, due to the absence of cargo and passengers. A rich catch of fish in the Lower Amur, about 1,600,000 poods, gave earnings to workmen and fishermen as well

as

as to the shipping, by transportation of fish cargo from
Nikolaevsk to Habarovsk and Blagovestchensk.

ECONOMICAL SURVEY OF HEILUNGKIANG PROVINCE: The development
of the Chinese steamer traffic on the frontier waters is
largely linked with that of the economical state of the
adjacent regions.

The frontier is still closed; the Russians
increased the number of frontier guards along the shore;
the ability of the Russian people to buy Chinese goods
is very low; Russian money is gradually falling; the
excise on Russian spirit and tobacco has been reduced;
the result of all this is that not only the regular
but also the contraband trade with Siberia definitively
ceased.   The output of gold was also considerably reduced,
because a great many Chinese workmen moved to the Russian
mines, where they hoped to find better conditions.

The crop in the Heilungkiang province was average,
but as the price for grain was very low the local
farmers are very hard up.

The amount of rafted timber and firewood from
the Upper Amur to Taheiho was reduced too, and many
traders were ruined because the price of wood was low
while taxes on it were very high.   Local merchants have
now raised the question of lower taxes on timber to
enable them to export it to Harbin and compete in the
timber markets there.

If this plan is favourably accomplished and the
hopes for raising of the ban on the export of grain to
Harbin

Harbin is brought about, local trading operations may increase as well as steamer traffic, and River Dues Collection may benefit.

CONCLUSION: Chinese authorities who are interested in the prosperity of Kirin and Heilungkiang provinces should give their attention to matters as follows:

1) To draw up a Technical Agreement for providing the Ussuri with Aids.

2) To raise the standard of Chinese ships; to elaborate "Sanitary Rules" and prohibit overcrowding of passengers.

3) To effect a stricter control of Officers certificates.

4) To strengthen the power of ships Captains.

5) To take up the question of "Rules for Navigation on Chinese Inland Waterways in North Manchuria".

6) To issue "Rules for Navigation on the Amur, Argun and Ussuri Rivers" in agreement with the U.S.S.R.

7) To remove stones from Chinese landing places along the Amur.

8) To consider Taheiho Harbour Concervancy.

9) To raise funds for Amur Aids work, as the River Dues Collection is insufficient.

10) To settle the question whether the Amur Navigation Office should have the right of operating dredging work on boundary rivers on their own account.

11) To develope an independent economic condition of trade by bringing in more settlers (reducing passenger fares on steamers), promoting mining and agricultural industries and reducing obstacles to the export of timber, grain etc., to Harbin. This would result in a larger collection of River Dues.

P. Tgnatieff.

Technical Adviser on Amur
Aids to Navigation.

呈海关总税务司署 313 号文　　　　　　　　　1927 年 4 月 22 日瑷珲关

尊敬的代理海关总税务司（北京）：

兹随函呈送附件：

附件 1：黑龙江航务专门顾问易保罗（P.I.Ignatieff）先生编制的 1926 年《黑龙江航务年度报告》

附件 2：1926 年黑龙江航路标志财务报表，包括：

1. 1926 年收支报表

2. 1926 年收支明细表

3. 1926 年俄阿穆尔水道局维护黑龙江航路标志支出报表（自波克罗夫卡至嘎杂克维池）

4. 1926 年航务专门顾问办事处支出报表

5. 黑龙江江捐账户自松花江航路标志账户预支款项报表（经海关总税务司署授权）

6. 黑龙江航路标志账户自松花江标志账户预支款项明细表

附件 2 中第三项，1926 年俄阿穆尔水道局维护黑龙江航路标志支出报表（自波克罗夫卡至嘎杂克维池）显示共计支出为 59800 金卢布，但瑷珲关第 263 号呈（附件 2）中的支出预算为 60031 金卢布。

1926 年的《黑龙江航路标志财务报表》中新增了两项，即附件 2 中第五项和第六项，以示自松花江航路标志账户所预支的款项及实际支用金额。兹请海关总税务司署指示，今后是否将自松花江航路标志账户收到的预支款项结转为账户 D 预支款。

如报表所示，至 1926 年末，经批准自松花江航路标志账户预支的款项，可用余额为 20000 银圆。但此后，黑龙江航路标志账户又提出了 5000 银圆的申请。瑷珲关第 311 号呈已汇报，预计江捐税收即将增长，希望随着航运季的到来，能够有足够的资金对预支款项进行偿还（只要满洲不发生政治变动）。

您忠诚的仆人

铎博赉（R. M. Talbot）

瑷珲关署理税务司

1926 年黑龙江航务年度报告

　　1926 年，在中俄黑龙江水道委员会的指导下，中俄双方继续共同维护黑龙江流域边界河道航路标志，总结如下。

　　1. 概览

　　1925 年早秋，黑龙江水道委员会双方委员于 1925 年合同到期前开始商讨，华方委员希望尽早签订 1926 年《地方工程协议》，俄方代表坚持同时签订黑龙江与乌苏里江协议，但是在商讨于乌苏里江新建航路标志时遇到了难题。根据 1858 年中俄旧条约，自额尔古纳河河口起沿黑龙江至乌苏里江段，黑龙江右侧被划分为中国管辖区域，但中俄边界委员会于 1911 年规定嘎杂克维池水道为边界线；黑龙江、嘎杂克维池水道与乌苏里江之间的岛屿属于俄国，并在嘎杂克维池水道与乌苏里江汇集处的中国河岸立了一块边界石碑，此石碑现已被移除。鉴于苏联谴责中俄先前签订的条约不平等，吉林省道尹认为黑龙江与乌苏里江至哈巴罗夫斯克的河段为中国与苏联的天然边界线，而嘎杂克维池水道则为中国内陆航道。

　　于 1925 年 5 月 31 日签订的中俄协议第七条规定："根据当前协议第二条，签约国双方政府同意召开会议，重新调整国界，但新协议签订之前，须遵守当前边界线。"

　　黑河道尹无权签订乌苏里江航路标志相关协议，须经吉林省政府授权或由其任命代表前来签约，但吉林省政府既未授权，亦未派代表前来，而道尹又已前往奉天关，因此乌苏里江航路标志相关协议已无签约可能。鉴于接近航运季，俄方代表匆忙拟订《黑龙江航路标志协议》，双方于 1926 年 4 月 21 日签订该协议。阿穆尔水道局提交的黑龙江航路标志工作预算总计 75000 金卢布，若早于 1925 年秋签订协议，预算便可定为 50000 金卢布，但是直至 1926 年春末协议仍未签订，然而 1926 年 2 月阿穆尔水道局职员及工人薪资上涨，遂将预算改为 60031 金卢布。经协商，预算金额的 50%，即 30000 金卢布由中国支出。

　　同时，俄方代表着手处理黑龙江上游的疏浚工作，该疏浚工作费用预算总计 81000 金卢布，此外，俄方代表还提交了需要标记出口方向的浅滩草图，但此事十分棘手，且中国船只不涉及此事，因此尚未决定。

　　2. 巡察

　　本人自航运季开始巡查黑龙江上下游，检查航路标志初始情况，沿途对海关测量师提出必要的指引及建议。

　　8 月底，本人与俄国委员会一同视察黑龙江航路标志完工情况，检查航道标桩是否准确。视察结果令人十分满意,故批准支出报表。

3. 支付阿穆尔水道局 1926 年夏季完工款项

全年向阿穆尔水道局分期付款,阿穆尔水道局提交完整账簿后经本人核验以及联合委员会批准后于 1927 年 1 月 12 日支付尾款。向阿穆尔水道局支付款项总计 29900 金卢布,因每次支付汇率不同,最终支付 29931.53 银圆。

1926 年初,苏联卢布价值高于中国银圆,但是年末时低于中国银圆,因此,1926 年银圆与卢布大约等值。

4. 签订 1927 年协议

1926 年春,阿穆尔水道局向中国水道委员会提交了 1927 年预算,计划如下:

（1）航路标志工事: a. 黑龙江 180000 金卢布

b. 额尔古纳河 12000 金卢布

c. 乌苏里江 180000 金卢布

（2）额尔古纳河石块清理费用 180000 金卢布

（3）黑龙江上游疏浚费用 12000 金卢布

总计: 338000 金卢布。

经多次交涉,阿穆尔水道局最终同意将黑龙江航路标志的预算从 180000 金卢布削减至 60000 金卢布。双方于 1927 年 1 月 10 日签订《临时地方工程协议》,协议签订一年自 1926 年 12 月 1 日起至 1927 年 11 月 30 日止。因嘎杂克维池水道与哈巴罗夫斯克的边界纠纷,未能与俄方就乌苏里江下游共同航路标志工作事宜达成协议,因此,在乌苏里江建立航路标志一事仍未解决。

阿穆尔水道局计划于 1927 年航运季进行黑龙江上游疏浚工作,此事仍在商讨阶段。

阿穆尔水道局申请 1926-1927 年冬于额尔古纳河进行石块清理工作,道尹已批准该请求并签发护照,相关经费由阿穆尔水道局支出。

5. 俄阿穆尔水道局

俄阿穆尔水道局当下的航路标志工作计划与近期的贸易需求、每年总体货物营业额及轮船运输减少无甚关联,只是急于将运营规模扩大至沙俄政权时期的规模,因此每年向莫斯科中央政府申请更多资金。1926 年俄阿穆尔水道局申请 120 万金卢布,但莫斯科只拨发 780000 金卢布。俄阿穆尔水道局可用此笔款项计划大型工事,而中国当前无需处理其辖内河道。

鉴于未与中国水道委员会就黑龙江上游疏浚工作达成一致,阿穆尔水道局于 1926 年夏季从铁路桥沿结雅河开展疏浚工作。

阿穆尔水道局已有资金充足,可在乌苏里江建立航路标志,遂于1926年春使用了部分资金在哈巴罗夫斯克与嘎杂克维池村庄之间的乌苏里江两侧建立航路标志,长36俄里(仅俄国侧嘎杂克维池村庄上游便长达20俄里)。

至1926年8月底,额尔古纳河水位一直较低,但俄方当时并未利用该优势于航道沿岸用桩子标记出需要于冬天清理的石块位置。工人于10月才开始做标记工作,但由于水位高、季节晚,也仅能在地图上大致标出最危险的石块位置,但是这远远不够,且还会增加成本、降低效率。

俄阿穆尔水道局重点完善了俄国内陆航道。

阿穆尔水道局于1927年申请220万金卢布,但是莫斯科只拨款100000金卢布。因距离哈巴罗夫斯克12俄里的旧冬季停泊处(乌苏里江一侧)现已阻塞,需进行大规模的疏浚工作,所以莫斯科随后又拨发90000000金卢布,用于在哈巴罗夫斯克另设新冬季停泊处及作坊。此外,黑龙江、乌苏里江与嘎杂克维池水道之间的岛屿(旧冬季停泊处所在地)的所有权如上所述——存在争议。因上述原因及其他许多不便之处,遂决定另设一个新的冬季停泊处。

莫斯科拨此巨款可供阿穆尔水道局处于1927年规划规模更大的工事。

6. 俄阿穆尔国家水运局

因奉天会议协商失败,中国商人又坚持抵制俄国船只通过松花江运输,该局通过松花江运输大量货物的大型计划全部搁浅。该局原打算于1926年夏季开展完整计划,依靠黑龙江支流运输货物,但是由于以下原因,计划失败:a.北满洲整个地区都没有降水,直到9月初额尔古纳河水位一直很低,阿穆尔水运局无法按苏联合作商铺要求自奥罗赤(Olochi)村庄(额尔古纳河上游)出口约20万普特小麦;而当河水水位涨高时,因整个额尔古纳河区域收成不好,亦无法出口小麦;b.官办采矿局冬季可通过陆路向谢列姆贾及布列亚矿山提供供给,轮船运输费用高,使用陆路运输获利更高;c.乌苏里江整个航运季只有3艘轮船及7艘驳船往返于兴凯湖与伊曼火车站,共运输313000普特豆类,因运输量过少,轮船运输未获利;d.往返于布拉格维申斯克与斯利坚斯克市的邮船与客轮整个夏天处于空载状况,这些船曾于秋季在斯利坚斯克市装载食盐,运输至尼古拉耶夫斯克(Nickolaevsk)渔场,后在尼古拉耶夫斯克装载糖类运输至斯利坚斯克市,期间轮船发生了几次事故,导致俄阿穆尔水运局该笔生意告败。

往返于结雅河运输的轮船收益更好些。

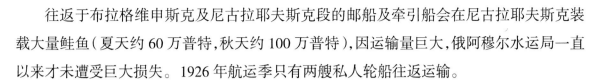

往返于布拉格维申斯克及尼古拉耶夫斯克段的邮船及牵引船会在尼古拉耶夫斯克装载大量鲑鱼（夏天约 60 万普特,秋天约 100 万普特),因运输量巨大,俄阿穆尔水运局一直以来才未遭受巨大损失。1926 年航运季只有两艘私人轮船往返运输。

7. 中国航运业

1925 年 9 月 1 日,戊通航业公司改组为东北航业公司（东北航务局）。东北航务局接管原公司全部轮船,并在冬季检修了部分轮船,于 1926 年春将轮船全部投入运营,欲在黑龙江、乌苏里江及松花江沿岸提供运输服务,以解决运输需求。

因形势良好、行程安排有序、卫生及技术完善、职员涨薪且发放及时、运货量及运客量剧增,整个航运业处于积极状态,此外,因松花江秋季水位适宜,故有大量货物运输至哈尔滨。

因东北航务局及私人船商都提高了运费,且如上述形势良好,中国航运业整体收益约 4000.00 银圆。东北航务局的收益足以发放职员 5 个月薪俸,因此即便在冬季依然有许多职员在岗,公司也得以在冬季进行加固检修工作,许多私人船商纷纷效仿。由于中国航运业驳船较少,现计划在大黑河建造两艘木驳船,一艘长 220 英尺、宽 38 英尺,另一艘长 160 英尺、宽 28 英尺。

航运季季末时,奉奉天关令,中东铁路公司运输轮船至东北航务局,东北航务局立即将一些船只投入使用开始运输货物。

中国航运业在黑龙江航道未能像在松花江及乌苏里江航道一样盈利。黑龙江因边境关闭,贸易减少,造成轮船运输量减少,然而,乌苏里江的轮船运输量与 1925 年相比,几乎增长了一倍。

从黑龙江上游运输木桦的木筏数量极少,但是民船运输了大量木桦至大黑河。道尹建议减轻对木料的征税,增加运输至哈尔滨的木料数量。

进入大黑河海关的船只数量及大黑河海关放行的船只数量

年份	水运轮船 （包括牵引驳船）		民船		总计	
	数量	运输量（吨）	数量	运输量（吨）	数量	运输量（吨）
1922	1543	436500	1796	25144	3339	461644
1923	605	192768	1315	36820	1920	229588
1924	407	113952	1352	20617	1759	134569
1925	263	59846	1490	25225	1753	85071
1926	334	107130	1240	21643	1574	128773

大黑河海关贸易总值

海关两	海关两	海关两	海关两	海关两
1922 年	1923 年	1924 年	1925 年	1926 年
6727105	5324035	4617175	3108210	3095322

出入大黑河的客运量

1922 年	1923 年	1924 年	1925 年	1926 年
30225	21800	19530	15083	15232

8. 黑龙江江捐征收

1926 年航运季开始之际，中国海关专门印制并发布了"黑龙江江捐征收"收费表，现在征税管理更加方便。

江捐征收的款额较少，难以负担阿穆尔水道局用于黑龙江联合航路标志工事的开支，因此，中国水道委员会命哈尔滨关税务司于航运季季末在拉哈苏苏向前往乌苏里江的乘客征收江捐。

1926 年江捐税收与 1925 年相比略有增长，主要因为从航运季开始便对货物征收双倍江捐，季末又对乌苏里江上的乘客征收江捐，此外，乌苏里江航道的运货量增加（几乎是 1925 年的两倍）且大黑河也有大量木料输出。

1926 年黑龙江江捐税收总计 35469.42 银圆，此外，自哈尔滨关松花江江捐账户贷款 20000 银圆，足以负担 1925 年部分债务及 1926 年开支。1926 年航运季季末贷款余额总计 3687.58 银圆。

黑龙江江捐税收（在大黑河瑷珲关及拉哈苏苏分关征税）				
1922 年	1923 年	1924 年	1925 年	1926 年
31137.19 银圆	23769.90 银圆	17291.25 银圆	28891.61 银圆	35469.42 银圆
黑龙江航路标志相关支出				
1922 年	1923 年	1924 年	1925 年	1926 年
20168.99 银圆	22156.86 银圆	30097.90 银圆	36408.96 银圆	43967.08 银圆

黑龙江江捐税收（在拉哈苏苏向往返于乌苏里江的轮船及民船征收）			
1923 年	1924 年	1925 年	1926 年
1371.32 银圆	1598.78 银圆	3496.50 银圆	10272.14 银圆 *

* 包括自 1926 年 8 月起征收的乘客船票税

1927 年预计支出约为 44600 银圆,其中不包括在乌苏里江安设航路标志的约 5000 银圆费用。

1927 年江捐税收预计为 30000 银圆,此外,经海关总税务司授权自松花江江捐账户贷款的余额有 20000 银圆,可抵消上述支出。

9. 1926 年航运状况

春天冰雪融化慢,流入河流的雪水并不多,黑龙江及其支流有浮冰但水位极低。4 月 30 日大黑河开始有浮冰,一直持续至 5 月 10 日。5 月 11 日从哈尔滨关出发的大兴号轮船首先抵达。1925 年黑龙江左侧的所有支流水位极低,而 1926 年额尔古纳河、松花江和乌苏里江右侧的所有支流水位都非常低。1926 年黑龙江河水充足,且黑龙江流域左侧支流都比右侧支流大,利于轮船航行。

额尔古纳河上没有中国轮船通行。一艘带驳船的俄国轮船在额尔古纳河行进了 140 俄里后因水位低返航。

6 月至 7 月,松花江水位极低——三姓浅滩水位只有 2 英尺——客船无法通行。8 月底松花江水位升高,直至航运季季末水位都非常利于轮船航行,松花江下游地区于 8 月至 10 月间向哈尔滨关运输了大量谷物。

乌苏里江水位也很低,但中国小型船舶仍可装载客货通行。

10 月 17 日结雅河开始结冰,10 月 20 日黑龙江开始结冰,"普江"号轮船于当日最后一个驶离大黑河。

10. 航运事故

中国轮船已经多次检修,规模虽不大但很彻底;关员尽职尽责,1926 年轮船事故很少。

（1）最严重的一次事故发生于乌苏里江航道,东北航务局的"圣阳（Shengyang）"号轮船吃水很浅,但由于乌苏里江航道上未安设航路标志,船只向右偏离航道过多,撞到障碍物后在外 – 尼亚耶夫斯基（Verhne-Kniajevski）浅滩沉船;之后被驳船打捞救出。

（2）"瑷珲"号轮船船舶轴破裂两次。

（3）"富江"号轮船气缸盖被吹掉。

（4）"绍兴"号轮船在水位低时两次撞上石头。

无论如何,中国轮船船身、发动机及锅炉的状况都应不断改良,该部门的负责人亦应于航行时注意提高工作标准,不断完善卫生条件。

任命船长及营造司时应注意,须聘用有资质证书、业务精通的职员,以免发生意外。例如,去年夏天两艘中国轮船相向而行时,未交换通过信号;此外,行往下游的轮船未按规定挂白色信号灯。

俄国"阿穆尔"号轮船在通过扎噶依安（Czagaian）峡谷时，中国大兴号轮船沿河向上也驶入峡谷，但未注意到对方信号。幸好俄国"阿穆尔"号轮船船长经验丰富，才避免了一场事故，

由于经验丰富的俄国船长及营造司日益年迈，现逐渐被经验不足的中国职员代替，因违反《俄国航务条例》引发的事故越来越多，故拟订《中俄轮船往来黑龙江、额尔古纳河及乌苏里江航务条例》乃当务之急。

11. 俄阿穆尔省经济调查

1926 年阿穆尔省降水充足，庄家收成高于平均值。虽然农民税收已减少，表面看来福利也有所提高，但生活必需品物价高，谷物售卖状况不佳，农民的购买力也因此严重下降。

由于金矿产量减少，现在几乎没有产出，矿主借贷困难，而银行又撤回贷款，以致所有金矿矿主几乎都已破产。

由于税收繁重、木料许可证难以申请，从黑龙江上游及结雅河运输到布拉格维申斯克的木料数量减少，运达的木料价格高涨。

由于运送货物量小且乘客人数少，俄国政府的商船在亏本经营。黑龙江下游水产捕获量高达 160 万普特，工人及渔民收益颇丰，通过将大量水产从尼古拉耶夫斯克运到哈巴罗夫斯克，航运业营收增加。

12. 中国黑龙江省经济调查

中国船只运输在边境水域的发展与邻近区域经济发展状况紧密相关。

边境关闭；俄国增加沿岸边境的卫兵人数；俄国人对中国货物的购买力低；俄币贬值；俄国烈酒及烟草消费税降低；因此，不仅正常贸易终止，与西伯利亚的违禁贸易也终止了。大量中国工人希望有更好的工作条件，去了俄国金矿矿山，因此黑龙江省金矿产量显著减少。

黑龙江省农作物产量中等，但是由于谷物价格非常低，当地农民并不赚钱，手头拮据。

从黑龙江上游运到大黑河的木料数量减少，由于木料价格低、征税高，导致许多木料商破产。当地商人提议降低木料税，这样才能使运至哈尔滨的木料在市场上有竞争力。

若能实现该提议，且不再禁止谷物输出至哈尔滨，则会促进当地贸易活动，提高轮船运输量，有利于江捐税收。

13. 总结

为保证吉林省和黑龙江省的繁荣发展，中国政府应关注：

（1）拟定关于乌苏里江设置航路标志的《工程协议》。

（2）提高中国船只标准；详细制定《卫生条例》，禁止乘客超载。

（3）严格把控关员资质。

（4）提高船长能力。

（5）处理《中国北满洲内陆水域航务条例》问题。

（6）与苏联签订并发布《黑龙江、额尔古纳河及乌苏里江航务条例》。

（7）移除散布在黑龙江沿岸中国码头的石块。

（8）考虑大黑河港口的管理问题。

（9）因江捐税收不足，为黑龙江航路标志工事筹集资金。

（10）确认阿穆尔水道局是否有自费于边界河道清理石块之权利。

（11）引入更多人口（减少乘客乘坐轮船的费用），促进矿业及农业发展，减少木料、谷物等运输至哈尔滨的障碍，推动贸易发展，使经济状况更加独立，由此，江捐税收将会大幅增长。

易保罗（P. I. Ignatieff）

黑龙江航务专门顾问

5. 为 1927 年黑龙江航务年度报告事

AMUR AIDS TO NAVIGATION:
Annual Report on for 1927, prepared by Mr. P. I. Ignatieff,
Technical Adviser on Amur Aids to Navigation, forwarding.

372.   Registered
        INDEXED

I.G.   Aigun   21st May, 1928.

Sir,

    I have the honour to forward, enclosed
herewith, the "Annual Report on Aids to
Navigation" prepared by Mr. P. I. Ignatieff,
Technical Adviser on Amur Aids to Navigation.
This report gives a comprehensive summary of
the activities of the Aids Commission during
1927 as well as an economic survey of conditions
in the Chinese and Soviet parts of the Amur
basin. A Chinese version is not being sent
to the Taoyin.

    At the request of the Taoyin Mr. Ignatieff
has also prepared a history comprising a summary
of the work done by the Aids Commission since
its inception in 1922. It is the intention of
the Taoyin to publish this in Chinese for
distribution to the authorities interested and as
the account should also be of general interest
I propose to prepare an English version in due
course to be forwarded to the Inspectorate and
Coast Inspector.

        I have the honour to be,

           Sir,

        Your obedient Servant,

           Acting Commissioner.

The Inspector General of Customs,

    Peking.

Enclosure to Aigun No. 372 to I. G.

Aids to Navigation on the frontier rivers of the Amur basin,
Annual Report for the year 1927.

    The history of the joint upkeep of Aids on the frontier rivers in the Amur basin, mutually maintained during 1927 by China and the U.S.S.R. under the direction of the Sino-Soviet Technical Aids Commission, Taheiho, may be summarised as follows:

1. GENERAL: On the 10th of January, 1927, the local provisional Technical Agreement for joint Amur Aids work was renewed and signed for one year, i.e. for the period from the 1st December, 1926 to the 30th of November, 1927; the estimated expenditure agreed to was Roubles 60,000.

    The question of providing the Ussuri with Aids was discussed during the whole winter, but the Agreement for Ussuri Aids was signed only on the 17th of June, 1927, for the period of 6 months, i.e. from the 1st June to the 30th November, 1927; the estimate for this work was fixed at Rbls.8,600, the Chinese to pay half.

    The question of dredging work on the Upper Amur is still unsettled. Owing to the fact that only one Chinese steamer and two Russian Mail steamers, the latter carrying very little cargo and passengers between Stretensk and Blagovestchensk, and one Russian tug with barges carrying firewood ply the Upper Amur, the Chinese Commission consider such expenditure as unnecessary.

    The question concerning rock removal work in winter time on the lower part of the Argun was agreed to by the Chinese and Soviet Authorities, the conditions being that the above mentioned work would be done by, and at the expense of, Soviet Russia, the Heiho Taoyin issuing the necessary Huchaos for the use of Russian workmen in crossing the frontier. The work has been very costly for
the

the Amur Navigation Office as the position of the rocks were poorly marked owing to high water level before freezing.

2. <u>INSPECTION TOURS</u>: During the navigation season I made trips on board the Chinese steamers on the Amur and Ussuri in order to examine the condition of Aids.   Toward the end of the season I was able to report favourably on the repairs to Amur Aids, which had been done by the Amur Navigation Office.   The work of removal of rocks on the Amur had been examined and approved in winter.   In August all the members of the Chinese Aids Commission together with the Ilan Taoyin (who controls that part of Kirin Province bounded by the river Amur below Lahasusu, and by the Ussuri river) made a trip of inspection on board Chinese steamers down the Amur and on the Ussuri. The members of the Commission had an opportunity of investigating for themselves the state of the Aids and study at first hand many difficult problems.   When the Commission arrived on the Ussuri, Aids had been erected for the lower half of the distance only (180 versts; the whole distance being 336 versts).   After the return of the Commission, a great flood occurred on the Ussuri so the Aids work had to be delayed for one month eventually being finished on the 18th of October.

3. <u>THE PAYMENT TO THE AMUR NAVIGATION OFFICE FOR THE WORK DONE DURING THE SUMMER, 1927</u>:   During the year instalments were paid to the Amur Navigation Office from time to time, and the final payment was made after a full account was submitted by that Office; the total sum for the Amur Aids work, paid according to the estimate, totalled Roubles 30,000 which, at various rates, amounted to $30,934.38. For the Ussuri Aids the estimate was Roubles 4,300 and the amount actually expended $4,445.

4. <u>THE SIGNING OF THE AGREEMENTS FOR THE YEAR 1928</u>:   Negotiations concerning the Agreements on Amur and Ussuri Aids work, to be continued for 1928, proceeded without great difficulties, the two

Agreements

Agreements being signed on the 11th of January, 1928.   The estimates as agreed to for the Amur and Ussuri amounted to Roubles 60,000 and Roubles 8,600 respectively.

On the 11th of January there was also signed an Agreement adopting mutual provisional "Rules of Navigation" for the frontier rivers to be in force from the beginning of the navigation season of 1928. The question of the joint erection of Aids on the Argun, after being discussed the past three years, was settled and an agreement signed on the 19th of January, 1928.   It was decided to provide Argun with Aids of a simplified type, on the stretch from the village Olochi to the mouth of the Argun (village Pokrovka), a distance of 420 kilometres (402 versts).   The estimate agreed to was Roubles 3,000. Rock removal work for the winter of 1927 - 1928 on the Argun was agreed to on the former conditions, and Huchaos issued.

The question of dredging work on the Upper Amur, a complicated one, remains still unsettled; but the last letter from the Amur Navigation Office states that the estimate for the above mentioned work may be cut to from Roubles 7,000 to 10,000 as compared with the previous figure of Roubles 180,000, only the most dangerous shallows to be partly dredged.

5. THE RUSSIAN AMUR NAVIGATION OFFICE: This Bureau has planned Aids work in the Amur basin for 10 years forward and does not pay much regard for the immediate needs of trade, the yearly turnover of cargo and steamer traffic in general showing a great decrease.   They are anxious only to enlarge conservancy operations to a scale comparable to that of the Czarist Regime when in 1916, more than 700 Russian ships were plying on the Amur with its tributaries, and when the amount of cargo transported from Nickolaevsk to Stretensk (3,018 versts) amounted to more than 30,000,000 poods, plus local cargo which amounted to 50,000,000 poods; the number of passengers carried for a year amounting to 600,000.   At that time the Czarist

Government

Government granted necessary funds for Aids work, dredging, etc., to an amount of more than Roubles 3,000,000 yearly; whereas the Amur Navigation Office asked the Soviet Government in Moscow for Roubles 2,200,000 for 1927 but received Roubles 1,200,000 only. For the year 1928, the Amur Navigation Office expects to receive also Roubles 1,200,000 though there are only about 70 - 100 Chinese and Russian ships altogether plying on the Amur and its tributaries and the tonnage of cargo has decreased to some 5,000,000 - 8,000,000 poods.

All the large estimates submitted by the Amur Navigation Office for joint Aids work are always cut down very drastically and new estimates have to be drawn up more in accord with the actual needs of steamer traffic and the funds available from Chinese sources.

Great attention was paid to, and funds granted for, the betterment of the winter port in Habarovsk by the Amur Navigation Office where the great flood of 1927 on the Ussuri spoiled the jetty made by the excavators.

Owing to the lack of material and to the bad output of labour, the S/S "Amur", used for inspection tours, could not be repaired by the beginning of May as was expected repairs only being completed at the end of July. The proposed trip of the joint Aids Commission on the S/S "Amur" was consequently cancelled and the Commission made the trip on Chinese steamers, as related in § 2.

The Soviet Government Amur Water Transportation Bureau took up the question of installing lighting on the whole Amur section, wishing to issue a regular time table for steamer traffic. This idea is not practical because there are many serious obstacles to navigating on the Amur such as shallow water, dark nights, and storms in the Lower Amur, while there is often dense fog which

cannot

,cannot be foreseen.   At times steamers are delayed from 12 to 24 hours.

6. SOVIET GOVERNMENT AMUR WATER TRANSPORTATION BUREAU: being in a very bad financial condition towards the beginning of navigation season, and not being able to pay workmen for the repairs to shipping done in winter, had to make loans at a bank mortgaging steamers. The number of steamers running was very small and many employees and crews were without occupation.   From the very beginning of the navigation season, all hope for the transportation of cargo to the gold mining regions was lost, as the whole amount of supplies wanted for the mines was transported overland beforehand during winter time, owing to the very high freight rates on steamers.

The amount of fish transported from Nickolaevsk up the Amur was also very small as fishing in the Lower Amur was forbidden during summer and the amount of salmon caught in autumn was not great, storms having destroyed all settings of nets.   So the freight rates collected did not suffice to cover all expenses.   In spite of the lack of cargo, the G. A. T. B. started running the S/S "Habarovsk", the most powerful tug on the Amur, of 900 horse power to show that she could tow 7 - 10 barges with 25,000 poods each.   This steamer did not ply for more than 20 years because, inspite of the previous great amounts of transported cargo, running her proved unprofitable. Having two machines and four boilers she burned 25 - 35 cubic sajens of best firewood a day and now when stocks of firewood are lacking, especially on the Middle and Lower Amur, it was necessary for her to tow two barges of firewood for her own use, in addition to her other tows.   Moreover the engine-room crew were ignorant, so this exhibition run failed.

There was one Russian Mail steamer plying on the Ussuri between Habarovsk and Iman (opposite Hulin) but she carried neither cargo nor passengers.   The export of beans from Lake Hanka was even

less

less than the last year.

Two mail steamers making regular trips between Blagovestchensk and Stretensk ran at a loss also, for there were no passengers and no cargo.

The Government Amur Navigation Bureau towed rafts from the Upper Amur to Nickolaevsk consisting of some 50,000 pine beams (3-4 sajens long and 8-12 vershok thick) for export to Japan.

A serious accident happened to the Russian mail steamer "Chicherin". By mistake she entered, on a dark night, a shallow side waterway. Another accident happened to a barge loaded with firewood which ran ashore on the Verhne-Chernayevski shallows; the result being that the current washed a direct channel on that shallows.

7. CHINESE SHIPPING: The North East Navigation Bureau (Tungpei Steamship Company), which took all private Chinese steamers into the syndicate, had a great quantity of grain cargo to transport, increased the freight rates, and had good profits.

The high water which lasted during summer was favourable for transportation of a great deal of grain from the Lower Sungari to Harbin, but towards the end of the navigation season the depth of water on the Sansing shallows decreased to 2 feet which did not permit the export of the new crop of the autumn of 1927; this affected badly the farmers as well as the work of the shipping syndicate. Some regulating dikes and dams making the channel more narrow should be constructed on the above shallows in order to insure a greater depth of water there.

It is only fair to say that, thanks to repairs done every year, and to much more business-like methods, a betterment of conditions of steamers both technical and sanitary, and improved order on them is to be noticed. Of course there are still many defects, but one may hope they will be overcome gradually and

Chinese

Chinese shipping will raise its standard in the direction required by Lloyds' Rules.

It is necessary to pay greater attention to the appointment of masters and engineers, in effecting a stricter control of Certificates and not allowing persons to be appointed who know little navigation; also not to allow steamers to ply without pilots.

For the purpose of preventing fires, more effective measures should be taken to limit the transportation of benzine and kerosene on board the steamers.

As the lighting of all beacons along the Amur would be too expensive and is not warranted because of the small amount of ships plying, every Chinese steamer should have a search light in order to make faster and safer trips.

Chinese shipping on the river Amur during the summer was not so successful as it was on the rivers Sungari and Ussuri. The closed frontier, which killed trade with Siberia, as well as the very high freight rates and passenger fares charged by the Tungpei Company decreased considerably the turnover of cargo and the passenger traffic on the Amur. On the Ussuri the steamer traffic might have increased two times, if military detachments had not destroyed all fields of poppy, there being no official permission to sow poppies in Kirin Province. The great flood on the Ussuri, which occurred toward the middle of August, affected badly Chinese farmers just settled along the Ussuri.

The amount of timber and firewood in rafts from the Upper Amur to Taheiho as well as that carried by junks was much less than last year. The price of inferior firewood on the Sungari being $50 per one cubic sajen, and large coal-pits with good coal having been discovered at a distance of 60 versts from the Sungari near the village Chia-mu-su, the Syndicate started using coal on some

steamers.

steamers, mostly tugs, which made the cost much cheaper.   The coal conveyed to the river by small cars cost only 8 cents per pood for the steamers belonging to the Syndicate (24 cents for the private ones).   Loading of coal also takes less time than that of firewood. But the mining of coal being done without proper methods, the quality supplied for steamers was greatly complained of; two barges were used exclusively for carrying coal to Harbin.   According to preliminary investigations a coal bed has been found near the town Hsing-tung-tao on the Amur.

Unexpectedly for the Syndicate, steamers leaving Harbin for the Ussuri have been overfilled with passengers, care should be taken, therefore, that steamers be fitted with sanitary cabins and first aid cabinets fitted with the most necessary medicines and bandages.   There should also be discussed the question of medical assistance to employees and crews, as well as that of compensation in case they are disabled whilst in performance of their duty.

During the 1927 navigation season, Chinese steamers were plying without any Russian pilots.   About 20 of these were living at Blagovestchensk, but as they, according to the order of their Labour Union, requested very stiff terms, plus payment of passports, (Roubles 300 each), the Syndicate refused to take them on.   The lack of Russian pilots made it difficult for shipping to carry on so now the Syndicate has again taken up the question of hiring pilots from Blagovestchensk for the 1928 navigation season.

As firewood is very expensive at Harbin ($60 - 70 per cubic sajen) the Syndicate bought firewood all along the shore of the Amur for $12 - 16 per one cubic sajen as well as about 1,500 pine timbers for building, 3 - 7 sajens long by 9 vershok thick at $4 - 5 per piece.   All this timber was carried on barges towed by 7 tugs.

8. AMUR RIVER DUES COLLECTION: The small balance in the River Dues
fund.

fund, amounting on the 12th of January, 1927, to $3,687.58, was
insufficient to cover the cost of expenses of the joint Amur Aids
work to the end of the year and the Chinese Aids Commission was
forced to ask the Inspector General, for a loan of $5,000 from the
Sungari Aids funds.   Simultaneously the Commission asked the local
Taoyin to increase the Amur River Dues Tariff from the beginning
of the 1927 navigation season.   After this question was agreed to
with the Taheiho Chamber of Commerce, the Taoyin sanctioned it.
As a result of the increased tariff the River Dues Collection
amounted to $50,427.53 instead of the $35,469.42 as compared with
1926.   These sums were sufficient to cover all expenses including
Ussuri Aids and the balance to the 1st of January, 1928, amounted to
$3,910.33.

The flood on the Ussuri had a bad effect on the autumn
turnover of cargo, so the figures of this year's River Dues
Collection, in spite of the increased rates, during September and
October were less than those of last year's on that river.

It is possible that River Dues Collection for the coming
year, in view of poor trade conditions, may not suffice by about
$4,000 - 5,000 for all the payments according to estimates for 1928
for Amur, Ussuri and Argun Aids work which amount to a total of
Roubles 71,600.   The share of China is 50%, or Roubles 35,800 plus
overhead expenses.   If the collection is not sufficient the question
of finding additional funds will have to be taken up.

9. CONDITIONS OF NAVIGATION DURING 1927:   The snow melted very slowly
   during the spring and did not supply much water to the rivers, the
   ice on the Amur and its tributaries drifting in very slow water.
   The ice moved for the first time in the Harbour on the 22nd of
   April, but the ice drift began on the 4th of May.   The first

                                                              steamer

steamer "Haicheng" arrived from Harbin on the 6th of May; S/S "Aigun" arrived on the 7th of May, and "Haicheng" left Taheiho on the 9th of May. But on the 10th the ice drift began again so the S/S "Aigun" could leave only on the 14th; she proceeded up the Amur.

On the Upper Amur the low water lasted for 3 weeks, the depth of water being less than 4 feet on the Permikinski shallows. In the middle of June it was 3 feet, 3 inches.

On the Sungari a favourable depth of water lasted during the summer, but towards the middle of September the depth decreased and by October on Sansing shallows there was only 2 feet. The water in the Argun was higher than for 1926 but there were no vessels plying there except junks. On the Ussuri the water was also very favourable and higher than in 1926. Towards the end of July the depth started increasing rapidly and by the end of August the banks overflowed. The Koslovski Water-gauge station showed a difference between the lowest level of water in 1926 and the highest level on the 22nd August, 1927, of more than 19 feet. The height established was a record for the Ussuri.

On the 20th of October the last steamer, the S/S "Haicheng", left for Harbin. The S/S "Hung-tai" was the last steamer to arrive from the Upper Amur on the 25th October and was laid up in Taheiho Harbour.

The Harbour closed on the 5th of November, when drifting ice appeared, the level of the Amur being very low. The river closed opposite Taheiho on the 18th of November. The last two steamers proceeded through Lahasusu from the Ussuri on the 25th of October; one of them, a small craft named the "Tung-shan" was over-filled with passengers, 402 in all.

The exceedingly warm autumn lasted into November, so that one Russian steamer with two barges came to Blagovestchensk on the

4th

4th of November, an extraordinary case that had not happened during 30 years experience of the Amur Navigation Office.

10. ACCIDENTS TO SHIPPING: Thorough repairs made to Chinese ships and a better grade of employees resulted in a much smaller number of steamer accidents in 1927.

1) A serious accident occurred to the S/S "Hu-shiang" on the river Ussuri on the 15th of October, 1927, which, after leaving Hulin and proceeding 3 versts down stream, struck a submerged tree trunk and sunk. She was beached but it will be difficult to float her. There was no loss of life and little of cargo. When the accident occurred the Aids were not yet completed - this spot was provided with Aids only on the 17th of October. Investigations showed that the steamer proceeded too close to the sandy bank and was out of the channel.

2) The main steam pipe in the engine room of the S/S "Fuchiang" burst when on a trip from Harbin to Taheiho, on the Middle Amur. If it had happened on the Sungari when there were about 800 passengers aboard (much above the limit) many lives could have been lost. Inspectors examining steamers should pay more attention to the steam pipes, most of which are already old.

3) The S/S "Aigun", which during the whole navigation season made trips on the Upper Amur, was robbed by bandits one evening while the crew was busy loading firewood. There were no casualties amongst the passengers and crew but some $10,000 of cargo and personal effects were taken.

4) On the steamer "Haicheng", proceeding with a barge through Hingan gorges, where there is a very swift current, one paddle in the wheel was broken. Two anchors were lowered but one cable broke, and the fluke of the second anchor broke also. Only the expert manoeuvring of her experienced Russian Captain saved the
steamer

steamer which was beached.

11. <u>WORK DONE IN THE TAHEIHO HARBOUR</u>:   A jetty (275 feet long) was
built in 1919 by the Wu-tung Company for the purpose of protecting
the wintering steamers.   This structure adversely affected the
Harbour the current being diverted to the Russian shore.   Owing
to the resultant lack of current in the Harbour shoals were formed
behind the jetty and the long gravel spit stretching from the
island up the river and lying between the Harbour and the main
channel, started increasing and began to threaten to silt up the
entire harbour.

          After the survey of the harbour was completed in 1922,
it could be seen quite clearly that the harbour was filling up
behind the jetty.   Accordingly in 1923, upon instructions from
the Customs, 89 feet of the jetty was removed.   It is to be
regretted that the entire jetty was not taken away as silting
still continues below it.   This complete removal could have been
accomplished easily during the autumn of 1927, as the water was
very low and the ground not frozen.   Owing, however, to the never
ending negotiations between the North East Navigation Bureau and
the Tsitsihar Bank which had sheltered a dredge behind the jetty,
and feared that any alterations in the jetty would expose the
dredge to danger from ice drifts in the spring, nothing could be
done.

          In spring of 1927, I proposed, as a palliative, to dig
a channel across the lower end of the gravel spit for the purpose of
increasing the current through the harbour. $2,000 from River Dues
Collection was granted for this work, the North East Navigation
Bureau refusing to assist.   The work was accomplished while the
water was low, the channel being 1,050 feet long and 84 feet broad,
the depth averaging less than 1½ feet.   While excavating many big
                                                            rocks

rocks were found and removed. During the summer this channel did not silt, the direction of the cut was ascertained properly, and the current through the harbour was increased. I may suggest that it is necessary and quite possible to deepen this channel some more. During the winters of 1927 and 1928, many large rocks carried in by the ice drift to the harbour were removed but not all of them.

The approach to the landing stage of the North East Navigation Bureau is now difficult because of the shoaling water while the place behind the jetty is not deep enough for the wintering of steamers. The consequence is that as usually in autumn the water there is very low steamers, after the navigation season, cannot get protection and are wintered in the fareway. This happened to the S/S "Hung-tai" this autumn, which came back too late to secure a protected anchorage.

At Blagovestchensk, there is a similar instance of a jetty built more than 30 years ago for protecting private steamers from the ice drift; now there is a large and high sand bank behind it which absolutely prevents steamers from approaching the adjoining quay, and the shoal has to be continually dredged.

The entire question of the Taheiho Harbour Conservancy should be thoroughly considered and early steps taken to prevent its ruining itself entirely.

12. ECONOMIC SURVEY OF AMUR PROVINCE: Crops in the Russian Amur Province, in 1927, were above the average owing to favourable rains. As taxes on peasants had been lowered, it would seem that their welfare would have improved, but the high prices of goods needed by them as well as bad conditions of sale of their grain products greatly reduced their purchasing power. The peasants are not permitted to bring their flour to the market and sell it cheaper

than

than the cooperative shops do; they must deliver grain to the Government mills where the price on it is very low: 80 cents per pood as compared with the former price of Roubles 1 - 1.20. At the same time one yard of simple printed calico costs now more than 80 cents, instead of 15, and even then is difficult to get. For all materials or products there are long cues people waiting for their turn to purchase. Private trade is persecuted. Collection of taxes is unsuccessful. The gold miners are now almost ruined; credit at bank, which was formerly extended to them, is now very limited and granted only on condition that all the gold shall be delivered up to the bank at a very cheap price; the output of gold has been reduced so much that it is almost nothing now. The Government, which is in need of gold, granted Roubles 13,000,000 to the Dalbank for the promotion of gold mining business but little had been done owing to ignorance of the Communists in charge of mining affairs.

Burdensome taxes and stiff conditions in getting timber concessions caused a reduced amount of rafted timber and firewood to arrive from the Upper Amur and Upper Zeya to Blagovestchensk and increased to five times (as compared to the Czarist Regime) the price on that which did arrive.

The Soviet Government commercial shipping every year runs at a loss, due to the absence of cargo and passengers.

13. ECONOMIC SURVEY OF HEILUNGKIANG PROVINCE: The development of the Chinese steamer traffic on the frontier waters is largely linked with that of the economic condition of the adjecent regions.

The frontier is still closed; the Russians increased the number of frontier guards along the shore; the ability of the Russian people to buy Chinese goods is very low; the excise on Russian spirit and tobacco has been reduced; the result of all

this

this is that not only the regular but also the contraband trade with Siberia definitely ceased. The output of gold was also considerably reduced because the conditions of work were very hard, the owners grossly overcharging for supplies issued; passenge fares on steamers were very high, tickets of the 4th class,(though the price on them was published) were not sold except at Harbin. The result was that almost no Chinese workmen arrived at Taheiho. Towards the end of the year 1927 there was discovered near Taheiho a very rich, although not large, gold mine; about 400 people are now working there. In the winters of the year 1923 and 1924 there were working on all gold mines surrounding Taheiho about 20,000 people.

Crops in Heilungkiang Province were good but as the pric for grain was very low and the demand very poor the local farmers are very hard up and the development of the country is hindered. Grain cannot be exported to Harbin and sold against competition there because of high steamer freight rates. That is why the latter should be lowered.

In spite of the reduced taxes on timber and firewood, the amount of rafted timber arriving at Taheiho showed a considerab falling off. During the past years all the good timber suitable for building purposes has been cut down along the shore and as there was no snow in the taiga the timber this year had to be carried a long distance without roads, which increased its cost. However, as the freight rates on steamers are very high, little of the timber could be sent to Harbin and the prices fetched in Taheiho were low.

Sowing of poppies for opium began to be permitted in Heilungkiang Province in 1927. The results have been poor, however, because of lack of experience of the farmers, unsuitableness of the soil and a too rainy summer.

Along

Along the Ussuri and the Amur the telegraph was established; this will certainly promote the development of the country and that of steam navigation.

Every year it is more difficult to get furs, and prices for them are always getting higher.

The question arose of the export of grain from Heilungkiang Province to Vladivostok by railway through Blagovestchensk, or by water through Habarovsk or Hulin, as well as that of rafting timber to Nickolaevsk. These projects are of a great importance, and if they could be put into operation the prosperity of the Chinese in this region would be greatly improved.

14. CONCLUSION: Chinese authorities who are interested in the prosperity of Kirin and Heilungkiang provinces should give their attention to matters as follows:

1) To raise the standard of Chinese steamers; to make a more strict examination of boilers and steam pipes, as they are all getting old.

2) To elaborate "Sanitary Rules" and, until this is done, to prohibit overcrowding of passengers; also to provide steamers with first aid appliances.

3) To effect a stricter control of Officers Certificates and raise the standard for qualification.

4) To strengthen the authority of steamer Masters.

5) To raise funds for Amur, Ussuri and Argun Aids work, as the River Dues Collection is insufficient.

6) To limit the transportation of kerosene and benzine on steamers, and to introduce stricter precautions against fire.

7) To have good search lights for steamers plying on the Amur.

8) Not to allow steamers to ply without pilots.

9) Since the "Rules of Navigation" will be put in force at the beginning of navigation in 1928, to introduce effective measures to insure their being observed by Chinese steamers.

10)

10) To pay attention to the strength of the anchor cables and steering gear chains as well as to the effectiveness of lanterns used on steamers when under weigh, anchored, or for signaling.

11) To settle the question concerning preparing maps for navigation.

12) To consider Taheiho Harbour Conservancy.

13) To develope an independent economic condition of trade by bringing in more settlers (reducing passenger fares on steamers and selling 4th class tickets to all intermediate points); promoting mining industry and trying to promote fair treatment by owners of workmen; promoting agriculture and reducing obstacles to the export of timber, grain etc. to Harbin by reducing the freight rates.   This would result in a larger collection of River Dues.

14) If financial conditions permit it would be timely to consider the question of purchasing a launch for the use of inspection and examination of Aids by the Chinese Commission as now Agreements have been concluded for joint Aids work on the whole frontier region of the Amur, Ussuri and Argun.

15) To issue Regulations concerning:

　　a) the respecting of beacons and lights by local inhabitants,

　　b) abridged "Rules of Navigation" for the plying of rafts and junks on the frontier rivers.

16) To prohibit the building of houses or stores in villages and towns at landing places and foreshores nearer than 10 sajens from the beach, in order not to impede landing and mooring as well as loading and unloading of steamers.

17) To consider the question of medical assistance to steamer employees and crews, and of giving them compensation in case they lose their ability to work while in the performance of duty

P. Ignatieff

Technical Adviser's Office,

Aigun/Taheiho,   21st May, 1928.

Technical Adviser on
Amur Aids to Navigation.

呈海关总税务司署 372 号文　　　　　　　**瑷珲关 1928 年 5 月 21 日**

尊敬的海关总税务司（北京）：

　　兹附黑龙江航务专门顾问易保罗（P.I.Ignatieff）先生编制的 1927 年《黑龙江航务年度报告》。该报告全面总结了黑龙江水道委员会 1927 年的活动情况以及中俄双方在黑龙江流域的经济形势。该报告中文版尚未发送至道尹。

　　在道尹的要求下，易保罗先生还编写了黑龙江水道委员会自 1922 年成立以来所做工作的总结汇编。道尹希望这部汇编可以出版中文本，并将之分发给各地有兴趣的主管部门。鉴于该报告涉及各方普遍关注之事，本署建议适时出版英文本，并呈报至海关总税务司及海务巡工司。

您忠诚的仆人

铎博赉（R. M. Talbot）

瑷珲关署理税务司

此抄件发送至哈尔滨关税务司及巡工司

录事：屠守鑫四等帮办后班

1927 年黑龙江流域边界河道航务年度报告

1927 年,在中俄黑龙江水道委员会的指导下,俄方与中方继续共同维护黑龙江流域边界河道航路标志,总结如下:

1. 概览

1927 年 1 月 10 日,关于中俄联合维护黑龙江航路标志的《临时地方工程协议》续约一年,协议自 1926 年 12 月 1 日至 1927 年 11 月 30 日有效;协定黑龙江航路标志工作的支出预算为 60000 卢布。

虽然整个冬季都在讨论乌苏里江航路标志问题,但是关于乌苏里江航路标志的协议却直到 1927 年 6 月 17 日才得以签订,且仅有六个月的效力,即 1927 年 6 月 1 日至 1927 年 11 月 30 日;乌苏里江航路标志工作的支出预算为 8600 卢布,中方摊款为预算额之半数。

而黑龙江上游的疏浚问题仍亟待解决。由于只有一艘中国轮船和三艘俄罗斯邮轮往来其上,而且其中的两艘俄罗斯邮轮仅仅是在斯列坚斯克与布拉格维申斯克之间往返,所载货物和乘客亦极少;此外就只有一艘带有驳船的俄罗斯拖船定期往返于黑龙江上游航道,以运输木桴,所以中方委员会认为暂时没有进行疏浚的必要。

中俄双方协定由俄方出资并负责进行额尔古纳河下游的冬季石块清理工作,由道尹为入境的俄国工人签发护照。但因该河段水位较高,以致俄阿穆尔水道局无法于结冰前标记出需要清理的石块位置,该项工作之费用亦因此而剧增。

2. 巡查

航运季期间,本人乘坐中国轮船至黑龙江及乌苏里江航道检查航路标志之状况,并于航运季结束之际,顺利完成了关于俄阿穆尔水道局航路标志维修工作的相关报告。黑龙江航道上的石块清理工作已于冬季通过验收。8 月,中国水道委员会的全体委员与依兰道尹(依兰道尹负责吉林省范围之内以拉哈苏苏下游的黑龙江河段及乌苏里江河段为界的河道)一起,乘坐中国轮船巡查了黑龙江下游和乌苏里江航道上的航路标志状况。借此机会,中国水道委员会的委员们不仅可以亲自视察航路标志之现状,亦可及时处理所遇之问题。委员们抵达乌苏里江之时,乌苏里江(全长 336 俄里)仅有下游河段(180 俄里)完成了航路标志的安设工作。在委员们返程后不久,乌苏里江即暴发了洪水,导致航路标志工作推迟了一个月,至 10 月 18 日才终于完成。

3. 支付阿穆尔水道局 1927 年夏季完工款项

全年定期向阿穆尔水道局分期付款，尾款于阿穆尔水道局提交完整账簿后支付。根据协议协定之预算，黑龙江航路标志工作费用总计 30000 卢布，按机动汇率换算，实际支付 30938.38 银圆；乌苏里江航路标志工作费用总计 4300 卢布，实际支付 4445 银圆。

4. 1928 年协议签订

关于 1928 年《黑龙江航路标志协议》和《乌苏里江航路标志协议》的协商进展顺利，最终两项协议均于 1928 年 1 月 11 日签订，协定黑龙江航路标志预算为 60000 卢布，乌苏里江航路标志预算为 8600 卢布。

1928 年 1 月 11 日航运季伊始，关于中俄边界河道的临时《航务条例》得以签订并即时生效。联合建立额尔古纳河航路标志一事历经三年协商之后终于得到解决，并于 1928 年 1 月 19 日签订了相关协议。根据协议，将于额尔古纳河上安设简易航路标志，范围为奥罗赤村至额尔古纳河口的波克罗夫卡村之间，全长 420 公里（402 俄里），协定预算为 3000 卢布。额尔古纳河 1927-1928 年冬季石块清理工作和与之相应的护照签发工作，此前已获得批准。

黑龙江上游的疏浚工作因较为复杂，仍然悬而未决。但是阿穆尔水道局最近来函表示，上述工作的预算将从之前的 180000 卢布削减至 7000 到 10000 卢布，如此，便只能于最危险的浅滩开展部分疏浚工作。

5. 俄阿穆尔水道局

阿穆尔水道局已完成黑龙江流域航路标志工作的十年计划，而对于当前的贸易需求却不甚重视，货物和轮船的年收益总体呈大幅下降趋势。俄方只是急于将航务活动扩大到 1916 年沙俄政权时的规模。沙俄政权时期，有多达 700 余艘俄罗斯轮船往返于黑龙江及其支流，自尼古拉耶夫斯克（Nickolaevsk）至斯列坚斯克之间（全长 3018 俄里）的总货运量达 3000 万普特，地方总货运量达 5000 万普特，总载客量达 60 万人次。当时，沙俄政府每年都会为航路标志的建设以及河道疏浚等工作拨发超过 300 万卢布的款项。然而 1927 年，阿穆尔水道局向莫斯科苏维埃政府申请了 220 万卢布预算，结果却只收到了 120 万卢布。1928 年，中俄两国虽仅有 70 到 100 艘左右的轮船往返于黑龙江及其支流上，而总货运量业已降至 500 万到 800 万普特，但阿穆尔水道局仍然向莫斯科苏维埃政府申请 120 万卢布的拨款。

阿穆尔水道局就联合维护航路标志工作所提交的预算金额遭到严重削减，只得根据轮船运输的实际要求以及中方的资金状况制定新的预算。

1927年，乌苏里江暴发洪水，冲毁了哈巴罗夫斯克（Habarovsk）冬季口岸处的码头，关于修复该码头一事，阿穆尔水道局已得到拨款。

用于巡查的"阿穆尔"号轮船本应在5月初修缮完成，但由于缺乏人力物力，一直到7月末才得以完成。因此中俄水道委员会原定的乘坐"阿穆尔"号轮船进行巡查的计划被迫取消，委员们改乘中国轮船完成了巡查。

俄阿穆尔国家水运局已着手研究于整个黑龙江流域安设灯桩，以期黑龙江流域的轮船均可按照固定的航运时刻表航行。但该想法有些不切实际，因为黑龙江上存在着很多危险因素，比如浅水、暗夜、下游的暴风雨以及无法预测的浓雾天气等，轮船有时会耽搁12小时乃至24小时。

6. 俄阿穆尔国家水运局

航运季初期，俄阿穆尔国家水运局财务状况十分糟糕，既无法支付工人的工资，也无法开展冬季的航路维修工作，不得已只能抵押轮船向银行贷款。因此能够用于运营的轮船很少，以致许多雇员和船员都没有工作。同时，所有向金矿地区运输货物的想法也都无法实现，因为受高昂的航运费用的影响，一般的矿区所需物品早在冬季就已经预先通过陆路完成了运输。

尼古拉耶夫斯克地区的水产运输量也非常低，因为黑龙江下游夏季禁止捕鱼，秋季的鲑鱼又不够肥美，安置的渔网还经常会受到暴风雨的破坏；因而所征收的航务运费并不足以负担所有的支出。不过，尽管缺乏可供运输的货物，但俄阿穆尔国家水运局还是尝试将"哈巴罗夫斯克"号拖船投入运营，这是黑龙江上动力最大的拖船，拥有900马力，可拖拽7到10条25000普特的驳船。虽然这艘拖船可以运载如此大量的货物，但是却已有20年未曾航行了，因为它的运营并不能获得任何利润。而且这艘拖船有两个引擎和四个锅炉，每天需要燃烧25-35立方俄丈的优质木桦，在航行过程中，一旦木桦不足，特别是当它行驶至黑龙江中下游的时候，则除了其他被拖拽物，还必须拉两驳船的木桦作为燃料。由于上述种种原因，加上它的引擎室目前也出现了问题，所以此次试运行以失败告终。

只有一艘俄方邮轮在自哈巴罗夫斯克至伊曼（与虎林相对）一段的乌苏里江上航行，但它既不装载货物，也不运载乘客。兴凯湖的豆类出口量比去年更少。

两艘在布拉格维申斯克与斯列坚斯克之间航行的邮轮因为既无乘客可供搭载，亦无货物可供运输而一直亏本。

俄阿穆尔国家水道局从黑龙江上游向尼古拉耶夫斯克拖运木筏，共计约50000根松木（长3到4俄丈，厚8到12俄寸），以供出口日本。

俄罗斯"奇切林（Chicherin）"号邮轮因于深夜意外驶入了浅滩一侧的航道而发生严重事故。另有一艘满载木桦的驳船搁浅于外 – 切尔纳耶夫斯基（Verhne-Chernayevski）浅滩，结果水流将该片浅滩冲刷出了一条笔直的河道。

7. 中国航运业

东北航务局（东北航业公司）集结了所有中国私人轮船，组成协会，同时拥有大量可运输的粮食，此外还提高了航路运费，由此赚取了高额的利润。

因夏季的高水位有利于航运，故而有大量的粮食自松花江下游运往哈尔滨；但到了航运季末期，三姓浅滩的水位下降到只有两尺深，以致1927年秋季的新产作物难以向外运输，这不仅给农民带来了极为不利的影响，也损害了船运协会的利益。应于三姓浅滩上建立一些可调控的堤坝，以调整河道的宽度和水位的深度。

由于每年均会检修轮船，且管理轮船之方法日益井然有序，因此轮船的技术、卫生以及航运秩序等方面均有所改善。当然，目前仍有许多不足之处需要逐渐克服，中国航运业也会继续按照劳埃德规则不断提高自身的标准。

人员方面，在船长和工程师的任用方面要更加谨慎，对工作资质的认证要更加严格，凡不懂航务知识的人概不任用，轮船上若无引水员，一律不准出航。

为防范火灾，应采取更为有效的措施以加强对运输汽油和煤油的管控。

由于点亮黑龙江沿线所有标桩的费用十分昂贵，加之来往的轮船不多，故此事暂未获得批准，因此所有中国轮船都务必配备探照灯，以确保航行的安全和便捷。

夏季时，中国航运业在黑龙江航道上未能像在松花江和乌苏里江航道上一样盈利，原因在于，边境的封闭阻断了与西伯利亚的贸易；另外，东北航路局收取的运费和乘客票费过高，也在极大程度上削减了黑龙江上货物运输和乘客运载的收益。吉林省关于播种罂粟虽无官方许可，但若不是军队摧毁了所有的罂粟田，乌苏里江上的运输量或可为实际运输量的两倍。乌苏里江在8月中旬暴发的洪水，也为刚刚在乌苏里江沿岸定居的中国农民带来极为不利的影响。

从黑龙江上游用木筏和民船运输到大黑河的木料及木桦数量也比去年大幅减少。在松花江流域，劣质木桦的价格尚且为50银圆每立方俄丈。不过后来在距松花江60俄里的佳木斯镇附近发现了许多具有优质煤的大型煤窑，于是东北航路局开始在一些轮船和大部分拖船上用煤来做燃料，遂使燃料费日益低廉。这些煤块通过小车就可以运至河边，对东北航路局船运协会的轮船，每普特燃煤只收取8个铜钱（对私家轮船收取24个铜钱）。而且装载煤的耗时也比装载柴火少得多。但是若开采方法不对，煤的质量便难以保证，以致引来轮船主们的抱怨。目前有两艘驳船专门负责向哈尔滨运送煤块。另外，根据最初的调查，黑龙江兴东道镇附近也发现有煤床。

出乎东北航路局的意料，从哈尔滨至乌苏里江的轮船载满了乘客，就连本可以坐车的乘客也都选择了坐船，因此轮船上也开始设有卫生室以及装满了必备药品和绷带的急救箱。不过除此之外，雇员和船员的医疗救助问题，以及工伤的补偿问题，也应该予以讨论。

至 1927 年航运季，中国轮船上已没有任何俄籍船员。虽然在布拉格维申斯克地区居住有 20 名俄籍船员，但由于该地区工会的僵化条款以及较高的护照费用（每份护照 300 卢布），东北航路局拒绝接收他们。然而俄籍船员的缺乏，却导致了航运的难以为继，于是东北航路局又决定在 1928 年航运季，再次雇用布拉格维申斯克地区的俄籍船员。

由于哈尔滨地区的柴火非常昂贵（每立方俄丈 60 到 70 银圆），因此东北航路局多从黑龙江沿岸购买柴火，其价格为每立方俄丈 12 到 16 银圆；除此之外，东北航路局亦于黑龙江沿岸购买了 1500 根用于建筑的松木，每根长 3 到 7 俄丈、厚 9 俄寸，价格为每根 4 到 5 银圆。所有木料均由驳船运载，由 7 艘拖船负责拖拽。

8. 黑龙江江捐征收

至 1927 年 1 月 12 日，江捐结余只有 3687.58 银圆，不足以支付年末联合维护黑龙江航路标志的费用，因此中国水道委员会迫于无奈向总税务司申请 5000 银圆的贷款（从松花江航路标志资金中支出）。同时，中国水道委员会要求地方道尹自 1927 年航运季伊始提高黑龙江江捐税率。在经大黑河商会协商通过后，道尹亦予以批准。相较于 1926 年 35469.42 银圆的江捐税收，税率提高后，1927 年江捐税收增加到 50427.53 银圆，这些钱款足以负担包括乌苏里江航路标志项目在内的所有支出。至 1928 年 1 月 1 日，江捐结余达到 3910.33 银圆。

乌苏里江的洪水严重影响了秋季的货物运输收益，尽管提高了税率，但今年 9 月至 10 月之间的江捐税收仍不及去年同期的金额。

在如此糟糕的贸易情况下，1928 年的江捐税收也许会不足 4000 到 5000 银圆。根据预算，1928 年黑龙江、乌苏里江与额尔古纳河航路标志工作的所需费用为 71600 卢布，华方须摊付一半（或许还要再加一些常规性支出）。如果江捐税收不足，则须着手寻找其他的经济来源。

9. 1927 年航运状况

由于春季冰雪融化得较慢，流入河中的雪水并不多，冰块大多在黑龙江及其支流中缓慢地漂浮着。4 月 22 日，大黑河港口的冰块开始移动，然而直到 5 月 4 日，冰块才开始漂浮。

5月6日,从哈尔滨关出发的第一艘轮船"海澄"号抵达大黑河,次日"瑷珲"号轮船也随之抵达;5月9日,"海澄"号轮船驶离大黑河。由于5月10日冰块再次漂浮起来,所以"瑷珲"号轮船直到5月14日才得以驶离大黑河而进入黑龙江。

在黑龙江上游,水位一连三个星期都很低,派米津斯基浅滩水深不足4英尺,到6月中旬已降至3英尺3英寸。

夏季的松花江水位适宜,至9月中旬便开始下降,到10月份时,三姓浅滩的水深已仅为2英尺。额尔古纳河的水位高于1926年同期,不过除了民船以外,河面上未见其他轮船往来。乌苏里江的水位情况也比较良好,同样高于1926年同期,且7月末,水位仍保持迅速上涨的趋势,至8月底,河水已溢过了河岸。根据克斯罗夫斯基水位观测站数据显示,1926年最低水位与1927年8月22日最高水位相差19英尺。该水位高度为乌苏里江的最高记录。

10月20日,大黑河最后一艘轮船"海澄"号驶向哈尔滨。10月25日,自黑龙江上游出发的最后一艘轮船"鸿泰"号抵达大黑河并停泊在大黑河港口。

11月5日,黑龙江上出现浮冰,水位变得非常低,大黑河港口随之关闭。大黑河对面的河道则于11月18日关闭。10月25日,自乌苏里江而来的最后两艘轮船经过拉哈苏苏关,其中较小的一艘"东山"号轮船共载客402名。

暖秋一直持续到11月,一艘带着两艘驳船的俄罗斯轮船于11月4日抵达布拉格维申斯克,阿穆尔水道局过去30年的航运经历中从未有过此类情况。

10. 航运事故

鉴于中国轮船已经彻底检修,且船员资质良好,因此1927年发生的事故屈指可数。

（1）1927年10月5日,"湖祥"号轮船发生了一起严重事故。该轮船离开虎林之后,在沿着河道下游驶出3俄里时,因不慎撞上水中的树干而沉没,且很难再漂浮起来。所幸并无人员伤亡,只损失了少量的货物。该事故发生时,航路标志还未完全建好,发生事故的地点于10月17日才建立起航路标志。据调查表明,事故发生的主要原因是轮船行驶时距离沙质河岸过近,偏离了原有的航道。

（2）由哈尔滨驶向大黑河的"富江"号轮船,在航行至黑龙江中段时,引擎室的主蒸汽管意外破裂。当时,船上的乘客多达800人（已远超其载客上限）,如果事故是发生在乌苏里江上,那必然会造成大量人员伤亡。所以稽查员在检查轮船时,应多加注意蒸汽管,因为有很多蒸汽管目前都已老化。

（3）航运季期间的某个夜晚,行驶于黑龙江上游的"瑷珲"号轮船,在船员忙于装运柴火时遭遇土匪抢劫。所幸乘客与船员皆无伤亡，但是约有价值 10000 银圆的货物及随身物品被土匪劫走。

（4）带着一条驳船的"海澄"号轮船，在驶入兴安峡谷时遭遇一股急流，一只轮桨被毁。当时该轮船曾放下两只锚，然而一只断了锚索，一只坏了锚爪。不过最终俄罗斯船长还是凭借自己丰富的航海经验成功拯救了该轮船。

11. 大黑河港口已完成工作

1919 年，戊通航业公司为保护于此过冬的轮船建立了一个码头（长 275 英尺）。然而该码头的结构却对港口造成了不利影响，致使水流转向了俄罗斯滨岸。由于港口缺少水流，码头后面遂形成滩涂，长长的砂砾沙嘴从岸边一直延伸至河道中，盘亘在口岸与主河道之间，并迅速扩大，造成淤塞，已威胁到整个口岸。

1922 年的港口测量结果显示，码头后面的港口淤塞程度日渐严重。1923 年，按海关指示，拆除了部分码头（89 英尺长）。然而令人扼腕的是，若不将整座码头拆除，码头下方的淤塞情况将会继续恶化。1927 年秋季，水位较低且地面也尚未冻结，因此码头拆除工作本可顺利完成，然而，齐齐哈尔银行因在码头后面放置了一台疏浚机，担心码头改建后，疏浚机会在春季浮冰期受到损坏，故与东北航务局之间的协商一直未有结果，码头拆除工作亦无法如期展开。

1927 年春季，本署提议在砂砾沙嘴的末端挖掘河道，以增加口岸的水流量。虽然本署已自江捐税收中拨款 2000 银圆用于该项工程，但东北航务局还是拒绝提供协助；不过，河道挖掘工程仍然借水位偏低的良机而得以顺利完成。新的河道长 1050 英尺、宽 84 英尺，平均深度不高于 1.25 英尺。在挖掘过程中，还发现并清理了很多大石块。新河道开通之后，港口的水流量果然增加不少。由于夏季河道并未发生淤塞，可以对挖掘方向做出准确的定位，故而本署认为可以将河道再挖深一些。1927 至 1928 年冬季，浮冰将很多大石块带入了港口，这些大石块目前仍未清理干净。

目前，因水位过低，轮船难以驶入东北航务局的浮动码头，且码头后面的水域过浅，根本无法供轮船停泊过冬。每到秋季，浮动码头附近的水位往往较低，以致轮船在航运季过后必须行驶到很远的地方过冬。今年秋季，"鸿泰"号轮船就是因为返航太晚，以致来不及在入冬前寻找到安全的停泊处。

在布拉格维申斯克也发生了类似情况。这里有一个已建成三十余年的码头，一直保护着私家轮船，使之免受浮冰的损害；但现如今，码头后面却因淤塞而形成了一片高大的沙岸，阻碍了轮船的驶入。该片滩涂同样亟待疏浚。

兹建议仔细考虑大黑河港口的管理问题，早日采取有效措施，以防止码头遭到进一步的破坏。

12. 俄罗斯阿穆尔省经济调查

由于降水充沛，1927 年阿穆尔省的庄稼收成远远高出平均值。然而，虽然已经减少了对农民的征税，农民福利本应有所提高，但是由于生活必需品的物价上涨，加上谷类产品的售卖状况不佳，因此农民的实际购买力仍然大幅下降。按照规定，农民不得将面粉带到市场，以低于合作社的售价售卖，而是必须将粮食运到政府的磨坊售卖，但政府给出的价格极低，每普特仅 80 分，市场价为 1 到 1.20 卢布。当下，买一码普通的白洋布就需要 80 分（过去一码只卖 15 分），而且购买十分困难；几乎任何物料和产品，人们都需要排很长的队去购买。私人贸易受到压制，征税亦不顺利。目前，黄金矿主已濒临破产，他们可以从银行贷款的额度十分有限，而且只有将所有黄金以低廉的价格交付给银行，方能获得贷款；然而，黄金的开采量已大幅减少，所剩无几。政府因急需黄金，已向远东银行拨发 1300 万卢布用以促进黄金开采业务，但由于忽视了矿业乃由共产主义者所控制这一事实，最终几乎一无所获。

因税收繁重，木料许可证申请困难，导致从黑龙江上游和结雅河上游运输到布拉格维申斯克地区的木料数量锐减，运达木料的价格暴涨了五倍（相比于沙俄政权时期）。

由于货物的运输量过小，而且乘客的人数过少，俄国政府商船已陷于亏本经营之中。

13. 黑龙江省经济调查

中国航运业在边境水域的发展与邻近区域的经济发展状况紧密相关。

边境仍然处于关闭之中，俄国增加了沿岸边境驻守的卫兵人数，俄国人对中国货物的购买能力甚低，俄国烈酒和烟草的消费税降低，这些因素不仅导致正常的贸易无法展开，就连与西伯利亚的违禁贸易也被迫终止。由于工作条件艰苦，黄金开采量锐减，黄金拥有者遂坐地起价。船票价格也涨得极高（尽管票面上已标明了常规价格），除哈尔滨以外，其他地区均不售卖四等船票，以致没有中国工人到大黑河工作。1927 年底，大黑河附近发现了一个储藏丰富的小金矿，目前约有 400 人在那里工作；而在 1923 年至 1924 年冬季，于大黑河附近金矿工作的人员达 20000 人之多。

黑龙江省的庄稼长势良好，但是由于粮价过低，需求不足，当地农民的生活仍然是举步维艰，地区发展也停滞不前。另外，由于航运费用高昂，粮食无法运至哈尔滨以对抗粮价的竞争，因此实有降低运费之必要。

虽然木料及木桦的税率已经降低，但运至大黑河的木料数量仍然大不如前。去年，岸边适用于建筑的优质木料已被砍伐殆尽；而今年,针叶林地带又没有下雪,因而所需木料都要经过远途运输,但又无法通过陆路来运输,航路运费便因此而大幅上涨。由于航路运费甚高,几乎没有木料能够运达哈尔滨；不过大黑河地区的运输价格却很低。

1927 年,黑龙江省开始允许种植罂粟以制作鸦片,但由于农民经验的不足,土质不适,以及夏季降雨量大等因素,其结果也只是差强人意。

乌苏里江与黑龙江沿线已建立了电报站,这对于航运乃至地区发展都将起到极大的促进作用。

目前,获取皮毛变得越来越困难,因此皮毛的价格也随之水涨船高。

关于黑龙江省粮食的输出,可以选择通过铁路经由布拉格维申斯克运送至符拉迪沃斯托克,又或者通过水路经由哈巴罗夫斯克或者虎林运送至符拉迪沃斯托克；而关于木料的输出,亦可由相同路线运送至尼古拉耶夫斯克。这些输出项目均十分重要,一旦得以运行,大黑河地区的中俄贸易一定能得到良好的发展。

14. 总结

为保证吉林省与黑龙江省的繁荣发展,中国政府应关注：

（1）提高对中国轮船的审核标准,特别是对于已经老化的锅炉和蒸汽管,要采取更为严格的检验标准。

（2）详细制定《卫生条例》,以杜绝拥挤现象,并为轮船提供完善的救生设备。

（3）严格审查驾驶员的驾驶资格,提高资格审核标准。

（4）提高船长之权威性。

（5）鉴于江捐税收不足以承担边界河道航路标志工作之费用,须为黑龙江、乌苏里江及额尔古纳河航路标志工作筹集资金。

（6）限制汽油和煤油的运输,更为严格地执行火灾预防措施。

（7）凡于黑龙江上航行的轮船,必须配备良好的探照灯。

（8）不允许轮船在没有引水员的情况下出航。

（9）自 1928 年航运季伊始执行《航务条例》,并采取有效措施以确保中国轮船遵守该条例。

（10）在轮船行进、停泊或者发送信号的过程中,须注意锚索、操舵装置的链条以及船上照明灯的情况是否良好。

（11）解决编制航运地图的相关问题。

（12）注意大黑河口岸的保护管理问题。

（13）引进更多移民，建立独立的经济贸易体系（降低乘客的船票费、允许所有代售点售卖四等船票）；促进矿业的发展，努力保障并提高劳工待遇；促进农业发展，降低航路运费率，以方便木料和粮食等物品向哈尔滨的出口；从而使江捐税收大幅增加。

（14）鉴于就联合维护边界河道黑龙江、乌苏里江以及额尔古纳河航路标志的协议已经签订，因此，若财政状况允许，希望可以为中国水道委员会购置一艘汽艇，以供巡查边界河道航路标志情况时使用。

（15）应颁布之章程包括：

a. 当地居民应注意维护标桩与灯塔；b. 删减《航务条例》中关于木筏和民船在边界河道航行的部分。

（16）为了保证轮船可安全靠岸、停泊以及装载货物，禁止在村庄的登陆地域以及距离海滩 10 俄丈的前滩范围内建房屋或商铺。

（17）解决雇员和船员的医疗救助问题，以及工伤的补偿问题。

易保罗（P. I. Ignatieff）

黑龙江航务专门顾问

航务专门顾问办事处

1928 年 5 月 21 日，瑷珲关／大黑河

6. 为 1928 年黑龙江航务年度报告事

AMUR AIDS TO NAVIGATION: Annual Report on for 1928,
prepared by Mr. P. I. Ignatieff, Technical Adviser
on Amur Aids to Navigation, forwarding.

I. G.

Aigun   1st   June,   1929.

Sir,

I have the honour to forward, enclosed
herewith, the "Annual Report on Aids to
Navigation for 1928" prepared by Mr. P. I.
Ignatieff, Technical Adviser on Amur Aids to
Navigation. As in his previous Annual Reports
Mr. Ignatieff not only summarises the activities
of the Aids Commission but gives an economic
survey of conditions in the Amur basin. A
Chinese version of this Report is not being
sent to the Chinese authorities.

I am forwarding this Report without
comment; it is fairly exhaustive and correct
in detail. The Aids to Navigation on the
Amur and Ussuri; and now on the Argun, rivers
were maintained by the Soviet authorities during
1928, as in former years, at a high standard of
efficiency and very little complaint, other than
of a routine nature, has been received from
Chinese shipping.

In Aigun despatch No.372, forwarding
Mr. Ignatieff's last Report, I mentioned that

he

THE INSPECTOR GENERAL OF CUSTOMS.
SHANGHAI.

he had prepared a history of the activities
of the Aids Commission for publication by the
Taoyin in Chinese and that I hoped to prepare
an English version in due course. The
manuscript is still in the hands of the Taoyin
for corrections and additions but will be
published shortly.

I have the honour to be,

Sir,

Your obedient Servant,

Acting Commissioner.

Enclosure to Aigun despatch No.423 to I.G.

Aids to Navigation on the frontier rivers of the Amur basin.
Annual Report for the year 1928.

The record of the joint upkeep of Aids on the frontier rivers in the Amur basin, as mutually maintained during 1928 by the U.S.S.R. and China, under the direction of the Sino-Soviet Technical Aids Commission, Taheiho, may be summarised as follows:

1. GENERAL: On the 11th of January, 1928, the local provisional Technical Agreements for joint Amur and Ussuri Aids work were renewed and signed for one year, i.e. for the period from the 1st December, 1927, to the 30th of November, 1928; the estimated expenditure agreed to was Roubles 60,000 for the Amur, and Roubles 8,600 for Ussuri Aids work.

On the 11th of January, 1928, an Agreement for the issue of Provisional "Rules of Navigation", to be mutually observed on the Frontier Rivers, from the beginning of the 1928 Navigation Season, was also signed.

On the 19th of January, 1928, an Agreement was signed for the river Argun providing it with Aids of a light type of beacons, on the stretch from the village Olochi (Shih-Wei-Hsien) (室韋縣) to the mouth (Lokuho), (洛古河), 402 versts. The estimate for this work was fixed at Roubles 3,000.

During the winter season of 1927 / 1928, the Soviet Amur Navigation Office was permitted to do some rock removal work on the Argun on its own account.

On the 19th of June, 1928, the Agreement for joint dredging work on the Upper Amur was signed and the estimate for this work was fixed at Roubles 6,000.

2. INSPECTION TOURS: During the navigation season I made trips on board the Chinese steamers on the Amur and Ussuri in order to examine

examine the condition of Aids.   Towards the end of the season I was able to report favourably on all repairs to Aids which had been done by the Amur Navigation Office.

The 34 beacons which were carried away by the flood on the Ussuri, during the spring ice-drift, have been renewed; others have been shifted, according to the notes of Masters and pilots of Chinese steamers.   Numbers had been put on all beacons there.

As the Soviet Authorities refused to furnish us with an up-to-date chart of the Ussuri river, I corrected, during my trips, the old one, marked thereon all beacons and numbers, and this chart will be printed for distribution to Chinese shipping.

On the Argun, on the stretch from the village Oloshi to the mouth (402 versts), the work of erecting Aids began on the 29th of May and was finished by the end of September; 203 new beacons of a light type were erected, and 176 of the old ones were repaired, total 379.   This work was done during low water, and was accomplished very late in the autumn, so I could not examine it then but the Amur Navigation Office has submitted Accounts which have been approved by myself and has marked the beacons on the chart of the Argun which was sent to them by the Chinese Commission for that purpose.

On the middle Amur, after repairs to beacons were already done, came the flood from the Zeya river which carried away many of them; but towards autumn, when the water was normal, all the beacons were renewed except the district of Michailo-Semenovsk and the Kasakevich Waterway, (160 versts) where the water covering the banks lasted to the end of Navigation Season.

Inspection trips may continue to be done on board private steamers but it would be much more useful to have our own inspection launch.

During

During my inspection tour on the Ussuri, I found that on the stretch from Hulin to the mouth of the river Sungacha (84 versts) the Amur Navigation Office, at the beginning of the 1928 season, had provided the river with Aids on the Russian side. In reply to a letter from the President of the Chinese Commission, the Amur Navigation Office replied on the 17th August 1928, that this was really done. The latter Office undertook this work independently, not having informed the Chinese Commission.

With reference to the Agreement spoken of above to dredge the Upper Amur, the Amur Navigation Office made surveys of the Beitonovski, Permikinski, Verhne-Chernayevski and Nijne-Chernayevski Shallows and brought down from the river Shilka dredge No.5, which began working on the Beitonovski Shallows on the 30th of July. The manager of this dredge was instructed to make a channel of a depth of 1.50 meter by the low water of 1913; the channel had to be 60 m. broad. As dredge No.5 was of poor capacity and its frame was very short the work, though the water was very favourable, lasted on these Shallows to the end of the autumn so the work on the Permikinski and Chernayevski Shallows could not be started at all this year. As it was very late in the season and we had no launch, I could not examine the work done on the Beitonovski Shallows.

Now that the "Rules of Navigation" have been issued there should be appointed an Inspector to enforce the Rules and to see that steamers and rafts are properly equipped and in good condition. During the inspection tours as well as when examining steamers and rafts moored to landing places, I found plenty of infringements of "Rules of Navigation", but not having any authority, I was not able to give instructions to Masters or to help them avoid some defects.

defects. Owing to this lack of control and of inspection officials
on the frontier rivers, many Chinese steamers did not give
statements of accidents and no inquiries could be made to discover
the causes of the accidents or the persons who were to blame for
them.

3. THE PAYMENT TO THE AMUR NAVIGATION OFFICE FOR WORK DONE DURING
   THE SUMMER 1928: During the year instalments were paid to the
Amur Navigation Office at regular intervals and the final payment
was made after a full account was submitted by that Office. The
Chinese Commission, according to the Agreements, has paid 50%
of the estimates, namely: Roubles 30,000 for the Amur Aids work;
Roubles 4,300 for the Ussuri, and Roubles 1,500 for the Argun;
total Roubles 35,800 which at various exchange rates, amounted to
Harbin dollars $21,679.50.

4. THE SOVIET AMUR NAVIGATION OFFICE: This Bureau receives from
its Government large sums (Roubles 1,200.000 for 1928) for Aids
works and plans large operations without taking into consideration
the necessity for them.   All estimates submitted by this Bureau
for joint Aids work are always considerably cut down.

        The Amur Navigation Office is still unable to complete
the work of building a winter harbour at Habarovsk as in 1927 the
flood which occurred on the Ussuri damaged the mole thrown up
by the dredge and this year the flood on the Amur entirely
covered all buildings, washed away the mole again and stopped
all work.

        The Chinese Commission refused to include in the
estimates about Roubles 10.000 to 20,000 for the expenses of
the steamer "Amur" intended to be used for the inspection toure.

5. SOVIET GOVERNMENT AMUR WATER TRANSPORTATION BUREAU AND GUNBOATS:
Owing to the lack of trade and a consequent shortage of cargo,
                                                    only

only a minimum number of steamers (12) have plied on the Amur
and even these few steamers generally sailed in ballast.

The Head Office of the Bureau has been transferred from
Blagovestchensk to Habarovsk, but this did not help matters as
the trade is getting less and less, the winter port was not ready
while the questions of dwelling and provisions there for the
staff were very difficult to solve. Moreover Blagovestchensk
remained the real centre of steamer navigation as the town is
built at the confluence of two large rivers, Amur and Zeya, the
latter of which has many important tributaries.

A very small amount of fish was transported from
Nickolaevsk because the flood prevented fishing. The
transportation of beans from Lake Hanka also did not realize
expectations because a great deal (about 100,000 poods) of
beans purchased during winter rotted owing to heavy rains. There
were no passengers and cargo on the Shilka and the Upper Amur.
There were almost no steamers running on the rivers Zeya,
Selemdja and Bureya as, owing to the lack of workers, the gold
mining business in those mountaineous regions entirely stopped.

The timber prepared for transportation through
Nikolaevsk was carried away by flood and only a very small amount
of it was shipped.

The running of steamers on the Argun was not undertaken
as there was no cargo.

The Soviet steamers never ply by the Kasakevich Waterway,
but their rafts coming from the Hingan mountain to the Ussuri
pass through it.

The accidents, which may be explained by the negligence
and inexperience of the ships' crews are as follows: the s/s
"Kalinin" with barge went ashore very badly on a high sand bank;
the

the launch "Otvajni", towed with open port holes, was sunk; and
the s.s. "Karataeff" and its barge, towed by the s.s. "Baliabin",
in arriving at a landing place, collided with a gunboat and was
badly damaged.　Soviet gunboats were plying on the Middle Amur;
towards the middle of the season one of them was sent to the
Upper Amur to the Permikinski Shallows.　On her way she got
ashore several times on Bussevski, Chernayevski Shallows and at
some other places.　Soviet guard boats came to the Ussuri to
watch the fishing, not allowing Chinese fishers to take fish on
the Soviet side of the fairway.　Some Chinese fishers were
killed and others wounded.

　　　　Opposite the mouth of the Sungari barracks were built
for soldiers of the G.P.U. (Frontier Guard).

6. <u>CHINESE SHIPPING</u>:　Chinese shipping on the river Sungari was
very successful because of lots of emigrants moving and great
amounts of cereals, coal and timber carried; the increased
freight rates also gave good profits; it was quite different on
the frontier rivers, owing to the closed frontier by the U.S.S.R.

　　　　As sound conditions of steamers are the best guarrantee
for their safe navigation, the authorities should pay more
attention to them.　All steamers hulls and machines are now
becoming very old.　Also they should not allow to be engaged
Masters, Engineers and Pilots without due certificates and
experience.　In order to prevent fires, steamers ought to be
supplied with proper pumps and other fire preventive apparatus,
and should have crews trained to fight fires on board.

　　　　There is almost no discipline on many steamers and many
of the Masters are subordinate to the compradores of their
steamers which makes the outturn of these steamers unproductive
to the owners.

　　　　　　　　　　　　　　　　　　　　On

On every steamer the crew and other employees are trading, when anchored, in goods that never paid freight, duty or River Dues; furthermore steamers are detained too long at the landing places.

The Tungpei Steamship Company put the s.s."Chiyang" on the Upper Amur run, although this steamer was not fit for this purpose being too long and of too deep a draught.

The s.s."Hungtai", the owner of which has a trading store in the village Wo-Hsi-men, on the Upper Amur, was not allowed by the local Authorities to ply there, a monoply for that run having been given to the Tungpei Steamship Company, so after having made one trip, the steamer was transferred to the Taheiho - Harbin run.

On the 26th of September, the s.s. "Chiyang", just mentioned, went ashore and could not be floated. The s.s. "Shanghai" was then sent to the Upper Amur on the 7th of October but after one trip the Tungpei Steamship Company refused to send her again on the plea that the river was about to freeze over. As the inhabitants on the Upper Amur had not yet received all their winter supplies the Taoyin made an arrangement with the Soviet Amur Government Water Transportation Bureau to send the Soviet s.s. "Murom" for conveying passengers and cargo. This steamer left on the 26th of October and had just time enough to run to the town of Muchan and come back with the ice-drift.

A new stern wheeled steamer constructed at Harbin named the "Weitung" 185' long, 35' broad, and 1' 3/4 draught, worked very successfully on the Ussuri, but as she was constructed of very short timbers she developed a bad list. This might also have happened because of faulty loading. All her partitions were made of veneer and were not strong. The construction of

steamers

steamers and barges should be controlled.

The fact is that the best profits came from steamers where the discipline was strong and the Master, by preference a Russian one, was the real master on his steamer.

During the great flood on the Amur in August, many steamers of the Tungpei Steamship Company and the private owned steamer "Hungtai", gave valuable assistance to those Chinese villages in distress.

At Lahasusu, by order of the local Authorities, there were detained on the s.s. "Peking" a party of Chinese workmen (about 200) who had been hired by Soviet authorities to be sent to the Ussuri to a place opposite the village Kasakevich, with the purpose of smuggling them across the river to the Soviet shore. They were engaged for work in the Siberian mines.

In the spring of 1928, the North Eastern Conservancy Bureau was formed at Harbin for the purpose of controlling the navigation of steamers and rafts on the Sungari and the regulation of the Sansing Shallows.

7. AMUR AND USSURI RIVER DUES COLLECTION: The stricter control over the Collection of River Dues on the Ussuri increased the total for the 1928 Season to $54,483.16; it was $50,427.53 in 1927.

According to the estimates drawn up and included in the various Aids Agreement for 1928, Roubles 35,600 were to be paid to the Amur Navigation Bureau for China's share of joint Aids work on frontier rivers. Owing to the low rate of the rouble during the year, however, there was a gain by exchange of some $14,000 which enabled the Commission to meet all its expenditure during the year.

8. CONDITIONS OF NAVIGATION DURING 1928: Thanks to the high

water

water on the frontier rivers as well as on the Sungari, the conditions of navigation may be considered to have been very favourable.

The hard storm that spread over the Sungari in the spring caused many accidents and much loss. 9 barges with coal and 60 junks were sunk.

Last summer the water continued high during the whole navigation season on both inland and frontier rivers. Steamers could pass the Sansing and other Shallows without difficulty and the question of improving the Sansing Shallows was left in abeyance.

On the 24th of April the first ice shifted at Taheiho the ice-drift beginning on the 30th of April. On the 8th of May the s.s. "Hungtai" left for the Upper Amur; on the 9th of May the s.s. "Tahsing" and "Haicheng" arrived from Harbin which port they left as early as the 19th of April, due to a misunderstanding and having to wait at Lahasusu for a long time for the Amur ice drift to stop. This caused great hardships to the passengers on board. The s.s. "Tahsing" was the first to enter the Upper Amur from the Sungari on the 4th of May. Steamers for the Ussuri began plying on the 22nd of April. The s.s. "Haicheng" was the last to leave Taheiho on the 23rd of October. On the 28th of October the ice started drifting at Taheiho and on the 11th of November the river froze over.

Towards the middle of July, owing to heavy rains, the Amur below Chernayevo and the river Zeya rose very fast and towards the end of July flooded the surrounding country. The Taheiho Water Gauge station showed 427.5' above the level of the Pacific, whereas the usual winter level is 398 feet. This is a record since 1872.

During

During the 1927 navigation season, a Soviet barge was
sunk in the Verhne-Chernayevski Shallows but unexpectedly this
accident was favourable as the current washed a new straight
waterway.   In 1928, there was noticeable also a straight
channel through Permikinski Shallows but towards the end of
the Season the waterway, close by the Chinese shore, which
before had been used to dump ground dug up by dredging, seemed
to be deeper and the s.s. "Shanghai", having $4\frac{1}{2}$ feet of draught,
passed through it there and back.   On the Shallows at the time
there was shown on the river Gauge $4\frac{1}{2}$ feet.

9. ACCIDENTS TO SHIPPING: Many accidents happened during the
year 1928 due to the bad repair of hulls and engines as well
as to the poor knowledge of their duties in navigating steamers
by some Masters and Pilots (s.s. "Chiyang", "Hungtai" and the
launch "Yungping" ran ashore, and afterwards the "Chiyang" was
burned).

Owing to the old hulls and steam pipes, as well as to
careless attention in the part of the crew, the following
Accidents happened: a steam pipe cracked on the s.s. "Shaohsing"
a steam pipe coupling broke on the s.s. "Shanghai" and some of
the crew were scalded; a cylinder cracked on the s.s. "Fuchiang".
Two anchors from the s.s. "Hungtai", two from "Haicheng" and
one from the barge "Wen-Chu" were lost because of very old cables
and bad steering.   As there was no report about these losses,
they could not be found and removed, the result was that the
s.s. "Shaohsing" struck an anchor on the Sansing Shallows and
was holed.

On the s.s. "Hungtai", when proceeding from Taheiho
to the Upper Amur, a bomb burst and killed a Russian who was
carrying it to present with malicious intent to the white refugees
living

living at Kuchan on Chinese territory.

The new Aids on the Ussuri improved the conditions of navigation on that river. No accidents like those of the last summer happened. The s.s. "Huchiang", which was sunk during the 1927 navigation season, on the Ussuri, because of a hole received when the steamer struck an obstruction, whilst out of the channel, was safely removed to the shore where the ice drift did not damage her.

10. WORK DONE IN THE TAHEIHO HARBOUR: In the spring of 1928, the water being very low, the remaining part of the Tungpei jetty was removed and this strengthened the current flowing through the Harbour. The channel that was dug across the gravel spit in the Harbour in 1927 was washed deeper on one side by the current. It would have been very useful if it had been cleaned during the spring when the water was very low, but $200 asked by myself for this work was not granted.

The great flood which occurred during the summer washed away from 7 to 18 feet of the bund in the Port, and there are places where it is now so narrow that a cart cannot pass. During the autumn a stretch of 472 feet long was bunded by means of fascines; the cost of the work was $406. In order to conserve the bund, the bunding should be continued farther on a stretch of 2520 feet; the cost of this work may be estimated at from $6.000 - $10.000 approximately.

11. ECONOMIC SURVEY OF THE AMUR PROVINCE: Crops in the Russian Amur Province in 1928 were expected to be average owing to favourable rains at the beginning of the summer, but when, towards the middle of July it started raining, the rain continuing to the end of autumn, quality and quantity of all crops were cut down by 50%. The enormous flood which ensued

on

on the river Zeya carried away not only hay, products of the fields and of vegetable gardens, but also houses, cattle and lots of people. In some districts on the Amur and Zeya, the flood extended from 30 to 50 versts across their valleys. Owing to this high water, that lasted to the end of the season, fishing was also poor.

The output of gold was nil because the "Dalsoloto" could not hire Chinese workmen, as it was not allowed by the Chinese Government. There were no Russian workmen, owing to the hard conditions of work on the mines.

The amount of cut and stored timber was great, but it could not be exported abroad through Nikolaevsk because the high water carried most of it away.

12. ECONOMIC SURVEY OF HEILUNGCHIANG PROVINCE: The great flood which occurred on the Amur in July affected very severely farmers and villages along the river. Many were entirely ruined and the Government must help them somehow. Lasting rains impeded the gathering of crops, the amount and the quality of which was very poor. The closed frontier and the absence of trade with U.S.S.R., snowfall and frosts on the 24th September, a month early, badly affected also all settlers along the frontier rivers. In the district between Taheiho and Moho (Lokuho – mouth of the Argun) trade is practically at a standstill. Cargo traffic was reduced during the 1928 navigation season, the figure amounted to 50,000 poods only. The export of timber from Taheiho, thanks to a casual demand from Harbin, increased to 500,000 poods. It is expected that the export of timber in 1929 will further increase.

The fur business until now has helped to support the

local

local population, the prices received for fur skins being high as furs were required abroad.   It seems likely to be different this 1928 / 1929 winter as there are fewer orders from abroad.

The output of gold greatly decreased.

On the Upper Amur there is no regular telegraph and mail communication and, furthermore, gangs of bandits make living there very difficult.

In August, in Heilungchiang Province, 200,000 poods of wheat were sold to the U.S.S.R. and exported on Soviet ships. At Taheiho there are now two saw-mills.

The Kirin Authorities ordered that no workmen, who had no direct work in the district Tuan-Shan-Tze, were to proceed there (vide § 6).   This reduced the passenger traffic on the Ussuri.   During the 1928 navigation season 19,000 passengers were carried, instead of 24,000 as compared with 1927.

The flood on the Ussuri during the spring ice-drift washed away a great deal of firewood from the shore and the great flood, which occurred in autumn inundated the whole country on the lower Ussuri and Kasakevich waterway almost ruining the settlers.

The telegraph line established in 1927, on the stretch from Lahasusu to Hulin, through Sui-yuan, will have to be repaired and some of the posts shifted.   The mail from Harbin to Hulin comes through Iman by the Russian railroad 3 times a week.

The first snow fell at Hulin on the 25th of September, (very early).

Timber wanted in the Lahasusu district for the use of building comes from Tai-Ping-Kow (in Hingan Mountains) by large rafts.

13.

13. CONCLUSION: Chinese authorities concerned in the prosperity
of Heilungchiang and Kirin Provinces should give their attention
to matters as follows:

1. To raise the standard of Chinese steamers, to require a more
strict examination of boilers and steam pipes, as they all
are getting old.

2. To elaborate "Sanitary Rules" and to prohibit overcrowding of
passengers.

3. To effect a stricter control of Officers' Certificates and to
raise the standard for qualification.

4. To strengthen the authority of steamer Masters.

5. To raise funds for frontier rivers Aids work, as the River
Dues Collection is insufficient.

6. To limit the transportation of kerosene and benzine on
steamers and to introduce stricter precautions against fire.

7. To introduce a River Inspector Staff to insure the "Provisional
Rules of Navigation" being observed by Chinese steamers on
the frontier rivers.

8. To pay more attention to the strength of the anchor cables
and steering gear chains.

9. To strengthen the bund in Taheiho.

10. To purchase or construct a launch for the use on inspection
tours by the Chinese Commission on the frontier rivers.

11. To pay attention to the conserving of 70 feet of the foreshore
at all the landing places.

Copy taken for archives:

P. Ignatieff.

Acting Commissioner.

Technical Adviser on
Amur Aids to Navigation.

Technical Adviser's Office,
Aigun/Taheiho, 15th May, 1929.

呈海关总税务司署 423 号文   瑷珲关 1929 年 6 月 1 日

尊敬的海关总税务司（上海）：

　　兹附黑龙江航务专门顾问易保罗（P. I. Ignatieff）先生编制的 1928 年《黑龙江航务年度报告》。与以往相同，该报告包括水道委员会的工作总结以及黑龙江流域的经济调查。该报告中文版尚未发送至中国政府。

　　该报告内容详实准确，本署无意见。1928 年依然由俄方政府负责黑龙江、乌苏里江以及现在的额尔古纳河上航路标志的维护工作，一如既往地效率高、投诉少，与中国船运例行公事之作风大不相同。

　　本署于瑷珲关第 372 号呈中呈送了易保罗先生的上一份报告，并提及易保罗先生已编制一份水道委员会活动史册，道尹将发行其中文版本，本署亦期可及时制作英文版本。底稿仍在道尹处做更正增补，不日将发行。

您忠诚的仆人

铎博赛（R. M. Talbot）

瑷珲关署理税务司

此副本抄送至滨江关税务司及海务巡工司

录事：黎彭寿 四等一级帮办

1928 年黑龙江流域边界河道航务年度报告

　　1928 年，在大黑河中俄水道委员会的指导下，中俄双方继续共同维护黑龙江流域边界河道航路标志，总结如下。

　　1. 概览

　　1928 年 1 月 11 日，关于联合维护黑龙江及乌苏里江航路标志的《临时地方工程协议》续约一年，协议自 1927 年 12 月 1 日至 1928 年 11 月 30 日有效；协定黑龙江航路标志工作预算支出 60000 卢布，乌苏里江航路标志工作预算支出 8600 卢布。

　　1928 年 1 月 11 日，签订发布《临时航务条例》之协议，边界河道双方自 1928 年航运季开始起执行。

　　1928 年 1 月 19 日，签订额尔古纳河航道协议，协定自室韦（Shih-Wei-hsien）县奥罗赤（Olochi）村至洛古河（Lokuho）口设立灯桩航标，全长 402 俄里，确定预算 3000 卢布。

　　1927/1928 年冬天，俄阿穆尔水道局获准于额尔古纳河航道做石块清理工作。

　　1928 年 6 月 19 日，签订黑龙江上游联合疏浚协议，确定预算 6000 卢布。

　　2. 巡查

　　航运季期间，本人乘坐中国轮船至黑龙江及乌苏里江航道检查航路标志之状况，并于航运季结束之际，完成俄阿穆尔水道局航路标志维修工作的相关报告。

　　乌苏里江航道上被洪水冲掉的 34 座标桩已于春天浮冰期换新；根据中国轮船船长及船员之记录，其他标桩已被转移。此前，该处所有标桩均已编号。

　　因苏维埃政府拒绝提供乌苏里江航道的最新航图，本人于巡查期间修订了原航图，标明所有标桩及其编号，修订后的航图印刷后将分发给中国船只。

　　5 月 29 日，额尔古纳河航道从奥罗赤村到河口段开始建立航路标志，9 月底完工，全长 402 俄里；新建 203 座标桩，修复 176 座标桩，共计 379 座标桩。因修建工作需要在水位较低时进行，至晚秋方完工，遂本人当时未能予以检验。但经本人核准后，阿穆尔水道局已提交账簿，同时亦在由中国水道委员会提供的额尔古纳河航道航图上标明所涉标桩。

　　黑龙江中游标桩修复后，又因为结雅河洪水来袭而被冲走许多；到秋天水位恢复正常，除了米开罗－塞米诺瓦斯科（Michailo-Semenovsk）地区及嘎杂克维池水道（160 俄里）因河岸至航运季结束一直被河水覆盖之外，中游其他地区的标桩均已换新。

　　虽然亦可乘私人轮船继续巡查，但若有自己的巡查汽艇会更有益处。

本人巡查乌苏里江航道时发现在 1928 年航运季开始时，阿穆尔水道局已经在虎林至松阿察河河口（84 俄里）段的俄国一侧建好了航路标志。阿穆尔水道局在 1928 年 8 月 17 日至中国水道委员会委员长的回函中称确有此事。阿穆尔水道局在未通知中国水道委员会的情况下，单独进行了该项工作。

根据上述黑龙江上游联合疏浚协议，阿穆尔水道局应勘查贝托诺瓦斯基浅滩，派米津斯基浅滩，外－切尔纳耶夫斯基浅滩以及内－切尔纳耶夫斯基浅滩之情况，并从石勒喀河撤下 5 号挖泥船。5 号挖泥船于 7 月 30 日开始在贝托诺瓦斯基浅滩工作，奉命按 1913 年的低水位，挖一条深 1.50 米、宽 60 米的航道。当时水位非常有利，但 5 号挖泥船容积小、支架短，以致该项工程延至秋末。因此派米津斯基浅滩和切尔纳耶夫斯基浅滩今年亦无法开工。因已是航运季末期，又无汽艇，故本人无法检验贝托诺瓦斯基浅滩之完工情况。

既已颁布《中俄边界河道联合航务条例》，则应委派巡官予以实施，确保轮船及木筏设备齐全、状况良好。无论是在巡查过程中还是在检查码头停泊的轮船及木筏之时，本人均发现很多违反《航务条例》的情况，但没有授权，本人无法向船长下达指令或助其避开问题。由于缺乏管制，而边界河道又缺少负责检查之关员，中国轮船大多没有汇报事故，因此也无法调查事故原因或事故责任人。

3. 支付阿穆尔水道局 1928 年夏季完工款项

全年定期向阿穆尔水道局分期付款，尾款将于阿穆尔水道局提交完整账簿后支付。根据协议，中国水道委员会已支付 50% 的预算，包括黑龙江航路标志工作 30000 卢布；乌苏里江航路标志工作 4300 卢布；额尔古纳河航路标志工作 1500 卢布；共计 35800 卢布，因汇率不同，共计 21679.50 哈尔滨银圆。

4. 俄阿穆尔水道局

俄国政府拨给阿穆尔水道局大量资金（1928 年 120 万卢布）用于航路标志工作，但阿穆尔水道局计划大型作业时并未考虑其是否必要，因此提交的联合航路标志工作预算总是被大幅削减。

1927 年，乌苏里江洪水冲毁挖泥船建造的防波堤，今年黑龙江洪水彻底淹没所有建筑，再次冲毁防波堤，工作全部停止，以致阿穆尔水道局无法完成哈巴罗夫斯克冬季停泊处的修建工作。

中国水道委员会拒绝将巡查所用的"黑龙江"号轮船之费用（约 10000 至 20000 卢布）纳入预算。

5. 俄阿穆尔国家水运局及炮艇

由于贸易减少，货物短缺，只有极少数轮船（12艘）往返于黑龙江，而这些轮船也往往空载航行。

俄阿穆尔国家水运局总局已从布拉格维申斯克迁至哈巴罗夫斯克，但也未能扭转局面。贸易越来越少，冬季停泊处亦未建成，职员食宿问题难以解决。此外，布拉格维申斯克立于黑龙江和结雅河两大河流汇集之处，结雅河有众多重要支流，故而仍是轮船航运之中心。

因捕鱼遭受洪水阻碍，从尼古拉耶夫斯克运输的鱼鲜量甚少。此外由于大雨，冬季收购的大豆大量（约100.00普特）腐烂，从兴凯湖运输的大豆也未达预期。石勒喀河及黑龙江上游既没有乘客也没有货物需要运输。结雅河、谢列姆贾河及布列亚河上几乎没有轮船往来。山区金矿生意亦因缺少工人而彻底停止。准备通过尼古拉耶夫斯克运输的木料被洪水冲走，仅有少量木料得以运走。

额尔古纳河航道上因无货物运输，无轮船航行。

俄国轮船从不在嘎杂克维池水道上航行，但俄国木筏从兴安岭至乌苏里江时需要经由嘎杂克维池水道。

因船员疏忽或缺乏经验而造成的事故包括："加里宁"号轮船及其驳船严重搁浅于一处较高沙洲之上；"奥特瓦尼"号汽艇在牵引过程中因舷窗打开而沉没；"卡拉塔耶夫"号轮船及其驳船在由"巴利亚滨"号轮船牵引至码头的过程中，与一艘炮艇相撞，损毁严重。俄国炮艇往返于黑龙江中游，临近航运季中期，其中一艘炮艇在被送往黑龙江上游至派米津斯基浅滩的途中，多次搁浅在布塞斯基浅滩、切尔纳耶夫斯基浅滩等处。俄国巡船至乌苏里江监察捕鱼时，不允许中国渔民在俄国水域一侧捕鱼，以致一些中国渔民受伤，甚至惨遭杀害。

松花江口岸对面建有营房，供政府政治部士兵（边境卫兵）使用。

6. 中国航运业

中国航运业在松花江航道上成果斐然，乘客、谷物、煤和木料的运输量都很大；运费上涨亦使收益增加。但因苏联边境封锁，边界河道之航运则大相径庭。

当局应高度重视轮船之状况，确保航行之安全，但目前所有轮船的船体及设备均已陈旧。人员方面，当局应保证凡船长、工程师及引水员无执照及经验者概不录用，还应训练船员的消防技能，同时为轮船配备合适的水泵及其他消防设备，以防火灾。

很多轮船上几乎都毫无纪律可言，大多数船长又服从于其所属轮船的买办，以致船主无利可得。

停泊时,每艘轮船上的船员和其他雇员都会交易那些未支付运费、税或江捐的商品,以致轮船长时间滞留于码头。

由于东北航路局已获得黑龙江上游航道之垄断权,虽然"鸿泰"号轮船船主在黑龙江上游倭西们(Wo Hsi Men)村有一家贸易店,但当地政府不允许其往来于此,因此"鸿泰"号轮船在黑龙江上游航道仅往返一次后便被转移至大黑河至哈尔滨航道。

东北航路局将"吉阳"号轮船派至黑龙江上游航道,但其船体太长、吃水太深,并不适合该航道,遂于9月26日搁浅后便再也无法漂浮起来。

10月7日,东北航路局又将"上海"号轮船派至黑龙江上游航道,但往返一次后,东北航路局便以河流即将结冰为由不再派送。

鉴于黑龙江航道上游的居民还未拿到所有过冬用品,道尹与俄阿穆尔国家水运局商定,派俄国"穆罗姆(Murom)"号轮船运送乘客及货物。"穆罗姆"号轮船于10月26日出发,时间刚好足够行至古站镇,并于浮冰期返回。

哈尔滨关建造了一艘新船"卫东(Veitung)"号,船尾装轮,长185英尺、宽35英尺,吃水深度1.75英尺,在乌苏里江航道上的航运工作成果颇丰,但因造船所用木料太短,轮船严重侧倾,或因为错误装货所致。该轮船隔断均用薄板搭建,不够结实。所以轮船及驳船的建造应受管控。

事实上,只有轮船上纪律严明,船长(最好是俄国人)能切实管理轮船,才能实现利益最大化。

8月黑龙江特大洪水期间,东北航路局的很多轮船以及私人轮船"鸿泰"号都曾向处于危难的中国村庄施以援手。

拉哈苏苏当地政府下令扣押了"北京"号轮船上的一群中国工人(约300人)。该批工人被苏维埃政府雇用到西伯利亚矿山工作,欲从乌苏里江嘎杂克维池村对面的一个地方偷运到俄国。

1928年春,哈尔滨关成立东北保护管理局,负责管理松花江航道上轮船及木筏的航运工作以及三姓浅滩。

7. 黑龙江及乌苏里江江捐征收

加强管理乌苏里江江捐征收工作后,1928年航运季总税收增至54483.16银圆;1927年航运季总税收为50427.53银圆。

根据1928年各航路标志协议拟订之预算,关于边界河道联合航路标志工作,中国应支付阿穆尔水道局35800卢布。因当年卢布汇率较低,委员会从兑换中约得14000银圆收益,恰好支付全年开支。

8.1928 年航运状况:

边界河道及松花江的水位较高,本应有利于航运,但春天暴雨侵袭松花江,造成多起事故,损失严重。9 艘运煤驳船及 60 艘民船沉没。

去年夏天整个航运季,内陆河道及边界河道水位持续升高,轮船可顺利通过三姓及其他浅滩,但三姓浅滩的改善问题却搁置下来。

4 月 24 日大黑河出现浮冰,4 月 30 日浮冰开始漂流。5 月 8 日,"鸿泰"号轮船前往黑龙江上游;4 月 19 日,"大兴"号轮船和"海澄"号轮船从哈尔滨关出发,中途因误解而滞留于拉哈苏苏等待黑龙江上的浮冰停止漂流,至 5 月 9 日方抵达大黑河,乘客也因此而受尽苦楚。5 月 4 日,"大兴"号轮船首先从松花江进入黑龙江上游。4 月 22 日,乌苏里江航道上开始有轮船航行。10 月 23 日,"海澄"号轮船最后一个驶离大黑河。10 月 28 日大黑河开始有浮冰,11 月 11 日河面结冰。

7 月中旬大雨来袭,"切尔纳耶瓦"下游的黑龙江以及结雅河水位快速上涨,至 7 月底,周边乡村被淹没。大黑河水位观测站显示水位为太平洋海平面以上 427.5 英尺,此乃 1872 年以来之最高记录,通常冬季水位为太平洋海平面以上 398 英尺。

1927 年航运季,一艘俄国驳船在"外 – 切尔纳耶夫斯基"浅滩沉没,但此次洪水冲出一条笔直的新航道,该事故迎来意外转机。1928 年,派米津斯基浅滩亦出现一条笔直航道,靠近中国海岸的航道以前是疏浚时倾倒泥土之处,航运季结束后似乎变得更深,当时水位标尺显示浅滩之水位为 4.5 英尺,"上海"号轮船,吃水 4.5 英尺,恰好可以通行。

9. 航运事故

1928 年事故频发,原因包括船体及发动机失修,一些船长及引水员不清楚其职责所在("吉阳"号轮船、"鸿泰"号轮船以及"永平"号汽艇搁浅,之后"吉阳"号轮船烧毁。)

船体和汽管老化以及船员疏忽所导致之事故包括:"绍兴"号轮船一汽管炸裂;"上海"号轮船一汽管挂钩断裂,一些船员烫伤;"富江"号轮船一气缸炸裂。由于锚索严重老化以及驾驶不当,"鸿泰"号轮船丢失两个船锚,"海澄"号轮船丢失两个船锚,"文储(Wen-Chu)"号驳船丢失一个船锚。因没有上报,丢失的船锚未能被发现并移除,以致"绍兴"号轮船在三姓浅滩撞到一个船锚后出现破洞。

"鸿泰"号轮船从大黑河驶向黑龙江上游时,一名俄国人恶意携带炸弹,欲对在中国境内古站(Kuchan)居住的白人难民不利,结果炸弹爆炸,致其身亡。

乌苏里江航道上新建了航路标志后,航运状况得以改善。去年夏天并无此类事故发生。1927 年航运季,"沪江"号轮船在乌苏里江航道撞到障碍物,出现破洞,以致沉船,离开航道后,被安全移上岸,轮船未受浮冰损害。

10. 大黑河港口已完成工作

1928 年春,水位很低,东北航路局码头剩余部分拆除后,通过港口的水流加强。1927 年穿过港口沙嘴挖掘了一条河道,如今河道一侧因水流冲刷而变得更深。清理工作最好在春天水位较低时进行,但本署申请的 200 银圆清理费用未得到批准。

夏天,口岸堤坝被大洪水冲掉 7 至 18 英尺,有些地方太过狭窄,货车无法通过,遂于秋天用梢捆将堤坝延长 472 英尺,花费 406 银圆。为保护堤坝,应将其继续延长 2520 英尺,预算约 6000 至 10000 银圆。

11. 俄阿穆尔省经济调查:

1928 年夏初雨水有利,俄阿穆尔省谷物产量理应达到平均水平,但 7 月中旬至秋末雨水不断,所有谷物的质量和产量都下降 50%。结雅河相继发生特大洪水,不但冲走了干草、田间作物和园中的蔬菜,还冲走了房屋、牲畜以及众多人口。黑龙江和结雅河的一些地区,洪水漫过溪谷,绵延 30 到 50 俄里。高水位持续至航运季结束以致鱼鲜产量很低。

中国政府不允许中国工人到"达尔索罗图(Dalsoloto)"矿山工作,而俄国工人又无法忍受矿山条件之艰苦,因此未产黄金。

木料砍伐量和存储量很大,但大多被洪水冲走,无法通过尼古拉耶夫斯克出口。

12. 黑龙江省经济调查

7 月,黑龙江发生大洪水,殃及沿岸农民及村落,很多村庄已成废墟,需要政府救援。谷物收获受到持续降雨的阻碍,产量低、质量差。因边境封锁,与苏联无贸易往来。9 月 24 日提前一个月开始降雪霜冻,严重影响了边界河道的沿岸居民。大黑河与漠河(洛古河至额尔古纳河口)之间的区域贸易几乎停滞。1928 年航运季货运量减少,仅有 50000 普特。所幸哈尔滨对木料偶有需求,大黑河木料输出量增至 50 万普特。预计 1929 年木料输出量还会增加。

皮革生意至今一直供养着当地人口,毛皮有出口需求,售价高。1928-1929 年冬天境外订单减少。金子产量大幅下降。

黑龙江航道上游生活非常艰难,电报和邮政通信不稳定,强盗成帮结伙。

8 月,黑龙江省向苏联出售 20 万普特小麦,由俄国轮船运输出口。如今大黑河有两家锯木厂。

吉林省政府规定,若工人本身在团山子地区没有工作,则不允许前往该地(参见 §6),

以致乌苏里江航道上的载客量减少。1928 年航运季载客 19000 人次，1927 年航运季载客 24000 人次。

春天浮冰期，乌苏里江河岸上的大量木桦被洪水冲走；秋天，大洪水又淹没了乌苏里江下游及嘎杂克维池水道沿岸的整个村落，村民也因此而变得一贫如洗。

1927 年，经由绥远从拉哈苏苏至虎林搭建了一条电报线路，现需要维修，一些巡缉站也要搬离。从哈尔滨至虎林的邮包由俄国铁路运输，经由伊曼，一周运送三次。

9 月 25 日虎林迎来第一场降雪（非常早）。

拉哈苏苏地区建筑所需木料取自"太平沟"（位于"兴安"岭），用大型木筏运送。

13. 总结

为保证黑龙江省和吉林省的繁荣发展，中国政府应关注：

（1）提升中国轮船标准，对于老化的锅炉及蒸汽管使用更为严格的检验标准。

（2）详细制定《卫生条例》，禁止乘客超载。

（3）严格把控关员资质，提升资质审核标准。

（4）提高船长之权威性。

（5）鉴于江捐税收不足以承担边界河道航路标志工作之费用，应筹集资金。

（6）限制轻汽油和煤油的运输，使用更为严格的火灾预防措施。

（7）委派一名巡江事务长，确保中国轮船于边界河道行驶时遵守《临时航务条例》。

（8）多加注意锚索及操纵齿轮链。

（9）加固大黑河码头。

（10）为中国水道委员会购置或建造一艘汽艇，以供巡查边界河道之需。

（11）注意确保所有码头前滩保留 70 英尺。

该副本存档

易保罗（P. I. Ignatieff）

黑龙江航务专门顾问

7. 为 1929 年黑龙江航务年度报告事

474

I. G.

AIGUN   27 February, 1930.

Sir,

With reference to your despatch NO. 75/9.74):

Amur Aids to Navigation: appointment of Mr.
Ignatieff as Technical Adviser on, notified:

and to Aigun despatch NO. 423:

Forwarding the Annual Report for 1928 on the
Amur Aids to Navigation prepared by Mr. P.I.
Ignatieff, Technical Adviser on Amur Aids to
Navigation:

I have the honour to forward, enclosed herewith, the
"Annual Report on Aids to Navigation for 1929" prepared by Mr. P.I. Ignatieff, Technical Adviser on Amur
Aids to Navigation. As in his previous Annual
Reports, Mr. Ignatieff not only summarises the
activities of the Aids Commission but gives an
economic survey of conditions in the Amur basin.
A Chinese version of this Report is not being
sent to the Chinese Authorities.

I have the honour to be,

Sir,

Your obedient Servant

Acting Commissioner.

THE INSPECTOR GENERAL OF CUSTOMS,
SHANGHAI.

Enclosure in Aigun No. 474/J.9.

Aids to Navigation on the Frontier Rivers
of the Amur Basin.

ANNUAL REPORT for the year 1929.

  The record of the joint upkeep of Aids on the
Frontier Rivers in the Amur Basin, as mutually maintained
during 1929 by the U.S.S.R. and China under the direction
of the Sino-Soviet Technical Aids Commission, Taheiho, may
be summarised as follows:

1. GENERAL: On the 9th of February, 1929, the local provisional
Technical Agreement for joint Amur, Ussuri and Argun Aids
work was renewed and signed for one year, i.e. for the
period from the 1st December,1928, to the 30th of November,
1929; The Chinese share of the estimated expenditure agreed to
for the upkeep of and repairs to Aids and for providing the
Ussuri with new Aids on the stretch between the town Hulin
and the mouth of the river Sungacha, was Chinese Harbin
$ 22,000.; monthly payment had to be begun from June.

As the dredging work on the Upper Amur was not accomplished
by the Soviet Amur Navigation Bureau during the summer of
1928, the Presidents of the Sino-Soviet Technical Commission
exchanged letters regarding the continuation of this work
during the navigation season of 1929, without increasing
the estimated sum of Roubles 6,000. sanctioned on the 19th
of June, 1928.

During the winter season of 1928/1929 some rock removal
work was done on the Argun by the Soviet Amur Navigation Bureau
on its own account, in accordance with permission given by
the President of the Chinese Aids Commission.

For the promotion of the steamer navigation on the Amur and
Ussuri rivers, navigation charts were drawn up and issued
          blueprints

blueprints, 1) between Taiheiho and the Mouth of Sungari, and

2) between the Mouth of Sungari and Hulin.

There was also prepared for issue a navigation chart, on a diminished scale (1000 sajen to 1"), of the Upper Amur between Taiheiho and Pokrovka (mouth of the Argun, 840 versts) For purposes of record I have compiled a " Description of the Amur District" in two volumes: 1) "Waterways", with enclosed charts, and 2) "The Activities of the local Sino-Soviet Technical Aids Commission", from 1922 to 1928. Now this book is being issued by the President of the Chinese Aids Commission, Mr. Chang-Shou-tsen.

As some Islands on the Amur are still in dispute, whether they belong to China or to U.S.S.R., I have drawn up a "List of Islands on the Amur" with maps of 1) Konstantin - ovski Shallows on the Amur (100 versts lower from Taiheiho) and 2) Islands Sang-Tsiao-chou, near Habarovsk, between the rivers Amur, Ussuri and Kasakevich Waterway.

2) INSPECTION TOUR. During the period from the 18th of May to the 28 of June, I made a trip on board some of the Chinese steamers on the Amur and Ussuri, in order to examine the condition of the Aids. Beacons were fixed correctly, and towards the middle of June the Amur Navigation Bureau began the repairs to Aids and dredging work on the Permikinski Shallows. The number of the lighted beacons was increased on the Upper and Middle Amur. The Shallows Lonchakovski and Kniajevski on the Ussuri were not kept up.

Thanks to the enforced " Rules of Navigation a better order could be seen on board the steamers and no infringements have been noticed. The newly issued navigation charts enabled steamers to navigate safely on the Amur and Ussuri rivers.

The rock removal work on the Argun was done by the Soviet Amur Navigation Bureau, but until now no steamers have sailed there.

After

After the conflict arose between China and U.S.S.R., the
Chinese Authorities issued an order for destroying all
beacons on the Chinese side of the frontier rivers, but
the execution of this order proved impracticable.

3. THE PAYMENT TO THE NAVIGATION BUREAU FOR WORK DONE in 1929. The
Amur Navigation Bureau was paid an instalment on the 28th
of February of $ 1,000., and on the 11th of July $ 3,000.
Further payments were not made owing to political complications.

4. THE SOVIET AMUR NAVIGATION BUREAU. This Bureau receives
from its Government large sums (Roubles 1,800000) for Aids
works and plans large operations on the waterways of the
Amur Basin without taking into consideration the necessity
for them. All estimates submitted by this Bureau for
joint Aids work were always considerably cut down and
many unnecessary works were protested against.
The Amur Navigation Bureau is still unable to complete
the work of building a winter harbour at Habarovsk, though
this Bureau had received Rls.700,000. for this purpose,
but the extremely high water on the Amur, which lasted
during the whole summer, prevented any work.

5. SOVIET GOVERNMENT AMUR TRANSPORTATION BUREAU & GUNBOATS. Owing
to the lack of trade and a consequent shortage of
passengers and cargo, either cereals or fish, the above
mentioned Bureau had no profits at all. The transportation
of beans from the Lake Hanka to the station Iman was
not realised.
At the beginning of the navigation season gunboats
displayed a great activity in plying on the frontier
rivers. In order to have control over the frontier and
waterways G.P.U. was provided with motor launches.

6.

6. <u>CHINESE SHIPPING</u>. The result of the great flood which occurred on the Amur and Ussuri in 1928 was that the settlers of those frontier rivers were entirely ruined and the traffic of cargo was considerably reduced; since July steamers ceased plying owing to political events. In order to provide work for the population after the flood, the Authorities of the Heilungchiang Province stored up, during the winter of 1928/1929, more than 6,000 sajen of firewood along the Amur for the Tungpei Co., but this firewood remained on the spot, thanks to the Sino-Soviet conflict.

The boiler and the engine from the burnt steamer "Chiyang" were taken to Harbin on a barge at the beginning of the season.

As the motor-launches had nothing to do on the Sungari, their owners have let them run on the Ussuri, but it was impossible to get any information concerning them.

The political Sino-Soviet conflict, the commandeering of many Chinese steamers and barges by U.S.S.R. and the consequent stopping of navigation since July greatly affected Chinese Shipping and led to an enormous loss.

7. <u>AMUR AND USSURI RIVER DUES COLLECTION</u>. As the turnover of cargo was reduced on these frontier rivers, so was reduced the River Dues Collection. The fare on passenger tickets between Lahasusu and Hulin was reduced, though the fare remained the same between Harbin and Hulin, and 4th class tickets were actually used for the first time. All this affected the Collection of passenger River Dues. Finally, in July, the stoppage of navigation by Chinese steamers on the frontier rivers suspended the River Dues Collection entirely. The total figures of River Dues Collection for 2½ months of 1929 navigation season amounted to $ 22,000. approximately.

8. <u>CONDITIONS OF NAVIGATION DURING 1929</u>. Thanks to the high

water

water on the frontier rivers, the conditions of navigation
may be considered to have been very favourable. The
ice in the Sungari broke up very early, but on the
Amur the first ice shifted on the 4th of May only. The
s/s "Hungtai" which was wintering in the Konstantinovski
Shallows (120 versts lower Taheiho) arrived at Taheiho on
the 10th May and left for Harbin on the 12th. From Harbin
the first s/s "Iching" arrived at Taheiho on the 16th May.
Towards July the water in the Upper Amur rose very fast
and caused many disasters. In the Zeya at the time there
was an average water, which fact was favourable for the
Middle Amur, where the level, though very high, still
was lower than that of the past year, and lasted during
the whole navigation season. Opposite Taheiho the Amur
closed towards the 18th of November.

9. ACCIDENTS TO SHIPPING. Not any grave accidents happened to
    Chinese steamers during the 1929 navigation season. On
    the 31 April the s/s "Tung-chang" ran ashore on the Lower
    Sungariski Shallows; this accident was caused by a very
    low water and by the wrong steering of the Master. On
    the 3rd May the s/s "Tung-ching" ran ashore in the Kasakevich
    waterway owing to low water and alteration of the channel.

10. WORK DONE IN THE TAHEIHO HARBOUR. In the spring of 1929,
    the work of bunding the shore and drainage in the Taheiho
    Harbour was done. The cost of this work was $ 5,874.01.
    After the remaining part of the Tungpei jetty was removed,
    the current flowing through the Harbour strengthened visibly
    and the channel that was dug across the gravel spit in
    1927 was washed deeper by the current very favourably.

11. ECONOMIC SURVEY OF THE AMUR PROVINCE. As the great flood
    in 1928 caused poor crops and consequently lack of sowing
    grain in spring, as well as episoty of cattle, the area

01

of sown fields in the Soviet Amur Province, in1929, diminished considerably.

The flood which occurred in 1929, and caused lots of damage on the Upper Amur, was not so ruinous as it had been in 1928 on the Middle Amur and Zeya, thanks to the low water in the Zeya. Owing to this high water on the Amur, that lasted to the end of the season thanks to the high water on the Sungari, fishing was also poor.

As there were no Russian workmen in the gold mines, and the Chinese Government did not allow Chinese workmen to be hired by the Soviet Authorities, the latter hired them illegally and lots of them crossed the frontier without permission.

The amount of cut and stored timber was great, but it could not be exported abroad through Nikolaevsk because the high water carried most of it away.

As the Transbaikalian and Maritime Provinces were in great need of cereal products and war was likely to start between U.S.S.R. and China, the Soviet Government was forced to confiscate all new crops. All these facts will certainly ruin the farmers.

12. ECONOMIC SURVEY OF HEILUNGCHIANG PROVINCE. The great flood which occurred in 1928 and 1929 on the Amur affected very severely and for a long period of time farmers and villages along the rivers; many were entirely ruined and moved away. The Heiho Taoyin has organised the storing of firewood for the use of the Tungpei Steamship Co.; this bettered to some extent the situation of some miserable people.

The closed frontier and the absence of trade with U.S.S.R. also badly affected all settlers along the frontier rivers. The high water which lasted during the two last years on the Amur and Sungari rivers was favourable for the export of timber from Taheiho to Harbin; there was no need to load and unload it in the shallows. During the
winter

winter or 1928/1929 there was prepared along the Upper Amur for export by rafts to Taheiho and by steamers and barges to Harbin, a considerably greater amount of timber that was done before. But political events prevented export.

A great hindrance to the development of the local timber industry was the export of timber to the Manchouli districts from U.S.S.R.; the latter, wishing to get foreign money, was selling timber at lowest prices, using all kinds of exemption on the Railway.

The fur business was bad, as few furs were required abroad.

The output of gold was almost nil.

The attacks made by Soviet soldiers on the villages along the frontier rivers entirely ruined settlers who fled away.

13. CONCLUSION. After the political conflict between China and U.S.S.R. is settled, there surely will arise lots of questions to be fixed in connection with: a) Boundary lines on the waterways; b) navigation on the frontier and inland rivers; c) ownership of some Islands in dispute; d) Joint Aids work, dredging and rock removal work; e) all kinds of Rules: technical, against fire and others; and f) the control over the sound condition of ships. The requests of the U.S.S.R. will certainly be excessive; and the submitted estimates on Aids and other works will be considerably increased, comparably to those of the formers years, whereas the River Dues Collection on the Amur and Ussuri will probably be reduced.

P. Ignatieff

Technical Adviser to, and member, of Chinese Aids Commission.

呈海关总税务司署 <u>474</u> 号文　　　　　　　　瑷珲关 1930 年 2 月 27 日

尊敬的海关总税务司（上海）：

　　根据海关总税务司署第 75/90949 号令：

　　　　"通知委任易保罗（Ignatieff）先生为黑龙江航务专门顾问。"

及瑷珲关第 423 号呈：

　　　　"呈送黑龙江航务专门顾问易保罗（P. I. Ignatieff）先生编制的 1929 年《黑龙江航务年度报告》。"

　　兹附黑龙江航务专门顾问易保罗（P. I. Ignatieff）先生编制的 1929 年《黑龙江航务年度报告》。与以往相同，该报告包括水道委员会的工作总结以及黑龙江流域的经济调查。该报告中文版尚未发送至中国政府。

您忠诚的仆人

富乐嘉（H. G. Fletcher）

署理税务司

此副本抄送至滨江关税务司及海务巡工司

录事：张远扬　三等二级税务员

1929 年黑龙江流域边界河道航务年度报告

1929 年，在大黑河中俄水道委员会的指导下，中俄双方继续共同维护黑龙江流域边界河道航路标志，总结如下：

1. 概览

1929 年 2 月 9 日，关于联合维护黑龙江及乌苏里江航路标志的《临时地方工程协议》续约一年，协议自 1928 年 12 月 1 日至 1929 年 11 月 30 日有效；协定中国为联合维护航路标志工作以及于乌苏里江航道（虎林县至松阿察河河口段）新建航路标志工作承担 22000 哈大洋的费用，自 6 月起按月付款。

鉴于俄阿穆尔水道局未能于 1928 年夏天完成黑龙江上游疏浚工作，中俄水道委员会双方委员长通过函件议定：俄阿穆尔水道局于 1929 年航运季继续进行疏浚工作，1928 年 6 月 19 日所批预算 6000 卢布则不再增加。

1928-1929 年冬季，阿穆尔水道局得到中国水道委员会的允准，自费在额尔古纳河航道做石块清理工作。为便于轮船在黑龙江及乌苏里江航道上航行，已编制并发放新航图，包括（1）大黑河至松花江口河段航道，以及（2）松花江口至虎林河段航道。

黑龙江上游自大黑河至波克罗夫卡村（额尔古纳河口，840 俄里）河段航图亦编制完成，航图比例为 1000/1 俄丈。此外，本人已编制《黑龙江地区介绍》一书以供记录，分为两卷：（1）《航道》附航图，（2）《中俄地方水道委员会之工作（1922 年至 1928 年）》。此书现已由中国水道委员会委员长张寿增先生发布。

鉴于中俄对黑龙江上一些岛屿的所属权仍有争议，本人编制了《黑龙江上的岛屿集》，收录地图包括（1）黑龙江上的康斯坦丁诺夫斯基浅滩，（2）黑龙江、乌苏里江以及嘎杂克维池水道之间的抚远三角洲（黑瞎子岛），靠近哈巴罗夫斯克。

2. 巡查

5 月 18 日至 6 月 28 日期间，本人乘坐中国轮船至黑龙江及乌苏里江航道检查航路标志之状况。巡查期间发现标桩已安装妥当，黑龙江中上游灯桩数量亦有所增加。阿穆尔水道局于 6 月中旬开始进行航路标志维修工作以及派米津斯基浅滩的疏浚工作，但未能进行乌苏里江上隆察可夫斯基浅滩和尼亚耶夫斯基浅滩的维护工作。

因施行《航务条例》，船上秩序得以改善，尚未发现违反《航务条例》之情况。新航图有助于轮船在黑龙江及乌苏里江航道上安全航行。

阿穆尔水道局已完成额尔古纳河航道上的石块清理工作，但迄今仍未有轮船航行于此。

中俄发生冲突后，中国政府下令将边界河道中国侧的所有标桩毁掉，但实际上却难以执行。

3. 支付阿穆尔水道局 1929 年完工款项

2 月 28 日向阿穆尔水道局支付 1000 银圆；7 月 11 日支付 3000 银圆。但由于政治纠纷，还未支付剩余款项。

4. 俄阿穆尔水道局

俄国政府拨给阿穆尔水道局大量资金（180 万卢布）用于航路标志工作，但阿穆尔水道局计划大型作业时并未考虑其是否必要，很多不必要的工作遭到反对，因此提交的联合航路标志工作预算总是被大幅削减。

阿穆尔水道局收到拨款 70 万卢布用于在哈巴罗夫斯克修建冬季停泊处，但去年整个夏天，黑龙江水位极高，所有工作都无法进行，该冬季停泊处未能建成。

5. 俄阿穆尔国家水运局及炮艇

由于贸易减少，乘客及货物（谷物或鱼鲜）相应减少，兴凯湖的大豆也未能运至伊曼站，因此阿穆尔国家水运局没有盈利。

航运季初，炮艇频繁往返于边界河道。为管制边境及边界河道，政府政治部配备了摩托艇。

6. 中国航运业

1928 年黑龙江及乌苏里江发生大洪水，以致边界河道沿线居民全部受害，货运大幅减少；由于政治问题，自 7 月以来轮船就已停止航行。为了洪水过后居民有工可做，黑龙江省政府于 1928、1929 年冬季在黑龙江沿线，为东北轮船公司囤积 6000 余俄丈木桦，但因中俄发生冲突，这些木桦仍留在原地。

航运季初，一艘驳船将烧毁的"吉阳"号轮船上的锅炉和发动机运送至滨江关。

因在松花江航道上摩托艇无所用处，船主们便将其转移至乌苏里江航道上航行，但无法获取这些摩托艇的相关信息。

中俄发生政治冲突后，俄方强占了大量中国轮船和驳船。7 月航运相继停止，中国航运业受到严重影响，损失惨重。

7. 黑龙江及乌苏里江江捐征收

由于边境河流货物成交量减少，江捐税收也随之减少。票价方面，拉哈苏苏至虎林河段的乘客票价下调,哈尔滨至虎林河段的乘客票价不变,四等舱船票首次投入使用。 这些都影响了江捐税收。 7月边界河道上的中国轮船停止航运工作,江捐征收彻底停止。 1929年航运季2.5个月的江捐税收总额约22000银圆。

8. 1929年航运状况:

松花江破冰较早,但5月4日黑龙江上才开始出现浮冰。 "鸿泰"号轮船在康斯坦丁诺夫斯基浅滩过冬(大黑河向下120俄里),于5月10日抵达大黑河,5月12日前往滨江关。 从滨江关出发的第一艘轮船"爱敬(Iching)"号于5月16日抵达大黑河。 边界河道水位较高,本应有利于航运,但到了7月,黑龙江上游水位迅速上涨,灾难频发。 当时结雅河的水位适中,对黑龙江中游比较有利,整个航运季中游水位非常高,但仍比去年同期要低。 黑龙江于11月18日关闭航运。

9. 航运事故

1929年航运季期间,中国轮船未发生重大事故。 4月31日,"东昌(Tung-chang)"号轮船因水位过低且船长驾驶不当在松嘎里斯基(Sungariski)浅滩较低处搁浅。 5月3日,"东青(Tung-ching)"号轮船因水位过低、改变航道而在嘎杂克维池水道搁浅。

10. 大黑河港口已完成工作

1929年春天,大黑河港口筑堤及排水工作已经完工,花费5874.01银圆。 东北码头剩余部分拆除后,通过港口的水流明显增强,1927年穿过港口沙嘴挖掘的河道如今因水流冲刷而变得更深。

11. 俄阿穆尔省经济调查

1928年的大洪水严重影响了谷物的产量,以致1929年春季缺少播种的谷物,阿穆尔省播种面积大幅减少。

1929年洪水再次来袭,黑龙江上游受害严重,但所幸结雅河水位较低,黑龙江中游及结雅河受害程度不像1928年那么严重。 直至航运季结束,黑龙江和松花江水位一直较高,以致鱼鲜产量低。

中国政府不允许中国工人为苏维埃政府工作,但苏维埃政府因雇用不到俄国工人到金矿工作,只能非法雇用中国工人。 这些工人大多数是未经许可偷渡过境的。

木料砍伐量和存储量很大,但大多被洪水冲走,无法通过尼古拉耶夫斯克(Nickolaevsk)出口。

沿海诸省对谷物需求量大,但中俄战争一触即发,苏维埃政府因形势所迫而没收所有新产谷物,农民将因此而变得一贫如洗。

12. 黑龙江省经济调查

1928 年和 1929 年，黑龙江沿线农民及村庄长期受到大洪水的严重影响。黑河道尹已经组织囤积木料以供东北轮船公司使用；一些难民的境遇也得到改善。

因边境封锁，中俄无贸易往来，边界河道沿岸的居民亦受到严重影响。黑龙江及乌苏里江过去两年水位一直很高，有利于轮船从大黑河向滨江关运输木料；轮船无需在浅滩装卸。1928-1929 年冬天，黑龙江上游沿线预计输出比以往更多的木料，准备使用木筏将木料运至大黑河，再使用轮船及驳船将木料运至滨江关。但因政治问题该计划受阻。

俄国向满洲里地区出口木料是影响地方木业发展的一大阻碍；俄国为得到外币，低价出口木料，以各种方式免除铁路征税。

由于国外几乎没有皮革需求，导致皮革生意惨淡。

黄金几乎无产量。

边界河道沿线村庄遭俄国士兵袭击，居民受害逃跑。

13. 总结

中俄冲突解决后，需要解决的问题有：a. 航道边界线问题；b. 边界河道及内陆河流航运工作；c. 受争议岛屿的所属权问题；d. 联合航路标志工作、疏浚工作、石块清理工作；e. 制定各种条例：工程类、防火类及其他种类；f. 船只状况管理工作。除此之外，俄国也会提出大量要求；已提交的航路标志及其他工作预算会大幅增加，而黑龙江及乌苏里江的江捐税收可能会有所减少。

易保罗（P. I. Ignatieff）

中国水道委员会成员

航务专门顾问

8. 为 1930 年黑龙江航务年度报告事

AMUR AIDS TO NAVIGATION: Annual Report on, for 1930,
prepared by Mr. P.I.Ignatieff, Technical Adviser on
Amur Iads to Navigation, forwarding.

543

543
I G

I.G.   A I G U N   5th March 1931

    Sir,

        With reference to Aigun despatch No. 474 :
forwarding the Annual Report for 1929 on the
Amur Aids to Navigation prepared by Mr. P. I.
Ignatieff, Technical Adviser on Amur Aids to
Navigation :

I have the honour to forward, enclosed herewith, the
Annual Report on Aids to Navigation for 1930 prepared
by Mr. P. I. Ignatieff, Technical Adviser on Amur Aids
to Navigation. As in his previous Annual Reports, Mr.
Ignatieff not only summarises the activities of the
Aids Commission, but also gives an economic survey of
conditions in the Amur basin.

        I have the honour to be,

           Sir,

        Your obedient Servant,

        (Signed) C. B. Joly

        (C. H. B. Joly)
        Acting Commissioner.

The Inspector General of Customs,

   S H A N G H A I.

AIDS TO NAVIGATION ON THE FRONTIER RIVERS OF THE AMUR BASIN.
ANNUAL REPORT FOR THE YEAR 1930

The record of the joint upkeep of Aids on the frontier rivers in the Amur Basin, as mutually maintained during 1930 by the U. S. S. R. and China, under the direction of the Sino-Soviet Technical Aids Commission, Taheiho, may be summarised as follows : -

1. GENERAL: The local provisional Technical Agreement for 1929 joint aids work on the rivers Argun, Amur and Ussuri became inoperative in July, 1929, as the result of the Sino-Soviet conflict over the Chinese Eastern Railway question, which led to seizures of Chinese vessels by the Soviets and to the closing of the frontier rivers to joint navigation. It was not till the 16th August 1930 that a local provisional Technical Agreement for two years from the 1st January 1930 to the 31st December 1931 - for joint aids work on the three frontier rivers and for the erection of new aids on the Hulin-Sungacha River section of the Ussuri River - was concluded.

    The Soviet Commission presented an estimate for aids and dredging work on the frontier rivers amounting to Roubles 481,000, but, after protracted negotiations, the estimate was reduced and the Chinese Commission agreed to pay Harbin $ 34,200.00, plus $ 4,000.00 for dredging work, yearly. Moreover, a sum of $ 7,000.00 was mutually agreed to as China's share of the cost of repairing damage done during the conflict.

    During the conflict all documents and charts belonging to the Chinese Commission were sent to Harbin for safe-keeping.

2. INSPECTION TOUR DURING THE 1930 NAVIGATION SEASON: After the Agreement was signed, during the period from 26th August to the 16th October, I made a trip on the

Amur

Amur and Ussuri Rivers and examined the conditions of the Aids and corrected all charts. At the beginning of the conflict, the Chinese Authorities ordered the demolition of beacons on the Kirin side of the Amur and Ussuri Rivers, according to which 70% of them were removed, and the Soviet, as an urgent measure, started immediately erecting aids on the Russian side only, and accomplished the work towards the end of the 1929 navigation season. Along the Heilungkiang bank of the Amur, beacons were not removed. The Aids on the Russian side were installed correctly and kept in good order and the number of lighted beacons was augmented by 60% above the pre-conflict figure. Instead of the red bearing-line beacons the Soviet erected corresponding white beacons having black stripes in the middle of white shields. At the Chahayen traffic station the signal posts were shifted. On the Ussuri there are no lighted beacons, but work on the most dangerous shallows, Lonchakovski and Kniajevski, was maintained. Passing through Lahasusu, I examined and corrected charts of the Ussuri River that were still in stock and these were afterwards sold to captains and pilots of steamers. The dredging in the Upper Amur on the Beitonovski Shallows during the 1928 and 1929 navigation seasons was not successful, so the Soviets last summer started dredging work in the side-water way, installed aids and opened a straight and safe channel.

During my trip, I noticed numerous infringements by masters of ships of the "Rules of Navigation".

3. PAYMENT TO THE SOVIET AMUR GOVERNMENT WATER TRANSPORTATION BUREAU: The Chinese Commission paid the following sums to the Soviet Consul at Taheiho for Aids work done during 1930: $ 22,600.00 (50%) in August and $ 11,300.00 in October. The final instalment of $ 11,300.00 will be

be paid after receipt of detailed accounts and
information from the Soviet Authorities.

4. THE WAY DEPARTMENT OF THE SOVIET AMUR GOVERNMENT TRANSPORTATION
BUREAU: In March 1930, the Soviet Amur Navigation
Bureau was suppressed and a Way Department, with the
Water Transportation Bureau to manage all waterways in
the Amur Basin, was inaugurated. The Amur Government
Water Transportation Bureau receives from the Government
a subsidy of more than Roubles 2,000,000.00, yearly for
aids work and these funds are spent on improvement to
Aids, lighting, dredging and the removal of rocks,
without taking into consideration the lack of cargo and
passenger traffic.

5. THE AMUR GOVERNMENT WATER TRANSPORTATION BUREAU: The running
of mail steamers and tugs was not very successful last
summer, as, owing to endless misunderstanding between
different departments, steamers were laid up at frequent
intervals and for long periods. Moreover, storms in
the lower Amur caused much damage and many vessels
which met with accidents were unable to reach their
winter harbours and to deliver cargo.

6. CHINESE SHIPPING: The seizure of Chinese ships by the
Soviet, during the 1929 navigation season, and the
uncertainty of the situation after the conflict, delayed
sailings on the frontier rivers until May, 1930, and
trade was adversely affected.

7. AMUR AND USSURI RIVER DUES COLLECTION. The great floods
of 1928 and 1929, the political conflict of 1929, and
the late start of navigation by Chinese steamers on
the frontier rivers in 1930, affected seriously cargo
and passenger traffic and the River Dues Collection
decreased during 1930 to $ 44,000.00, as against
$ 54,500.00 collected in 1928.

8. CONDITION OF NAVIGATION DURING 1930: Thanks to the high
water on the frontier rivers, the conditions of

navigation

navigation may be considered to have been very favourable. On the 4th May, the ice at Taheiho commenced to move as a result of very high water which rose to 19 feet above the winter level. On the 12th May, the first junk left for the Upper Amur; the first steamer, the S. S. "Suchow", arrived from Harbin with all the Customs Staff on the 30th of May. The last steamer, the "Yang Hu", left Taheiho on the 22nd October. The S. S. "Suchow" plied on the Upper Amur and the S. L. "Yungping" down the Amur as far as Chik'ot'e. On the 28th October, the first ice-drift appeared in the Taheiho Harbour, and on the 10th November the Amur closed.

9. ACCIDENTS: No accidents occurred to shipping during the navigation season on the frontier rivers.

10. WORK DONE IN THE TAHEIHO HARBOUR: The trenches made during the conflict damaged the bund road, and the ice-drift during the high water caused some damages to the embankment built in 1929, but repairs were successfully completed. The ice-drift also damaged the jetty of the Tungpei Company, and repairs will have to be taken in hand in the spring.

11. ECONOMIC SURVEY OF THE AMUR PROVINCE: The great floods experienced during two successive years, the poor crops of 1929, disease amongst horses, repression of the rich farmers and the organisation of collective farming and agriculture, caused a great decrease in the agriculture in the Amur Province. The Soviet built new villages along the frontier rivers, erected five cisterns in the village Nagibovo for the storage of kerosene oil, cut down timber along different rivers and rafted it to Haberovsk and Nickolaevsk in tow of tugs for export abroad. These activities gave an impression of the feverish effort to accomplish the five

five years' plan, but official information proves that
less than 50% of the work planned has so far been
done. The output of gold, owing to the lack of
Chinese workmen, reached only 45% of the estimate;
charcoal 50%, because of labour troubles. Very rich
fisheries exist, but, as insufficient barrels had been
provided for, only a part of the catch could be
salted. Much of the timber was not rafted from small
rivers in due time and much was lost through storms
in the Lower Amur. It is doubtful whether the good
crops of last summer will help to improve economic
conditions in the Amur Province as, apart from a
certain fixed ratio, all surplus must be handed over
to the Government.

12. ECONOMIC SURVEY OF THE HEILUNGKIANG PROVINCE: The great
floods of two summers, the political conflict of 1929,
and the activities of bandits ruined Chinese farmers
along the Amur and many of them migrated from their
farms. As the roads and the telegraph lines are in
bad condition, there is, except for shipping, no
regular means of communication along the Amur.
Government assistance, favourable conditions for navigation
good crops of cereals as well as of fungus and
cranberries and the transportation of timber to Harbin
without loss of time on the Sansing Shallows, thanks
to high water, all contributed towards local improvement
and revival. The drop in the value of the Soviet
rouble led to an exchange of goods on a basis of
barter. On the Upper Amur and in the region of the
Kaikuk'ang river gold mining was begun. Fur bearing
animals were plentiful, but it is difficult to approach
the hunters (Orochen tribe) because of the lack of roads
and the presence of bandits. There was very little
demand for furs on the local market. Owing to the
conflict no timber was prepared during 1929 and the
amount

amount rafted to Taheiho in 1930 was very small. The old stocks of timber having been exported to Harbin, Taheiho was left without timber and no replenishment of stocks is possible during the winter. A great hindrance to the development of the local timber industry is the export of timber to the Manchouli districts from U. S. S. R., the latter, using all kinds of exemptions on the railway, sells timber at prices about 50% lower than those current on the Harbin market.

13. <u>CONCLUSION</u>:- The Chinese Authorities concerned with the prosperity of the Heilungkiang and Kirin provinces should give their attention to the following : -

1. To organise a regular Mail and Passenger Service on the frontier rivers Amur and Ussuri.

2. To organise a Mail Service during the winter.

3. To instal a telegraph line along the Middle Amur.

4. To repair the telegraph lines along the Upper Amur.

5. To ensure compliance with the "Rules of Navigation" on the frontier rivers.

6. To elaborate "Sanitary Rules" and to prohibit overcrowding of passengers; also to enforce the provision of medicine chests on steamers.

7. To conserve 70 feet of the foreshore at all the landing places for the storage of firewood and for the repairing of rowing boats and junks.

8. To start preparations for an independent Aids Service.

9. To acquire a steam launch for inspection tours on the frontier rivers.

P. Ignatieff

(P. I. Ignatieff)

Technical Adviser on Amur

Aids to Navigation.

Custom House,

A I G U N, 20th December 1930.

呈海关总税务司署 <u>543</u> 号文　　　　　　　　　　瑷珲关 1931 年 3 月 5 日

尊敬的海关总税务司（上海）：

根据瑷珲关第 474 号呈：

"呈送黑龙江航务专门顾问易保罗（P. I. Ignatieff）先生编制的 1929 年《黑龙江航务年度报告》。"

兹随函附上黑龙江航务专门顾问易保罗（P. I. Ignatieff）先生编制的 1930 年《黑龙江航务年度报告》。与以往相同，该报告包括水道委员会的工作总结以及黑龙江流域的经济调查。

您忠诚的仆人

周骊（C. H. B. Joly）

瑷珲关署理税务司

此抄件发送至滨江关税务司及海务巡工司

录事：陈培因　三等二级税务员

1930 年黑龙江流域边界河道航务年度报告

1930 年,在大黑河中俄水道委员会的指导下,中俄双方继续共同维护黑龙江流域边界河道航路标志,总结如下:

1. 概览

中俄双方在中东铁路问题上发生冲突后,俄国不仅扣押了中国轮船,还关闭了中俄共用的边界河道,1929 年就联合维护额尔古纳河、黑龙江及乌苏里江航路标志所签订的《临时地方工程协议》亦因此于 1929 年 7 月失效。直至 1930 年 8 月 16 日,中俄双方才再次就联合维护三条边界河道上的航路标志以及于乌苏里江自虎林至松阿察河河口段建立航路标志等工事签订了一份为期两年的《临时地方工程协议》,即自 1930 年 1 月 1 日起至 1931 年 12 月 31 日止。

针对边界河道上的航路标志及疏浚工程,俄国水道委员会最初给出的预算为 481000 卢布,经过漫长的协商后,中国水道委员会最终同意每年支付 34200 银圆用于航路标志工程,以及 4000 银圆用于疏浚工程。此外,中俄双方协定,中方为冲突期间所造成的损害支付 7000 银圆的修复费用。

冲突期间,凡隶属于中国水道委员会的文件及图表均已被发送至哈尔滨收存。

2. 1930 年航运季期间的巡查

中俄双方签订《临时地方工程协议》后,本人于 8 月 26 日至 10 月 16 日期间前往黑龙江及乌苏里江航道检查航路标志状况,同时校准全部航图。中俄双方冲突开始时,中国政府下令将黑龙江及乌苏里江航道吉林省一侧的标桩全部拆毁,最终有 70% 的标桩被拆除。而黑龙江航道黑龙江省一侧的标桩则幸免于难。俄国随后采取紧急措施,单于俄国一侧竖立航路标志,但并未使用红色条纹标桩而是竖立了带有黑色条纹的白色标桩,至 1929 年航运季结束时,此项工程已圆满结束,俄国一侧的航路标志均得以准确安置,井然有序,且灯桩之数量比发生冲突前增加了 60%。

此外,察尔岩(Chahayen)通行信号站的标杆位置已发生改变。乌苏里江上未竖立灯桩,但隆察可夫斯基浅滩及尼亚耶夫斯基浅滩上的施工仍未停止。

经由拉哈苏苏时,本人对现有的乌苏里江航图进行检查校准。之后,这些航图被售卖给轮船船主及引水员。

俄方于 1928 年至 1929 年航运季期间在黑龙江上游贝托诺瓦斯基浅滩进行的疏浚工

程并不成功,故又于去年夏天在此浅滩边开展疏浚工程,竖立航路标志,并挖掘了一条安全笔直的航道。

此外,本人巡查期间发现多起船长违反《航务条例》事件。

3. 支付俄阿穆尔国家水运局 1930 年完工款项

中国水道委员会向驻大黑河俄国领事支付 1930 年的航路标志工程款项为:8 月支付 22600 银圆(50%),10 月支付 11300 银圆。最后一笔分期款项 11300 银圆将于收到俄国政府详细账目及通知后予以支付。

4. 俄阿穆尔国家水运局航路部

1930 年 3 月,俄阿穆尔河水道局终止运行后,开始由俄阿穆尔国家水运局航路部接管阿穆尔河流域的全部航道。俄阿穆尔国家水运局每年从俄国政府领取 200 万卢布以上的拨款用于航路标志工程,包括改善航路标志、安装照明,疏浚及石块清理工程,但实施此类工程时其并未考虑到乘客及货物的稀缺问题。

5. 俄阿穆尔国家水运局

由于各部门间误解不断,轮船频繁长时间停运,以致去年夏季邮轮和拖船无法顺利航行。此外,阿穆尔河下游遭到暴风雨袭击,受损严重,许多船只均受牵连,未能抵达冬季停泊处交付货物。

6. 中国航运业

1929 年航运季期间,中俄发生冲突,局势动荡,随后俄国又扣押了中国轮船,以致在 1930 年 5 月前,中国轮船一直未能于边界河道上航行,贸易亦因此大幅减少。

7. 黑龙江及乌苏里江江捐征收

1928 年和 1929 年接连发生大洪水,1929 年中俄两国发生政治冲突,1930 年中国轮船在边界河道上的通航时间又遭延误,客货运输受到了十分严重的影响,黑龙江及乌苏里江江捐税收亦因此从 1928 年的 54500 银圆减少到 1930 年的 44000 银圆。

8. 1930 年航运状况

边界河道水位较高,对航运非常有利。5 月 4 日,大黑河地区的黑龙江因水位较高(比冬天水位高出 19 英尺),开始出现浮冰。5 月 12 日,大黑河第一艘民船驶往黑龙江上游;5 月 30 日,载有瑷珲关全体关员的"苏州"号轮船自滨江关抵达大黑河,此为首艘抵达大黑河的轮船;10 月 22 日,"扬湖"号轮船最后一个驶离大黑河。"苏州"号轮船往来于黑龙江上游;"永平(Tungping)"号汽艇往来于黑龙江下游至奇克特河段。10 月 28 日,大黑河开始出现浮冰,11 月 10 日黑龙江关闭航运。

9. 航运事故

航运季期间，边界河道上未发生航运事故。

10. 大黑河港口已完成工作

中俄冲突期间修建的战壕对堤岸道路有所破坏，高水位期间的浮冰亦对 1929 年修筑的堤岸造成损害，此等损害均已修缮完毕。此外，东北航路局的码头亦因浮冰受损，但修缮工程须于春季开展。

11. 俄阿穆尔省经济调查

连续两年的大洪水，1929 年谷物的歉收，马匹的染疾以及对富农和集体农业组织的镇压，均使得俄阿穆尔省的农业产量大幅下降。当地居民已沿边界河道兴建新村庄，并在纳吉博沃（Nagibovo）村建造了五个水塔以储藏煤油，此外，还沿河砍伐木料，以木筏载之，再用拖船拖着木筏运送到哈巴罗夫斯克（Habarovsk）和尼古拉耶夫斯克（Nickolaevsk），向国外出口。此番种种应是为完成五年计划而为之，但官方资料证明，迄今为止所计划之工作只完成不到 50%。此外，由于中国工人短缺，黄金产量仅达预期的 45%，木炭产量又因劳资纠纷仅达预期的 50%。

俄阿穆尔省渔业资源丰富，然而，由于所供腌鱼桶不足，无法盐腌全部渔获。

另外，沿小河砍伐的木料大多未能及时用木筏运出，而阿穆尔河下游的木料又因遭遇暴雨损失良多。

因除去一定固定比例外，所有盈余必须移交给政府，故去年夏季谷物之丰收是否有助于改善俄阿穆尔省的经济状况，仍值得怀疑。

12. 黑龙江省经济调查

黑龙江沿线的中国农民因连续两年遭遇大洪水，又受到 1929 年政治冲突和土匪猖獗的影响，已是一无所有，很多人已迁至别处。此外，因道路及电报线路状况不佳，黑龙江沿线的通信只能依靠船运。幸得政府援助，谷物、菌类及越桔的收成又较好，另因水位较高利于航运，木料得以顺利运至滨江关（未在三姓浅滩延误时间），形势终得以改善复兴。

此外，俄国卢布贬值导致易货贸易兴起。

黑龙江上游及开库康（Kaikuk'ang）一带已开始开采金矿。

黑龙江沿线毛皮动物虽多，但道路较少，土匪猖獗，猎人——奥罗赤（Orochen）部落——难寻，好在当地市场对毛皮需求量极少。

1929 年因中俄冲突，大黑河未能储备木料，1930 年用木筏运至大黑河的木料亦寥寥可数，而此前储藏之木料均已运至滨江关，大黑河已无余留之木料，冬季亦无法补充库存。

俄国利用各种方式免除铁路征税,以低于哈尔滨市场价50%之价格向满洲里地区出口木料,已然成为影响大黑河木业发展的一大阻碍。

13. 总结

为保证吉林省和黑龙江省的繁荣发展,中国政府应注意以下几点:

（1）在黑龙江及乌苏里江边界河道沿线设立固定的邮寄及客运服务机构。

（2）在冬季设立邮寄服务机构。

（3）在黑龙江中游沿线安装一条电报线路。

（4）修理黑龙江上游沿线的电报线路。

（5）确保轮船于边界河道上航行时遵循《航务条例》。

（6）详细说明《卫生条例》,禁止乘客超载；在轮船上供设医药箱。

（7）在所有码头预留70英尺前滩,以作存放薪柴及修理划艇及舢板之用。

（8）着手准备成立独立的航路标志管理机构。

（9）为边界河道之巡查工作准备一艘汽艇。

易保罗（P. I. Ignatieff）

黑龙江航务专门顾问